Li Dazhao

SUNY series in Chinese Philosophy and Culture
―――――――
Roger T. Ames, editor

Li Dazhao

China's First Communist

PATRICK FULIANG SHAN

SUNY
PRESS

Cover: Li Dazhao when he served as the chief librarian at the Beijing University Library, between 1918 and 1922.

Published by State University of New York Press, Albany

© 2024 State University of New York

All rights reserved

Printed in the United States of America

No part of this book may be used or reproduced in any manner whatsoever without written permission. No part of this book may be stored in a retrieval system or transmitted in any form or by any means including electronic, electrostatic, magnetic tape, mechanical, photocopying, recording, or otherwise without the prior permission in writing of the publisher.

For information, contact State University of New York Press, Albany, NY
www.sunypress.edu

Library of Congress Cataloging-in-Publication Data

Name: Shan, Patrick Fuliang, author.
Title: Li Dazhao : China's first communist / Patrick Fuliang Shan.
Other titles: China's first communist
Description: Albany : State University of New York Press, [2024]. | Series: SUNY series in Chinese philosophy and culture | Includes bibliographical references and index.
Identifiers: LCCN 2023029200 | ISBN 9781438496818 (hardcover : alk. paper) | ISBN 9781438496801 (ebook)
Subjects: LCSH: Li, Dazhao, 1889–1927. | Communists—China—Biography.
Classification: LCC DS777.15.L5 S53 2024 | DDC 324.251075092

10 9 8 7 6 5 4 3 2 1

To my former doctoral advisor,
Dr. David Barrett

Contents

List of Illustrations — ix

Acknowledgments — xi

A Note on Romanization — xiii

Introduction — 1

Chapter 1 Family and Early Years — 13

Chapter 2 Pursuing a Modern Education — 29

Chapter 3 The Japan Years — 53

Chapter 4 Editor and Writer — 81

Chapter 5 Beijing University — 105

Chapter 6 Embracing Communism — 133

Chapter 7 The United Front — 159

Chapter 8 The Last Years — 185

Epilogue — 213

Abbreviations — 225

Glossary	227
Notes	233
Bibliography	279
Index	299

Illustrations

Figure 2.1 One of the earliest known photos of Li Dazhao was taken when he studied at the Yongping Prefectural Academy between 1905 and 1907.   32

Figure 3.1 Li Dazhao studied in Japan between 1913 and 1916, during which he was admitted into Waseda University.   59

Figure 5.1 Li Dazhao served as the chief librarian at Beijing University Library between 1918 and 1922.   108

Figure 5.2 Li Dazhao was employed at Beijing University beginning in early 1918.   119

Figure 8.1 Li Dazhao was arrested by the warlord Zhang Zuolin in Beijing on April 6, 1927.   208

Acknowledgments

While focusing on this project for nearly a decade, I have received support from a large number of colleagues, friends, librarians, archivists, and others. The limited space does not allow me to offer a full list of all of their names, yet I must express my gratitude to some who have significantly helped me in the process of my research, writing, revision, and publication of this book. First, my colleagues in the Department of History at Grand Valley State University (GVSU) set up a collective example for me in my pursuit of scholarly excellence. The academic environment my colleagues have created profoundly impacts me and nurtures me to be a mature learner of history. The East Asian studies program (EAS) at GVSU is equally important in my scholarly life, and my EAS colleagues have assisted me in various ways in the past two decades. The Center for Scholarly and Creative Excellence at GVSU has supported my research, sponsored my travels to retrieve useful sources, and assisted me with presenting my scholarly findings at conferences. Amber Dierking, the librarian for the East Asian collection, and Leigh Rupinski, the librarian for the history collection, helped me acquire monographs. Dr. Yi Zhao, the EAS librarian liaison, assisted me with purchasing books for my projects. The document delivery department borrowed books for me from other libraries with an efficient approach.

The librarians at the Asia Library of the University of Michigan are helpful whenever I visit Ann Arbor to borrow books. Dr. Neil O'Brien proofread the manuscript and offered valuable suggestions, for which I am grateful. Dr. Arthur Waldron, a famous China historian, invited me to talk to his students at the University of Pennsylvania on October 19–20, 2019, and his encouragement of my project was inspirational.

When I did my research in China, I got support from librarians, archivists, and scholars, to whom I am indebted. Professor Chen Linghai helped me purchase *Li Dazhao yu guxiang* (Li Dazhao and his hometown) when I needed it as a collection of primary sources for writing my chapter on Li's early years.

In the past years, I have presented my research on Li Dazhao at national and international conferences, notably those held by the American Historical Association (AHA), the Chinese Historians in the United States (CHUS), and the Association of Chinese Professors in Social Sciences (ACPSS). I have obtained useful feedback and inspirational comments from the following commentators, to whom I am thankful: Xiansheng Tian, Yi Sun, Jingyi Song, Guo Wu, and Shaorong Huang, whose thought-provoking questions and insightful comments prompted me to think more critically. I presented a paper on Li Dazhao at an international conference hosted by Pacific Lutheran University on October 29–31, 2021, where I received warm support from Drs. Geoff Foy, Paul Manfredi, Mikel Edwards, and Jun Zhou, to whom I want to express my thanks.

I am thankful to the following individuals whose help is greatly appreciated during my research for this project: Dr. Gao Hong, Dr. Sun Lingling, Dr. Chen Hongmin, Dr. Yang Hu, Dr. Xi Wang, Du Jianhui, Shan Fumin, Zhang Huafeng, and many others.

I am grateful to my family for years of support; in particular, my son Matthew helped me load many piles of books into the car and carry them back home from the University of Michigan's Asia Library.

Finally, the editors, staff, and other professionals at SUNY Press have done an excellent job and provided their efficient work, without which this book could not have been produced. In particular, Mr. James Peltz's professionalism with my manuscript deeply impresses me. Dr. Roger Ames's support is greatly appreciated. Also, I want to thank the following individuals for their support in the past months: Diane Ganeles (senior production editor), Aimee Harrison (cover coordinator), Julia Cosacchi (assistant manuscript editor), John Britch (marketing director), and Megan Zid (copyeditor). Of course, I am grateful to the three anonymous reviewers whose comments, suggestions, and support helped me revise my manuscript.

A Note on Romanization

Throughout this book, the pinyin system is used to romanize Chinese names, places, historical terms, and other terminologies, following the current scholarly trend. For important phrases, pinyin versions are offered in parentheses and their Chinese characters are provided in the glossary. For important nomenclatures, the Wade-Giles versions are given in parentheses in the first instance, such as *Guangzhou (Canton)*, for the purpose of clarification. For personal names, the Chinese tradition is respected: the surname appears first, then the given name; for Li Dazhao, for example, *Li* is his surname and *Dazhao* his given name. For Chinese Americans or overseas Chinese individuals, however, full names are rendered according to the Western convention, which means that the given name appears first and the surname the next.

For those special names that are well known in the West, their Wade-Giles versions are retained, such as *Sun Yat-sen* instead of *Sun Zhongshan* or *Sun Yixian*, *Chiang Kai-shek* instead of *Jiang Jieshi*. However, Li Dazhao's former rendering of *Li Ta-chao* is changed into its pinyin version. As for Peking University, where Li Dazhao worked for years, its pinyin version, *Beijing University*, is used. For the pinyin renderings in footnotes, the Chinese phrases are grouped together. The title of a Chinese publisher or a Chinese journal is treated as one single phrase.

Introduction

Communism was not Chinese; rather, it was a by-product of the Industrial Revolution in mid-nineteenth-century Europe. Despite its status as an influential ideology that eventually spread throughout the entire global community, communism was not introduced to China instantly. Only during the early twentieth century was it imported by a group of radical Chinese intellectuals. In just three decades after the first Chinese scholar embraced this foreign creed, this alien ideology propelled the Chinese Communists to score a stunning victory through a major national revolution, triumphantly turning what was then the world's most populous country into a communist state. Because communism has significantly reshaped modern Chinese history, it has attracted the attention of Western scholars, who devote their scholarship to the Chinese acceptance of this foreign ideology. Now, a number of questions naturally pop up: Who was the first communist in China? Why did he embrace communism? When did he become a communist? Where did he find this foreign ideology? Through what approach did he spread the communist doctrine? What role did he play in the early communist movement? How did he impact twentieth-century China?

These questions are all fundamentally scholarly issues. Without a deeper understanding of this particular man, the evolution of modern China would be elusive and the defining moment of Chinese history ambiguous. Hence, it is imperative to study this man, his personal odyssey, his individual pursuit, his faith in communism, and his leadership role in the early communist movement. In other words, this man's conversion to communism and his dedication to the communist revolution must be scrutinized in order to trace the historical trajectory of his nation.

This man was Li Dazhao (1889–1927), who did not live a long life but exerted a significant influence upon his country. At first, however, he was not a communist at all; rather, he was a democrat who pursued Western-style democracy for a long time. Yet he was the man who became China's first communist in 1919 and who blazed a path steering his country in a new direction. In many ways, his acceptance of communism symbolizes the Chinese search for a new approach to state building and nation building. As Sun Yat-sen lamented, the Chinese seemed befuddled at "the way" of national reconstruction after the collapse of the old imperial system.[1] Indeed, Li Dazhao was also seeking "the way," working as an intellectual in Beijing (Peking) and later treasuring communism as "the way." He accepted this foreign ideology just a few years after the establishment of the Republic of China, at which time he organized study groups, drew in young students, and guided them into the communist path. He used the media of the time, such as newspapers, journals, and magazines, to disseminate the communist creed and doctrine. His large quantity of publications exhibits his passion for this ideology. More importantly, he was not only a theorist but also an activist. It was Li who organized one of the first communist cells. Immediately afterward, he became a cofounder of the Chinese Communist Party. He was instrumental in forging a united front with Sun Yat-sen's Nationalist Party for the National Revolution against warlords and the imperialist powers, for which he sacrificed his own life. Li was much more than an ordinary historical figure; he was a catalyst for China's ongoing revolution and the nation's quest for a new identity.

Li Dazhao's salient status has long been recognized by scholars, who have bestowed upon him various glowing sobriquets. Outside China, he has been called "the father of Marxism in China," which acknowledges his indispensable role in initiating the communist movement.[2] Inside China, he is portrayed as "China's Prometheus" who dedicated his life to his cause, disseminated the communist ideology, and impacted a generation of Chinese youth.[3] Consequently, Li was a "bell-man" (*zhuangzhongren*) who struck the alarm bell to inform the people of the coming of daybreak and to press them to cradle the fresh new morning.[4] He was extolled, because of his heroic deeds, as "a brave gunman" (*yonggandeqiangshou*) who fired his shots at the old culture and as the disseminator of a new ideology.[5] He was depicted as "a seed-sower" (*bozhongzhe*) who planted the seeds that grew and bore fruit.[6] For communists, Li has attained a saintly status. Mao Zedong in March 1949 praised Li as his teacher, just before his proclamation of the establishment of the People's Republic of China. Communist leader Jiang Zemin respected Li as an erudite "scholar."[7]

Chinese scholar Hu Qiaomu granted Li multiple titles: "patriot, revolutionary, educator, scholar, writer, and intellectual."[8] While celebrating the one hundredth anniversary of Li's birthday, Chinese historian Hu Sheng commended Li as "a tree planter" (*zaishuren*) and remarked that "we commemorate Li Dazhao, as if we are remembering the tree planter in front of the tall tree he had planted."[9]

Glorious titles aside, Li Dazhao's role in directing the path of modern China must be highlighted. This book, however, is not a hagiography to glorify him; rather, it is a scholarly inquiry into his life in which he is presented as a man, as a democratic intellectual, as China's first communist, and then as a professional revolutionary. To the dismay of modern liberals, China's march towards communism, which was initiated by Li, was a big loss for China's bourgeoning liberalism during the early postimperial era.[10] Regardless of whether it was a bewildering and unexpected occurrence, it was the path modern China took. A close examination of this road demonstrates Li's crucial role in setting his foot on it and leading others onto it. As a cofounder of the Communist Party, he was a key figure in all major events of the early communist movement. Li's life symbolizes his nation's development, signals the dramatic transformation of Chinese intellectuals, and represents the modification of one of the oldest cultures in the world.

In fact, Li Dazhao's conversion to communism was a lengthy journey that requires a thorough study. Yet the dominant paradigm in mainland China emphasizes the magic moment of the Russian Revolution and its role in inspiring the Chinese to accept communism. This simplistic perspective lacks an in-depth analysis because it elevates the trigger of the Russian factor and neglects the long-term pursuit that shaped Li's embrace of the foreign ideology. This book traces Li's life vertically and connects his life horizontally with Chinese history in order to situate him at the intersection of multiple national events. It differs from the existing literature that focuses on his thoughts; instead, this study tracks his odyssey as well as his ideas, aiming to avoid obscuring his individual experience and intending to underscore his gradual travel to communism.

The historical era in which Li Dazhao lived, the family within which he grew up, the social milieu he endured, the national condition he encountered, and the international situation he experienced all helped remold him into what he would become. Li was born during the late Qing dynasty, in a period of theatrical transformation from empire to republic. It was a time of imperial decay, political chaos, foreign invasions, social instability, and rising nationalism. His upbringing seemed similar to that of his contemporaries. Yet he had his own distinctive childhood: his parents passed away when he was very young, which led him to a special life. His early education in classics enabled him to absorb traditional culture and to become an erudite individual and an effective writer. Li was also exposed to modern education, and he adroitly combined his classical expertise with the newly introduced Western learning. He used his pen to deliver poignant writings and to spread new ideas. Experiencing China's decline and witnessing China's sufferings, Li became nationalistic in his pursuit of national salvation. Growing up, he was an enthusiastic learner and demonstrated a sharp mind; he became a sarcastic critic, a loud proponent and a sonorous mouthpiece for national salvation. He wrote extensively, published prolifically, and publicized his opinions constantly, from which we can glean information to trace his long path toward communism.

Li Dazhao's life was deeply impacted by what happened in the late Qing and early republic eras, which were imposed upon by a large number of so-called unequal treaties (*bupingdengtiaoyue*) engendered by the imperialist powers. China not only suffered from its territorial cessions but also bemoaned the loss of national interests. Consequently, the underpinning political culture of the time was rising nationalism. By the beginning of the twentieth century, three sides of nationalism coexisted, as elaborated by Jonathan D. Spence: xenophobia, official nationalism, and Han nationalism.[11] Chinese scholars confirm this new trend, and one claims that Chinese nationalism emerged at the start of the twentieth century.[12] Li Dazhao was impacted by all three of these political sentiments. He lamented his nation's impotence in the face of imperialist invasions, although he was not a xenophobic zealot. He supported the late Qing constitutional reform but quickly became disillusioned with it. He soon switched to Han nationalism to topple the Qing dynasty but gave it up after the establishment of the republic. In postimperial China, he continued to witness imperialist invasions, from which he acquired a national trauma syndrome, which impelled him to become a radical intellectual seeking national resurgence and cultural renaissance.

Li outgrew those three types of nationalism but continued to carry on his nationalist fervor to champion national independence and cultural revival. The emphasis on nationalism might seem irrelevant when we focus on Li as China's first communist, but it is pertinent because nationalism was a potent force in his thinking. To analyze his long odyssey to communism, nationalism must be deliberated, reconceptualized, and reinterpreted. For Li, nationalism not only meant a genuine love for his country but also denoted actions necessary for the modernization of his nation, the reform of its culture, and the extreme makeover of the existing regimentation by destroying the old evils, wiping out the woes, and leading the people to pursue a new identity. Although his nationalism was originally a patriotic sentiment, it evolved into a zeal for transforming China into a constitutional, democratic, and modernized republic, then into an anti-imperialist and anti-warlord independent nation-state, and finally into a modernized country with communism as a guiding ideology. Even on his very last day, Li remained adamant in defending his nationalistic stance. His communist ideology relied as much on his nationalism as on his political pursuits and social quest. In a unique way, his nationalistic sentiment compelled him to move onto the path of communism.

Although the underlying motivation of Li Dazhao's ideological pursuit was his ardent nationalist enthusiasm, he picked up diverse ideas in the process of his quest for national salvation, including anarchism, nihilism, liberalism, constitutionalism, democracy, and other elements. Ultimately, he turned to communism. His nationalism, like other forms of nationalistic sentiment, was so cohesively adhesive that it easily bonded with other ideas to make his thought a potpourri of diverse origins and an intermixture of sundry elements that comprised multiple forms, exerted multiple impacts, and nestled within multiple functions. A close examination shows that Li mainly absorbed new ideological imports from the West, even if sometimes through the detour of Japan. He kept hold of the essence of China's traditional culture while relinquishing undesirable elements, selecting valuable ingredients, pursuing a new culture, and ultimately choosing communism. He did not completely abandon what he had previously acquired, which blotted his version of communism with assorted elements—in particular, nationalism, which continued to be the constant binding force in his discourse of communism for national liberation, national revival, and national modernization.

Since his death, the study of Li Dazhao has undergone a few different periods, each possessing its own characteristics. The first period ranged from 1927 to 1949, during which the communist movement faced the relentless extermination campaigns of Chiang Kai-shek (Jiang Jieshi) while the communists continued to carry on their revolution. During those years, the study of Li was limited to sporadic publications. As soon as Li died, Gao Yihan wrote a biography of Li Dazhao for *Central News Daily* (*Zhongyangribao*) in Wuhan on May 23, 1927, which is regarded as the first biography of Li.[13] In 1934 in Tianjin, Wang Senran published a short biography of Li Dazhao in *Ta Kung Pao* (*L'Impartial*), a famous newspaper, in which Li was praised as an erudite scholar. In 1935, Guo Zhanbo praised Li as a great philosopher in his monograph on modern Chinese philosophy. Amazingly, those latter two publications came out during Chiang Kai-shek's merciless anti-Communist censorship.[14] Under these unfavorable circumstances, the compilation of Li Dazhao's writings was conducted secretly by Li Leguang, who packed what he had gleaned into *The Complete Works of Li Dazhao* (*Li Dazhao quanji*); it was published in April 1939 by Beixinshuju in Shanghai, and the famous Chinese writer Lu Xun contributed a preface. Lu Xun applauded Li's writings as "a heritage of the pioneer and a giant monument of revolutionary history."[15] Nevertheless, the Nationalist government immediately banned its publication and confiscated the printed copies. It was not until June 1949 that it was republished by the same publisher, soon after the communist forces occupied Shanghai.[16]

It is wrong to assume that the study of Li Dazhao immediately reached a climax after the victory of the communist revolution, although the post-1949 political situation became favorable for it. Nonetheless, the period between 1949 and 1966 witnessed publication of related books and articles. Zhang Cixi authored the first book-length biography of Li Dazhao in Beijing in 1951, tracing Li's life from birth to death. Zhang called Li "a giant" (*juren*), hoped that his book would "cast a brick to attract jade," and expected to see more Li biographies.[17] In spite of Zhang's optimism, not many books on Li were published before 1966. It is worth mentioning that a couple of books indeed were issued to celebrate what would have been Li's seventieth birthday in 1959. One was *The Collected Works of Li Dazhao* (*Li Dazhao xuanji*), which included Li's major articles. Another was a long epic offered by the poet Zang Kejia, which served as a biographical sketch of Li's life. In this saga, Zang utilizes modern free verse to spotlight Li's life and showcase him as an amicable figure and as an example of a great revolutionary.[18] During this period, the Chinese were much preoccupied by Mao Zedong's fervor to construct a socialist state, for which Li was utilized as a heroic martyr to foster socialist zeal.

The ten-year Cultural Revolution from 1966 to 1976 was a setback for the study of Li Dazhao. Not only did the national upheaval create an adverse scenario, but also the political mentality of that era forestalled an objective inquiry into the history of the Chinese Communist Party. During the Cultural Revolution, an unprecedented cult elevated Mao Zedong to demigod status, and any positive assessment of other communist figures became a taboo. Mao loomed large, and then appeared gigantic and brooked no rivals, while others such as Li were quarantined in the backstage. Many have blamed the Gang of Four led by Mao's wife Jiang Qing for this detrimental milieu. Indeed, Kang Sheng, an abettor of the Gang of Four, intended to remove Li from history, as he viewed Li as an insolent opponent of Mao's holy prominence, for which Li was even smeared with a distorted image.[19] Li's contributions to the communist cause vanished from the historical annals during this time. No longer was Li viewed as in the vanguard of Chinese communism; on the contrary, he was regarded as a liability and even as an apostate. Li's children suffered from persecution; his daughter Li Xinghua was seriously beaten, lost her eyesight, and was hastened to an unfortunate death in 1979. Those who studied Li Dazhao were victimized, and some among them were persecuted to death.[20] Rarely was anything about Li published during those ten years, marking an ill-fated disruption to the study of Li Dazhao. Only when the post-Mao era started was Li's reputation restored.

The post-Mao era has witnessed an upsurge in the study of Li Dazhao. The removal of the Mao cult led to a tolerant milieu in which scholars could study other communist figures, which gave rise to the admiration of "the red martyrs" through printed materials, mass media, and governmental support.[21] In particular, Li drew special attention as China's first communist. In 1989, the nationwide Li Dazhao Study Association was established to promote scholarly inquiries. Chinese scholars have investigated Li's contributions to modern Chinese culture and his legacy upon the nation. As a result, recent publications on Li tend to be exhaustively detailed and widely circulated. Almost all of them adopt a positive stance to eulogize Li, highlight his glorious life, emphasize his enduring influence, and underline his immortal status. About ten book-length biographies were published, over one thousand articles came out, and other forms of related literature also appeared. According to a statistical source, besides monographs, seventy articles on Li were published each year between 1978 and 1994, peaking in the two years 1979 and 1989: 140 in 1979 and more than two hundred in 1989. Between 1994 and 2005, more than forty articles came out each year.[22] In the past decade, monographs, dissertations, and theses on Li have continued to enrich the growing literature.

Interesting to note is that more of Li Dazhao's own writings have been discovered and identified in the recent decades, not only in mainland China but also in Taiwan, Russia, Japan, and other countries and regions. For example, in 1985, the Russians published four articles Li authored during his visit to the Soviet Union.[23] Li's articles were also found in Taiwan's archives. One letter to Sun Yat-sen, coauthored in 1923 by Li Dazhao, was discovered in a Dutch archive.[24] The tallies of Chinese characters in different editions of Li's works help us to underscore the quantity of the new findings. In the 1959 edition of *Selected Works of Li Dazhao*, the total word count was 390,000, but it increased to 1,100,000 in its 1984 edition.[25] The new edition of *Li Dazhao quanji* (*The Complete Works of Li Dazhao*) published in 2013 is counted at two million words.[26] In other words, more than half of the trove of Li's writings were newly found in the post-1976 era. Of course, scholars have debated their authenticity, purporting to figure out whether or not they were truly his writings given that he used numerous pen names.[27] Scholars have challenged one another and defended their own approaches to identification.[28] This assessment of apocryphalness may well continue, and perhaps more new articles by Li will be recognized in the future.

Li Dazhao's voluminous writings have attracted the gaze of Chinese scholars, who have devoted their expertise to the study of his works. Some sift the writings to ascertain their truthfulness, while others examine the contents to highlight their canonical value. The recent efforts amount to a new level of hermeneutical studies. Textual criticism aside, they have started to annotate Li's writings with detailed commentaries, while other scholars criticize one another in their elucidation of footnotes to Li's original writings.[29] Some scholars have reproached the editors of his works for offering insufficient information in footnotes.[30] This exegetical criticism has compelled the publisher to not only update Li's writings but also add more information to the footnotes in the new edition; consequently, the 2006 edition of *The Complete Works of Li Dazhao* was republished in 2013 with newly revised and added footnotes.

Given his prominent role in the shaping of twentieth-century China, Li Dazhao's name has not gone unnoticed outside China. Japanese scholars have devoted considerable scholarship to him, while European scholars, particularly those in Italy, Germany, and France, have written pamphlets and articles on Li's role in the communist movement as well as his philosophical ideas. In contrast, only one book has been published in English, by Maurice Meisner in 1967, although a few articles have come out exploring Li's career and thought. Meisner's monograph remains a classic in terms of its interpretation of Li's ideas. According to Meisner, Li was the "first true leader and . . . martyr" of the Chinese Communist Party.[31] However, this book lacks biographical information. Of course, the skin-deep recognition of Li as a historical figure can be found in the newly published monographs, textbooks, and encyclopedias that highlight Li's role during the May Fourth Movement and the early communist movement. The absence of a badly needed biography is due to the pre-1976 lack of relevant primary and secondary sources; most of the valuable sources concerning Li's life were published after 1976, including Li's daughter Li Xinghua's memoir about her father. Nevertheless, Li Dazhao's major articles could be found in libraries before 1976, which allowed scholars of the period, such as Meisner, to study Li's philosophy but not Li's life. Consequently, Li was not accorded a truly sensed and full-blooded biography. Since 1976, abundant primary and secondary sources have been published, including memoirs, collections of reminiscences, Li's own writings, scholarly monographs, and journal articles, all of which contain anecdotes, his activities, and vignettes concerning Li's life. Altogether, the sources now are so rich that it is an opportune time to obtain a fuller view of Li as a historical figure and to confer on him an informative biography.

This biography rests squarely upon rich primary sources and abundant secondary sources, including Li's personal writings, Li's friends' and family members' memoirs, and recently published monographs and articles. During the investigative process for this project, a large amount of data was examined, especially those post-1976 publications. The exceptionally large quantity of valuable sources opens up an entire new world, broadening the scope for viewing Li and shattering the previously simplistic assessment. Of course, the values of those sources have been incorporated into this book through assessment, reflection, and interpretation. This book does not follow any dogmatic rules; rather, it adopts a critical approach for a rational analysis that hopefully will stimulate the reader to ponder more deeply Li's role in his nation's transformation. Although countless materials were read, assessed, and used, it is to be admitted that the limited space cannot allow all to be directly cited. Consequently, only a small portion of those sources are utilized, unfairly leaving out numerous important ones—a regret and apology surely shared by other scholars in their own scholarly endeavors.

Two dichotomous approaches have coexisted in the study of Li Dazhao: one pursuing his philosophy, and the other examining his life. Neither are static, because his thought advanced as he grew older. Chinese historians have achieved much in both modes, but Western scholars lag behind. The urgent need to understand modern China necessitates a careful study of Li in those two categories. Western scholars so far have explored Li's thought, but his life has not been fully examined. A critical biography should reveal the track of his life and demonstrate the evolution of his unique ideas. This biography traces Li's life and integrates his personal odyssey with his ideological transformations. An overall evaluation demonstrates that he went through several periods marked by personal maturation and ideological progress. The first period ranged from 1889 to 1905, during which Li was nurtured in the classics while imbibing his initial simplistic patriotism. From 1905 to 1913, Li acquired a modern education and developed his patriotic zeal. His study abroad in Japan from 1913 to 1916 was an opportunity for learning more about Western civilization, yet Japan's harsh demands on his home country heightened his nationalism and turned him into an activist. From 1916 to 1918, while serving as an editor of various newspapers in Beijing, he became passionate about national resurgence, constitutional rule, and the democratic system. Beginning in 1918, Li worked at Beijing University and became a rising star in China's cultural arena. His pursuit of national salvation continued to lead him along the communist path. From 1921 to 1924, Li participated in establishing the Chinese Communist Party and led its early operations. Between 1924 and 1927, he was instrumental in forging a united front with Sun Yat-sen and then served as a leader of the ongoing National Revolution. The last period comprises the remaining days of his life, during which he was arrested, secretly put on a trial, and promptly executed by Zhang Zuolin. Each of those periods represents a milestone in Li's life, underlining his role in the shaping of his country, and thus they lend themselves well to structuring the chapters of this book.

Li Dazhao's short life of less than thirty-eight years mirrored his nation's transformation from empire to republic and reflected his country's move toward the communist revolution. Although he died young, his legacy has persisted. This study provides a window into the time during which Li lived, worked, and died. In a sense, this biography is concerned more with modern China than narrowly with Li's life. To understand China's national transition, we have to familiarize ourselves with the genesis of the communist movement for which Li was indispensable. Western readers, in spite of their traditional stance against communism, need to know its genesis in China in order to attain a deeper comprehension of it, for which Li Dazhao truly requires a fresh look and demands a new inquiry. The writing of such a biography should be a welcome undertaking in today's international situation, as the demand of reassessing Chinese communism is an urgent necessity in the West. It should not be ignored due to traditional anti-communist sentiment, which is one of the reasons so much less ink has been spilled over Li in the West. The author here believes that Li's odyssey would rightly help anyone understand the trajectory of modern China and expects that this biography will serve to fill the gap in Western academia. Li Dazhao deserves a serious scholarly exploration, warrants a deeper analysis, and merits a comprehensive biography that does not so far exist.

Chapter 1

Family and Early Years

Introduction

Scholars have developed diverse theories in their analyses of the inseparable tie between childhood and adulthood, but they concur on the enormous impact of the early years upon adulthood in a person's life.[1] While the role of childhood leaves much room for further exploration, scholars generally agree that children develop their attitude, contract their habits, and foster their social ties during the early years, all of which are carried into adulthood. Children's family upbringing, social network, natural environment, and communal background all shape their idiosyncratic traits. Children predispose to local culture, partner with their peers, and acquire distinctive habits, all of which persist through their entire life. Adults always live under the shadow of their childhood, which is why childhood attracts scholars to devote their expertise to it. However, the study of a person's early years always poses a tough task, as the insufficiency of sources often forestalls a serious and well-arranged scholarly study.

In the same vein, the topic of Li Dazhao's childhood has experienced a long process of scholarly exploration. It was not until more memoirs, more investigative reports, and more primary sources become available after 1976 that a relatively unblemished portrait of his early years gradually appeared. Since then, scholars have interpreted Li's early years through careful inquiries. Today, all agree that Li had an unfortunate childhood. He was orphaned as a baby. As a young child, he was put under special care. It was through the meticulous intervention and watchful guardianship of his foster grandfather (who was in fact his great-uncle) over his at-risk life that Li Dazhao was able to gain protection, grow up soundly, and acquire a classical education. In recent years, scholars have examined Li's ties with his local culture, his family pedigree, his early education, and his initial patriotism during his early years. All emphasize that the sixteen years from 1889 to 1905 significantly remolded him as an independent mind, an enthusiastic learner, an erudite youngster, a patriotic person, a moral individual, and a responsible man. His familiarity with the rural setting enabled him to become acquainted with peasants and form a unique perspective in which he had faith in the rural folks, who he believed would be an extraordinary force for the Chinese revolution. It was this belief that prompted him to write about Chinese peasants, to engage in peasant-related activism, and ultimately to impact the future path of the Chinese revolution.[2]

Family Background

The region where Li Dazhao was born and grew up shaped his personal character. His county, Laoting (or *Leting* in Mandarin), in Zhili Province (Hebei after 1928), is located in the far northeastern corner of the North China Plain. The county of Laoting sits astride a number of converging geographical areas, including North China and Manchuria, with Mongolia nearby and Korea across Bohai Bay. His village is 140 miles from Beijing, one hundred miles from Tianjin, thirty miles from Beidaihe, a few miles from the coast, one mile from the Luan River, and twenty-five miles from Mount Jieshi to the north. The local landscape affected Li's passion for nature, as he remarked in 1913: "I have an inborn love for the mountain. I saw Mount Jieshi in the distance daily during my childhood, which had such a profound allure for me that my affection for the mountain was long since clinched."[3] Li spent vacations during the decade 1910–20 on the summit of Mount Jieshi, known as Wufengshan, writing his nationally known articles inside an isolated house. To the south of the mountain lay the plains of Laoting County, which consist of alluvial soil from rich deposits of the Luan River. Although the annual floods sometimes inundated the local residents, in Li's eyes, "the Luan River is a destroyer of the old life, but it is also a creator of a new life."[4]

Although Li Dazhao was a native of Laoting County, he and his family were the descendants of immigrants to this region. According to the oral history of Li's family, Li Dazhao's ancestors first arrived there in 1404, following the order of Emperor Yongle of the Ming dynasty to repopulate North China after a fierce civil war during which Yongle seized the throne from his nephew and the local population was decimated and displaced. However, the question of Li's ancestors' original locale (*zuji*) poses a quandary, for which several conflicting interpretations have been offered. Some argue that the Li family came from Shandong, some claim that they emigrated from Shanxi, some assert that they moved in from Henan, some maintain that they came from Anhui, and some even contend that the Lower Yangtze River Valley was the original domicile of the Li clan.[5] Perhaps this problem can never be solved, as internal migration has been a frequent phenomenon throughout the long sweep of Chinese history. However, historically speaking, in general immigrants to a new settlement from diverse origins quickly intermingled and produced a new community with a new identity. The Li family history states that two Li brothers settled down in Laoting but one of them returned to their ancestors' locale. It was that permanent settler, Li Guoqiu, who made Laoting his home, got married, and became Li Dazhao's remote ancestor.[6]

The Li family lived in a settlement called Daheituo Village and became an extended clan of a hundred heads by the time Li Dazhao was born. The village earned its odd name, which means "big black lump," because of a big heap of sandy soil in its northeastern corner. It is said that its original color was black, but it had turned yellowish and finally became the silvery color it appears as today. In spite of the color changes, the village retained its original name. The settlement is about ten miles from the county seat, a few miles from the coast, and just one mile from the Luan River. As new immigrants settled down and intermingled, a number of large clans took shape, including Gu, Zhao, Li, and Yang. By the time Li Dazhao was born in 1889, the village had begotten 250 households with twelve hundred residents.[7] The total acreage of land for the villagers was around one thousand, with which the residents engaged in farming. A great change took place when the Manchus conquered China in 1644, after which Laoting was under Manchu control. Consequently, Manchu bannermen (*qiren*), through the so-called enclosure (*quandi*) policy, occupied the choice land while the Han farmers had to rent land in order to survive.[8] The Manchu oppression sowed the seeds of aversion among the local residents and generated anti-Manchu nationalism in Li Dazhao's young mind, which he dubbed "the nine-generation hatred" (*jiushichou*) in a poem he composed in 1909. In the poem, he counted the Manchu conquest in terms of generations, each lasting roughly thirty years. This anti-Manchu sentiment inspired him to participate in late Qing constitutional reform aimed at limiting Manchu power and ultimately to support the 1911 Revolution to overthrow Manchu rule.[9]

Li Dazhao's nationalism had its roots in the local culture of North China. Laoting County is located in the zone of the Yan-Zhao culture (Yan-Zhao wenhua), so labeled for the two ancient states in the region. The Yan-Zhao culture is of course a part of greater Chinese culture, but it retains myriad dynamic local values featured in substantial regional elements. As a result, residents identify themselves in an internally circumscribed sphere in which they cherish shared conventions, value similar conduct, and follow parochial thinking modes. One example is the patriotic sentiment derived from Jing Ke, who attempted to assassinate the First Emperor of China (Qin Shihuang) just before latter's war to unify China. To the Chinese people who have lived in the Yan-Zhao cultural zone, Jing Ke embodies selfless devotion to his state, for which he sacrificed his life. No wonder Li Dazhao wrote articles supporting assassination so long as it was in the pursuit of justice, to defend national interests, or to eliminate wicked evils. Li was fond of local shadow plays (piyingxi), for which he selected well-known stories. One story he used focused on the assassination of Ito Hirobumi by An Jung-geun. Although An was a Korean, his assassination of Ito resembled Jing Ke's story, purporting to halt the Japanese conquest of Korea.[10] Of course, not all elements of the Yan-Zhao culture were desirable; for example, the Flower Association (huahui) is regarded as a gambling network that attracted local residents into squandering precious time, consuming prized energy, wasting valuable savings, and relishing a profligate livelihood. Indeed, Li Dazhao directed tenacious efforts to fighting against this local tradition.[11]

The claim that Li Dazhao's family did not have any special religious faith is not accurate.[12] As a matter of fact, like many other Chinese, the Li family practiced all traditional religions in a syncretic approach, which may seem meaningless and unimaginable to some Westerners. The Chinese have allowed each of the traditional religions a special space, while all of the belief systems share a common realm as a collective setting for a spiritual benefit. In a special way, the Chinese denote the coalescence of religious practice in a broad sense to allow different tenets and diverse faiths to fulfill numerous functions in order to alleviate tough issues in daily life. The fact that Li Dazhao, his father, and his foster grandfather were well versed in Confucian classics demonstrates their faith in Confucianism, from which they derived political and social values. Li's foster grandfather's purchase of land near the Huayan Buddhist Temple in Daheituo Village to allow local residents to enjoy folk culture proves his tie to Buddhism. That Li Dazhao's father offered his calligraphy as a stele inscription for the temple confirms the family's affinity to Buddhism. Nevertheless, Li Dazhao supported converting this temple into an elementary school to educate young children, benefit local villagers, and enrich communal life. In the spring of 1920, he helped hire a female teacher for this school and contributed twenty yuan for her travel expense to the village. The traditional syncretic religious practice encouraged Li to explore diverse ideas, including his study of Christianity when he was in Japan.[13] Ultimately, however, the syncretic approach prompted him to move closer to other foreign doctrines, including communism, while not totally relinquishing the previously acquired ideas.

The Li family members had been farmers in Daheituo Village, yet the elevation of Li Dazhao's foster grandfather, Li Ruzhen, to elite status significantly impacted Li Dazhao's young life and enabled him to acquire an early education. A close look at the Li family tree shows that Li Dazhao's great-grandfather Li Weimo begot three sons: Li Ruzhen, Li Ruzhu, and Li Rubi. Li Ruzhen read classics but got involved in commerce. He went to Manchuria to run a grocery store, engaged in business, and led a sojourner's life between Manchuria and his village. Fortunately, he reaped considerable wealth; unfortunately, he was assaulted by bandits who forced him to return to his village. At the age of forty, he still had not begotten a son, although he had fathered three daughters. In traditional society, the lack of a son meant that a man would suffer the extinction of his line, a taboo for anyone to bear. Consequently, he pleaded with his brother Li Ruzhu to allow him to adopt Ruzhu's second son, Li Renrong (Li Dazhao's father), which enabled Li Ruzhen to retain his patriarchal line.[14] Li Ruzhen, upon his return with his remaining fortune to his village, bought a piece of land of fifteen acres, purchased a title as a lowest-level recipient of the Civil Service Examination System (Kejuzhidu), and led a relatively well-off life. With his purchased title, he was officially endorsed as a local elite by the government. He was a competent, eloquent, and well-connected man and often served as a judge to settle local disputes. However, he could be stern, critical, and obstinate, which earned him the nickname "Iron-Mouth Li" (Litiezui).[15]

Li Ruzhen established a reputation as a contributor to the local community. On one occasion, he donated 460 yuan from his own pocket and persuaded others to donate an additional 1,200 yuan to purchase a piece of land (1.5 acres) in front of Huayan Temple in Daheituo Village, which he named "the Prosperity Land" (xianghuodi), and built a performance stage for the local communal life; it served as a venue for religious events, popular entertainment, festival celebrations, and other communal activities.[16] Li Dazhao was impacted by his foster grandfather's leadership skills, which young Li Dazhao inherited and carried on to his future political life. With his fortune, Li Ruzhen constructed a new house for his family in 1881. The house, a compound, was named by Li Ruzhen "Morality Nurturing Hall" (Huaidetang), and it consisted of three big yards with walls around them to indicate that it was an elite's residence. The front yard was intended to be a private school, the central yard included six bedrooms, and the backyard included a huge storage area for grains, tools, utensils, and other items. Because Li Dazhao was born in the central yard and grew up inside the compound, this house was designated as a museum in 1958 by the Chinese government. It became a provincial historical heritage site in 1982 and was further defined as a national historical site in 1988.[17]

Early Years

A mounting concern regarding Li Dazhao in recent decades has been rectifying the mistaken dates for his birthday and birth year. At least a few different dates can be found in diverse sources.[18] In his own autobiography, which Li wrote in English for his American teacher in Japan in 1914, he claimed that he was born in 1890. The American scholar Maurice Meisner claims that Li was born on October 6, 1888,[19] which is a wrong date that still appears in Western publications to this day.[20] Thus, a question naturally comes to mind: Why are there so many conflicting dates even though Li had only one birthday? This would not have been a problem at all in the West, as after birth a baby is registered with the government in the modern age, before which the parents most likely logged the baby's birth with a prebendary office, with the local parish priest, or with their local city ward. In traditional Chinese society, no such registrations with government or church were required, and it was the duty of the family members to remember birth dates. The lack of administrative and religious registrations put the recording of an accurate birthday in disarray, so much so that individuals sometimes could not confirm the date of their own birth. According to one argument, Li pretended to be younger, while he was actually a much older student among his peers in Tokyo. Hence it becomes apparent that a primary source might orient a researcher in the direction of an inaccurate date—a warning to all to read an original document more critically. The Li Dazhao fervor after the Cultural Revolution compelled Chinese researchers to carefully examine those conflicting dates. Through scholarly research, on-site interviews, and correlational scrutiny, Li Dazhao's birthday has now been ascertained as October 29, 1889.[21]

The fact that Li Dazhao led an unfortunate young life supports the validity of the theory of childhood that important individuals are often those who experience misfortunes during their early years. It is their adversity that prompts them to be more assertive and more valiant in their quest for a successful career. As for Li, the available sources bring to light several grief-filled episodes in his childhood. These fateful occurrences were so deeply lodged in Li's memory that he lamented his sorrowful infancy in the autobiography he authored in 1914. Just before his execution in 1927, he still bemoaned his wretched childhood in his own last statement.[22] One fatal tragedy was his bereavement at losing both of his parents around the time of his birth. Li's father, Li Renrong, was adopted by his uncle. Renrong was a talented and promising young man. His marriage to Lady Zhou was arranged at a nearby village. Both husband and wife enjoyed nuptial happiness, but Renrong fell sick due to a lung disease that became exasperated by exhaustion during the earthquake of 1888 because he carried his birth mother from her residence to a safe place. Fright and overtiredness soon ended his life, and he died in March 1889, making Li Dazhao a posthumous son of his late father.[23] In her grief, Lady Zhou, newly widowed, found herself pregnant and gave birth to Li Dazhao seven months later. Another disaster befell Li at the age of a little over one year old, when his mother passed away on March 7, 1891.[24]

What followed these bereavements was Li Dazhao's injurious experience of constraint, isolation, and animosity within the household. An orphan without parental love, young Li Dazhao was surrounded by hostile family members who deemed him a thorn in the flesh. His foster grandmother, Lady Cui, harbored no feeling for him because she regarded him as an outsider and a usurper. Lady Cui had three daughters, among whom two had been married off to reside faraway. The youngest daughter, known as Third Aunt (Sangu) to Li Dazhao's children, remained with the family, although she was married to a man named Mr. Wang who also lived in the same house. Lady Cui, Third Aunt, and Mr. Wang forged an alliance and conceived a plan to seize the inheritance of family property. Third Aunt paid no heed to young Li Dazhao, nor did she assist in raising him. Even worse, according to one testimony, she plotted a scheme to murder him because she viewed him as a hurdle to her bequest of her father's property.[25] With such intimidating individuals living in the same compound, young Li Dazhao entered a harrowing realm of abuse, negligence, and hatred. In a traditional family, blood ties determined social relationships and distant blood ties meant a remote relationship, which rooted deeply in the mindset of Third Aunt, her husband, and her mother. Consequently, young Li Dazhao suffered from long-term psychological maltreatment, which left a bitter memory deeply etched in his mind. After his acceptance of communism, Li Dazhao utilized communist doctrine to interpret his early years and argued that the private ownership of property was the origin of his early family problems. His bitter childhood experience was a factor in his move onto the path of communism, as his daughter Li Xinghua has claimed.[26]

In spite of such an ill-fated family setting, Li Dazhao did not grow up to be a desperate youth; rather, he outgrew the insalubrious environment and made strenuous efforts to move on to a better life. During the process, his foster grandfather played a role in guarding, nurturing, and educating him. According to his daughter Li Xinghua's memoir, "the old grandfather labored diligently to feed him mouthful by mouthful."[27] At first, the old man tried to find a wet nurse to provide milk for young Li Dazhao, who had just lost his mother. But young Li refused any other woman's milk except for his aunt's. Although Third Aunt could have been an ideal substitute, she declined to offer any help. As a result, the foster grandfather chewed all kinds of foods carefully to feed the baby. The grandfather selected "Simpleton" (Hantou) as the first name for the baby, following the local tradition of choosing an undesirable name to expect good fortune in return. This turned out to be a special caregiver-infant relationship, in which the grandfather lavished young Li Dazhao with abundant affection, emotional gentleness, and cautious safekeeping. Without hesitation, he shielded the boy from abusive family members and defended him from bullies. He understood that only in this way could young Li Dazhao survive and grow well. However, he occasionally allowed his sister-in-law, Li Dazhao's own grandmother, whom he trusted as a reliable person, to come over to take care of the baby.[28] Thus, young Li Dazhao was brought up by his foster grandfather, who invested all his hopes in him, because of which Li Dazhao did not sink into limbo. Li gratefully acknowledged this in his last statement: "I lost my parents while I was a baby. Without any brothers and without any sisters, I was raised up by a gray-headed grandfather."[29]

This special bond enabled young Li Dazhao to enjoy his foster grandfather's love, yet the old man's overprotection limited Li's social activities. Of course, the grandfather had reasonable justifications; he feared that young Li Dazhao might be harmed by bullies, influenced by detrimental habits, or abducted by wicked villains. It was this fear that led Li's grandfather to confine young Li in the family compound and to subject him to a specially designed custody. From today's perspective, this would not be considered a healthy parenting practice. Yet it was the grandfather's commitment that directed young Li onto a path to reach his full potential. The grandfather's decision was not made without reason, as local residents indulged themselves in gambling, which led many young children down that profligate path. Once, young Li went to watch such gambling, and his grandfather penalized him by having him do heavy chores. Ever since, Li never contacted any of those gamblers.[30] The grandfather's stark emphasis on protection was meant to ensure that young Li would not squander his time and would not befriend decadent individuals. Instead, young Li, accompanied by his grandfather, raised flowers and plants in their yard and kept dogs and cats in the compound.[31] The lack of outside social contacts strengthened their mutual bond. In the mind of young Li Dazhao, his foster grandfather occupied an irreplaceable place as an extraordinary guardian. In this way, a psychological seed was sowed in his mind that would bloom much later as he continued to seek a similar kind of care for his nation, which motivated him to search for an ideological protector, eventually settling on communism.

The foster grandfather's protective guardianship was not meant as an act of pampering; rather, he designed for young Li Dazhao a path toward a successful life through rigorous early education in preparation for his participation in China's Civil Service Examination System. This was an inseparable component of traditional Chinese elite culture, for which Laoting County had scored considerable success. In the 170 years between 1706 and 1876, the county produced sixteen *jinshi*, 142 *juren*, and

226 *xiucai* degree holders. Li Dazhao's grandfather felt it a necessity for young Li to acquire an early education, and he himself acted as Li's first mentor. No professional curriculum was designed; rather, a rudimentary knowledge of selected Confucian classics, such as *The Three-Character Classic* (Sanzijing) and *The Thousand-Character Classic* (Qianziwen), was taught through memorization of Chinese characters by rigid rote and repeated recitation. From three to six years old, young Li was under the tutelage of his foster grandfather in these basics of Confucianism. Without a doubt, this act of early intervention benefited the young boy, who in turn amazed his grandfather with his acumen for acquiring literacy. Thus, young Li's personal paradise included a desk on which he placed his classics, notebooks, ink, and pens, along with a nearby family garden with flowers, plants, and pet animals.[32] In this way, Li Ruzhen's desire to tap into his foster grandson's potential prepared young Li to be an educated individual and an efficient writer.

Li Ruzhen's overprotection can also be found in his arrangement of Li Dazhao's early marriage, which has long spawned substantial attention, as it was rare for a ten-year-old boy to be a groom. More strikingly, Li's bride was almost six years his senior. The bizarre marriage may seem sensational to today's audience. A careful examination demonstrates again the foster grandfather's unusual care for young Li, as his marriage was meant to be a survival strategy. Unlike other marriages that involve social, economic, and political interests, young Li's marriage was shepherded for his personal survival. When Li got married in 1899, his grandfather was already seventy-two years old and knew his own days were numbered. Unless his foster grandson contracted a viable marriage with an older woman, the boy would be at risk once the old man passed away.[33] In other words, an older wife would function as a responsible caretaker for young Li. Truly, this marriage was intended to benefit young Li's vulnerable life, alleviate his possible adversity, and turn a disadvantageous situation into an advantageous one. Despite the age difference, the marriage conformed to local tradition, as the bride was the daughter of the foster grandfather's friend Zhao Wenlong. Through a business partnership in Manchuria, Li Ruzhen and Zhao Wenlong developed an increasing friendship. The Zhaos, a well-to-do family, being driven by this strong tie, sympathized with young Li's situation and agreed to marry their daughter off to a much younger boy. Since the two families lived in the same village and because the bride and the groom knew each other well, the Zhaos believed that the marriage would be a perfect fit.

It is obvious that the foster grandfather's primary concern was the survival strategy, and fortunately for him the marriage panned out well. The bride, Zhao Renlan (1884–1933), proved to be a virtuous and responsible wife. She arrived in Li's home in 1899 and started to take care of Li's foster grandparents and perform chores inside the house. It was this young lady who escorted young Li Dazhao to a private school for his classical education, and it was this new bride who acted as a young motherly figure.[34] She had been taught by her own father so that she was able to read simple books and write short letters. Upon marriage, she became obligated to undertake her duties as a wife and was subsequently praised as a diligent, honest, and kind woman. She gave birth to nine children, of whom five grew to adulthood. To support young Li's scholarly pursuits, she bore hardships at home, sold a portion of the family land to pay Li's tuition, and encouraged Li to complete his college education. Obviously, Li felt indebted, remained loyal to her, and endorsed monogamy throughout his life. His gratitude was explicitly articulated in his last statement, written in jail in 1927, in which he said, "My family is not wealthy, and my wife managed the family land diligently. Sometimes, she had to pawn our family belongings to acquire money to pay my tuition in order for me to graduate from the college."[35] What ought to be mentioned also is that Zhao Renlan raised their young children alone after Li Dazhao's tragic death in 1927 so that they would be prepared for their upcoming careers.

A Classical Education

From 1895 to 1905, Li Dazhao attended three private schools for his ten-year education in the Chinese classics, an essential component in the life of the traditional elite. It was a rigid preparation for the civil service examinations with which the imperial court and its different levels of administration selected talented literati from a large pool of capable candidates to fill vacancies in the imperial bureaucracy. On one hand, it trammeled the growth of hereditary nobles and prevented aristocratic intervention into government affairs, and on the other hand, it encouraged all gifted men, despite their humble backgrounds, to aspire to participate in an openly equitable examination for a job as an official.[36] It was a meritocracy in which well-educated individuals were chosen to be administrators, allowing them to become officials assisting the imperial family in governing the huge Chinese empire. As Benjamin A. Elman elaborates, it allowed the ordinary people "to achieve elite status and wield political power."[37] For over a millennium, it served as a national program to such an extent that it permeated the core organs of the dynastic regimentation, diverse levels of imperial rule, and the lowest echelon of the grassroots community. During the Qing dynasty, "the civil service examination system in late imperial China became a dominant force in determining the character of Chinese society."[38] Viewed from the bottom up, it is obvious that well-to-do families acted vehemently and responded keenly to it by educating their male children to be qualified candidates for the triennial examinations held at county seats, provincial capitals, and the imperial headquarters. Li's grandfather had already homeschooled him in rudimentary classical education; nevertheless, he felt that young Li should be sent to a private school for intensive training under the guidance of an experienced tutor in order to be able to pass the upcoming county-level examination.

Despite the lack of detailed records about Li Dazhao's early education, scholars in recent decades have obtained a large quantity of empirical information about it, including personal recollections, individual memoirs, and oral historical accounts. For three years beginning in 1895, Li Dazhao attended a private school at the west end of his village, which was run by the family of Gu Zonghai, who allowed other children in the village to enroll as well. The tutor was Shan Zi'ao, a *xiucai* degree holder, who taught the *Analects* and the *Mencius*. It was in this school that young Li got his formal name, Qinian (old age), and his scholarly name, Shouchang (booming longevity), from Shan, who sympathized with young Li as an unfortunate orphan and wished him a long life. To his teacher's satisfaction, Li was the youngest but the smartest. Li was not only diligent in his work but also tried his best to help other children. According to one testimony, Li converted a small wooden box made by his grandfather into a small library, stored his books inside, brought it to school daily, and read those books whenever he had spare time. Later on, he presented this box as a gift to his classmate Gu Xingsan, whose family had kept it until they donated it to a local museum in recent years. In Shan's eyes, Li was the best student in his forty-year career. Li respected Shan and kept a cordial relationship with him for the rest of his life. It is said that Shan wept profusely over Li's execution in 1927 and wrote a eulogy dedicated to his former student and condemning the warlord who killed him.[39]

Upon Shan Zi'ao's recommendation, Li Dazhao was transferred to another private school located in Xiaoheituo, about a mile south of his village. Li walked daily to this school. The tutor, Zhao Huidou, was a *xiucai* degree holder, a poet, and a well-regarded classics teacher. Li Dazhao's father had once been his student. Seeing Li's extraordinary intelligence, Zhao invested his time in his former student's son, hoping that young Li could excel in the upcoming civil service examinations. The school was run by a rich man named Zhang Gongpu for his only son, Zhang Chunjiong. This school was ranked the best in the area in terms of facilities, equipment, and resources. Within a few years, under Zhao's meticulous tutelage, Li Dazhao did so well that he became a brilliant prodigy, according to Zhao.[40] Unfortunately, Zhang Chunjiong suddenly died, and the school was subsequently shut down. To continue assisting Li Dazhao, Zhao went to Li's house to tutor him. With all this preparation, Li took his first examination at the county level in 1902. It is said that he did very well, but he spilled his ink on his essays by accident, which caused his unfortunate failure.[41] By this point, Zhao was an old man and recommended that Li attend another private school in a faraway village where Li would stay to continue his pursuit of classical learning.

The third private school was located at Jingjiatuo Village, about six miles away. It was established by a *juren* degree holder, Song Senyin, who once served as a county magistrate in Shandong Province. Song hired a famous scholar, Huang Baolin, as the tutor. Huang was an acclaimed instructor among the *xiucai* degree holders in Laoting County because he studied at the Imperial Academy (Guozijian) in Beijing for a number of years. Under Huang's supervision, Li Dazhao made rapid progress. Although the classics remained the same, the tutor's resourceful expertise enabled his students to interpret the classics from different perspectives, to compose elegant essays, and to author sophisticated poems. According to Huang's testimony, "Li Dazhao is always obsessed with reading. His hands are always accompanied by books. He becomes knowledgeable and he has a superb memory. He excels in both moral cultivation and scholarly aptitude."[42] Not surprisingly, Li achieved one of the highest scores in the county-level examination in 1905, for which he should have been awarded a *xiucai* degree. But, surprisingly, the imperial government suddenly decided to abolish the Civil Service Examination System at this very critical moment as a part of the ongoing reform known as the New Policy (Xinzheng). This abolition left Li's dream in shards, like a pane of glass falling from the roof to the ground. It seemed to Li that the bright light suddenly grew dim; nevertheless, the abolition of the Civil Service Examination System only proved to serve as a turning point in his life.

It is reasonable to underline the importance of Li Dazhao's classical education because he was immersed in the traditional culture, which contributed to the cultivation of his early patriotic awareness. The Confucian emphasis on individual responsibility to the state and the Confucian stress of personal obligations to society require a gentleman to aim at a high target, to act according to moral principles, and to reflect frequently over his own conduct for the purpose of self-rectification. Although Confucianism is an all-embracing ideology that intends to remold every aspect of human life, one of Confucianism's determining elements is its accentuation of personal duty as integral to the wholesome function of the entire country, which serves as a desideratum necessitating individuals' dedication to their nation. This sort of accountability becomes so pertinent that it engenders the high criterion of being a gentleman whose burdens are much broadened beyond the restrictions of family, community, and region. Li's writings prove that his exposure to the classics drew a burst of spontaneous reactions, as he encountered a decaying empire and a shattered nation. At the private schools, he asked questions about national affairs, inquired about foreign invasions, and demonstrated his concerns about his country. The ancient patriotic examples elicited his innate response, exhorting him to emulate those precedents. Li would extricate himself from the Confucian shackles by veering away from this traditional paradigm while he was constantly searching for a newer ideology. Nevertheless, it was the traditional sense of personal bond to the state and his initial patriotic urge to serve his country that provided an intrinsic driving force compelling him to pursue a more suitable ideological approach for his nation's salvation.[43]

China's current events at that time equally served to foment young Li Dazhao's nationalistic awareness. While pursuing his classical education, Li found that his private schools functioned well as information hubs to receive the news about what was happening in the country. First of all, the Hundred Days' Reform of 1898 inspired young Li. The courageous deeds of Kang Youwei and Liang Qichao, although unsuccessful, exerted an influence upon on him, as he venerated the reformers' patriotic audacity. To strengthen Li's understanding of the reforms, his tutor Huang Baolin presented him with Kang and Liang's articles and books as gifts.[44] Li was therefore impacted by the ongoing official nationalism that aimed at learning from the West in order to modernize China. However, young Li was open to other diverse ideas. For example, he was strongly captivated by Han nationalism, as he himself was an ethnic Han. Perhaps the most gripping evidence was his high regard for Hong Xiuquan, the leader of the Taiping Rebellion, which happened three decades earlier. Huang Baolin introduced the Taiping Rebellion to him and narrated its history at the school. Upon hearing the stories, Li lamented Hong Xiuquan's failure. To young Li, Hong was a hero trying to topple a corrupt dynasty. It is said that Li voiced his resolve to emulate Hong emphatically and unwaveringly.[45] His evocation of the Taiping insurgents, his admiration of Hong Xiuquan, and his determination to pattern himself after the rebel leader all demonstrated his concord with Han nationalism.

Most salient to historical reality, besides the corruption of the Qing regime, was Li Dazhao's witnessing of foreign invasions into his country and especially his province. This was not a faraway event; on the contrary, it happened just nearby while Li was attending the private schools. In particular, the eight industrialized powers dispatched a huge number of troops to suppress the Boxer Rebellion in 1900, inflicted on the local people unspeakable sufferings, and brought about an agonizing trauma throughout Li's province. When the news of the local people's appalling sorrows arrived, Li Dazhao sympathized with his fellow provincial folks. He angrily asked his tutor, "Why can the foreign powers be so domineering in our land?"[46] Of course, the answers are multiple, but his anti-imperialist sentiment was partially fostered as a repercussion to foreign aggression. His animosity toward foreign atrocities did not turn him into a Boxer-type xenophobe; on the contrary, Li admired Western culture, according to the available sources. At the age of nine in 1898, at his private school, it is said that Li used his regular-script calligraphic skills to copy down the Chinese translation of Adam Smith's *The Wealth of Nations*.[47] These two contradictory attitudes, an aversion for foreign invasions and a passion for foreign ideas, coexisted within Li's mental world. It was the interplay of these two conflicting ideas—one resisting and one embracing—that became an endless theme throughout his future life. While Western imperialism was his enemy, Western ideas must be accepted so long as they could fulfill his goal of national salvation.

Conclusion

The perennial problem in the study of any historical figure's early years is the dearth of relevant materials and, in particular, primary sources. Fortunately, the voluminous post-Mao publications on Li Dazhao have offered a clearer portrait of his early life. Li led an unfortunate life during his childhood, not only because he lost his parents when he was a baby but also because he lived among abusive family members. It was his fortune that his foster grandfather took care of him as an earnest and devoted endeavor. This pair of extraordinary individuals, the foster grandfather and the foster grandson, created a special tie between a guardian and a minor. Besides the daily guardianship, his foster grandfather set high expectations for Li to accomplish: preparing for the civil service examinations and scoring higher in the upcoming tests. Yet the abolition of the examination system in 1905 shattered young Li's dream and diverted him to a new path. If time were frozen and there had been no major changes, Li might have become a village elite playing an important role in his local community, just like his foster grandfather had. Nevertheless, Li Dazhao moved on to explore the outside world. His early marriage at the age of ten may seem a bizarre union, but he faithfully stuck to the marriage his grandfather had arranged. Interestingly, throughout his life, Li was looking for a new guardianship as a replacement after the death of his foster grandfather, even an ideological guardianship, such as communism, not only for his life but also for his nation.

It is fair to argue that Li Dazhao's ten-year classical education at the three private schools in Laoting County under the tutelage of three excellent Confucian scholars laid a solid foundation for Li to be a future scholar. More importantly, from the Confucian classics, he inherited a sense of individual responsibility to the country, which could be better interpreted as a special type of traditional patriotism. His provincial culture exhorted him to seek justice, gallantry, and uprightness. Given the circumstances of the invasion of his country by the imperialist powers while the Qing dynasty was declining, it was not strange to see him adopt a strong sense of nationalism at such a young age. Nonetheless, his nationalism was multifaceted: he was influenced by official nationalism, by anti-Manchu sentiment, and by an anti-imperialist attitude. In his young psychological world, those nationalist underpinnings took root but could be modified, and he would be enriched by new ideas from new sources. Overall, it is fair to argue that his nationalist feelings during this early stage were rudimentary, simplistic, natural, and spontaneous and did not become systematic, complicated, sophisticated, or all-inclusive. The dramatic shift to a new form of nationalism occurred after his departure from Laoting County to experience Western-style learning at two new educational facilities, from which he received his modern education, acquired new knowledge, and accepted new ideas.

Chapter 2

Pursuing a Modern Education

Introduction

Between 1905 and 1913, Li Dazhao was nurtured in a modern education in two new schools: one was an academy in Lulong Prefecture, and the other was an elite college in the city of Tianjin. This was the first time he had left Laoting County, lived away from his family, led an independent life, and expanded his social network. More importantly, at the two schools, he acquired newly introduced knowledge gleaned from the outside world in the expanding educational system of the late Qing dynasty and the early republic, embracing new ideas, adopting new outlooks, and being inculcated with new values. In contrast to his nation, which underwent a dramatic disruption between empire and republic during these years, Li's personal journey shows an amazing continuity in terms of his uninterrupted pursuit of a modern education. In this way, he was a perfect example, revealing China's educational reforms and encounter with inflowing Western learning.

While pursuing modern education, Li Dazhao's patriotic consciousness was strengthened rather than weakened. His innermost nationalist urge is visible in both his writings and his participation in national events intending to transform his country into a modern state. At first, he got involved in the movement calling for constitutional reform, for which he was a student leader. Then, he supported the 1911 Revolution that toppled the Qing dynasty. After the establishment of the republic in 1912, he championed constitutional rule, democratic institutions, and Western civilization. In the most straightforward terms, his nationalist underpinnings were interlaced deeply with his thoughts and his actions.

As his country faced domestic and international difficulties during the early republic, his nationalism propelled him to search for a newer approach, to find a newer solution, and to seek a newer paradigm for his country's modernization.

One way to save China, according to Li Dazhao's understanding, was to fully establish the democratic system, and in his writings and actions he interpreted its merits, elaborated its values, and pushed for its materialization. While supporting democracy, he condemned tyranny, emerged as a proponent of constitutional rule, and became a sharp critic of the despotic tradition. In a sense, he was one of the precursors among the young generation fighting for the bourgeoning republicanism. His writings during those years expose his blueprint for transforming China by following the Western way, for which he created a vision of democracy, borrowed Western terms to interpret its values, and advised his countrymen on its acceptance. Lamenting the chaotic national disorder during the early republic, he defended the newly established republican system, called for national revival, and promoted democratic ideals. In many ways, he was a democrat, or more precisely a patriotic democrat, during those years.

The Yongping Days

The abolition of the Civil Service Examination System in 1905 dashed Li Dazhao's dream of obtaining a traditional degree but served as a turning point of his personal life. The fact that he passed the county-level examination at such a young age demonstrated his extraordinary ability.[1] The ensuing governmental policy of allowing successful examinees at the county level to attend the prefectural academy offered him a new chance of receiving a modern education. It proved vital to his life, as it was an opportunity for him to step out of the old way. In 1905, Li went to the Yongping Prefectural Academy (*Yongpingfuzhongxuetang*) and studied there for two years, which was a rewarding experience. Yet scholars who write on Li mention those two years in just a few sentences. This negligence, naturally enough, was caused by the lack of primary sources. His short stay there perhaps also contributed to this indifference. As a transition period in Li's life, his Yongping years were likely deemed unimportant, so much so that little was written on them.

Indeed, patchy sources make it difficult to trace Li Dazhao's life during those two years; nevertheless, recent studies point to the impact the local culture had upon the shaping of his personal character. Yongping was a prefecture, a level of imperial administration between province and county, that oversaw six counties: Lulong, Qian'an, Funing, Changli, Linyu, and Laoting. The prefectural seat was located at Lulong, which was also the county seat, and the academy sat right in its urban center. Historically, Lulong was the place of epic stories, including that of the Guzhu Kingdom, a vassal state of the ancient Shang dynasty, whose two princes Boyi and Shuqi refused to submit to the Zhou dynasty and starved themselves to death to flaunt their loyalty to the Shang. Both men were hailed by Confucius as models of loyalty, integrity, and bravery, which inspired local folks, including the new resident Li Dazhao, to be patriotic, straightforward, and intrepid.[2] This local tradition reinforced the local residents' nationalism, in particular in reaction to the recent wake of imperialist invasions. During the suppression of the Boxer Rebellion in 1900, the foreign powers sent troops to occupy all strategic locations in the region, including Lulong, where British soldiers killed seventy residents in one action. The atrocities of alien troops aroused local animosity and poignantly impacted Li Dazhao.[3]

The academy Li Dazhao attended was a new learning facility. To guarantee its quality, the government only admitted successful county examinees of the civil service examinations along with other talented individuals. The academy was a part of the provincial educational reform initiated by Yuan Shikai, who was at that time the governor-general of Zhili Province. It was established at the traditional imperial prefectural learning center (shuyuan), which was remodeled into an official training school in 1902 and later also incorporated the nearby charity school. This enlarged facility became the Yongping Prefectural Academy, established to train talented individuals from the prefecture. The academy dislodged the dominance of the Confucian curriculum in favor of Western learning, but it did not completely engulf the old by the new, as the classics remained a portion of the new curriculum. Its real value, though, was in its offering of courses in Western learning, including English, mathematics, science, global history, world geography, international politics, and physical education. It also owned a library that allowed students to browse a variety of collections, including books, journals, newspapers, and magazines.[4]

Figure 2.1. One of the earliest known photos of Li Dazhao was taken when he studied at the Yongping Prefectural Academy between 1905 and 1907. It was in this school that Li started to be exposed to Western learning, before which he had studied Chinese classics. (Public domain)

China's newly established educational facilities were still porous, shapeless, and inadequate during the transitional era, yet the new academy at least rolled out a new vision for modern education by endorsing an interdisciplinary curriculum with a mission of introducing Western learning. In addition, the ethos of this academy was to encourage students like Li Dazhao to pursue scholarly excellence. It was this new school that contributed to Li's academic progress, as he initially found it fit his needs and suited his taste. He was regarded as a gifted young man, respected as a diligent individual, and praised for his excellent academic performance. According to his classmate Han Xiangting, Li had accomplished so much but led a simple and self-disciplined life. Another testimony states that Li read whenever he had time and often studied without a break.[5] More strikingly, Li indulged himself in the writings of Kang Youwei and Liang Qichao and was deeply influenced by the two reformers' progressive ideas for changing China into a modern country.[6]

As Li Dazhao moved toward the verge of maturity in his life, he built a new social network at Yongping. Not a large number of students had enrolled there, though. Including the upper classes, less than a couple hundred students in total studied at the academy, while Li's class for that year (1905) admitted fifty students. Nevertheless, Yongping granted the young men an opportunity to develop their fraternal ties. The collective mood was their high spirit for national salvation through diverse means, including modern education, frontier defense, military reform, and so forth. For example, Bai Meichu, a Manchu who was in the upper class, became Li's good friend. Bai would become a geographer and draw the first solid line to declare China's sovereignty over the South China Sea, which was the origin of today's nine-dashed line.[7] Song Zhongbin, Li's classmate, became a military commander and once served as Sun Yat-sen's personal logistics assistant.[8] Liu Yulou, another classmate of Li's, would become an educator in Beijing. Liu Yulou's grandson, Liu He, a Harvard graduate, was the chief Chinese negotiator for the US-China trade war of recent years.[9] Among Li Dazhao's classmates, Jiang Weiping can be singled out to emphasize the common mood of the ever-expanding nationalism of that time. Jiang Weiping (alias Jiang Datong) was seven years Li's senior but became his good friend. Jiang was extremely nationalistic, with the particular aim of defending China's frontier in Manchuria, for which he studied the Russian language. Jiang quit Yongping, studied briefly at a military school in Baoding, and then migrated to Manchuria, where he secretly joined Sun Yat-sen's Revolutionary Alliance. He crossed the Amur River, purporting to restore the occupied Chinese enclaves on the Russian side. Unfortunately, he was captured by Russian soldiers, but he was released the first time. Once again, he tried to assist the Heilongjiang provincial government to reclaim the Chinese settlements inside Russia, but this time he was killed by Russian troops. The Nationalist historian Feng Ziyou praised Jiang Weiping as a saint of the Nationalist Party.[10] Although Li Dazhao and Jiang Weiping studied together at Yongping for just three months, their friendship did not fade out. In young Li's mind, Jiang was a model to be emulated. In 1909, Li Dazhao wrote two poems in tribute to Jiang Weiping's loyalty to China. Upon hearing of Jiang's death in 1910, Li felt an enormous loss and composed another two poems to honor Jiang as a gallant warrior who sacrificed his life for China's border fortification. Li wrote in commemoration of a dear friend, a lost idol, and a respected national hero; his elegantly crafted lyrical lines were intended to bring back to life a daring patriotic individual.[11]

During Li Dazhao's Yongping years, one tragic loss was the death of his foster grandfather in 1906. The grandfather and the grandson had forged an intimate psychological tie ever since young Li was an infant. To him, the old man played an all-encompassing role in his life, embodying love, benevolence, humility, support, and protection. According to Li Xinghua's testimony, Li Dazhao rushed back home upon hearing that his grandfather was dying. For days, he accompanied the old man until the latter breathed his last. Although the grandfather's last will stipulated clearly that the family should avoid an expensive funeral in order to save money for young Li's education, the ensuing family dispute unfortunately resulted in the holding of an extravagant burial upon Third Aunt's insistence. The excessive expenditure on this lavish funeral exhausted the family's fortune and caused a heavy financial drag on young Li's education. Li's grief as well as the subsequent financial burden imposed an unbearable weight, making young Li's life fraught with quandaries. At this crucial moment, however, his supportive wife fearlessly bore the heavy load. She encouraged him to continue his education while she pawned family belongings and borrowed money from relatives, including her own father, with a determination to sponsor her husband's scholarly pursuit.[12]

After he returned to Yongping, Li Dazhao found that the academy could not fulfill his expectations, and thereafter he decided to quit it for a new outlet. The prefectural academy was supposed to be a venue for young Li to secure a decent job as a staff member or even an official in the local administration. Since Li had already received accolades by scoring the highest of any at the academy, this venue should have been a guarantee of such a job. But Li was inspired by his patriotic friends. It was this increasing nationalistic consciousness that prompted him to choose a new path. According to Li's own testimony, "I felt a paramount pressure from the national crisis, for which I was zealous in studying political theories, and I was eager to seek a better way of saving the country and rejuvenating the nation."[13] Obviously, Yongping could not help him reach those goals. Thus, a gap existed between Li's existing reality and his nationalistic objectives, as Li explicitly explained. To close the gap, he believed, only a more comprehensive and more liberal college could consummate his aspirations. Consequently, one year before his scheduled graduation from Yongping, he abruptly dropped out and traveled to the provincial capital Tianjin to take the examination for admission to a college.

The admission into a college meant that Li Dazhao had terminated his two-year stint at Yongping. Upon his arrival in Tianjin, he faced three options, according to his own memory. The first was a military medical college, the second a banking institution, and the third a college specializing in law and politics. He recalled, "I had no interest in military medicine, for which I did not even take the examination. I tried to pass the exam for the banking institution, which offered me admission. Yet my appetite was not to handle money or to get rich for myself. Therefore, I gave up that opportunity. Finally, I took another examination for the third option, and fortunately I was accepted by North China College of Law and Politics."[14] Without graduating from Yongping, Li embarked on the new path of his college education.

It should be noted that Li Dazhao's journey from Yongping to Tianjin and his return home begot a by-product: an infatuation with natural adventure, which would accompany his future intellectual life. When he traveled to Tianjin, he first took a boat on a waterway from Yongping to Luanzhou and transferred at its railway station. On the waterway, "the meandering mountainous paths and the high peaks . . . presented an extremely beautiful spectacle."[15] This was the first time he had taken the railway, which enabled him to see the landscape of the countryside on both sides. On his way back home, he visited Wufeng Mountain, the peak of Mount Jieshi, which he had previously fallen in love with. He called it "a wonderland in the human world," glorifying its splendor.[16] This trip had an enduring effect, as it became his hobby to come to Wufeng Mountain to appreciate nature's beauty, release heavy burdens, seek temporary seclusion, write scholarly pieces, and escape political persecution. His celebration of natural beauty along with his passion for the untamed wilderness was an essential part of his adventurous spirit, and it was closely linked to his patriotism, as his affection for the country also included his fondness of its beautiful landscape.

The Tianjin Years

Li Dazhao's Tianjin years, from 1907 to 1913, comprised a huge milestone in his life. It was in Tianjin that Li obtained his college education, exposed himself deeply to Western learning, and familiarized himself with more foreign ideas. From the new imports of the outside world, he absorbed unfamiliar information, embraced modern values, and assumed broad perspectives. It was in Tianjin that he achieved his only complete college education, became a well-educated man, and turned into a globally oriented intellectual. He benefited significantly from the newly established educational system, relished his hunger for imported knowledge, imbibed the shared mood of absorbing new cultural elements, and delighted in the nationalistic sentiment for salvaging the waning Chinese civilization. It was in Tianjin that his nationalistic commitment to making China a strong country through adoption of the democratic system was further developed. While obtaining his accredited baccalaureate education during those six years, Li witnessed Chinese social elites' efforts in a push for constitutional reform and experienced the violent revolution that overthrew the moribund dynasty. In this turbulent time, he became a participant in the nationwide political uproar that resulted in China's transition from an empire to a republic.

Li Dazhao's college was a six-year higher education institution called the North China College of Laws and Politics (*Beiyangfazhengzhuanmenxuexiao*), which had been built in 1906 by Yuan Shikai and became a nationally reputed institution, admitting students from all over China through its rigorous entrance examination. It was distinct from the previous Civil Service Examination System in that it followed a new didactic philosophy and adopted a reformed pedagogy. In fact, it was one of the first modern universities established during the late Qing dynasty. Of Li's six-year program, the first three years constituted the preparatory stage, and the next three years the formal training. Li selected politics as his major, intending to realize his dream of saving his country through studying political theories. He was benefited by the college's comprehensive curriculum, its flexible pedagogy, and its vibrant community, in which he was exposed to an open, liberal, and internationalized milieu. Besides the courses that focused on Chinese-style learning, such as Chinese literature and Qing laws, Li took more Western-style courses, which included politics, economics, finance, sociology, constitutional law, criminal justice, regional autonomy, world history, international law, and more.[17] During the first three years, Li was immersed in learning two foreign languages, Japanese and English, in which he made quick progress. His instructors included Japanese scholars, such as Yoshino Sakuzo and Imai Yoshiyuki, who taught at the college for years without interpreters, challenging Chinese students including Li to experience the Japanese style of education in a Chinese classroom. Li was soon well versed in both Japanese and English, which enabled him to absorb information about national and global issues from foreign publications.

The daunting issue for Li Dazhao was not his capability for acquiring knowledge or sharpening his skills; rather, it was the high expense of the college, which required him to pay a monthly tuition of three yuan that had to be paid every three months. In addition, the monthly cost for food was five yuan. Along with miscellaneous fees, the monthly expenses could be more than ten yuan. The annual expenditure, including travel fees and other overhead, could be an astonishing amount of one to two hundred yuan, which was a huge sum for a rural family like Li's to afford. He was perplexed at such a cost, and it amounted to a serious financial burden for his family, while his wife was laboring diligently at home. At this critical moment, according to his daughter, his uncle (the brother of Li Dazhao's own father) encouraged him to continue his higher education. More luckily, his wife promised to offer hard-bitten support, paying his tuition and expenses, handling the family budget, and raising the two little children they had begotten by then.[18] Given such a hardscrabble situation and the accompanying stress, it would have been unsurprising if he had dropped out, which might have been a practical solution. It was his wife's assistance that allowed him to concentrate on his scholarly pursuits, for which he felt indebted. Perhaps his wife's incessant aid and his beholden gratitude to her continued to strengthen their marital tie.

It is impossible to browse Li Dazhao's student file, as the site of his college was totally ruined during the subsequent wars and the college's archives were lost. Yet, from the surviving materials and personal memoirs, we still can glean sufficient information about his excellent performance and his prominent standing. His numerous notes in the margins of his own books displayed in museums demonstrate his assiduousness in learning and his thoroughness in reading. It was during those years that he started to publish essays and poems, with which he began to accumulate an amazing body of work, considering his status as an undergraduate student. Although publications should be seen as a relatively minor, unimportant matter to a college student, Li's writings underscore his extraordinary ability among his peers. His elegant lettering skills and his unique ideas came to define his impending fame as a critical thinker, an effective author, and a prolific writer. His classmate Yu Shude commented that "Li Dazhao was the one who excelled in essay writing, for which he enjoyed an envious reputation throughout the entire college."[19] Moreover, Li was a diligent truth seeker, a sarcastic commentator, and an honest individual. For his excellent academic performance and moral conduct, he was acclaimed as one of "the Three Brilliant Talents" of his college (Beiyangsanjie).[20] To extol his writing skills, his classmate Yu Yi commented that Li's elegant, farsighted, and poignant essays "are so glaring that they can penetrate the towering clouds, so mysterious that they can arouse gods to shed tears like rain, and so sharp that they can cut metals and stone into pieces," a very lavish compliment.[21]

A quick glimpse over Li Dazhao's works could immediately create an incorrect impression that he was just an essayist, because he authored so many articles during his college years. But a careful reading of his works shows that he was also a poet. Among his twenty-five surviving poems, nineteen are traditionally styled lyrics, and the remaining ones are the free verses he authored after 1915. From his poems, it is evident that Li devoted some of his time at the college to crafting lyrics. Not only did he master the established literary modus operandi, but he also integrated his patriotic mood into those inspirational lines. He often cited ancient anecdotes to articulate his passion for his country, to demonstrate his concerns about his nation, to vent his anger at the imperialist invasions, and to show his anxiety over thorny issues. He displayed his admiration for patriotic heroes, including his own friends, in his exquisite verses. He integrated local culture into his lines and considered his poems a tool to resonate patriotic sentiment, exhibit the people's valor, and highlight popular veneration for ancient heroes such as Jing Ke.[22] A reader can easily extract the thought-provoking messages from his patriotic verses and identify his anguish over his suffering nation. By utilizing historical precedents, he intended to extend the logical continuity of China's patriotic tradition, purportedly to embolden his peers and to arouse his countrymen to action. Yet his poems might not be comprehensible to foreign nationals if they were translated verbatim into other languages, since Li composed them by following the traditional Chinese lyrical pattern of citing facts concerning historical figures, classical anecdotes, and ancient events.

It should be noted that Li Dazhao forged a new social network among a group of energetic, ambitious, and nationalistic young men during his college years. All of them were well-educated individuals in Tianjin, where they pursued knowledge together, discussed national affairs together, and expressed shared feelings together. Many of them would retain a lifelong friendship, although some broke off relations because of future diverse political orientations or deviation from their initially communal mindset. Yu Yi, a Hunanese, came to Tianjin and became Li's best friend. Yu and Li collaborated on a number of projects and forged a fraternal bond. Yu would go on to serve as a university professor and once was appointed as an official in his home province. Bai Jianwu was also Li's intimate friend and kept a narrative of Li's activities in his diaries. Li and Bai exchanged their views on national affairs frankly. But their relationship broke off in the early 1920s due to their conflicting political interests. More tragically, Bai later became a collaborator for the Japanese invaders in the 1930s, for which he was executed by General Feng Yuxiang.[23] Some of Li's classmates, under his influence, went on to follow the path of communism, such as Yu Shude, who served as a high-ranking official of Maoist China. From the existing primary sources, we can see that Li kept on good terms with his peers. For example, two of his classmates, Ni Dingyun and Liu Xiling, were assigned by the Beijing government in 1913 to escort the transport of weapons and ammunition to Xinjiang to defend the frontier region. When the two set off, Li composed two heartrending poems to voice his concerns over their long journey, to extend his best wishes for their travel to a chaotic borderland, and to proclaim his support for national defense, declaring that each inch of the national territory must be guarded. In this way, patriotism and personal intimacy were intertwined tightly in his stylish verses.[24]

More importantly, Li Dazhao put his patriotic zeal into actions that transformed him into an activist, leading the promulgation of a local petition for constitutional reform in 1910. In the early years of the twentieth century, Chinese elites advocated constitutional rule and launched a nationwide petition movement to demand that the Qing dynasty adopt a constitution, establish a national legislature to pass laws, and set up a cabinet to handle routine state affairs. The Manchu rulers, however, refused any erosion of their own power and treated the challenge with disdain. After the failure of the first three petitions, the fourth petition made Tianjin a hub of this movement. According to Li's testimony, his college became one of the centers.[25] The petition movement lasted for days in December 1910, during which massive rallies were assembled at the college as well as in the city. Li witnessed the patriotic moves of his schoolmates; one cut his finger and used his outpouring blood to write a supplication, while another student used a knife to slash his arm, letting blood out to demonstrate his determination. A petition association was organized with Wen Shilin, a local elite, as its president, while Li served as a student leader. On December 21, 1910, about three thousand students and urban residents marched to the office of the governor-general in a colossal rally.[26] Unfortunately, Qing bigotry compelled the local government to take actions of suppression. Wen Shilin was arrested and sent into exile in Xinjiang. Although the movement failed, according to Li, it bequeathed the nation a rare gift, because it exposed the stubbornness of the Manchu rulers who now pushed the people to the opposite side in the upcoming revolution. Ultimately, this movement, which predated the 1911 Revolution, spurred the Chinese to contribute to the Qing's downfall through a new, groundbreaking action in a little less than a year.

Whether or not Li Dazhao participated in the Luanzhou Uprising, which was an event in the 1911 Revolution that overthrew the Qing dynasty, remains a controversial topic, because the existing primary sources, strangely enough, can be used to confirm it and also to deny it. Ling Rong, in his memoir, states that Li was a member of a revolutionary organization called the Northern Republican Association (Beifanggonghehui), which participated in the Luanzhou Uprising in Zhili in early 1912. Yet other memoirs by Wu Shousheng, Nan Qinxuan, Yu Shude, Hu Egong, and others do not mention Li when they discuss the history of this association.[27] Because the Northern Republican Association existed secretly and its members wrote memoirs years or even decades later, the accuracy of their memories poses a problem, which prompts us to not solely rely on those conflicting sources.[28] In any case, it is unreasonable to deny Li's participation. Some assert that Li never mentioned his role in the revolution, which might seem to automatically deny his participation. However, he never mentioned his participation in the 1910 petition movement either, but in fact he was its leader. A simple employment of a source to validate or deny his part in the 1911 Revolution would seem to be unlikely. Until further convincing evidence is found, we have to be cautious in our interpretation. Whatever happened, we can rationally argue that Li supported the 1911 Revolution, either in action or in spirit, as his anti-Manchu attitude reveals. Perhaps he did not personally take part in the Luanzhou Uprising, but he assisted it in a particular way. What we do know is that his friends, such as Yu Shude and his teacher Bai Yayu, got involved in the uprising. Bai Yayu, Li's geography teacher at the college, sacrificed his life for it. Bai's heroic death in front of the Qing troops always lingered in Li's mind. Li mentioned Bai in his writings a number of times. Once, he suggested establishing a shrine or erecting a bronze statue in honor of Bai at the site where he was executed by the Qing troops.[29]

From Li Dazhao's early writings, we know that he was not happy with the national situation of the early republic because he believed that the central government was weak in front of the local elites' defiance, which led to numerous national issues. Li's discontent prompted him to become a member of the Chinese Socialist Party (Zhongguoshehuidang) in November 1912. Although the republic established in 1912 could be called China's first democracy, the country in reality was run by strongmen and manipulated by opportunistic politicians. The two largest political parties, the Nationalist Party and the Progressive Party, had adopted different political agendas; according to Li, however, each was motivated by its partisan egoism. Profoundly disillusioned, Li agonized over the ill-fated republic, even though he continued to celebrate the 1911 Revolution as an epochal event. While he criticized the major political parties for their selfish insatiability, he valued the agenda of the Chinese Socialist Party, built in November 1911 by Jiang Kanghu and his followers such as Chen Yilong. This party upheld "absolute liberty, absolute equality, and absolute fraternity." It supported republicanism, endorsed ethnic harmony, promoted public education, respected individual freedom, and advocated the abolition of hereditary property. By early 1913, this party claimed to have a membership of half a million, which must be an exaggeration. In any case, Li found the party's ideals appealing, especially its emphasis on public education and its promotion of gender equality. Li developed a personal tie with Chen Yilong, whose selfless devotion to the public good might also have been a factor prompting Li to join the party. Unluckily, Chen's application to register the party's Tianjin branch was abruptly rejected by the government. Defying the official disapproval, the Tianjin branch held its founding ceremony on February 2, 1913, with Li Dazhao as one of the leaders, but the local police dispersed the rally and issued an order to prohibit any further meetings. Soon, Chen Yilong was killed by the government, and no further partisan operations were conducted. Despite the party's failure, it was the first political party with which Li had affiliated.[30]

Li Dazhao's leadership role at the college could also be seen in his organization of students' activities to foster nationalistic sentiment, uphold patriotic zeal, and provide timely information to the public. In 1912, Li helped establish the North China Society of Law and Politics (Beiyangfazhengxuehui), which recruited two hundred members and placed them into divisions, of which the largest was the editorial board, consisting of fifty students. This board assumed the responsibility for translation, publication, and dissemination of useful information. Li was elected as one of the two directors, which highlighted his irreplaceable role and his recognized writing ability. Within a year, he and his fellow editors translated two foreign books into Chinese. One was Nakajima

Tan's *China's Destiny of Partition*, in which the Japanese author predicted China's inevitable fate of being carved up by powers because of the Chinese people's inability to embrace republicanism, Chinese leaders' ineptitude, and conservative Chinese culture. Nakajima's book was published in Tokyo in early 1912 but was quickly translated and published in Tianjin in December 1912. In the Chinese edition, Li and his fellow editors employed harsh rebuttals to counter Nakajima's vilification of the Chinese people, defended the Republic of China, lambasted Japan's jingoistic imperialism, and condemned the author's blatant discrimination against the Chinese people.[31] Li and his fellow editors also translated a Russian book titled *Mongolia and the Mongols* by A. M. Pozdneev, who traveled into Mongolia in 1892–93, wrote the book, and published it in 1896. Li exposed Pozdneev's ulterior motive of supplying the czarist government with information for Russia's invasion into Mongolia and alerted the Chinese about their northern frontier crisis. Because only four foreign languages were offered at the college and Russian was not one of them, Li and his classmates must have translated Pozdneev's book from its Japanese or English version. In any case, the translators intended to warn their countrymen of the relentless foreign aggression. The achievement of two translations in one year won Li and his classmates praise, because the books served as a forewarning to alert the Chinese about their national crisis and notify them of incessant foreign incursions. In a harsh nationalistic tirade, the translators, including Li, called on their countrymen to rise up and defend their national interests.[32]

As one of the two editors in chief for the journal *Yanzhi* (The political review), the official publication of the North China Society of Laws and Politics, Li Dazhao took charge of launching the journal on April 1, 1913. In total, six issues were published. The journal assumed a broad-minded attitude and published essays, novels, short stories, biographies, translations, miscellanies, legal codes, and other items, purporting to support republicanism, offering analysis of national issues, and proposing constructive advice to the nascent republic. Under Li and the other editors' careful management, the journal enjoyed a circulation of four thousand copies for its second issue alone.[33] Sources show that Li devoted himself wholeheartedly to the journal's first three issues by reading manuscripts, copyediting texts, arranging colorful insertions, handling printing issues, coordinating nationwide distribution, and reaching out to the public. He continued to assist with the subsequent three issues even after his graduation from the college in July 1913. The journal's publication dragged on until early the following year, although its sixth issue was marked as being published on November 1, 1913. The delay underlines the special connection between Li's dedication and the journal's initial success. Li's involvement begot a windfall of sorts, and he published a barrage of over thirty articles in the journal. As a leading editor, Li reached a wide readership through citations, quotes, and wholesale reprints of the journal content by newspapers, magazines, and others. His writings touched upon diverse issues in a more or less straightforward approach, advancing his comments on national affairs and providing his advice to the young republic for its nation-building and state-building efforts.

Li's Early Thought

It would be an exaggeration to claim that Li Dazhao became a mature theorist during those years as he pursued a modern education, yet it is undeniable that he had turned into a skillful critical thinker, and his acumen, alertness, and erudition empowered him to convey his innermost feelings, innovative views, and insightful remarks. Whenever he focused on national issues, he did not vacillate but candidly propounded his solutions and painstakingly offered his recommendations. It is true that he was a young college student and that he had not yet established his distinctive ideological framework; nevertheless, he had sharpened his critical thinking skills and made remarkable progress in rational inference. The more he exposed himself to foreign culture, the more he chose to rely on a wide lens, maintaining his priority for an approach to national salvation, a goal from which he never flinched. Just as John King Fairbank argued that modern Chinese history is but the process of China's response to the foreign, especially Western, impact, so too was Li's ideological growth during those years his personal response to the national crisis resulting from imperialist invasions and domestic troubles.[34] Assuming an open mind, Li was inclined to incorporate new ideas into his nationalism and apply his procured knowledge to tackling practical issues. His nationalism suffused his reasoning and saturated his discourses. Like most Chinese intellectuals of that time, he did not lag behind but rather enhanced his patriotic fervor by championing the common goal of the revitalization of his weakened country.

It should be noted that Li Dazhao did not break with Chinese culture in his pursuit of Western learning while he was acquiring a modern education. In fact, his enthusiasm for traditional patriotism never faded.

His incursion into the historical domain to retrieve patriotic models was to reverberate among his compatriots, as these bygone examples could catalyze nationalistic fervor, strengthen the collective bond, and reinforce a shared identity. In a 1908 poem, he cited the patriotic stories of Jing Ke, Fan Li, Xian Gao, Zhong Yi, and other heroic figures to inflame the people's affection for their motherland and to challenge the imperialist powers.[35] Li did not rely on mysterious hearsay; on the contrary, he banked on truthful historical facts. To arouse patriotic sentiment, he studied Ming loyalist Zhu Shunshui, who led a ferocious but futile resistance against the Qing conquest and who later died in exile in Japan. Li first learned about Zhu in 1912 from a Japanese newspaper that covered the Japanese celebration of the 250th anniversary of Zhu's arrival in Japan. Utilizing Japanese sources, Li published three articles on Zhu in Chinese in early 1913. Through his fascinating narratives, elegant language, and poignant commentaries, Li accentuated Zhu's enduring loyalty, unyielding spirit, and unbending faith in the Ming dynasty.[36] In choosing Zhu as a model, Li expected that the Chinese could emulate such a brave man with their own devotion, passion, and allegiance to their country. With a circumscribed scope focusing on one historical figure (Zhu), he underscored one main point, which was an eternal theme in his mind: Chinese patriotism.

Li Dazhao's nationalism evolved during those years to mirror the changing national situation. At first, he held a simplistic patriotic feeling coupled with the local culture to foster an affection for his country. Then, it was peppered by anti-Manchu sentiment, with which he provoked his fellow Han Chinese to take action for "raising the Han flags [*hanjiaqi*] throughout the country."[37] Later, it advanced into an anti-imperialist rhetoric against foreign invasions. Li's multiple patriotic layers reflected the historical transformation of the times, from empire to republic, and shaped a common psyche for the majority of Chinese people, who adopted these deep-seated yet changing moods. After the 1911 Revolution, however, Li followed the new trend of regarding the Manchus as an inseparable member of the five major ethnic groups (Han, Manchu, Mongol, Hui, and Tibetan) in the newly established republic. By this point, his nationalism aimed to serve a Chinese nation of all ethnic stripes and to invite an upbeat and cooperative endeavor for national salvation. On the personal level, he demonstrated his passion for his fellow citizens. According to Zhang Cixi, Li Dazhao himself endured poverty at the college and endeavored to earn money by publishing his articles in newspapers. Once, he received a royalty of twenty yuan from *Ta Kung Pao*, a famous liberal newspaper in Tianjin. Upon seeing a very sickly old man on his way back, his sympathy prompted him to offer all he had received to the poor old man without even asking his name.[38]

Li Dazhao's passion for his country, an essential element of his nationalism, led him to show his utmost concern for the postrevolutionary national situation. Taking a fresh look at the existing problems, Li felt that China had encountered an unprecedented nightmare rather than the rosy dream the people had expected and that the people must tackle those tough issues. Less than half a year after the imperial abdication, Li enumerated six grave challenges to the republic, including the frontier crisis, military disorder, fiscal anemia, a food shortage, the commercial predicament, and the scarcity of well-educated citizens.[39] With all those worries in his mind, Li became an indefatigable champion for a stabilized political and social order as a support for his country. Despite his qualms over imminent issues, he remained optimistic about the long-term national prospect. He remarked that "our country has a huge territory and a large population. It is a heavenly ordained land, as its rivers flow in a knitted web and fertile soil is interlocked inside its watery grids. If China adopted a sound approach to governance, it could become a prosperous country within ten years."[40] The future should not be in despair, even if China was currently facing serious problems. The key for a better country, as he explained, was to espouse a reasonable way to run the state.

Li elaborated that the approach to managing the republic must exclude the tyrannical remnants of the old days, because traditional despotism had inflicted so much suffering upon the people for so long. The old system was dismantled and the new one must be upheld. Of course, anti-tyranny was not Li Dazhao's invention; nevertheless, it became iconic in his thought, and he termed it a "monarchical catastrophe" (*junhuo*). In early 1913, Li alerted the Chinese to the misfortune caused by the thousand-year-old despotism and called for its total repudiation. According to his analysis, the Chinese people had grieved under this despotic system for the past millennia, as it sanctioned the concentration of power in one man's hands and turned that man into a primary evil (*yuan'e*) who wielded his absolute power to oppress the people and ruined fundamental human rights. Consequently, the people did not have a chance to voice their opinions, the society was stifled under a yoke, the education system became lifelessly stagnant, and even knowledgeable scholars became thoughtless individuals. Whenever the tyrant's vicious power waned, however, lawless bandits emerged, and the people continued to bear sorrow. In the past millennia, one tyrant was replaced by another and violence was supplanted by ferocity in a vicious cycle, which Li attributed to the hereditary autocracy. As China accepted republicanism, the old tyranny must be precluded at all costs. Thus, his anti-tyranny rhetoric was a part of his recommendation for China's state building. While rejecting despotism, he called for initiating a new path for the young republic. His denunciation of the tyrannical system posed a sharp contrast to his glorification of traditional patriotic heroes since both belonged to the same traditional domain.[41]

Some scholars have mistakenly assumed for a long time that Li Dazhao opposed Yuan Shikai's early presidency due to his anti-tyrannical ideas. A theory well circulated before the early 1980s was that Li hated Yuan's dictatorial power and contested his autocratic rule from the very beginning of Yuan's presidency. The truth, however, was quite different. Li at first rested his hope in Yuan as a promising leader of the republic. According to Zhu Chengjia's interpretation, Li intended to persuade Yuan to take actions for national salvation and to defend the republic, which differs from the view that Li resisted Yuan from the beginning of the republic.[42] One of Li's poems, composed in August 1913, was regarded as evidence of his anti-Yuan posture, yet this same poem is now reinterpreted as proof of his pro-Yuan stance.[43] Indeed, a mix of factors led Li to defend Yuan. The potential national breakup by local strongmen made Li worry. Li was impressed by Yuan's unprecedented reputation as an indispensable man in the establishment of the republic, for which Yuan was being hailed as China's George Washington. Personally, Li himself was a beneficiary of Yuan's educational reform, not to mention the fact that his college was established by Yuan. For over a decade, Li continued to live under Yuan's shadow. Li leaned toward Yuan in the public forum, but he did not flock to Yuan's side as a lackey. Li's writings indicate his insinuated backing for Yuan and attest to his explicit criticism of Yuan's rivals. Only in 1915 did Li become an anti-Yuan activist, because of Yuan's monarchical pretensions. Prior to this, Li gave his support to Yuan, for which the evidence is not spotty and the proof not unconvincing.

What concerned Li Dazhao most was national unity under the republican system, which led him to criticize Yuan Shikai's rivals and regard them as troublemakers. To him, the partisan conflict in the political arena became a vicious struggle as "one party supports its leader while the other parties immediately condemn him as a bandit or a public enemy."[44] Li coined a phrase, "partisan egoism" (*dangsi*), to depict this scenario. While he recognized the importance of partisan politics as a necessary republican apparatus, he viewed partisan egoism as a national disaster, because a political party only defended itself without caring much about national interests.[45] Li slammed both radicals (the Nationalist Party) and moderates (the Progressive Party) for wasting national resources without contributing anything to the public good.[46] He lamented the theft of people's democratic rights, which, in his view, slipped into the hands of powerful hegemons and unscrupulous politicians who behaved like bandits waylaying the people for booty.[47] He threw his weight behind national unity by condemning military governors (dudu) who built their military rule in the provinces during the 1911 Revolution but refused to obey the republican government after the revolution. They acted as arrogant and presumptuous hegemons, monopolized regional authority, and brought forth "provincial egoism" (*shengsi*). Li straightforwardly proposed abolishing military governorships. Without any guile, he condemned the Nationalist military governors of Anhui, Jiangxi, Hunan, and Guangdong just before the Second Revolution.[48] By venting his outrage over partisan self-centeredness and provincial arrogance, he showcased his incorruptible attitude and his attempt to unify the nation as a wholesome republic and to penalize partisan politicians and military governors for their irresponsible behavior.

Commenting on the assassination of Song Jiaoren, Li Dazhao differed sharply from the majority of the Nationalists, who pointed their fingers at Yuan Shikai. Li condemned the murder, lamented Song's death, and eulogized him as "a contemporary hero." Yet Li did not reproach Yuan; on the contrary, he denounced the declining moral standard of the time for causing the tragedy. While Song worked diligently for the nation, the evil of declining morality had deprived him of his young life. As the public conscience faded, the evil force emerged like bandits and beasts.[49] Li called the Song assassination a national catastrophe, just as if "nature had lost its normal function, humans had lost their normal conduct, and the cosmos had lost its normal course."[50] If this continued, China would move in a more ominous direction and would step into a more disastrous situation. Imbued with the standard of a noble moralist, Li delivered his messages advising his compatriots to enhance their ethical lives rather than resorting to returning violence for violence. Simply put, Li offered his diagnosis of the Song case and refused to support Sun Yat-sen's Second Revolution, which, in his opinion, would create new chaos and lead to more bloody mayhem. Viewed from hindsight, we can reason that Li's solution to limit the Song case within the moral scope was not very helpful. At least, however, he had voiced his unique opinion on the case, underscored his firm stance for national unity, and articulated his idea on how to avert a new national crisis.

In spite of his dissatisfaction with the national political reality, Li Dazhao remained firmly dedicated to republicanism and constitutional rule. His modern education granted him the opportunity to read a large number of publications, with which he familiarized himself with the theories of the representative system. Although he had never visited the West and had obtained related information from the library, media, and classroom, Li's enthusiasm for democracy and his appreciation of republicanism opened an avenue for his discourse on republican life. When he introduced the Western representative system, he argued that only fair elections could guarantee the success of constitutional rule.[51] In order to ensure the effective operations of congress, Li compiled appropriate data concerning legislators' salaries in a number of countries.[52] He paid attention to the civil service system, viewed it as a vital mechanism of democracy, and regarded it as a serviceable organ of republicanism.[53] He was absorbed in diverse topics regarding democracy, got excited over more relevant information, and became fervent about its implementation. He did research on the practice of impeachment, drew attention to its long history, explicated his endorsement, and forewarned about its risks.[54]

Although Li Dazhao admired Western democracy and aimed to transplant it in order to consolidate the Republic of China, he did not hide his disagreement with certain Western democratic elements when he ruminated over their improper applications in a different national situation. Through his study of legislative systems, whether congress or parliament or diet, he recognized that most of them were bicameral bodies. However, the British Parliament, according to his understanding, was a unicameral institution because the House of Lords was basically nominal. Respecting China's national circumstance, Li preferred that the legislature of his country should be unicameral to allow more ordinary citizens to be elected as lawmakers.[55] This modification should not be seen as a constitutional deficiency; rather, as Li argued, it was a suitable alteration to satisfy China's national needs. As indicated earlier, Li supported Yuan Shikai and expected him to be a defender of the republic, just as

Yuan had loudly so proclaimed himself. However, Li did not want Yuan's power to be unrestricted. Through his study of balance of power, Li made it clear that a distinction should be drawn between the proclamation of a constitution and the implementation of laws. While the president had the right to implement the law after its passage by congress, he did not have the right to proclaim a constitution. On the contrary, the constitution must be issued by a specially organized constitution-making body. If the president was allowed to proclaim a constitution, as Yuan's followers planned, it would become farcical nonsense, much like "the son giving birth to his mother" (*zichanmu*).[56]

In the realm of rational thinking, Li Dazhao did not confine himself within just one single frame, and he did not view mixed ideas as anomalous; instead, he regarded ideological absorption as a process of fluidity. As no rigid boundary was circumscribed to curb his free thinking, he did not set up formality as a stereotype, nor did he alienate himself from any ideas. The readers of his articles may encounter a great deal of surprise at the diversity of his world of thought, which comprised traditional Chinese concepts, Western notions, and other thoughts. One striking absorption was his acceptance of the philosophy of Leo Tolstoy. Like Tolstoy, Li promoted practicing repentance, through which the Chinese would reach peaceful enlightenment, encourage nonviolent contrition, and enhance social morality and national advancement.[57] Li translated an article by Tolstoy from a Japanese version rendered by Nakano Kaizan that highlighted noble labor, personal repentance, social justice, and an antigovernment posture.[58] Among a flurry of foreign ideas, Tolstoy's cooperative spirit and stirring anarchism exerted a strong impact on Li. Indeed, Li's articles contained a call for repentance with which the Chinese could achieve social impartiality and accomplish social progress.[59] Li continued to open his mind to more ideas in the years to come, but he did not drop all of those he had internalized, as long as they were helpful to his vision of national salvation.

Conclusion

Li Dazhao's eight years at Yongping and Tianjin epitomized his personal dramatic transformation from a rural teenager to an educated modern intellectual. This time span served as a springboard to transform this young boy with a classical education into a pursuer of Western learning.

This special period of study served as a bridge; it did not change who he was as a patriot, and neither would it be duplicated in the future. If Li had not attended these two modern schools, he could have been a local elite in his village just like his foster grandfather. It was during these eight years that he received the modern education that transformed him into a learned man. Lured by Western learning and urged on by his burning nationalism, he became an industrious learner, a productive writer, and an ardent activist. If he had followed the path taken by his classmates after his graduation from this college, he might have ended up as an employee of the local government, living a relatively stable life. However, he despised the officialdom of that period, portraying "an official's life as a ghost-muddling life (*guihundeshenghuo*)" and describing the country as "a fraudulent republic (*guihundeminguo*)" because of the misbehavior of unabashedly amoral politicians.[60] He refused to join them; on the contrary, he was determined to pursue his own noble goal. Li's writings demonstrated an alert awareness of national crisis and his thoughtful recognition of national issues, for which he endeavored to find a solution. It was his instinctive sense of national responsibility that pushed him to jettison the springboard to officialdom offered by his eight-year modern education.

Those years witnessed China as a country truly undergoing significant changes, including dynastic reforms, constitutional petitions, a violent revolution, and the early republican chaos. Paralleling those significant events during the transition from empire to republic, Li Dazhao became not only a witness and an observer but also a participant and a leader. Interestingly enough, he did not lose much during those turbulent years, as he continued to receive his modern education, absorbed new ideas, accumulated new knowledge, and assumed new outlooks. Li shared ubiquitously communal moods with fellow Chinese citizens of that time, including anti-Manchu sentiment, pro-constitutional zeal, and revolutionary passion. After the 1911 Revolution, his mind continued to be marked by patriotic upwellings, which compelled him to pursue democracy. He gave his support to the republic, but he became cognizant of its ineffectiveness, for which he offered his proposals. He condemned dishonest politicians and slammed conceited local hegemons who, in his eyes, became dangerous troublemakers. Seeing that the republic did not solve national problems and believing that those issues only became worse, Li used his newly acquired knowledge and newly shaped worldview to explore a way of achieving his higher hopes by embracing Western-style democracy.

During the early years of the republic, Li Dazhao turned his increasingly ardent zeal to Western democracy, on which he read widely, wrote productively, and disseminated writings in a timely manner. From his writings, we can perceive his intention of imitating the representative system with certain reservations and modifications to make it fit well into the Chinese national circumstance. Although he had not gone abroad by then, as an educated man, he grasped the gist of democracy and vehemently endorsed it for his country to become a truly democratic republic. His intense study of democracy was driven by his desire to resuscitate his country. As far as we can ascertain, his nationalistic eagerness was the keystone of his quest for democracy. Yet Li was not confined to just one ideology, and his mind was porous and uncluttered. His world of thought should not be conceptualized as merely static or monolithic but rather as changeable and multifarious. What emerges from reading his writings is the clear portrait of a young intellectual with diverse and intermingled ideas, as his mind held an uneven and loose synthesis of Western and Chinese notions. For a while, he was briefly swept up by the Buddhist "pure land" (jingtu) sect and even considered living like a carefree recluse after his friend Chen Yilong was killed, which caused Li to experience a miserable spell of depression and a dizzying spiritual low.[61] With respect to his philosophical values, Li was deeply impacted by Leo Tolstoy's anarchist philosophy. Such a remarkable mix of ideological elements, not unusual among college students, would exert a profound influence upon Li's incessant pursuit of new ideas in the upcoming decade.

Chapter 3

The Japan Years

Introduction

Commenting on Li Dazhao's study abroad experience in Japan from late 1913 to May 1916, Chinese scholar Zhu Chengjia uses the phrase "breaking through the North Chinese palisade" (*chongchu beiyang de fanli*) to depict Li's exit from the thrall of the northern regime led by Yuan Shikai.[1] Although Zhu's point helps portray Li's life after his departure for Japan, it does not holistically reflect Li's Japan experience. Indeed, before he left for Japan, Li had benefited from Yuan's progressive policies and had grown up under the shadow of Yuan's educational reform, for which he admired and generally supported Yuan. However, Li did not belong to Yuan's Beiyang clique, as his membership in the Socialist Party demonstrates. Furthermore, he lamented the death of his friend Chen Yilong, who was killed by the Yuan regime. Therefore, Li did not need to break through Yuan's "palisade." However, his Japan experience did redirect him and set him adrift to some degree from his past. The refreshingly different milieu in Japan drove him apart from his previous setting, decreased his attachment to the political norms under the rule of Yuan Shikai, and ushered him into a new historical stage. Nevertheless, he did not encounter a sudden break from his past; rather, the new cultural setting gradually enabled him to view Yuan's regime from a different perspective by living a different life, establishing a new social network, and acquiring a new education. Indeed, it was in Japan that Li started to stumble in his acceptance of Yuan, whose authoritarian policies disgruntled him. Ultimately, he turned against Yuan because of the latter's move towards imperial pretensions. In this sense, Li Dazhao broke through an old barrier while remolding himself into a new individual.

Needless to say, Li Dazhao's study abroad in Japan was a life-changing experience. Not only was he exposed to Japanese culture, but he also learned more about Western civilization through the burgeoning Taishō Democracy. Differing from other young Chinese students who also studied in Japan, Li cherished his opportunity as a much older learner. Indeed, the liberal milieu granted him a chance to familiarize himself with liberalism, democracy, and constitutionalism. He attended Waseda University, a famous Japanese institution with a first-rate faculty and rich resources, which allowed him to be immersed in a nonconformist ambiance. Nonetheless, he continued to care for his country and did not keep his nationalism under wraps; on the contrary, he was a broker of information with which he swayed his compatriots toward nationalistic actions.

The events happening in his country during those years were, in part, what motivated Li Dazhao to become an overseas activist. To him, what occurred in China constituted a new round of national crises, which included Japan's Twenty-One Demands and Yuan's imperial pretensions.[2] While harboring a deeply embedded nationalism in his heart, he saw those developments as perilous threats. In his eyes, the foreign belligerence seeking to subjugate his country was catastrophic, and Yuan Shikai's attempted dynastic restoration, which Li viewed as an act of betrayal to the republic, was quite destructive. More sadly, Yuan, a man whom Li had once admired, now endeavored to build a new dynasty. Prior to the establishment of Yuan's Empire of China, Li participated in the debate over the potential change of China's political system and soon became an activist in the war against Yuan's infidelity to the republic. In this way, he entered the public spotlight in Japan, not through his excellent academic performance but because of his role in mobilizing his countrymen for patriotic actions. Fortunately, many of his writings during those years have survived, and more of the articles he published in Japan have been discovered in recent years, which grants us a chance of examining Li's Japan years.[3] In addition, the publications by Chinese and Japanese scholars enable us to fathom his academic performance, his personal life, his nationalistic stance, his political activities, and the creative ideas he brought forth during these years.

Studying in Japan

It seems paradoxical that Li Dazhao, who disliked the Japanese invasions into his country, went to Japan to pursue his higher education. His abhorrence was first fomented as a consequence of Japanese troops having ravaged his province during the Boxer Rebellion. Further loathing was incited by his own witnessing of the killing of five Chinese policemen by the Japanese soldiers at the Changli Railway Station a couple of months before his departure for Japan. Seeing the five corpses, Li furiously wrote that it was "an unbearable humiliation." The Japanese troops had committed a heinous crime on Chinese soil. This atrocity, according to Li, generated "a detestable hatred which is as stony as the nearby Mount Jieshi."[4] On his way to Japan, the tempestuous waves in the Yellow Sea reminded him of the dead souls killed by the Japanese during the First Sino-Japanese War (1894–95). The forlorn scene, as he stated, meant that the raging sea was still lamenting his country's tragic war.[5] His recollection of recent occurrences strengthened his ill will toward the country he was heading to. Be that as it may, he had always viewed the First Sino-Japanese War as a demarcation line in China's foreign relations, because his country was defeated by the small neighboring country that inflicted upon his nation an unbearable trauma.[6]

Why, then, did Chinese citizens, including Li Dazhao, who did not harbor any love for Japan, go there to pursue higher education? The answer is that Japan's swift modernization led to its rapid rise as a strong power, which was seen as a stunning achievement that prompted the Chinese to emulate it. To them, Japan might offer a lesson for their own modernization. The Japanese policy of enticing young Chinese individuals to study in Japan served as a lure by way of a specially designed program providing express training for a speedy diploma and a degree from an accredited college. The low cost, in comparison to the pricey tuition and living expenses in the West, also attracted the young Chinese to Japan. The geographical adjacency meant convenience. The abolition of the Civil Service Examination System compelled many young Chinese to go overseas to earn a degree or obtain a special training diploma in order to land a decent job at home. The Chinese were so positioned to learn from their recently modernized neighbor that they sailed across the sea to get there. According to a study, the first group of thirteen students went to Japan in 1896, but the numbers increased yearly: two hundred in 1899, five hundred in 1902, one thousand in 1903, eight thousand in 1905, and thirteen thousand or twenty thousand in 1906, which was the peak year. The disparity among the figures in 1906 was caused by the fact that many enrolled in multiple schools. According to one scholar's analysis, at least 8,600 went to Japan in 1906.[7]

Concerning Li Dazhao's motives to study abroad in Japan, a number of other decisive factors should not be ignored. For years, Li had admired the West, which meant that a Western country would have been an ideal destination for his study abroad plan. But the financial barrier was a hurdle. Even for studying in Japan, he would not have been able to afford it without using available financial aid. Although Japan was not "an ideal destination," he chose it because he could "indirectly learn" about the West in order to seek a way of national salvation.[8] His classmate Yu Yi commented in 1913 that "Li wants to go to Japan to focus on the theories about society and economics, in order to figure out the origins of Chinese poverty, to explore the ways of restraining powerful hegemons, and to relieve the suffering of the weak."[9] Obviously, Li was motivated by his nationalistic fervor. Another potential factor, as one scholar claims, might have been Li's intention of studying the Ming loyalist Zhu Shunshui, on whom he had published some articles.[10] This might seem a possible motive; however, he did not do any further research on Zhu after his arrival in Japan, and there is no evidence whatsoever to prove otherwise.

Financial support from Tang Hualong and Sun Hongyi, two leaders of the Progressive Party, was crucial to Li Dazhao's study abroad plans. Tang, the speaker of congress, and Sun, a famous congressman, viewed Li as a promising young man who might become a potential talent for their party, even if Li was not a member yet. Sun came from Tianjin and was a leader of the constitutional movement during the time when Li got to know him. They started a lifelong friendship from that point on. Through Sun Hongyi, Li established a tie with Tang Hualong. Presently, Li was offered an annual package of three hundred Japanese yen out of a regular public fund for individuals to study in Japan from the budget of the Progressive Party.[11] Since a Japanese family needed about twenty-four yen for typical monthly expenditures in the early twentieth century, Li would not need to worry about his life there with such a sum.[12] Without Tang and Sun's support, it would have been impossible for Li to have traveled to Japan, as he had exhausted his family's financial resources for his college education and he could not have afforded another round of higher education, especially in a foreign country. Tang Hualong's support, however, had strings attached; namely, he requested that Li take care of his young children and supervise their learning. In fact, Tang had already sent his wife along with his two children to Tokyo. His young son, Tang Peisong, barely ten years old by then, would eventually become a Chinese scientist after he earned his doctorate degree from Johns Hopkins University. Li took his obligation seriously in carrying out his duty as a supervisor and demanded a weekly academic progress report. Li's stern supervision and constructive advice enormously benefited his young charge, as Tang Peisong himself testified years later.[13]

From the available yet diverse sources, we might be confused about Li Dazhao's arrival date in Japan. Since Li did not keep a diary, no records were left about his landing date. From his own writings, only a couple of vague time spans, such as "last winter" or "last fall," could be found.[14] The lack of verifiable sources and the existence of diverse claims make it hard to ascertain the date.[15] Nevertheless, several claims have been offered, including "late 1913 or the winter of 1913," "the fall of 1913 or October 1913," and even "January 1914."[16] To make the matter more complicated, landing in Japan and the arrival in Tokyo were two different things, as students from North China first sailed from a port near Tianjin and landed in Kobe, from which they transited via train to Tokyo. Yet many viewed their entry into Tokyo as their arrival date. Without a precise date and with multiple claims, much to our dismay, Chinese scholars now adopt a vague phrase, "the winter of 1913," to chronicle Li's arrival in Tokyo.

The place where Li Dazhao lived after his arrival in Tokyo, however, was never in question. He resided in the Young Men's Christian Association (YMCA) center, which was at that time roughly five hundred meters south of the campus of Waseda University. The center was sponsored by American churches for the purpose of assisting Chinese students to adapt to a new life, introduce Christianity to them, and attract potential converts. The center was a three-story building; the first floor held classrooms, a dining hall, a bookstore, and a grocery stand, and the two other stories were dormitories.[17] It was in this building that Li lived for more than two years. Like other Chinese students, Li planned to enroll in the nearby university. To do so, he had to prepare for an examination to earn admission. For more than eight months, Li studied

Japanese, English, and other subjects at the center. During this period, Li was tutored by his American teacher, Arthur G. Robinson. Their teacher-student relationship has been discussed by the American scholar Maurice Meisner, who might have created an impression that Robinson taught at the university where Li was a student.[18] The Japanese scholar Tomita Noboru, through his archival study, found that Robinson was not hired by Waseda University, which means that Robinson served as a teacher at the YMCA center.[19] In any case, Li wrote "My Autobiography" for Robinson's class, which remains a valuable primary document stored at the Harvard University library.

With his solid scholarly foundation, strong portfolio, and careful preparation, Li Dazhao passed the examination and was admitted into Waseda University on September 8, 1914. He was a student at this well-reputed school until February 2, 1916. According to Waseda's policy, a student needed to stay in the preparatory stage for one year prior to his formal entrance into a major. Li, however, enjoyed a direct admission into his major in political economics because of his status as a college graduate in China. Li's academic performance has come to light thanks to the careful study of Japanese scholar Mori Masao. During the first year, Li tried his best. His second year was incomplete because of his very active involvement in the anti-Yuan war. This means that Li's file only contains his first year's scores.[20] During this first year, Li took eleven courses, for which he earned the following grades: Principles of Modern States, 77 percent; Imperial Constitution, 75 percent; Economics, 85 percent; Finance and Economic Principles, 65 percent; History of Modern Politics, 70 percent; Civil Laws, 60 percent; Criminal Jurisprudence, 55 percent; Political Classics Readings, 40 percent; Economic Classics Readings, 87 percent; English, 66 percent; and Japanese Composition, 56 percent. The total score was 736, with an average of 66.9 percent for each course, which earned him a class ranking of number 40 among 106. To put this into context, we should consider that among the 106 students, six students failed and another thirty-seven missed a number of examinations.[21] Considering all this, we can argue that Li remained in the middle range among his peers. Because his classmates were mostly Japanese, his medium ranking verifies his accomplishment. During the first semester of his second year, Li took more courses in politics, economics, history, sociology, statistics, and other subjects, although no scores were recorded. In addition, Li took elective courses, which were not included in his transcript, according to the university's regulations.

Figure 3.1. Li Dazhao studied in Japan between 1913 and 1916, during which he was admitted into Waseda University. Here, Li is shown dressed in the Japanese fashion. He lived in a dormitory run by the American Christian mission, through which he learned more about the United States. Li was expelled from Waseda University because of his political activities against Yuan Shikai. (Public domain)

Beyond his classroom interactions, Li Dazhao befriended Waseda's academics, who supported his scholarly inquiry. Among his professors, Li was familiar with Yoshino Sakuzo and Imai Yoshiyuki, his former teachers in Tianjin who were now professors at Waseda University. From his professors, he obtained new information and new knowledge and, more importantly, accepted new ideas. In particular, Yoshino's and Imai's championing of democracy made a long-term impact upon him.[22] The intrepid espousal of constitutional rule by his professor Minobe Tatsukichi inspired him. Abe Isoo, a devout Christian who espoused Christian socialism, also left an impact upon Li's life, as Li often visited Abe.[23] Obviously, Li's hatred toward Japanese imperialism did not get in the way of his personal friendships with Japanese intellectuals. He continued to maintain his friendship with his professors and endeavored to promote Sino-Japanese cultural exchange in the years thereafter.[24] When his colleague Chen Duxiu was arrested in 1919, Li wrote an urgent letter to Yoshino, appealing to him to use his reputation to press the Chinese government for Chen's release.[25]

Li Dazhao's ties with Japan's progressive intellectuals suited his nationalist fervor. While he did not develop any relationship with conservative professors who backed Japanese imperialism, he fostered ties with those who sympathized with China. A good example of this was his relationship with Imai Yoshiyuki. Imai had been Li's teacher in Tianjin and earned his doctoral degree by investigating foreign invasions into China with a particular focus on consular jurisdiction, from which Imai published a book entitled *China's International Laws*. According to Li's testimony, when he visited Imai in the spring of 1914, he saw the latter's manuscript. During their conversation, Imai informed Li that the barrier to China's legal predicament was consular jurisdiction, or extraterritoriality, a component of the unequal treaties that China had signed with the powers. Without its abolition, Imai argued, China would not be able to achieve the status of an independent nation. To Li, consular jurisdiction was China's painful trauma that had to be eradicated. Its obliteration would allow the Chinese people to retrieve, at least partially, their lost national interests. The premise of Imai's contention was aligned with Li's nationalism, and because of this Li opted to translate Imai's book into Chinese, along with his cotranslator Zhang Runzhi, also a student at Waseda. To his delight, the Chinese version of Imai's book, for which Li also authored a preface, was published in China in April 1915.[26]

While studying at Waseda, Li Dazhao made full use of Waseda's vibrantly internationalized scholarly milieu, within which he tried to explore global issues. According to Li's testimony, American scholar Shailer Mathew's public lecture titled "Democracy and Public Opinion" was inspirational. He listened to Mathew's speech and admired his ideas concerning the role of schools, media, churches, theaters, workers' organizations, and women's clubs in the shaping of public opinion. Later, Li brought Mathew's ideas back to China and organized theater performances to sway China's public opinion in favor of modernization.[27] At Waseda, Li read Western classics, such as the works of John Stuart Mill, Albert Venn Dicey, Woodrow Wilson, Thomas Carlyle, and Ralph Waldo Emerson, whom he would quote frequently in his future writings.[28] Those Westerners' liberal, democratic, and creative ideas influenced him. It was during this period that the Great War broke out, which plunged the entire globe into unprecedented turmoil. Li carefully monitored the war. Sadly, he found that his country was similar to the Balkan Peninsula, where the struggle of the great powers led to global conflict. Li remarked that "China and the Balkan are two foci which have attracted the great powers" and that the Chinese should not neglect the danger to their national status, so as to avoid the unfortunate fate of the Balkans. For that reason, Li planned to write a pamphlet titled *The Changes in the World and China* to arouse Chinese patriotism and to alert them to the myriad national crises their country encountered.[29] Although Li made the announcement of this forthcoming book in April 1915, no evidence proves that it was actually published. Nevertheless, the announcement itself provides us a snapshot of Li's perceptive feelings toward his nation and his desire to deal with the urgent issues his country faced at that time.

To be sure, Li Dazhao's nationalism was not grounded in any supernatural belief system; neither was his nationalistic sentiment integrated with a religious commitment. Nevertheless, his relationship with Christianity deserves our attention. Not only was he influenced by his Christian professors at Waseda University, but also the culture at his domicile deeply impacted him. At the YMCA center, Li attended Bible-study sessions, learned English from American teachers, and became familiar with Christian values. He very likely learned to play the accordion while there. His daughter Li Xinghua wondered, "We do not know where my father learned to play the accordion. However, he played it whenever he had spare time."[30] She continued, "My father did not believe in any religion, but he liked to sing a hymn which was popular in the church."[31] Li Dazhao attended the services offered by Japanese pastor Maruyama Koichiro, read the Bible, and participated in religious activities.[32] Li played the accordion and sang hymns, which were part of the program at the center. According to Yasuzo Shimizu, a Japanese Christian, Li played the accordion to accompany Japanese children singing hymns. Yasuzo exclaimed decades later that "it was an incredible scene in which the future great communist accompanied the singing of Christian hymns at this Sunday school."[33] Li continued to keep a close tie with Yasuzo, who visited him in Beijing in 1918.[34] Li's familiarity with the religion did not result in his conversion, as no evidence shows his acceptance of Christianity as a faith. Yet Li admired Jesus, in whom he found a moral paragon and the highest good. Li's connection with Christianity, scholars have argued, enabled him to absorb humanist ideals from this religion.[35]

Although Li Dazhao defied the odds in his pursuit of higher education at Waseda University, as his first year's transcript attests, he was suddenly expelled from the school on February 2, 1916, after having traveled back to Shanghai for a couple of weeks to support the anti-Yuan war. When he returned to Tokyo, he encountered the shocking news that he was no longer a student. Perhaps he filed his explanation, negotiated with the administrators, or lodged a protest, but the university seemed to refuse to revoke its decision. Consequently, no remedy was offered, no lenience granted, and no probation extended. Needless to say, Li was sadly disappointed, as his dream of becoming a Waseda graduate had been shattered. To the university, his long absence was inexcusable because it meant that he was not a committed learner and not a responsible student. The expulsion nominally was triggered by his protracted absence, but it invites a question: Just how long was this "long absence"? If Li was away for just a couple of weeks, the university could have accepted his explanation and allowed him to resume his status. However, two additional interpretations may provide potential answers. The first is that Li actually missed a lot of classes besides those two weeks. The second is that the conservative administrators at Waseda University detested Li and regarded him as a thorn in their flesh, in particular after witnessing his anti-Japanese activities resisting the Twenty-One Demands just a few months before. Han Yide argues that "the long absence was just a pretext to oust Li."[36] This point is not offered without a reason; the prime minister of Japan at that time, Okuma Shigenobu, who imposed the Twenty-One Demands upon China, was the founder and a former president of Waseda University, where his followers might have found a convenient excuse to drive Li out.[37] If this was true, Li's dismissal was politically motivated rather than because of poor performance, legal violation, rebellious behavior, moral depravity, or even a long absence.

An Activist

Li Dazhao's physical presence in Japan did not detach him from the ongoing national affairs in his country. On the contrary, he continued to monitor China's domestic issues and its relationship with the international community. He was not comfortable with the new political trend, and Yuan Shikai's authoritarian moves made him worry about China's future. Li was aware of his country's backwardness, and he always compared China with its more developed Asian neighbor. Indeed, Li and other Chinese students often discussed China's status quo, lamented its serious problems, and reached a consensus that their country must catch up. Li remarked that "we students often sighed and bewailed the decline of China's political mores."[38] Even though he was away from his own country, he continued to contribute articles to Chinese journals to express his ideas by elaborating different aspects of national issues.

Li Dazhao was in awe of Japan's quick modernization, but he did not develop an admiration for Japanese imperialism; rather, he loathed Japan's aggressions in his country. His tours in Tokyo sparked his self-reflection and reminded him to heed the recurring call for his nation's modernization. His visit to the Yushukan, a museum inside Yasukuni Shrine for the purpose of glorifying the Japanese Empire, exacerbated his hostility to Japan's invasions. Inside the museum, he saw Chinese weapons and military auxiliaries captured during the Sino-Japanese War as Japanese trophies. From the vantage point of the other end of the equation, Li was not enticed by them but rather conceived his nationalistic response to them. He wrote, "I became heartbroken while viewing those artifacts. My sadness held me right there, as I paced up and down without leaving for a while . . . the Japanese keep the trophies from their victory, but we must keep them in our minds as reminders of our national shame."[39] He lashed out at the shameless Chinese politicians who had become insensible to the recent humiliation, who only engaged in vicious power struggles, and who added new woes to burden the Chinese people. Li strongly admonished his countrymen to remember China's defeat at the hands of imperialist powers—in particular, the belligerent neighbor at the door.

Li Dazhao was sensitive to foreign intrusions into China's political life. In late 1914, he published an article titled "The National Condition" to criticize two of Yuan Shikai's foreign advisors: Frank Johnson Goodnow, an American man, and Nagao Ariga, a Japanese man, because they claimed that the Chinese people were so used to monarchy that they were not ready for republicanism so suddenly and so quickly. They implied that constitutional monarchy might be a better fit for China's needs. Refusing to agree with the two, Li argued that foreign advisors' opinions did not reflect the Chinese mindset and that the Chinese people dearly held their newly established republic. Much like Americans' call for building a representative system during the American Revolution, Li contended, the Chinese had fought for democracy, sacrificed their lives for the republic, and cherished the newly established republican system. He stated that Goodnow's and Ariga's views reflected their own perspectives but were not congruent with the Chinese national mood because they offered inaccurate, hyperbolic, and distorted assertions.[40] Li told his countrymen that foreign intervention into Chinese politics should not be permitted because foreigners did not work for China's national interests. He warned Yuan Shikai to halt his collusion with the foreigners and to throw into the trash any idea of relinquishing republicanism. Li's nationalistic commitment urged him to respond immediately to the new phenomenon just popping up in China's political arena. Unfortunately, Yuan turned a deaf ear to it and continued to move along the path of his monarchical pretension.

While Li Dazhao was a serious learner, he was also a sociable and gregarious individual. The new social network he established in Japan had an impact on his future life. Through this new communal web, Li retrieved information, exchanged ideas, received advice, and cooperated in nationalist activities. Li benefited from his friendship with Zhang Shizhao, a Hunanese, who ran a journal called *Jiayin* (The tiger) in Tokyo that focused on China-related issues. Soon after his arrival in Japan, Li started to read this journal and to submit his own articles to it. After reviewing Li's manuscripts, Zhang found in Li a talented writer, as his articles were elegantly composed, articulately expressed, and soundly organized. He invited Li to a meeting, during which the two began a lifelong friendship. According to Zhang, the two at first shared common ideals, but later they drifted away onto different paths. Nevertheless, their differing political standpoints did not harm their friendship, as the two families in Beijing later became so close that they informally "adopted" each other's children. Zhang portrayed Li as a daring, resolute, simple, and slow-speaking person.[41] This friendship benefited Li's scholarly life, enriched Li's thoughts, and assisted Li's career. It was Zhang Shizhao who recommended that Li be installed as the chief librarian at Beijing University, a job that changed Li's life.

Li Dazhao's new social circle included individuals of diverse backgrounds: students, scholars, reformers, and revolutionaries. Being extremely susceptible to the nationalistic spirit, Li was often swept off his feet by patriotic individuals, with whom he tried to collaborate for their common goal. Together, they built a distinctive community inside which they addressed their concerns and issues, such as career, future life, family, and, most of all, the nation. Besides their shared patriotic zeal, Li forged fraternal ties and durable friendships with these individuals. For example, when Lin Boqu, a future prominent communist, returned to China, Li organized a party in Tokyo to bid him farewell. Li composed a poem for Lin, to whom he extended his brotherly feeling.[42] He dedicated a poem to Liu Xiangwu, in which Li regretted that they knew each other too late and that their undesirable parting saddened both of them.[43] In a poem to Huo Lubai, a Cantonese and a future colleague on a newspaper in Beijing, Li stated his tender emotion and disclosed his utmost concerns for Huo, who was away at that moment.[44] In each of those pieces, Li enjoined his friends to honor their country, to contribute to their nation, and to defend the republic.

Li Dazhao's nationalist voice became louder in early 1915, in an urgent response to the Japanese aggression, which he decried as more lethal than ever. As the ongoing First World War was in progress, the Japanese government took advantage of the vacuum left by the Western powers in East Asia and delivered the Twenty-One Demands to the Chinese government on January 8, 1915. The Japanese government requested that Japan take over German colonial privileges in Shandong and enjoy special rights in Manchuria, prohibited China from renting out territories to any third country, and demanded that the Chinese government hire Japanese advisors throughout China's government, military, police, and financial administrations. The thrust of the Twenty-One Demands, if enacted, would have turned China into a Japanese protectorate. To cover their injustice, Japan requested that China handle the demands confidentially, but Yuan Shikai leaked the demands to the media for the purpose of inciting a national outcry as a strategy of counteraction.[45] Needless to say, those demands arrived as a thunderclap to Li and his fellow Chinese students in Tokyo.

Outraged at the demands, nearly three thousand Chinese students in Tokyo held a rally on February 11, 1915, to protest against the Japanese government, to press the Chinese government to reject the demands, and to implore the Chinese people to safeguard their national interests. At this rally, the General Association of Chinese Students in Japan (Liurixueshengzonghui) was established, and Li Dazhao was elected as one of its leaders. His duty was to take care of propaganda: publishing pamphlets, circulating information, and editing a journal. The association authorized Li to write its proclamation, entitled "A Warning to All the Chinese People." Although Japanese scholar Tomita Noboru argues that this proclamation was written after the February 11 rally, Chinese scholar Zhu Chengjia asserts that it was written by Li before the rally and distributed at the rally.[46] In any case, the document alerted the Chinese of their country's imminent crisis and condemned Japan's demands as venomous. Li denounced Japan for its trickery in seizing the German colony of Qingdao as a ploy for its first step in colonizing China. He lashed out at Japanese troops for their recent atrocities in Shandong and labeled Japan's invasion as China's national humiliation. By citing traditional Confucian values, Li condemned the Japanese government for its unrighteousness (*buyi*), malevolence (*buren*), injudiciousness (*buzhi*), gutlessness (*buyong*), and dishonesty (*buxin*). He alerted the Japanese people that the demands would result in nothing but bringing forth disasters to East Asia. More exigently, Li solemnly beseeched his countrymen that it was their obligation and duty to act in order to save their country.[47]

It is a mistake to assume that Li Dazhao opposed Yuan Shikai at this critical moment; on the contrary, Li expected Yuan to defy Japan. As Yuan was negotiating with Japan, Li wrote to persuade Yuan to resist the expansionist neighbor. Even after Yuan accepted the demands after multiple revisions, Li's denunciation still targeted the Japanese Empire rather than Yuan Shikai. One month later, Li published "The Concealed Vengeance" to vent his rage toward Japanese imperialism. He condemned Japan's belligerence, enumerated Japan's wrongdoings, and denounced Japan for tossing China onto the brink of an abyss of national disintegration. To Li, Japan's declaration of war against Germany was a façade to cover its ulterior motive to subjugate China. In this article, Li narrated the recent history of Japan's offenses, accused Japan of abusing China as a weak neighbor, and censured Japan for coercing China to accede to an intolerable ultimatum. Li emphasized that the Twenty-One Demands along with other virulent actions would raze China's nationhood because they would "completely ruin China's chance of national revival, obliterate China's national dignity, and ensure that China would not gain any momentum for national growth."[48] Li did not criticize Yuan but urged Yuan to seek a new way of national survival, for which he offered his advice: implementing democracy, accepting popular education, reforming the military, counterattacking Japanese imperialism, and liberating the Chinese from the Japanese yoke.[49]

Only in late 1915 did Li Dazhao start to oppose Yuan Shikai, after he received the news that Yuan endorsed the monarchical movement, decided to change the republic into a monarchy, and had accepted the title of emperor. It was Yuan's imperial pretensions that exasperated Li, whose dedication to republicanism turned him into an anti-Yuan activist. It would be an ahistorical exaggeration to exalt Li's role in the national war against Yuan, but it is also unfair to downplay his status as an enthusiastic anti-Yuan campaigner. Answering the call of Tang Hualong, who had sponsored his study abroad, Li rushed back to Shanghai in January 1916. In Shanghai, Li served as Tang's liaison officer to communicate with other political groups, highlighting Tang's role in the anti-Yuan war. Tang seldom went out in public due to his fear of assassination, harassment, and unwanted trouble.[50] In this way, Li was Tang's stuntman, facing potential dangers but working to derail Yuan. On his way to Shanghai, Li wrote to slam Yuan for "stealing the country" (*qieguo*), lamented the national turbulence Yuan had created, but saw hope in the anti-Yuan war.[51] In this way, Li vehemently supported the National Protection War (Huguozhanzheng). Besides his propaganda efforts, Li's journalistic contributions demonstrate his anti-Yuan stance, but he also donated cash. To the one-time donation of twenty Japanese yen by students from the General Association of Chinese Students in Japan, Li's contribution was two yen. In the spring of 1916, Li donated another five yen, which was a big sum for a student, to the National Protection Army led by Cai E.[52] His donations demonstrated his anti-Yuan determination and shed light on the role of overseas Chinese students in the anti-Yuan war.

It was during the anti-Yuan war that Li Dazhao felt the need to unite Chinese students into specialized groups in order to explore various ways of saving their nation. He organized the Chinese Scholarly

Society (Zhonghuaxuehui) in Tokyo, which soon incorporated the Year of the Rabbit Society (Yimaoxuehui) established by Yi Xiang. These two groups merged into one group under the new name the China Society (Shenzhouxuehui) on January 30, 1916, and elected Li as president.[53] The group's goal was to promote scholarly research, advocate personal cultivation, and awaken the Chinese people to labor for their country. The society gathered together fifty members in a short time, and some sources indicate that the membership exceeded one hundred.[54] This society was not a purely academic group; rather, it was a revolutionary coterie aimed at toppling Yuan Shikai, defending republicanism, and revitalizing China.[55] Whether it was a secret revolutionary organization, as some scholars have claimed, is open for further investigation.[56] The available sources, however, reveal that the society sponsored meetings every Saturday featuring a presentation on a particular topic by a speaker, which was followed by an open discussion among attendees. The society published a journal called *Shenzhouxuekan* (The China journal) and built other branches in China and in overseas Chinese communities. The fact that its Beijing branch was still operating in 1917 demonstrates the widespread geographical scope of its activities.[57] Unfortunately, the organization did not last long, because it functioned mainly as an anti-Yuan group. When its goal was reached as Yuan's imperial endeavors failed, the society's existence became unnecessary, although its sporadic activities lingered.

To enhance understanding about fiscal and commercial issues among the Chinese people, Li Dazhao established the Chinese Society of Economy and Finance (Zhongguojingjicaizhengxuehui) in March 1916 in Tokyo. According to its proclamation, Li and other members perceived it as urgent that the Chinese people learn more about the principles of economics and finance. Citing the success of Western countries, Li highlighted the role of Western economic thought and financial theories in the progress of Western modernization. Japan after the Meiji Restoration also emphasized the role of these two fields, which helped turn Japan into a rapidly industrialized country. In contrast, ordinary Chinese people ignored economic and financial theories, and Chinese officials seldom cared about them. After the establishment of the republic, Chinese officials still did not pay attention to them. Li decided to organize this society to disseminate the relevant information, investigate China's existing problems, and provide constructive advice for China's wealth acquisition.[58] The prime objective of this society was to advocate national growth by supporting related studies, spreading appropriate information, and prioritizing the two disciplines. Yet no evidence proves the society's long existence, except for its books being on display at Li Dazhao's old residence, now a museum, in Daheituo Village.[59]

Li Dazhao was not discouraged by his expulsion from Waseda University. He became passionate about editing *Minyi* (People's sovereignty), the official publication of the General Association of Chinese Students in Japan, and he was elected the director of its editorial board. After his dismissal from Waseda, he moved out of the YMCA center to a dormitory in the suburb of Tokyo called Tsukinin Seiki, which was surrounded by natural beauty and which provided him a quiet place to edit the journal and to write his own articles. From early February to early May, about three months, Li devoted himself to the journal's mission of upholding justice, promoting scholarly research, disseminating modern civilization, and enhancing national wellness. Although its mission was broad, the journal at that moment served as an anti-Yuan mouthpiece. Under Li's directorship, the editorial board attracted a group of talented writers with a wide range of intellectual traits to dedicate their enthusiasm, expertise, and experience to the cause. Together, they opened the following columns: articles, commentaries, news, a forum, translation, miscellany, association services, and other items.[60] Li was, in a sense, the soul of this journal, and his commitment was crucial. Although he returned to China when its first issue came out on May 15, 1916, his significant contributions to it were widely acknowledged.[61]

Why did Li Dazhao return to China in May 1916? His own explanation was that he returned because of his sense of nationalistic obligation. He felt that "the remaking of China" (*zaizaozhongguo*) was urgent, while a citizen's ability to help in transforming the country was limited if living overseas. Li's friend Gao Yihan confirmed this account: "Li Dazhao, for the purpose of national salvation, resolutely relinquished his academic pursuit and returned to his motherland in early 1916, without the slightest care for a college diploma anymore."[62] Truly, a bundle of national crises remained and the stakes were high, because Yuan Shikai continued to stay in power while the anti-Yuan war raged on. A patriotic man like Li had to return in order to work to address the multiple challenges and to accommodate the urgent national needs of China. Of course, his expulsion from Waseda University was another major reason for his return. However, he could have applied for admission into another school, as many others in similar situations did. Unfortunately, we do not know if he applied for a transfer due to the lack of original sources. Furthermore, his financial situation might have been a problem because it is unclear whether Tang Hualong continued to support him. In any case, it is safe to argue that diverse factors led to Li's return. Similar to his arrival in Japan, the date of his return to China requires further study, as no sources so far can verify it. From Bai Jianwu's diary, a rough time span between May 2 and May 19, 1916, for Li's landing in Shanghai can be found.[63] After reading other primary sources, one scholar claims that Li arrived in Shanghai between May 10 and May 19, 1916.[64] Upon a cautious calculation, another scholar further narrows down Li's arrival date to the time span between May 12 and May 19, 1916.[65] Whichever the date might be, it is reasonable to argue that Li rushed back to China in May 1916 intending to defend the republic and topple Yuan Shikai, against whom the national maelstrom lingered.

Ideological Changes

Li Dazhao's Japan years granted him the opportunity to absorb diverse ideas, in particular those of the West, from which he imbibed necessary nutrients, strengthening his reasoning capabilities and reinforcing his dedication to democracy. From his nearly twenty surviving articles, poems, and the letters he authored during his Japan years, we can be sure that he continued to place a high premium on nationalism. The transparently expressed intent beneath all of his writings was his nationalistic conviction around which he made it crystal clear that his country was his utmost concern. However, his nationalism underwent a process of gradual transformation, from defending the nation to embracing democracy, and on to more expanded thought. He integrated his patriotism into his newly acquired ideas and committed to making his nationalism the underlying force for his activities. His blueprint to change China, his criticism of unscrupulous politicians, his open anti-Yuan stance, his hatred toward imperialist powers, and his optimistic view of the prospects of his country's future were couched in his poignant nationalistic vocabularies. It would be an exaggeration to claim that Li had created a systematic ideology at that time. What we do know is that he continued to absorb, learn, and widen his reflective reasoning, with which he became more valiant and more vocal in his actions against whomever he regarded as a liability for his country.

After his arrival in Tokyo, during his preparation for admission to Waseda University, Li Dazhao wrote articles to expound his ideas on China's situation and offered his advice on multiple issues. In his article titled "The Custom," Li lamented the declining social and political morality in China, expressed his worries about ethical degeneration, and condemned politicians' thirst for power, which had caused the country to plunge into chaos. He emphasized the sustainability of national custom in the process of safeguarding China's culture, survival, and development. National custom was the soul of a country, without which a state might perish. A salubrious national custom could propel a perished state to revive. The nation consisted of individuals whose exemplary behaviors could sway others to preserve the best of national custom. At the extreme end of the spectrum, Li tried to find brilliant exemplars in order to underscore the tie between individuals and the nation and to stress the relationship between paragons of national virtue and the country. He did not limit those models to China. For example, he presented a lofty portrait of George Washington as an ideal example, because the latter's righteousness dramatically shaped the national custom of the United States. Li called on his fellow citizens to obligate themselves to carrying out their duty to follow Washington's example and maintain a high standard of national custom.[66] Aiming at the Chinese as a huge ethnic group, Li advised them to stick to their own social norms, cultural conventions, and national customs and to avoid inhabiting a social vacuum or living in a narrowly selfish space, which often led to national disunity and social disorder. He did not promote utter conformism; rather, he encouraged the Chinese to keep away from bad behavior, to eliminate criminal attitudes, to promote a wholesome life, and to keep pace with the national progress toward modernity.

Having witnessed China's vicious political struggles for years, Li Dazhao viewed the existing partisan fighting as a serious national problem. To redress the issue, he advanced the idea of political tolerance, which would be essential to constitutional rule. Referring to Western and Japanese political theories and practices in his article entitled "The Formation of Opposing Political Forces," published in late 1914, he advocated constitutional rule via tolerance. He affirmed that the existence of opposing political parties should be beneficial to the country if their partisan struggle followed the constitution and produced equilibrium by peaceful deliberation. He criticized the political organizations of that time for creating national chaos. First, he labeled Yuan Shikai as a powerful generalissimo who implemented coercive and repressive policies, and he advised Yuan to be less harsh on other political groups. Li reproved Liang Qichao's Progressive Party for being dishonest by entertaining the powerful and catering to bad manners without any moral standard. Li warned Liang to redress his behavior in order to play an honorable role in national politics. Li censured Sun Yat-sen's Nationalist Party for continuing to resort to unnecessary violence and admonished him to give up his lethal weapons. Li proposed that all political groups should respect the people, relinquish the old ways, and create a healthy environment for all.[67] According to Li, well-managed political confrontation under constitutional rule should not exhaust national resources or disturb social order; rather, it should be a mechanism for the country to avoid troubled circumstances and to circumvent hostile situations.

Li Dazhao highlighted the importance of education in China's national progress toward modernization. The traditional education system was torn apart by the impact from the West; as a consequence, a modern education system was being established. However, the number of students in the new system was so tiny that it was not proportional to the large population, because only a small sector of the Chinese people got a chance to go to school and, even worse, fewer went to college. Education was a means of national salvation, and Li advised the Chinese to support a modern education and regard it as a national urgency. If more people received an education, Li remarked, the quality of citizenry would be enhanced. Consequently, educated citizens would become knowledgeable, endorse righteousness, cherish humility, and avoid shamefulness.[68] Healthy national customs could be developed and a new nationhood cultivated. However, it would not be easy to reach this goal, for which the entire nation should work together.

Facing multiple national crises, a lot of Chinese people became pessimists, but Li Dazhao was not one of them. Those defeatists felt a high level of frustration, anxiety, and desperation and were full of complaints, magnifying the worst side of things. More sadly, the suicide rate among Chinese citizens, particularly the youth, had increased. This type of hopelessness could be spotted in the writings of Chen Duxiu, a Chinese intellectual who also lived in Tokyo at that time. In his article "Patriotic Mind and Self-Consciousness," Chen showed his despair and revealed his distrust of the Chinese state, society, and people. Chen remarked that a bad state was no better than a perished state, for which patriotism was worthless and useless. To counter Chen, Li published an article titled "The Sick of Life and Self-Consciousness" in August 1915, in which he condemned Chen's self-abandonment. Li argued that "China at this moment is at the brink of despair. However, we should not allow our people to be crestfallen as long as we still have breath." He promoted an exalted national spirit, patriotic passion, and high-minded self-consciousness. He denounced the widespread pessimism that caused young citizens to commit suicide, and he expected the Chinese to cherish life, assume a positive mindset, and adopt an optimistic attitude. Otherwise, "the defeat of our country will not be caused by others but by ourselves. The guilt of national demise will not be triggered by others but by ourselves."[69] Li's optimism was grounded in his faith in national rejuvenation so long as the Chinese would be patriotic, endeavor to find solutions, and labor hard for national revival. Although the Chinese status quo was not perfect, the people should challenge difficulties, espouse the right outlook, and strive for a better future.

It was in Japan that Li Dazhao walked a path departing from Yuan Shikai, whom he had previously regarded as an indispensable leader because of his talent, accomplishments, and prestige. For a long time, Yuan's reputation as a reformer drew Li's admiration. Yet Li's writings prove that his support of Yuan was not without conditions. For years, Li circumscribed his trust in Yuan with the preconditions of upholding republicanism and safeguarding national unity. When these conditions no longer obtained, Li openly opposed Yuan. Before late 1915, Li seldom pointed his finger directly at Yuan and only occasionally criticized Yuan's policies with critiques couched in ambiguous language. But Yuan's imperial endeavors enraged Li so much that he proclaimed that Yuan's Chinese empire could not be an alternative for the country and that republicanism should not be replaced by family rule. Li articulated the rationale for his stance: "Freedom and tyranny cannot coexist. Therefore, when monarchy survives, the citizenry becomes dead. When tyranny revives, liberty is lifeless." He furiously branded anyone who supported monarchy as "the public enemy [*gongdi*]."[70] He condemned Yuan for his betrayal of republicanism and for his egotism in embracing hereditary rule. Indeed, his breakup with Yuan prompted him to move on to a new way of national salvation.

It was during the anti-Yuan war that Li Dazhao brought forth his creative notion of "people's sovereignty" (*minyi*), which is viewed as a milestone in the history of Chinese philosophy, as Li utilized traditional Chinese cultural resources to interpret Western democratic concepts, values, and practices. This notion appeared in Li's article entitled "People's Sovereignty and Politics," published on May 15, 1916, in Tokyo shortly after his return to China. But he advanced the idea of *minyi* in Japan; it represented a crystallization of his continual pursuit of democracy, liberalism, and progressivism. He specifically coined the phrase *minyi*, which can be translated as "people's sovereignty" or "people's will," to deliver his discourse on democracy. Literally, *min* means "people" and *yi* means "vessel." It was not a careless lexicographical error, although it could be misunderstood as such; rather, it was deliberately concocted by Li to depict the universal significance of democracy. The term seems obsolete, but Li endowed it with new connotations. Through his elucidation, *minyi* became a sinicized version of Western humanism and liberalism and demonstrated his profound commitment to the democratic system. According to Li, *minyi* resembled a holy vessel for religious sacrifice. Likewise, the people collectively became a sacred entity, similar to a religious vessel, which must be deemed so divine that it should not be desecrated. *Minyi* also means people's normal regularity (*minchang*), which had been abused by the rulers for so long. Yet this normal regularity was comparable to human freedom and the people's awakening power. *Minyi*, as Li commented, further meant the people's natural longing for constitutional rule (*minxian*), as the people possessed an innate instinct to proceed toward democracy.[71]

By championing people's sovereignty, Li Dazhao abjured the tyrannical tradition. Through an interpretation of his notion of democracy, he evoked an image of an unfettered individual who was able to initiate a breakthrough in trailblazing a path for freedom. Unfortunately, this individual was posited under despotic dominance, with the influential ideology of Confucianism as an apparatus of dominance. Li commented that "it was fortunate for China to beget Confucius; but, at the same time, it is a misfortune for China to continue to own Confucius. . . . Since Confucius was born, China has gradually declined."[72] According to Li, Confucianism deprived the Chinese of freedom, robbed them of independence, and stripped them of autonomy. Because of the long tyrannical tradition, the Chinese faced four enemies of freedom: a hefty historical burden, a tenacious reliance on power, a stifling political worldview, and an impediment to new laws.[73] Furthermore, this tyrannical tradition gave rise to ambitious individuals who took advantage of the tradition, employed trickeries, utilized duress, and distorted the sage's philosophy to establish an oppressive political system.[74] Disastrously, the disrespect for people's sovereignty resulted in people's uprisings, which allowed bandits and rebels to appear in such chaos and which shaped a vicious cycle of perennial problems. Nevertheless, Li was confident that "people's sovereignty can create history, but history cannot constrain people's sovereignty permanently." And he entreated the people to create "a new history of new citizens."[75]

In a sense, Li Dazhao's article on people's sovereignty was a proclamation against Yuan Shikai's move to restore the monarchical system. Having condemned Yuan as the national thief who stole the country, Li warned the Chinese of their psychological tie with heroes, because Yuan had been respected as such a hero in the recent past. He remarked, "While Yuan was regarded as China's George Washington or China's Napoleon Bonaparte just a few years ago, he suddenly was deeply hated by the people, grinding their teeth in anger." The reason for the spectacular change was Yuan's own lethal mistake. Li argued that "heroes cannot be separated from the people, and heroes become powerless if they drift away from the people."[76] In the same vein, Yuan was admired as a hero and respected as an indispensable leader a few years ago, but his fatal move to establish a new dynasty led to his own disgrace. Li repudiated heroism, which he saw as the origin of tyranny, and he strongly supported people-centered sovereignty under constitutional rule.[77] He called on the Chinese to give up the hero-worshipping tradition, relinquish the hero-focused cult, and eliminate the hero-centered mentality. Only in this way could the Chinese people be liberated from a strongman's manipulation, dominance, and hegemony.

In contrast with Li Dazhao's criticism of tyranny and its infliction upon the people, he assumed a positive attitude toward democracy, about which he presented his understanding and displayed his conviction. He regarded the British parliamentary system as the manifestation of the British people's sovereignty. He implored the Chinese people "to be courageous in following the spirit of the time to pursue constitutional rule and to build the democratic institution."[78] He advised them to respect people's free will and cherish people's autonomous rights. Freedom of speech must be guaranteed by law and secured by a constitution.[79] At the same time, he emphasized the importance of social order and human progress. While order was guaranteed by law, progress was assured by reason. Li argued that both law and reason reflected people's wisdom to maintain a healthy society, but it was the latter that would be more essential for human progress. Li commented that "if one day a state exists without law, it loses its authority. On the day a man loses reason, he loses his worth and value."[80] He called for the Chinese to respect both law and reason. He said that tyranny stifled reason while democracy reassured it. While tyranny discarded law, democracy refined it. It was reason vested in the people's sovereignty that could allow democracy to retain its vitality.

In addition to his intention of transforming China through the establishment of democracy, Li Dazhao brought forth his unique idea of national rejuvenation through the building of a "Young China," according to an article he authored in Japan between April and May 1916. This article was titled "Qingchun," or "The Youth," which can also be translated as "Spring," as Italian scholar Claudia Pozzana does. Indeed, it can be understood from two perspectives: either an age or a season. In this article, Li's tone was philosophical, his attitude optimistic, and his language elegant. No wonder Pozzana praises it as "one of the best literary texts produced in the 1910s."[81] Japanese scholar Ishikawa Yoshihiro, after a meticulous examination, concluded that Li drew his idea from the writings of Kayahara Kazan.[82] This means that Li utilized Kayahara's notions to craft this article on the concepts of cosmology, worldview, outlook on life, and nation building, which attests to the transnational ideological inflows of that time. Li's article advocated that the Chinese people, particularly the youth, step out of pessimism and that they participate in the New Culture Movement, which is why Chinese scholars deem this article to be a proclamation of Young China.[83]

In "The Youth," Li Dazhao brought forth a new cosmological worldview about the unlimited universe through a dialectical discourse: The world is endlessly infinite and constantly changing. Whereas the universe is without beginning and without end, its vitality lies in its being eternally and energetically juvenile. Although an individual's youth is relatively short, humans can enjoy unlimited youthfulness. From this stance, Li brought forth his notion of life from a positive attitude, as he encouraged the Chinese to take faith in recreating youthful time, rejuvenating youthful life, refashioning a youthful family, rebuilding a youthful country, and reconstructing a youthful nation. All these were not only a potentiality but also a certainty. Li assured his countrymen that "our nation's standing in the world does not rely on its feeble existence during the last leg of the Old China, but must depend on the resurgence of a Young China."[84] Therefore, "Old China is the essence of the embryo of Young China, while Young China is the rebirth of the white-haired Old China."[85] Li expected the youth to be the crack force of Young China by assuming a confident attitude, developing an expectant self-awareness, and attaining a hopeful self-consciousness. Li heartened the Chinese, especially the youth, to "break the yoke of past history, destroy the rotten dogma, never be confined by the ruinous tradition, and attain a youthful self."[86] The youth should bear the responsibility of "striving to build a youthful family, a youthful state, a youthful nation, a youthful mankind, a youthful earth, and a youthful universe."[87] Li's notion of Young China moved along an ever-ascending line to overcome pessimism, challenges, and obstacles by liberating the Chinese people from the remnants of Old China and by reaching a Young China free from repression, oppression, and constraint.

One often-neglected area in Li Dazhao's thought is the economic ideas he developed in Japan. While his articles mostly aimed at national rejuvenation, his other notions have not been given sufficient attention. As his energy was devoted to nation building, he did not write much on other topics. Yet, after his arrival in Japan, he engaged himself in a scholarly debate on economics, which occurred in August 1914, before his admission into Waseda University. It was caused by his reading of an article authored by Kang Shuaiqun, a student at Waseda and a future colleague at Beijing University. In mid-1914, Kang proposed in the article that "the phenomenon of national poverty is proportionately related to the paucity of currency." Upon reading it, Li found himself at loggerheads with Kang. In his own article, Li argued that "more currency in circulation will cause the lowering of purchasing power."[88] Li shed light on inflation in much the way we see it today. He further analyzed the relationships between currency, monetary purchasing power, the value of goods, and the price of commodities. In fact, this topic was part of a heated debate among Japan's academia at that time, and Li's unique perspective shows that he had not detached himself from the scholarly world. He read so widely, prudently, and critically that he was able to render his unique point of view on the topic.[89]

Whether or not Li Dazhao maintained in Japan any association with Marxism, the communist doctrine, cannot be firmly ascertained. The lack of evidence does not allow us to find a definite answer. Gao Yihan claimed that "Li Dazhao started his contact with the Marxist doctrine while he was in Tokyo," leading many to believe it. As he was Li's close friend, Gao's words naturally sway the reader. Gao further specified that "Li got to know Marxism through Kawakami Hajime, who translated

Karl Marx's *Das Kapital* into Japanese."[90] Yang Shusheng affirmed that "Marxism was introduced to China via the Japanese contour through Li Dazhao."[91] Other Chinese scholars contend that Li got to know socialism from his readings of Kotoku Shusui as well as through his personal tie with Abe Isoo. Some Japanese scholars deny the influence of Kotoku and Kawakami upon Li in terms of the dissemination of either socialism or Marxism but affirm Li's acquisition of socialism through his special relationship with Abe.[92] It is true that Kawakami translated *Das Kapital* into Japanese, but his translation was not published until 1927. However, we cannot simply deny his contact with Marxism over there, as there is no proof that can be used for a denial. The irrefutable fact is that Li's intellectual horizon was broadened in Japan, and this doubtlessly included Marxism and communism to some degree, although the dearth of substantial evidence thwarts our efforts to draw a crystal-clear inference concerning his attraction to communism while he lived in Japan.

Conclusion

Li Dazhao's study abroad experience in Japan remarkably reshaped his life, as it erected a colossal milestone in knowledge acquisition, political pursuits, nationalistic activism, and ideological progress. He received an opportunity to join the ongoing national craze for studying overseas and reaped a windfall by securing financial aid, without which his overseas odyssey would have been out of the question. After arriving in Tokyo, fortune continued to shine on him in his successful admission into Waseda University. Needless to say, this stroke of luck came as a result of his painstaking preparation for the examination and as an outcome of his own scholarly aptitude. His luck continued in that he was able to obtain a specially granted approval of his direct entrance into a major, which was a rare exception even for most Japanese freshmen. His first-year transcript divulges a good performance, although he did not tower over his peers. If his godsent luck had persisted, Li would have become an esteemed graduate of Waseda University. But misfortune befell him and brought a sudden halt to his academic objectives. He was expelled in early 1916, not because of an academic fiasco but because of his long absence from class necessitated by his own nationalistic drive to help shape China's salvation at a time of impending danger: Japan's Twenty-One Demands and Yuan Shikai's attempt at monarchy. Despite this dismissal, his overseas experience was an asset that would be valued in Chinese society at the time and that helps explain why he was later hired as a professor at Beijing University.

Regardless of his failure in reaching his academic goal, Li Dazhao acted as a leader among the Chinese students in Japan. After monitoring the news concerning national issues and international affairs, Li organized protests in early 1915 against Japan's Twenty-One Demands upon China. By using his pen, Li became a loud voice among the Chinese students, urging their country's government to resist Japan's demands and entreating the Chinese people to defy the expanding Japanese Empire. Enraged by Yuan Shikai's imperial pretension in late 1915 and early 1916, Li passionately supported the anti-Yuan war, which resulted in his long absence from classes and led to his expulsion from Waseda University. As an activist, he added his expertise, insight, and fervor to those campaigns. Li's leadership role was multiple: organizing mass rallies, assembling a student association, establishing student groups, writing proclamations, and editing a journal, through which Li reinforced the momentum of those nationalist movements with his vigor, knowledge, and commitment. By flaunting his patriotic zeal, he inspired his fellow students to be participants. More importantly, his decisive role prepared him to become a talented organizer, an effective writer, and a rational thinker. In a sense, his Japan years served as a prerequisite for him to emerge as a leader of China's radical movements in the decade to come.

Li's deep engagement in nationalistic movements unfortunately deprived him of the chance to accomplish his academic objectives; nevertheless, this misfortune did not prevent him from bringing forth original ideas. On the contrary, his adversity prompted him to ponder more deeply and work more diligently to find a solution to save his ill-fated nation. Evidence collected here makes it clear that his intensifying nationalistic sentiment remained the backbone of his mindset. While taking pleasure in reading widely, he developed an array of unique and creative ideas. As he continued to insist on democracy and viewed it as a must for his country, he regarded the people as a collectively sacred entity and deemed the people's rights as a naturally blessed privilege. For that, he defended constitutional rule, promoted freedom of speech, upheld the representative system, promoted popular education, and beseeched his countrymen to realize a Western-style democracy. Differing from some Chinese individuals at that time, Li was not a pessimist but rather an optimist about his nation's future. Being optimistic, he forecast the renaissance of the old civilization in becoming a Young China, for which he encouraged his compatriots to achieve a new nationhood through tenacious endeavors, fervent enthusiasm, and durable confidence. The innermost core of his mind contained a diversity of notions from multiple sources, such as democratic doctrine, evolutionary theory, Tolstoy's ideas, traditional creeds, and patriotic precepts, all of which intermingled to serve his goal of national revival.

Chapter 4

Editor and Writer

Introduction

Li Dazhao's short life poses a challenge to scholars who seek a clear-cut periodization; nevertheless, the time span between May 1916, when he returned to China from Japan, and January 1918, when he landed a job as director of the Beijing University library, should be seen as a special period. Though it was only a little over one year and a half, this transitional period prepared him for a professional career. Li involved himself deeply in the ongoing New Culture Movement and contributed significantly to it as an editor and a writer. It was a time of precarious living for him, because he encountered challenges including financial pressure, broken relationships, and political persecution. Although he was not far away from his wife and children, who remained in Daheituo Village, he stayed with them for a total of only two months during his two short visits. The primary sources confirm that he was a busy man, jumping from one job to another yet publishing as a prolific author to give voice to his ideas.

Nationalism remained the most salient theme in Li Dazhao's world of thought. Unlike his previous active participation in defending his nation and challenging the imperialist powers, he was relatively serene during this period. Beneath the tranquility, however, he utilized his pen to arouse his countrymen to strive for national revival and cultural renaissance. On this nationalistic ground, he intended to raise China's status, reform China's old culture, and remold China's identity. He brought forth a new notion of his country as a reborn nation, while his remedies for China were intended to advance an extreme makeover of one of the oldest continuously developing civilizations on earth. In the international community, he defended China's status as an important country and tried to enhance its image by persuading the Beijing government to join the Great War. He disseminated what useful concepts he got from the West, but his diverse ideas had not yet coalesced into a concrete ideological system. His mixed thoughts epitomized his continual search for a newer model for his country.

Li Dazhao reaffirmed his belief that the rejuvenated China should be a democracy. Tracing the history of Western civilization, he expressed his admiration for Athenian democracy, his appreciation of British constitutional rule, and his reverence for the American representative system. By citing the works of Western thinkers, he expounded his commitment to universally appropriate democratic values. Facing China's messy political situation, republican in name but warlord-ruled in reality, he blasted those strong military commanders who turned provincial or county military bases into private fiefdoms with his virtuoso linguistic dexterity. Aiming to help materialize constitutional rule, Li did not flinch in his moves to safeguard republicanism. He linked Confucianism to despotism, viewed it as a backbone of tyranny, and resolutely rejected the proposal of some conservative politicians to make it part of the national constitution. For a healthy political life, he advocated trustworthy compromise and opposed malicious confrontation. He regarded tolerance as a political virtue. Seeing the whole world plunging into the chaos during the Great War, he reiterated his belief in democracy as the common destiny of mankind, for which he was confident and optimistic. Viewing the war as a chance for mass participation leading to the sophistication of democracy in Europe, he envisioned a democratic world in the near future. Without a doubt, he established himself as a staunch champion for democracy in China's cultural arena during this period when so many young Chinese were longing for a new culture.

The Editor in Chief of the *Morning Bell*

Li Dazhao's journey from Japan back to China was accompanied by downhearted sorrow. His incomplete academic pursuit at Waseda University was one reason, and the touchy volatility of China's national situation was another. After his departure from Tokyo, he boarded ship in Yokohama. During his stopover at Nagasaki, he wrote a letter to his friend Huo Libai to express his woes: "In front of beautiful natural sceneries, my quest for even a single line will not pop up because my heart is full of tears."[1] Upon his arrival in Shanghai in mid-May 1916, his melancholy blues worsened after looking over the perilous national situation. His underlying feelings of gloom embittered him upon seeing his countrymen continuing to fight in the ongoing civil war. In another letter to Huo, he introduced what had happened in China by focusing on the anti-Yuan maneuvers among local politicians, the centrifugal forces in Sichuan, Hunan, and the Lower Yangtze River Valley, and a potential inhouse clash among Yuan's own followers.[2] Although Yuan Shikai "abdicated" in March 1916, the anti-Yuan war was prolonged, simply because Yuan did not leave office and instead continued to stay on in his position as president, which was roundly condemned as illegal. It was a bleak time, during which China was tarnished in the relentless conflict, which Yuan did nothing to mitigate but rather intensified.

In the wake of national crises, Li Dazhao continued to be associated with Tang Hualong and Sun Hongyi, the two former sponsors of his study abroad in Japan. After his return, Li became Tang's secretary, assisting his political maneuvers. It was during this time that Li also participated in a group called the Constitutional Study Association and attended its meetings in Shanghai to discuss which approach to constitutional rule to follow after Yuan's "abdication." Detailed information about this group cannot be found due to the loss of its meeting minutes. According to Bai Jianwu's diary, at least three meetings were held, on May 21, May 24, and May 31, 1916, and Li might have attended all of them.[3] At these meetings, this group deliberated over the national situation, resolved to continue their support of republicanism, and intended to search for solutions for national issues. It was Sun Hongyi who organized this group purporting to play a role in national affairs. Yet this group never became a long-term political organization. It was assembled all of a sudden and disappeared soon after Yuan's death. The existence of such a group shows Li's political activities after his return from Japan and his involvement in the new maneuvers for China's state building.

After his return, Li Dazhao became an intellectual who quietly used his pen to sway the public; however, one episode reveals his rage as he encountered a British policeman in Shanghai. According to Zhang Cixi, it happened prior to his departure for Beijing in July 1916. When Li and his friends took a walk around the Bund and sat on a bench, they were ordered to leave by the policeman, who exclaimed that the bench was not reserved for the Chinese. Li was incensed. As his departure time approached, he did not quarrel with the policeman; rather, he took out his revenge on the nearby statue of Charles Gordon, who epitomized British imperialism. Li angrily pointed his finger at "Gordon," fulminating with the following words: "There will soon be a day on which we will demolish you!"[4] Chinese scholar Zhang Jianguo romanticized this story, featuring Li's confrontation with the policeman whom Li sternly warned that colonialism would be over, scaring away the Briton.[5] Whether or not Li challenged the policeman requires further study; however, it is a fact that he continued to be a nationalistic and anti-imperialistic intellectual.

Scholars have verified Li Dazhao's departure date from Shanghai to Beijing, as he and his friends took a ship sailing northward on July 11, 1916.[6] His travel to Beijing was not to seek a job to eke out a livelihood but to edit a newspaper upon Tang Hualong's invitation. As soon as he arrived in Beijing, he started to assume his role as editor in chief. He was promised freedom in running the daily newspaper, which of course would serve as a mouthpiece for Tang Hualong. Li named it the *Morning Bell* (Chenzhong) and published its first issue on August 15 after a month's preparation. This newspaper contained six pages, half of which were occupied by advertisements. Li designed the image of a bell on which a short motto was inserted daily to encourage the Chinese to be optimistic, positive, and assiduous. Besides a daily editorial, the newspaper covered local, national, and international news; incorporated stories; published translations; and relayed newly released governmental documents. Li was himself an active contributor, publishing many articles in the newspaper.

In the inaugural issue, Li Dazhao elucidated the mission of this newspaper and exhorted the Chinese—in particular, the youth—to labor for their country. The old China in decay was ill prepared for a great transformation; rather, the country should discard the old shell and enjoy a rebirth through a cultural renaissance. He explained why he chose the title of the *Morning Bell*, for he expected to alarm his countrymen that they must work for national rebirth, resuscitation, and reconstruction. He relied on the youth for this goal and remarked that "the country cannot exist for a single day without the youth." He insisted that the youth must live up to this ambition. "A youth is the king of life, the spring of life, and the essence of life. In the dictionary of youth, there is no word for 'difficulty' and there is no term for 'barrier' among their vocabularies."[7] He hailed the Enlightenment, Junges Deutschland, and the Young Turks to stress the importance of the youth in national renaissance and that it should be viewed by the Chinese youth as their mission, for which he intended to use the newspaper as a platform.

With his deafening call for building a Young China, Li Dazhao became one of the pioneers promoting national renaissance during the ongoing New Culture Movement. It is true that some of his ideas were what he brought back from Japan, yet he needed a forum to spread his ideas, which the *Morning Bell* facilitated. With this daily newspaper, he shed a ray of light upon China's gloomy, dim situation. Seeing traditional culture stretched out thinner and thinner while imported ideas poured in thicker and thicker, Li started to reflect profoundly over the possible combination of the two existing civilizations. In his eyes, the first civilization in the East leaned too much toward spirituality, while the second civilization in the West relied too much on materialism. The best approach was to embrace what he called the third civilization, which would harmonize, integrate, and balance the two existing civilizations. He proposed to merge the cutting edges of the two into a coherent, vigorous, and complementary civilization for perpetual progress and continuous advancement.[8] Li's exposition of the third civilization was a rousing and enlightening call to his countrymen.

It was during this period that Li Dazhao's article "The Youth" ("Qingchun") was published, not in the *Morning Bell* but in an influential journal titled *New Youth* (*Xinqingnian*), edited by Chen Duxiu. This article instantly enjoyed a wide readership throughout the country and beyond because of its exhortation to build a young nation, a young state, and a young civilization. It set up a model for the Chinese to be optimistic and confident in their capabilities as well as in their nation's potential. Although Li had high hopes for the young Chinese and encouraged them to act, he argued that the term *youth* was not confined within a specific age range; rather, it should be regarded as a psychological age.[9] Li's "The Youth" attested to vitality and impact and served as a mighty proclamation to the Chinese people of all ages, in particular the youth, to retain a high spirit, rekindle the national glory, and hold this noble task in their hands. Many testimonies demonstrated that this article resulted in "proselytizing" the Chinese to adopt a self-assured, encouraging, and hopeful outlook.[10]

As the editor of his newly launched newspaper, Li Dazhao endeavored to utilize it as a platform to boost the national morale for the reconstruction of a reborn country. Although this might be seen as a future-oriented effort, Li dug into the past to retrieve examples to encourage the youth to embark on the path of a noble enterprise and to cope with potential difficulties. The youth should stand firm, be faithful, and surrender to no pressures. For this purpose, Li created a column in the *Morning Bell* to introduce successful individuals and trace their roads to triumph. He did research on American entrepreneur Horace Greeley, on whom he published a long article. As Li showed, Greeley led a miserable early life due to his father's bankruptcy when he was barely ten years old. Suffering from poverty, the Greeleys moved around seeking survival. Yet Horace Greeley was not intimidated but braved his way to an independent life. As a teenager, he started to work as a child laborer. As Li narrated, Greeley tried to acquire knowledge by himself. Later, he went to New York City to be a typist. At the age of twenty-three, he inaugurated his own magazine, which later turned into the *New York Tribune*, which had a daily circulation of 100,000 during the mid-nineteenth century.[11] By introducing Greeley's successful story, Li aimed to inspire the young Chinese to pursue an independent life, value individualism, and to never lose hope, all of which would lead not only to personal accomplishment but also to national renaissance.

By introducing thinkers from other countries, Li Dazhao presented a rubric of diverse versions of liberal thought, with which he persuaded the Chinese, especially the youth, to be more positive and more confident. When he presented Leo Tolstoy, he underscored Tolstoy's aristocratic background but also emphasized his ordinary life. According to Li, Tolstoy had in his mind noble ideas championing universal love and fighting against tyrannical rule.[12] In the same vein, Li hailed Rabindranath Tagore for his passion for love as the utmost happiness, as the spirit of humankind, and as the apogee of truth.[13] Li admired Francis Bacon for endorsing the destruction of idols and pursuit of truth, and Li entreated the Chinese to do the same for a free life.[14] In regard to Friedrich Nietzsche, Li considered his philosophy helpful to the Chinese to smash the barriers to personal liberation. Li believed that Nietzsche's ideas could assist Chinese youth in enhancing their spirit in order to become high-spirited members of society.[15] Li created an ideological smorgasbord with his all-inclusive presentations of diverse ideas for the

Chinese to select from, live by, and use to accomplish their task of national revival through personal cultivation.

Without hesitation, Li Dazhao kept on pursuing constitutional rule, condemning tyranny, and defending democracy. He prolonged his castigation of Yuan Shikai, denouncing his imperial ambition and condemning him for harming the fledging republic.[16] He endorsed open politics and opposed secret political deals. He remarked that "political contest of civilized nations has been conducted on the oratory platform," and thus he demanded Chinese politicians publicize their plans and avoid undisclosed dealings behind "the black curtain" (*heimu*), which inevitably triggered conspiracy.[17] Unfortunately, politicians struggled for power and engaged in conflicts that often led to civil wars. To remedy this, Li requested that these politicians put a brake on their chase for unlimited power. "Power without a limit results in tyranny, and power without a clear-cut perimeter causes struggle"; both should be prevented in order to guarantee constitutional rule. Li was firm on the need to eradicate the long despotic tradition.[18] He was aware of the importance of newspapers in political life, but he worried about their overflow. The number of newspapers in Beijing, according to Li, was far larger than those in any other capital city in the world. The surplus of newspapers generated "hooliganism," as Li termed it, because a servile owner usually struck a deal with unscrupulous politicians, bargained with shameless manipulators, and then spread deceitful information. Li called for the regulation of the media in order to achieve a healthily transparent political life.[19]

A first glance at the *Morning Bell* exposes its status as a venue for Li Dazhao to realize his goal of a rejuvenated China. Unfortunately, his dream was shattered three weeks after the launch of this newspaper. The problem was his disagreement with Tang Hualong, who now leaned toward Duan Qirui, the premier of the republic and the de facto ruler of the Beijing government. Li planned to write articles criticizing Duan as a warlord but was halted by Tang, who suddenly demanded approval before publication. It was impossible for Li to continue working with such a boss under such a restrictive precondition. Venting his anger, Li published a short story, "Bye-bye with Tears," on September 4, 1916, in which he compared Tang and himself to a pair of former lovers. As the man associated himself with powerful hegemons and committed serious mistakes, the woman became so despairing that she resolutely ditched him.[20] Obviously, the story exposes Li's rage at Tang for tying himself to

Duan. The next day, Li announced his resignation and left the newspaper. Another reason for Li's split from Tang was the rift between Tang Hualong and Sun Hongyi. Tang pressed Li to write an attack on Sun Hongyi for joining the Nationalist Party, but Li's long friendship with Sun would not allow him to comply with such a request. Whatever the reasons for his breakup with Tang, Li's short stint on the newspaper was productive, as he published fourteen articles in just three weeks.

An Editor of the *Public Review of the Constitution*

After his resignation from the *Morning Bell*, Li Dazhao became virtually a jobless man. He went back to Laoting to stay with his family for three weeks. His friends in Beijing, however, asked him to return to launch a new journal called the *Public Review of the Constitution* (Xianfagongyan). The reason for this publication was to offer comments on issues concerning the constitution, because a national council was being convened at that time to either draft a new constitution or revise the existing constitution. Suddenly, diverse political groups became active, all intending to add their political values into the upcoming constitution. For this journal, Li and his friends organized a team to handle the editorial chores. They delimited the journal's mission to studying constitutions, strengthening the rule of law, eliminating tyrannical rule, and lobbying for a better constitution. They informed the public that the journal would welcome diverse opinions, of which they promised a fair dissemination. They decided that their journal would be issued every ten days and that the first issue would come out on the fifth National Day of the Republic of China: October 10, 1916.

Although the editorial team included a group of independent minds, including Li Dazhao, the sponsorship for the journal bares its political bent. The general manager, Qin Guangli, Li's classmate in Tianjin and once a member of Sun Yat-sen's Revolutionary Alliance, came from Heilongjiang Province and became a congressman during the early years of the republic. Qin was responsible for raising the funds, for which he himself donated two thousand yuan after selling his own property. Other donors were mostly Nationalists or individuals friendly to the Nationalist Party; for example, Sun Yat-sen donated five hundred yuan; Tang Shaoyi, three hundred; Sun Hongyi, one hundred; Li Qingfang, one hundred; and Peng Jieshi, fifty. Others were small donors, such as Wen

Shilin and Wang Zhengting, each pledging twenty yuan.[21] In post-Yuan politics, Liang Qichao's Progressive Party moved closer to Duan Qirui, while Sun Yat-sen's Nationalist Party operated as its opposition. From the list of above donors, it is obvious that Li and his team favored the Nationalist Party as they drifted away from the Progressive Party and became more critical of Duan Qirui's regime.

It is wrong to assume that Li Dazhao became a partisan individual at this moment. In fact, he did not hold a membership with any political party. He remained an independent mind, pursuing democratic institutions, promoting constitutional rule, and defending republicanism. Personally, however, he led a precarious life, because his status as a coeditor could not guarantee him a steadfast income. Yet he continued to pursue his habit of reading, researching, and writing. Gao Yihan remembered those days: "Li maintained a normal state of mind, even during his unemployed days. He read widely and did his research on important issues. His strong resolve enabled him not to surrender to any difficulties."[22] During the short stint of working for the journal, Li wrote five long articles to interpret the significance of constitutional rule, defend individual liberty, and fight against any schemes of espousing old values for the new constitution. He leaned towards the Nationalist Party, and he endorsed its stance and defended its values so long as they suited his standpoint. His close relationship with the Nationalist Party was also shown by his attendance of the funeral for Huang Xing in Beijing on December 1, 1916.[23]

Another piece of evidence to show Li Dazhao's tie with the Nationalist Party was his support of provincial power as a clause of the constitution, for which he published an article on November 9, 1916. In it, Li traced the separation of power in Chinese history and argued that provincial power bestowed by the imperial court was prevalent throughout China's long civilization. Such a special balance of power between the central government and the provincial administration was a benefit to the country. Rejecting the view that federalism would divide the country, Li employed the American federal example and the German federal case for his defense. He was confident that federalism that licensed local autonomy was a serviceable way of eradicating domestic division and strengthening national unity. It is difficult to claim that Li became a federalist, as this was a one-time stance; however, his support for provincial autonomy demonstrates his leaning toward the Nationalist Party. Hailing the Yunnan Proclamation (Yunnanxuanyan) issued during the anti-Yuan war as a model document, Li favored its advocation of local autonomy as a principle for

China's new constitution. According to Li, the proclamation supported the balance of power between the central government and the provincial administration, without which China would encounter conflicts and with which China could avoid unnecessary troubles.[24]

Li Dazhao resolutely repudiated Kang Youwei's call to incorporate Confucianism into China's new constitution. He was enraged by Kang's appeal to enshrine Confucius by exclaiming that "Heaven bestows us knees, and why don't we kneel down?" To Li, Kang was echoing "strange noises from the tomb." Li felt that Confucius's teachings contained values but that they should not be elevated to such a sanctified status in the constitution. According to Li, Confucianism denigrated self-independence, choked individual autonomy, and stifled citizens' creative thinking. He likened Confucianism to the rotten backbone of China's long tyranny. To seek the rebirth of China, traditional values should be retained, but Confucianism should not be a part of the constitution. For ideological liberation, the Chinese must smash the shackles of Confucianism, regard it as a failed apparatus, and disclaim it officially in advance of republicanism. Because Confucianism assisted imperial rule, it was not suitable for democracy, and the insertion of Confucianism into a republican constitution was ridiculously unacceptable.[25] To Li, Confucianism did not possess eternal usefulness; neither did it retain infinite values. Rather, its imperfect relativity posed a perilous hurdle to China's modernization.[26]

To Li Dazhao, the national constitution should be a guarantee of the freedom that was obtained through the bloodshed of revolution. Citing Western constitutions as examples, Li contended that the French constitution came into being after a long, violent revolution and that the American constitution sprang up from the blood of American revolutionaries in the thirteen colonies. Similarly, Chinese fighters battled for years, and Li recounted relevant events such as the anti-Manchu uprisings during the Qing dynasty, the 1911 Revolution, the Second Revolution in 1913, and the National Protection War in 1916. Li's allegory was poignant: "history is the field, and freedom is a plant in it. The blood of citizens irrigates the field and nurtures the plant's growth." China so far had begotten a preliminary constitution, but ignorant men, including Yuan Shikai, crudely disdained it as "a mere scrap of paper" and ruined it at will. Li admonished the members of the constitutional council to take a look at the bloodstains of revolutionary martyrs and to become more determined to draft a new constitution to safeguard the republic and to protect freedom.[27]

Cherishing freedom, Li Dazhao demanded that individual liberty be insured by the constitution. To him, it would be unbearable for humans to live without freedom. He proclaimed that "freedom is a prerequisite for human existence. Without freedom, it is meaningless to live. Freedom guaranteed by the national constitution is a necessity for citizens to subsist. Without freedom being guaranteed in the constitution, citizens' lives have no worth."[28] Although freedom was defined diversely, Li specified a number of important elements of it, including freedom of speech, freedom of education, freedom of publication, and freedom of faith. Li condemned China's long-standing tyranny, stretching all the way back to the Qin dynasty, and blamed Confucianism for fostering despotism after the Han dynasty. Promoting citizens' liberty, he urged the incorporation of freedom of speech as an essential component of the national constitution. Criticizing China for being a country without freedom of publication for so long, Li supported free dissemination of knowledge and opposed harsh governmental censorship. He emphasized the importance of religious freedom for guaranteeing a harmonious communal life. He highlighted the value of educational freedom and endorsed free diffusion of knowledge by the modern educational system.

While the constitutional council was deliberating over constitutionally related issues, Li Dazhao published his articles to advise the councilmen to work hard and to discuss thoroughly and objectively all of the clauses. He hailed the United States Constitution as a model and praised the American elites who gathered in Philadelphia for years, who labored hard to produce a general law, and who then presented a classical constitution.[29] China's national constitution, starting with the Provisional Constitution of 1912 and then Yuan Shikai's revision, represented the beginning of the process. Li advised the council to follow the American example to achieve a similar accomplishment. In particular, Li offered two important suggestions. The first was a balance of power for political compromise among diverse yet opposing political forces. The council should pay attention to the needs of the existing political groups and incorporate their good ideas into the constitution. The second was the coexistence of the formally written constitution and the customarily unwritten constitution; according to Li, both should be respected in the making of a new constitution so as to produce a resilient general law.[30] The national constitution was so sacrosanct that it could only be amended through deliberatively popular approval, enabling it to adapt to new national needs in the future. However, in a cruel and sudden shock to the hopes and expectations of Li and many others, the council never offered a new constitution, because it was soon suspended by the Beijing government.

A Contributor to the *Tiger Daily*

Financial difficulties compelled the *Public Review of the Constitution* to terminate its operations upon publishing its last issue on January 10, 1917, after which Li Dazhao once again became an unemployed man. Just in a nick of time, however, Zhang Shizhao resumed his *Tiger* in Beijing after a year's suspension from its Tokyo days, though he changed it into a daily newspaper with the new title of the *Tiger Daily* (*Jiayinrikan*). Zhang cherished Li's talent, appreciated his insight, and invited him to be a contributor. With Li's and others' efforts, the *Tiger Daily* published its first daily issue on January 28, 1917, which kicked off Li's five-month stint as a writer for this newspaper. During those months, Li worked diligently and published about seventy articles altogether. At first, Li focused on domestic issues and attacked the Beijing government and Liang Qichao's party. According to Gao Yihan, Li's criticism startled Zhang Shizhao, who had now befriended Liang. Zhang asked Gao to persuade Li to change his stance but was rejected. After reaching a compromise, they decided that Li would cover international issues from that point on.[31] As a result, Li's seventy articles could be roughly partitioned into two categories, the first covering domestic issues and the second reporting on international affairs; in both cases, Li offered his rational analysis and instilled his nationalistic sentiment into his discourses.

To construct a Young China, Li Dazhao offered a new definition of China's citizenry within the national boundary by coining a new term, the New Chinese Nation (Xinzhonghuaminzu). He explained that "at the beginning of the republic, the nomenclature of five ethnic groups came into being. In my observation, the culture of the five have become indistinguishable. In fact, all citizens now have no separate boundaries among them. The people of the republic have forged a new identity as the New Chinese Nation."[32] Li spoke highly of this new nation for its qualities of "excellence" and "strength," two prominent features possessed by France and Germany, respectively. In China, however, the two were combined into one inseparable national characteristic.[33] To Western readers, this notion might denote a type of Han chauvinism, as it did not recognize ethnic differences among the five groups, but that was indeed how the Chinese viewed their country during the early republic. Yet Li elaborated that Chinese citizens had undesirable habits; for example, he stated, the Chinese acted upon emotion rather than reason and tried to solve problems by power rather than law.[34] The Chinese lacked politeness in how they treated one another. He cited Japanese social courtesy as an example for his fellow citizens to emulate.[35] He urged the Chinese to respect Tolstoy's way and advised them to repent conscientiously, correct their bad habits, and shun evildoing.[36] The Chinese should live a simple life, avoid luxuries, abjure extravagance, and despise wastefulness. A simple life could guide the Chinese on a normal track, avert unlawful behaviors, and rebuild a healthy society.[37]

While sympathizing with people of low incomes, Li Dazhao simultaneously saw their potent strength and recognized their innate power. As Ping Zhu points out, like other Chinese intellectuals in Beijing, Li had paid his sympathy to rickshaw drivers.[38] As Li lived in Beijing, he called on the local residents to commiserate with rickshaw drivers who "have devoted all their might and sacrificed themselves to the society to earn a few cents a day, while the survival of their families relies on that petty income." Indeed, rickshaw drivers were the pillars of transportation in Beijing, as tens of thousands of rickshaw drivers provided a low-priced service before the introduction of automobiles. Li enumerated their sufferings: contracting lung diseases by inhaling dirt along the road, enduring year-round inclement weather, earning barely a small fraction of others' income, and being subjected to police harassment.[39] Traveling on the train in May 1917 back to Laoting County, he saw a large number of poor migrants heading toward Manchuria to seek a better life due to its available land and opportunities. Yet he saw those emigrants as powerful national defenders. He remarked that their settlements would enable them to defend the frontier region to counterbalance Japan's invasion.[40] While taking care of his sick wife in Laoting in May and June 1917, Li studied the local community and was convinced that the true public opinion should be coming from the grassroots society rather than from the great urban metropolis; because of this, he advised the Chinese not to ignore the potential of the rural folks.[41]

Li Dazhao conceived and developed his thoughts on the role of the youth in national reconstruction, for which he encouraged the youth to bear their responsibility. He called on the whole society to empathize with the youth, treasure them, and nourish them.[42] Young students, as a special sector of the society, encountered numerous difficulties, as they were often despised for their radical ideas, belittled due to their progressive minds, and rejected because of their liberal behaviors. According to Li, the student issue became one of the most urgent national problems.[43] More pressingly, many young people, after graduation from schools, became jobless, distressed, and disappointed, which led some to commit suicide. Li cautioned the Chinese to take care of the youth, create jobs for them, and lend a hand to them. If the young people were mobilized, they would be a benefit to the nation.[44] Li championed free love among the youth and condemned parental interference into their marriages. Upon viewing a drama in Beijing that deliberately distorted the youth's free love by alleging its disastrous consequence, Li saluted free love, hailed it as a barometer of social progress, and warned the conservatives not to spread their toxic messages.[45]

Li Dazhao remained ardent as ever in his support for the republican system for which he rendered his new ideas. He enumerated three existing political forces in the Republic of China: the military power, which had controlled the government for so long but now declined; the moderates who took advantage of the situation but now became freebooters; and the radicals who played a role in revolution but now continued to champion unnecessary violence. Unfortunately, as Li remarked, moderates and radicals turned out to be two vicious enemies who had already caused national troubles. Thereafter, Li expected to see a new central political force (*zhongxinshili*) spring up from the middle class to steer the country toward a normal republican life.[46] Future political rivals, no matter their backgrounds, should all be patriotic opponents.[47] As he did previously, he continued to rule out a possible insertion of Confucianism into the constitution, declaring that "its insertion will generate a dead constitution" because Confucianism was a dehydrated skeleton belonging to a time several thousand years ago.[48] He stuck to open politics and transparent social life; in particular, he promoted the accessibly oratory speechmaking in order to fairly disseminate information in the public sphere.[49] In April 1917, China as a nation encountered a crunch as the minister of the Department of the Treasury, Chen Jintao, was dismissed due to his involvement in a bribery case. Chen earned his doctorate from Yale University and had become a talented official. Yet a large bribe had lured him to commit a crime. The conservatives who stuck to the old way immediately utilized this case to derail republicanism.

Li blamed them for implicating the republic rather than pointing their fingers at a single wicked individual.[50]

In the political realm, Li Dazhao recommended compromise, tolerance, and reconciliation, because he deemed the intensely malicious partisan struggle a cause of China's fiasco. He remarked that "those who follow the way of compromise will run into vitality and success, while those who reject compromise will face the chance of entering a dead end."[51] The world was made up of diversity, for which tolerance was proportionate to harmony. Li remarked that "delicious taste is desired by all, but the most delicious taste should be the combination of all kinds of tastes. Attractive color is loved by all, yet the most beautiful one is the mix of all different colors. The same thing could be said about political life."[52] Li's idea of compromise was aimed at coexistence rather than self-sacrificing for others' benefit. Compromise did not mean making a distinction between the old and the new but negotiating between them. Compromise should be viewed as ideological rapprochement instead of a petty matter to be dealt with privately. Compromise did not need a third party as an arbitrator, and sincere bilateral or multilateral reconciliation should be managed peacefully and magnanimously.[53] In applying compromise in the democratic system, the centrifugal force must be tolerated, although the centripetal force is treasured by those in power. Ideally, the two forces should reach an agreement and create a congruent political life.[54]

In the realm of China's foreign relations, Li Dazhao paid special attention to the Chinese role in the Great War. He believed that China should support the Allied powers in order to elevate its own international status. As soon as the United States severed its diplomatic ties with Germany, Li urged the Chinese government to take the same action. He argued that it was China's "second nature" (*di'ertianxing*) in the past to apologize to foreigners, relinquish national interests, and pay whatever the powers demanded whenever an incident occurred.[55] For the ongoing Great War, the Chinese should take the initiative to display their national vitality. Although he knew that China was not a strong power, he argued that "diplomatic victory means using our strength not to challenge Germany but to develop our friendship with the Allied powers."[56] China would at least be able to supply manpower to those potential allies for their war efforts.[57] To Li's dismay, Chinese officials were divided on this issue. President Li Yuanhong opposed joining the Great War, but

Premier Duan Qirui supported declaring war against Germany. Facing this situation, Li warned politicians not to use diplomacy as a means of power struggle at home and advised his countrymen to be united in order to establish a new international image of their country.[58] After China took actions against Germany, Li called on the Chinese to rally behind the government. He urged Chinese officials to study diplomacy-related issues in order to safeguard national interests. He advised the Chinese government to treat with grace the 336 German employees who worked in China as engineers, customs inspectors, railway technicians, and in other capacities. The German concessions, after China's declaration of war, should be retrieved by the Chinese government. The German property in China should not be confiscated by any nation other than China. Li pointed out that China should fortify its northwestern frontier, which was inhabited by Muslims who kept ties with Turkey, an ally of Germany, because he reasoned that Germany and Turkey might collaborate with those Muslims to retaliate against China by inciting a revolt in the northwestern region.[59]

As an admirer of Western civilization for so long, Li Dazhao carefully monitored the changing political situation in the West during the Great War. He was watchful of the reshuffling of cabinets and other governmental changes. Even minor administrative shifts did not evade his eyes; for example, he offered his comments on the British government that had created an enlarged cabinet with a special addition of the War Committee.[60] Li wrote four long articles to spotlight the socialist parties in Europe, their changing attitudes toward the war, their recent maneuvers, and their special roles in wartime politics. According to Li's observations, European socialists were originally anti-war activists who opposed entry into a general war but became cooperative with their governments after the outbreak of the Great War. As the conflicts dragged on, those socialists played a particular role in national politics and in leading revolutionary movements.[61] As a believer in democracy, Li was hopeful that democracy would not be weakened by the war. His study satisfied him, because he found that ordinary citizens' participation in politics in Britain and France became so widespread that it strengthened democracy there.[62] From the economic perspective, Li stressed the important role of food in the course of war. A shortage of food would not lead to peace, and he deemed bread holy, powerful, peaceful, and lovable.[63] Li introduced Western patriotism in order to inspire his fellow citizens, and he made the Chinese aware of Theodore Roosevelt's plan to send his four sons as soldiers to the front.[64] Another inspiring case, as Li cited, was that of a French mother who had already lost two sons on the battlefield but still called back her other son, a Harvard University student, to return to France to defend her country.[65]

One of the foci of Li Dazhao's coverage was the revolution in Russia that overthrew the czarist government in early 1917. Li regarded it as a case of the ongoing global revolution and warmly received it as a triumph over tyranny. He was elated at the new government led by Georgy Lvov and exclaimed that the new Russia was "a neighboring republican sister" of China.[66] To satisfy the curiosity of his readers concerning the origins of this revolution, Li did research on it and determined eleven causes: ideological clash, thriving nihilism, German influence, liberal literature, mass poverty, tyrannical government, the czarina's conspiracy, the arrogance of reactionaries, conservatives' resistance to reform, food shortages, and the rising Labor Party.[67] Although many more causes could have been listed, Li's analysis was quite comprehensive. Li was confident that the revolution in Russia would exert a positive impact upon China because it would inspire the Chinese to follow the global trend to defend their own republican system.[68]

Li Dazhao was vigilant over issues concerning Japan, as he had personally studied in Japan and had participated in the campaign against Japan's Twenty-One Demands a couple years before. Li noticed the profits Japan reaped from its exports to other countries during the Great War, which was depicted by the Japanese as "the deluge of gold" (*huangjinzhihongshui*). Japan's newly acquired wealth, Li warned, would help it manufacture more battleships for its more aggressive actions.[69] Upon hearing that a Japanese official proposed a "Far Eastern Monroe Doctrine" in early 1917, Li exposed it as Japan's ambition to dominate East Asia.[70] Reading a Japanese article on pan-Asianism in April 1917, which described Western civilization as a predatory culture and portrayed Japan as the Asian leader, Li immediately criticized its ulterior motive. Viewing China as the pillar of Asia, he argued that Asia could not exist without China. He exhorted his countrymen "to create a new civilization, rebuild a new state, stand firm in the world, and be a peer of the Western civilized countries."[71]

Li Dazhao persisted in admiring Western civilization, about which he continued to elaborate and publish. In April 1917, he did a comprehensive study of the differences between the East and the West and found striking disparities: Eastern civilization featured quietness, while Western civilization was characterized by its mobility; the East relied on agriculture, while the West depended on commerce. "In the past one hundred years, the way of Western mobility swiftly invaded the noiseless life of the East. It was this incursion that awakened the sleeping Eastern continent."[72] Li proposed to pursue the Western way and "to turn our noiseless state into a moving one, change our silent civilization into a dynamic one, and reform our soundless life into a noisy one."[73] This does not mean that Li endorsed everything in the West. For example, he criticized the theory of population by Thomas Malthus in early 1917, on which he wrote two articles. He condemned the Malthusian notion of solving the population issue by resorting to wars.[74] By quoting recent global demographic data, Li relegated Malthus's theory to the dustbin of false hypothesis. Rejecting Malthus's claim, Li reasoned that the developed nations had experienced demographic declines due to low fertility rates, which Li termed "the disease of civilization" (*wenmingzhibing*).[75] More importantly, food production could be significantly increased, he argued, disagreeing with Malthus's assertion about its mathematical growth. Li was confident that the earth, with its immeasurable capacity, would be able to sustain sixty billion human beings.[76]

Li Dazhao's thought continued to reveal its hybrid nature with mixed ideas from diverse sources, although some notions sprang up from his careful observation and his own creative thinking. All were to serve his nationalistic fervor, though. As the Great War raged on, Li noticed a strange phenomenon: China's copper coins, a traditional currency, were collected and sold abroad. Li worried about the potential inflation it might cause, for which he advised the Chinese government to take actions to protect the ordinary people.[77] After his careful examination, he found that the outflow of copper coins was related to the Great War. He calculated that the Allied powers consumed 600,000 tons of copper per year for weapon making. He noticed the fluctuating price of copper in the international market and cautioned the Chinese to value its vital utility. Even if the war ended, he argued, copper would continue to be an indispensable metal. Thus, he advised the Chinese government to collect the old copper coins, store them up, and prohibit their outflow, because copper would be treasured as a prized commodity and a valuable military material.[78]

A Domestic Political Refugee

The second half of 1917 was an unfortunate period for Li Dazhao, as China's political turmoil turned him into a domestic refugee. After staying with his family for more than a month in Laoting, he returned to Beijing on June 22, 1917. No sooner had he arrived than he found that the struggle between President Li Yuanhong and Premier Duan Qirui had spiraled into a political crisis. Li Yuanhong requested that Zhang Xun bring in his troops into Beijing for mediation but only found that Zhang tried to profit by the opportunity. Zhang's arrival in Beijing added volatility to China's political life, as he began to revile the republic and flaunt his hostility to progressive intellectuals. To Li, Beijing suddenly became a dangerous place to live. To make matters worse, Zhang, who openly championed the restoration of the Qing Empire, suddenly staged a coup and installed the abdicated Qing emperor, Puyi, as a reinstated emperor on July 1, 1917. Almost predictably, Li fled the capital and traveled to Shanghai. The reasons for Li's escape to the south might have been multiple, but the major one was certainly his strong support for the republic, because of which he became a target of Zhang's persecution. Zhang's army was a notoriously conservative force, so much so that his troops still wore the Manchu queue more than five years after the Manchu abdication. Although Zhang was a Han Chinese, his stubborn loyalty to the Manchu dynasty provoked terror in anyone who had supported the republic. Li was jobless at this point, which meant that his travel to the south did not cost him his employment; rather, it might offer a chance for him to land a job there. Perhaps, as the conservatives suddenly flocked to Beijing to serve the monarch, Li felt stifled by the suffocating atmosphere, which compelled him to leave.

Zhang Xun's act proved to be a debacle for him as well as for his soldiers, as his restoration of the Qing dynasty lasted barely twelve days. However, this event left an aftershock echoing through Chinese politics. The former president did not return to politics, while Duan Qirui, who had suppressed Zhang Xun, started to promote himself as a hero who had rescued the republic. Duan continued to serve as premier but started to clash with the new president, Feng Guozhang. The two factions, along with other military leaders, dragged the country into a state of constant conflict. In the political arena, Liang Qichao started to collaborate with Duan. After his travel to the south, Li stayed with his friend Sun Hongyi, who owned a house in Shanghai. Reasonably, after the failure of Zhang Xun's restoration, Li should have returned to Beijing seeking a new life. Yet he continued to stay in Shanghai for four months. His long stay has not been well studied and requires further scholarly inquiry. Perhaps Li's dislike of Duan Qirui and Liang Qichao was the major reason. Possibly, he was busy assisting Sun Hongyi, who was now a member of the Nationalist Party, in a maneuver to derail Duan. He might have been looking for a job in Shanghai. From his letters to his friends, we can see that Li's faith in republicanism did not change, his commitment to democracy endured, and his aversion to warlords was renewed.[79] He continued to do research, but he was not as prolific as he was in the past year. In fact, he only published three articles during those four months, all of which appeared in the *Pacific Ocean*, a journal edited by Li Jiannong in Shanghai, in which he lashed out at the new power holders of the Beijing government.

In this new situation, Li Dazhao first vented his anger at Liang Qichao, the leader of the Progressive Party. After Zhang Xun's failure, Liang was selling his idea of political reconciliation in the name of benefiting the republic. To Li, however, it was a masquerade behind which Liang retained a strong tie with Duan. According to Li, "In politics, there must be an opposition without which there is no compromise for even a single day." But Liang's compromise was conducted without principle because he surrendered himself to the warlord regime. Liang's reconciliation was a pseudo compromise (*weitiaohe*), which mirrored his long pattern of acting as a capitulator to strong power holders. Citing Western thinkers on the topic of compromise, Li argued that true compromise should be conducted with self-dignity and shepherded by moral principle. Only by holding firmly to one's standpoint could one reach compromise for peaceful coexistence with others. In contrast, Liang's compromise was to commit political suicide and to ruin himself. Consequently, Li demanded that all political groups reflect, repent, open up their hearts, and behave properly to reach meaningful and genuine compromise.[80]

Li Dazhao himself was not a member of the Nationalist Party by then; however, he was combatting a common enemy along with it. After Duan Qirui refused to convene congress and rejected working on the constitution, Sun Yat-sen launched the Constitutional Protection Movement (Hufayundong) in September 1917 and condemned Duan as a tyrant. Li soon wrote an article titled "Violence and Politics" to upbraid Duan and his regime. Li remarked, "Neither a normal state nor conventional politics exists in today's situation. What we have got are power grabbers who have snatched power through violence. . . . In the despotic world, the state is built by the strong force, while in a constitutional world, the state is established upon the people's will."[81] He denounced Duan for ruining the constitution, bullying the people, and resorting to military might. According to Li, violence led to the emergence of responsive hostility, and repercussive ferocity channeled the nation into a disastrous situation in which the people lived in a constant fear. Citing Tolstoy's ideas, Li urged the powerful men to listen to the people's pleas, to repent by self-criticism, and to act with self-conscientiousness.[82] Obviously, Li's advice was ignored by Duan; nevertheless, it served as a highly principled criticism of the Beijing government and as strong support for Sun Yat-sen's ongoing revolutionary movement.

Encountering such a perplexing national situation, Li Dazhao did not lose confidence in the republican system. On October 10, 1917, he wrote an article titled "The Day" to celebrate the National Day and to honor the sixth anniversary of the 1911 Revolution. In this article, Li made it clear that democracy should be fully established through people's continual efforts. He articulated that the American Revolution succeeded because the American people persistently fought during eight long years. France's freedom was achieved through decades of the French people's sacrifices. While the road ahead for the republic might be bumpy, Li cautioned his countrymen to repent over their wrongdoings, cherish democracy, and protect the republican system. The National Day of China was the crystallization of blood from the revolutionary martyrs who had given up their lives for it. The day should be deemed as an annual reminder of those martyrs' sacrifice and as a yearly recurrent occasion to fortify the people's will to protect democracy. Urging the Chinese people to defend the republic, Li borrowed the then-current German military catchphrase "The Day," a popular expression voicing loudly German soldiers' resolve, to encourage the Chinese to strengthen their willpower for democracy, enhance their understanding of republicanism, and dedicate themselves to the young republic.[83]

Most of Li Dazhao's activities during those four months in the south were not formally recorded. Yet, from his articles, letters, poems, Bai Jianwu's diary, and other sources, we know that he was busy challenging the Beijing government. As a domestic political refugee, Li persisted in his belief in republicanism. Although he was not a member of Sun Yat-sen's party then, he wrote to condemn the common enemy. He might have served as Sun Hongyi's messenger to urge Jiangsu military governor Li Chun to resist the Beijing regime. Indeed, during those four months, Li Dazhao went to Nanjing to meet Li Chun two times. During his first visit, between October 18 and 22, 1917, he met Li Chun, discussed issues with him, and toured the nearby scenery with him. During his second visit, between November 9 and November 11, he met Li Chun again. The details of those meetings will never be known, but the claim that Li Dazhao served as Sun Hongyi's go-between to press Li Chun to resist Duan is a reasonable argument.[84] As an important general under Feng Guozhang, Li Chun belonged to the Zhili clique, which differed from Duan Qirui's Anhui clique. After his second visit to Nanjing, Li Dazhao did not return to Shanghai; rather, he proceeded to Beijing by the railways to accept a new job as the chief librarian at Beijing University, which would open a new page of his life.

Conclusion

The brief time of a little over one year and a half after his return from Japan was a special period in Li Dazhao's life. Although semi-employed and semi-jobless, he offered a large number of impressive publications, which account for 20 percent of all his writings so far known. Nearly one hundred articles that he wrote during this period have survived, which allow us to understand his life and his thought around this time. A close examination exhibits Li's involvement in the print media to influence his fellow citizens. Through both newspapers and journals, he disseminated the ideas he acquired from the West and Japan and infused them with his nationalistic zeal in an attempt to sway public opinion. By publishing on a variety of topics, Li established himself as a prolific author, a competent editor, and an inspiring intellectual. His passion for the media and his copious works earned him the splendid epithet of "the shining pearl" in literary circles. His articles, in uneven lengths, showcased his refined writing style, elegant linguistic dexterity, smooth fluency, provocative thinking, and persuasive analysis. That is why he was praised by his contemporaries, such as Bai Jianwu, who commented that Li was "a man of high quality and scholarly excellence [*pinjiexuecui*]."[85]

In fact, a number of stimuli pushed Li Dazhao to continue reaching his lofty goal of national salvation. Being elated at Yuan Shikai's demise in mid-1916, Li was hopeful for China's renaissance as a new country, a new nation, and a new civilization. His burning desire for this nationalistic objective prompted him to write down and spread his ideas for the purpose of turning his country into a rejuvenated, resurrected, and reborn nation. Differing from the prevalent pessimism of that era, Li assumed a high-spirited, positive, and optimistic attitude in which his ongoing nationalism remained a driving force. To change China, Li vehemently defended the republican system. To Li, constitutional rule must be upheld, democracy strengthened, and people's well-being upgraded. His adoption of Western democratic concepts and his versatile adaptation of foreign notions into Chinese vocabularies displayed his firm conviction in supporting democracy. In Li's view, democracy would assist China's national renaissance. Witnessing China's unhealthy political phenomena, he became a sharp critic of diehard conservatives, powerful warlords, and unscrupulous politicians, while he used his pen to motivate his countrymen to obligate themselves to carry out their duty to help establish a salubrious and modernized nation.

Up to this moment, there were no signs of any strong connection to Karl Marx's theories from Li Dazhao, nor could Li's writings verify a familiarity with communist doctrines. However, his increasing interest in the socialist parties of the West proves his curiosity about the socialist ideology and his profound appreciation of Western civilization. Up through this time, his mindset continued to be a hodgepodge of diverse ideas, including nationalism, democracy, traditional culture, and other constructs. Socialism had infiltrated silently into his mind. Tolstoy's promotion of social change through individual repentance reshaped Li's outlook. In a number of ways, Li was a cultural bridge connecting his country with the outside world, in particular the West. He intended his introduction of foreign ideas to solve tough issues in his own country. Nevertheless, murky spots and gray spaces in his mind still existed without clear-cut perimeters, which compelled him to work more diligently to seek an unblemished view and to redefine a faultless outlook for his nationalistic ambition.

Chapter 5

Beijing University

Introduction

In January 1918, Li Dazhao started his job as the director of the Beijing University library (Tushuguanzhuren), the chief librarian and the head librarian in diverse translations, which was a professional appointment in academic circles. Before this he had led a precarious life as an editor and a writer; after his appointment, however, he became an employee at the most prestigious university in his country. He served in this position for about five years, during which he was also hired as a professor in the summer of 1920. Until his death in 1927, his title remained professor at Beijing University, although his salary was frozen during his last years because of his inactivity in teaching.[1] This was the first time Li held a long-term professional job, and it enabled him to fend off financial pitfalls since the income allotted him allowed a stable life. More importantly, under the auspices of the liberal policies of Cai Yuanpei, who was president of the university, Li enjoyed academic freedom in his own scholarly endeavors. Li's own motto for the university, "scholarly achievement is the only criterion," compelled him to do new research, explore new topics, and publish new findings.[2]

Li Dazhao's prolific publications and creative ideas garnered him the stature of a well-known intellectual during the ongoing New Culture Movement. As a scholar, Li advanced progressive thoughts on a number of issues, intending to transform his country in myriad fields. His role in pursuing a new culture was not a nebulous process but could be traced clearly in his writings. The underpinning of his thoughts, however, remained his strong nationalism. In particular, his loathing of foreign infringement prompted him to be an activist.[3] As the Paris Peace Conference threw the Chinese into a flux of despair and fury over the Shandong issue, he ramped up his activities and took the lead in agitating young students for action. He guided them in the nationwide demonstrations that are known as the May Fourth Movement in modern Chinese history.

An examination of Li Dazhao's wide-ranging roles at Beijing University delineates a broad parameter to his diverse activities. Li put theory into practice by getting involved in a number of social and political movements. To protect his colleagues, he became a leader in challenging the warlord government. To explore a feasible blueprint for China's renaissance, he assisted in establishing civilian societies to encourage the Chinese, in particular the youth, to seek an ideal way. He championed civil liberty, defended republicanism, endorsed the scientific approach, and supported women's rights. On the personal level, he inspired the Chinese to live a moral life by forsaking pleasure and relinquishing coarse habits. In a number of ways, Li left an indelible mark on various fronts of the New Culture Movement, in particular within the Beijing University community.

The Chief Librarian

Scholars in recent years have explored Li Dazhao's employment at Beijing University but are still unclear about when he took up the job as the chief librarian and when he ceased to work at the university. Fragmented primary sources do not allow us to be sure of those two dates, yet there is a bulk of evidence to prove his long-term employment. Diverse views have been offered about his initial appointment around the beginning of 1918, but none of them point to an accurate date. One photo taken on December 17, 1917, with Li inside the university proves his arrival on the campus. In any case, most scholars today agree that he started to work at the library in January 1918.[4] Li became the director of the library not because he was a professionally trained librarian. He was appointed to the position because of his close friend Zhang Shizhao's strong recommendation. Indeed, the Western-style library had just been established in China, and whoever served as the chief librarian could not be a previously trained professional. Li Dazhao was further appointed as a professor at Beijing University to teach history, politics, and economics in July 1920. He resigned from the position of chief librarian on December 2, 1922, but continued to teach as a professor.[5] According to Jin Yufu, Li formally left Beijing University in August 1925, after which his salary was suspended.[6] Other scholars contend that Li's name remained on the university payroll even after his death.[7] The above debate may seem pointless to Western scholars, but it reflects Chinese scholars' seriousness in probing Li's employment at the university. In any case, it is reasonable to argue that Li had developed a professional career at Beijing University since early 1918 and that he did not fulfill his teaching duty during his last years because he chose to be a professional revolutionary.

As soon as Li Dazhao became the chief librarian, he started to investigate the existing issues in a bid to facilitate the effective use of all available resources at the library. Beijing University, as China's first public institution, enjoyed a prestigious status throughout the entire nation. Yet its library as an organ of education was but a new business. Although China had imperial and private libraries in its long history, the traditional approach of management was not to serve a large number of public readers. After his arrival, Li also found that he encountered serious issues, such as the insufficiency of books and journals, ineffective management, unprofessional staff training, and other perplexing problems. Li was not intimidated by any of these; he took measures to redress the existing issues and to implement precautionary measures to thwart any further hazards.

Perhaps the most distressing issue for the library was its management, in particular the loaning practice. The fact that faculty and students did not return books on time had negatively impacted their effective circulation and efficient use. After examining the problem, Li Dazhao authored "The Revised Library Loan Rules" in April 1918 and revised it again in December 1920. He published public notices concerning his library in university bulletins. He classified all books into the most valuable items and the common readings. For the first category, the readers would only be allowed to read them inside the library. He limited the number of loans but allowed members of the faculty to borrow more. He ordered the timely return of borrowed books before the due date, after which the clients, whether faculty members or students, would be prohibited from further borrowing.[8] Yet some remained tardy, for which Li implemented even stricter measures by granting faculty members only a two-week loan period, while students were granted one week. In case

Figure 5.1. Li Dazhao served as the chief librarian at Beijing University Library between 1918 and 1922. He was also hired as a professor by the university in 1920. The Chinese characters are translated as "the photo of Mr. Li Dazhao who is the director of the library." (Public domain)

of violations, Li ordered the suspension of privileges and imposed fines, which would be deducted from a faculty member's salary or added to a student's account to be paid. Book damages and losses were to be penalized by charges. The university bulletin on October 21, 1921, announced that seventy-two students were suspended from further registration and another sixty-nine were punished by no further book loans for a year due to their violations of the library regulations.[9]

Although the university library was ranked as the largest among higher institutions in China, its 140,000 volumes around the time of Li Dazhao's arrival were mainly Chinese classics. Li intended to change the situation through acquisitions of foreign publications. Through his efforts, the Western collection increased from 9,930 volumes in 1917 to 19,846 volumes in 1920. The number of journals jumped to six hundred, among which two hundred were foreign titles.[10] After the relocation of the library from Mashenmiao to Shatan, near the Forbidden City, in late 1918, the university allotted the first floor of the newly built Red Mansion (Honglou) on the new campus to become the university library. Li allocated reading rooms for readers to browse newspapers, journals, magazines, and books. He adopted the Western cataloging system to classify all books, both Chinese and foreign, at his library. He permitted faculty members and other individuals to share their collections with the library and encouraged private donations to the library. He prolonged library hours during the summertime. He took precautions to prohibit smoking to avoid fire.[11] Seeing that some pages in journals or magazines were torn away, Li circulated a campus-wide notice criticizing the act of vandalism and warned potential violators to exercise "self-restraint" (*zizhong*).[12]

To build a modern library, Li Dazhao broke the traditional mode by enhancing the staff's professionalism. Li often conversed with his librarians and advised them to familiarize themselves with modern library practices. He was aware of the complaints at the paucity of information concerning Western libraries. Upon receiving a request to visit Western-style libraries built in China, Li arranged a field trip on March 15, 1918, to the Qinghua (Tsinghua) School Library at the now famous Qinghua University, which was established on the American model. According to Li, he and his librarians spent most of their time at the library and were impressed by its unique architecture, which allowed fresh air to flow in and let the sunlight penetrate into the interior. Qinghua's cataloging system and its large number of foreign items amazed them. Its acquisition approach astounded them, as it involved faculty members, administrators, and librarians collectively. Its penalties were striking; even foreign professors were not exempted from penalties for damages and losses. During this trip, Li interacted with Yuan Tongli, the chief librarian at Qinghua, who later became a staff member at the Library of Congress in the United States.[13]

Li Dazhao recognized the importance of opening up to the global community and the peril of narrow-minded isolationism. As a result of his comparative studies between China and the outside world, he lamented China's stark shortage of library professionals and China's sluggish progress that was dwarfed by the West.[14] He took the lead in studying Western library enterprise. Having studied the history of Western libraries, he extolled the establishment of the international library association in Britain in 1877 as a milestone in the modern age. American libraries often came to his mind, on which he authored articles for Chinese readers. He paid attention to the training of professionals at library schools in the United States. He hailed American efforts to enhance the public good through building more libraries. Even summer schools, training classes, and short-term seminars on the library enterprise did not elude him; they enabled the American people, according to Li, to enjoy the most recent cultural achievements. He spoke highly of American library management, including the open-stack policy, book classification, and high-tech facilities. Seeing American women's active role in library science, he encouraged Chinese women to become librarians in order to initiate a new epoch in modernizing Chinese libraries.[15]

Li Dazhao sought exchange opportunities with foreign librarians, with whom he endeavored to forge an international tie, in particular with those from the United States. In June 1921, he met Katharine H. Wead, a librarian at the Library of Congress, and showed her around his library, including storage, reading rooms, and other facilities. From Wead's letter to Li, dated September 17, 1921, we can see his interactions with his American colleagues. In the letter, Wead expressed her gratitude to Li for his hospitality and praised Li's management of his library. She assured Li that she had requested her library to send him American cataloging cards while expressing her gratefulness to Li for allowing her to borrow his Chinese classification cards.[16] After acknowledging Li's achievements, the Library of Congress in 1922 donated a million blank catalog cards to Li so that he was able to register the items at his library.[17] Li also studied Japanese libraries and their acquisition, classification, and preservation of books. He asked Yin Rugeng, a Chinese student in Japan, to collect relevant information, for which Yin replied with a long letter that was published in the university bulletin on August 8, 1918.[18]

The Beijing University library, which was perched in the cradle of China's most prestigious university, through Li Dazhao's reforms became the destination of visitors who respected it as an important center for disseminating information, spreading new ideas, and attracting enthusiastic readers. In a number of ways, the library was improved under Li's directorship through its interplay in national and global communities. Japanese journalist Watanabe Minojiro visited Li Dazhao on June 1, 1920, and he had a favorable impression of Li and his management of the library: "His hair was cut extremely short. His round face appears to fit his handsome mustache and a long black robe that he wears. At the first glimpse, he looks like a Japanese. He is an amicable middle-aged gentleman. Speaking fluent Japanese and couching his opinions in a quick-witted tongue, he never conceals his emotions; rather, he justifies his stance with reasoning and demonstrates his lofty spirit through his persuasive rhetoric. He leaves us the best impression and pleasure." More importantly, Watanabe observed Li's library and "was amazed at Li's orderly arrangement of the library and his skillful management of it."[19]

It is an exaggeration to claim that Li Dazhao developed a systematic theory of library science, but it is also unfair to downplay his unique ideas on it. He labeled China's traditional librarians "book protectors" (*shoushuderen*) whose job was to preserve books but not to maximize their use. In his view, a modern library should not only be a place to keep books; it should function also as an educational organ. Chinese libraries must be modernized to meet the needs of the changing educational system. He even suggested "turning the whole country into a library" and "offering the entire nation an opportunity for doing a scholarly investigation at any time and in any place." He specified two kinds of libraries: one for society in general and one for schools. He smashed the isolated-book-keeping approach and promoted the open-stack policy. To his dismay, after the relocation of his library to Shatan, the Red Mansion's small rooms limited the open-stack practice. To redress this problem, he created reading rooms near the storage areas.[20] Li helped establish a library association in Beijing and sponsored seminars to train professionals. By doing so, he earned a reputation as a pioneer of library science, and, as Jing Liao claims, 70 of China's modern academic libraries by 1927 were "managed by librarians with whom he [Li Dazhao] had maintained close contact."[21] Li's legacy can be viewed by his fame as "the father of modern Chinese librarianship," as the American scholars Diane M. Nelson and Robert B. Nelson maintain.[22] According to some scholars, Mao Zedong, who worked as Li's assistant at the library, eventually brought Li's ideas into the library management of the People's Republic of China.[23]

A Professor and a Scholar

Given Li Dazhao's solid knowledge, critical thinking skills, prolific publications, and outstanding performance at the library, it is not a surprise that he was appointed as a professor by Beijing University in July 1920 to teach history, politics, and economics. It is unimaginable for a twenty-first-century professor to teach courses across such a wide scope of disciplines; however, his appointment reveals the liberal milieu at Beijing University during Cai Yuanpei's presidency. According to one study, Li was never appointed a professor of economics; rather, he just taught a course in the department of economics. In September 1921, he stopped teaching politics and remained just a professor of history ever since.[24] Although he was a popular teacher, his background drew disdain because of the campus ethos then of profiling faculty members in line with their educational background, which was not a talented-oriented criterion featuring scholarly accomplishments. According to Zhang Shizhao, most members of the Beijing University faculty held degrees from Western universities, while Li did not even earn anything from Waseda University, for which he was scorned as a low-grade dumbbell. Yet, as Zhang observed, Li's talent, creativity, and prolific work soon turned him into a renowned scholar with a respectable status throughout the entire nation.[25]

Apart from his principal role as a faculty member at Beijing University, Li Dazhao also taught at four other institutions in the city of Beijing. For Li, it was not a compulsory duty; rather, it became a rewarding experience to not only increase his income but also educate more young minds. Li's part-time jobs allowed these universities to maximize the benefits of pooled resources in the national capital and to increase their share of scholars in order to save in the stringent budget for hiring full-time faculty members. Unfortunately, detailed archival materials concerning Li's teaching at these schools have been lost, although we can garner relevant information from his writings, from local newspapers, and from student reminiscences. For example, he taught a course on historiography at Beijing Higher Normal College. He offered courses on sociology at Chaoyang University, which trained legal professionals. He lectured on politics, socialism, and other subjects at China University, established by Sun Yat-sen.[26] He was a professor of sociology, feminism, and other courses at Beijing Female Higher Normal College, which specialized in training female teachers. Li's residence was just a few blocks away from this women's college, which conveniently allowed him to teach young girls there.[27] Sun Guidan remembered her first class with him: "The whole class welcomed him with curiosity and warmth. Students learned things that they had never heard about. He spoke slowly, in an orderly fashion, and clearly, from which he left us with an unforgettable impression."[28]

The wide recognition of Li Dazhao as a revolutionary overshadows his accomplishments as a historian.[29] Indeed, he taught history courses at the abovementioned universities, published articles on historical issues, and authored a book on history for which he was acclaimed as "a great historian."[30] Challenging the traditional narrative approach, Li encapsulated his creative ideas on the meaning of history, the nature of history as a discipline, and the philosophy of history. He placed an emphasis on living history instead of on a pile of lifeless records in the classics, archives, registers, and other places. He defined history as a subject that was essential to life, culture, and society. He argued that history as a discipline was a branch of science because it required historians to investigate social changes, seek truth, and figure out the link between causation and consequence. Li enumerated six kinds of histories: individual history, clan history, communal history, national history, ethnic history, and global history. While he did not downplay the values of the traditional approach of collecting valuable facts, he accentuated the importance of the philosophy of history, which demanded that historians "study more general, more profound, and more essential issues" and offer "fundamental analysis and insightful interpretations."[31] In a sense, his pursuit of the philosophy of history gradually led him to study historical materialism, which led to his final acceptance of Marxism.

It is worth noting that Li Dazhao intended to reconstruct history with his optimistic approach. Refusing to glorify the "golden age" of the past, he spearheaded his concept of building a golden age in the present time and for the future. He criticized the act of exalting an ancient time as the golden age and considered it a pessimistic and degenerative attitude.[32] As he bluntly put it, "the concept of the golden age is wrong."[33] Li asked historians to ditch their belief in a past golden age. According to Li, "New historians should first discard this wrong notion and then endeavor to build a present or future golden age. The golden age is not behind us but always lies in front of us."[34] Li vividly portrayed history as a grand waterfall streaming down and never reversing its course.[35] He argued that contemporary history should be an optimistically loaded site to help the people construct a brighter future. He said that "history is created by humankind. While ancient history was created by ancient humans, today's world is created by modern humans. . . . It is our responsibility to make full use of today's life to create a golden age and to benefit the future generations."[36] In a similar vein, Li linked the learning of history with daily life and argued that the benefit of learning history was to pursue pleasure and happiness.[37] The utility of history was to solve problems and at the same time to help "enrich and cultivate human life."[38]

Li Dazhao's voluminous publications on diverse historical topics reveal his wide-ranging interests, but he was inclined to study modern history—in particular, modern Chinese history. He tried to reconstruct it from his nationalistic perspective, through which he could promote national salvation. In his view, the history of modern China should be viewed as a national history of sheer exploitation by the imperialist powers.[39] It was imperialist aggression that caused China's national crisis, in response to which the Chinese people had launched mass movements to achieve national independence. He viewed the First Sino-Japanese War as the demarcation line that divided modern Chinese history into two periods, because this war led to China's foreboding crises and ensured political changes.[40] To expose foreign aggression, Li selected pertinent topics, among which was German control of the railways between Qingdao and Jinan from 1898 to 1915. This was one of his interests on which he had published an article. The purpose of this study was to urge the Chinese to restore its sovereignty from the Japanese, who had seized the railway line during the Great War.[41] Of course, Li also paid selective attention to ancient history as well. His articulation of ancient economic thought demonstrated his unique analysis of the differences between the East and the West. By highlighting the economic ideas of Confucius, Laozi, Han Feizi, Mozi, and others, Li displayed the Chinese frugality through the control of human desires in contrast to the Western way of indulging human desires for maximum satisfaction.[42] Li explored frontier history by focusing on the tea trade between the Han Chinese and other ethnic groups, particularly the Mongols and the Tibetans. He argued that the tea trade served as a medium between the agrarian Han and nomadic ethnic groups with which they forged a long-term political, cultural, and economic tie in the long flow of Chinese civilization.[43]

Li Dazhao spent much of his time in 1923 studying Western historiographical theories, authored a number of articles, and offered in-depth analysis in an effort to modernize China's historiography. After introducing Jean Bodin, a French historian, Li spoke highly of him for his rejection of the notion of human degeneration and his recognition of human advancement.[44] As for Montesquieu, Li acclaimed his creative ideas, in particular his unique thoughts concerning law and history. Li praised Montesquieu for repudiating fatalism, condemning divine outcomes, and offering rational discourse on historical causations.[45] Li hailed Giovanni Battista Vico, an Italian historian, as a pioneer of the philosophy of history for his insistence on deducing from facts in order to reach a comprehensive analysis and a rational conclusion.[46] Li investigated Marquis de Condorcet and his periodization of human civilization. He was impressed by Condorcet's rationalism, his emphasis on facts, his support of peace, his promotion of social equality, and his endorsement of the people's role in history.[47] Even though Li left out many other Western historians, he had broadened the scope of Chinese examination of history and urged Chinese historians to adopt an interpretive approach rather than solely sticking to the traditional narrative paradigm.

By the mid-1920s, Li Dazhao had established himself as a progressive educator, a prolific scholar, and a well-known historian.[48] Despite his increasing reputation, he was willing to assist others' scholarly endeavors. For example, in the preface he authored on December 11, 1923, for Xiao Yishan's *A History of the Qing Dynasty*, Li praised Xiao for retrieving rich sources, commended him for his unique perspectives, and acclaimed him for his pioneering endeavors in rewriting Qing history.[49] Li treated his students well and encouraged them to visit him in his office and even his home for a direct dialogue. In this way, he intended to help them achieve academic progress, and his children remembered that his study at home was often crowded with visitors, in particular his students.[50] He became a successful intellectual and earned a considerable income, but he continued to live a simple life. According to one estimate, his initial income as the chief librarian was about 120 yuan per month, which was raised to a monthly salary of more than two hundred yuan when he became a professor. By then, his monthly earnings were almost equivalent to the yearly salary of an ordinary laborer in Beijing. However, he often donated a part of his salary to support poor students. Consequently, he was not able to purchase a house during his decade-long residence in the capital city.[51] Bao Huiseng reminisced that "no flowers and grasses were planted in his yard, and no exhibitions and displays could be found in his house. Not even a decent piece of furniture stood inside, which evidently proves Li Dazhao's simple lifestyle."[52]

The May Fourth Movement

Beijing University, where Li Dazhao worked, was the center of China's pursuit of a new culture. In fact, it became the cradle of two closely knit events that have been viewed collectively as the May Fourth Movement (Wusiyundong). Strictly speaking, the broadly defined May

Fourth Movement should also be called the New Culture Movement (Xinwenhuayundong), which started with the publication of *New Youth* in 1915. Yet its ending date is a topic of debate. If the termination of the journal's publication is used to mark the date, then the New Culture Movement ended in 1926. The more narrowly defined May Fourth Movement occurred during May and June 1919 as a special response to the decision made by the major powers at the Paris Peace Conference in which students staged a nationwide demonstration to compel the Chinese government to refuse to sign the Treaty of Versailles. These two movements, interconnected yet different, pose a perpetual scholarly issue, and Chinese scholars have struggled to interpret their connections.[53] For convenience of analysis here, we will treat the broad one as the New Culture Movement and designate the narrow one as the May Fourth Movement; in both, Li Dazhao played a leading role. As soon as Li returned from Japan, his championship of democracy, constitutionalism, and freedom of the press turned him into a famed figure of the New Culture Movement. After taking his positions at Beijing University, he continued to pursue a new culture, and, more importantly, he influenced his students to become activists.

Having encountered the paramount national crisis in the postimperial period, the Chinese intellectuals, including Li Dazhao, grappled with the essential question of national revival by embracing a new approach to nation building, state building, and culture building. The general direction for their country, as many intellectuals advocated, was to reconstruct the Chinese civilization. Li's intention was to learn from the West, adapt Western culture to the Chinese landscape, negotiate the differences between the two cultures, and select the best from both to fashion a new civilization. The urgent task for reaching this goal was to awaken the Chinese citizens to develop a consciousness in order to strive for national cultural renaissance.[54]

By the time Li Dazhao started his employment at the university, Chinese scholars were elaborating the cultural issue, purporting to "locate China within increasingly multicultural dimensions of space and time," as Leigh Jenco points out. "The trans-historical, trans-cultural multicultural comparisons" led to "the East-West dichotomy."[55] As for the discourse of the civilization issue, as Ya-pei Kuo asserts, "Li Dazhao was one of the initiators."[56] In one article he authored in the summer of 1918, Li Dazhao argued that Eastern civilization was featured by its quietness, while Western civilization was characterized by its motion.

Each was shaped by its tradition, geography, and climate. Although the East had its merits, its civilization possessed a number of disadvantages, including a pessimistic attitude, less motion, less respect for individualism, an emphasis on collective missions, a negligence of personal rights, a low opinion of women, a lack of sympathy, superstition, and despotism. Li argued that "the illness of Chinese civilization has reached its apex while the fate of the Chinese nation is lingering in the dying stage" and its renaissance would be the only solution.[57] Li "urged a blending of civilizations . . . in order to create a wholly new syncretic civilization in locales both Chinese and Western."[58] In so doing, he also continued to pursue democracy, constitutional rule, liberty, and other commonly cherished values.

To dismantle the old culture and to construct a new one, progressive intellectuals endorsed the use of the vernacular language. In their view, the classical Chinese language had blocked the dissemination of information, served as a barrier to public education, and lowered literacy. It helped create a handful of literary elites who had monopolized culture and politics. Although Hu Shi always pops up as the champion for the vernacular language whenever this topic is mentioned, the truth is that Li Dazhao was also a strong advocate. Challenging the accusation of using "the soiled language" (*tuyu*), Li openly supported the vernacular language and promoted its unprecedented scale of use. Li took the lead by adopting it for his own writings as soon as he started his employment at Beijing University.[59] Yet he did not intend to eliminate classic language; rather, he viewed it as a bridge with which the Chinese could explore their long civilization. Nevertheless, he opposed any efforts to uphold solely the old classical language. In late 1919, the warlord Qi Xieyuan petitioned the government to forbid the use of the vernacular language. Li immediately condemned Qi for prohibiting the Chinese people from speaking out, labeling Qi as "an intimate of the Qin tyrant."[60]

Too much attention has been paid to Lu Xun and Hu Shi whenever the revolution in literature during the New Culture Movement is discussed, while Li Dazhao's achievements in the field are commented on surprisingly little. In fact, Li offered his distinctive opinions on the ongoing radical change in Chinese literature. He did not consider the use of the vernacular language itself as a new form of literature and rejected the literature of advertisement (*guanggaodewenxue*) for intentionally charming the audience. Rather, the new literature required authors to write about social life, universal love, and the humanist spirit.[61] Given the traditional literary focus on the upper class, Li believed that the pressing need was to focus on true life in order to underscore literature's social utility. He termed the new literature a "living literature" and entreated the Chinese to throw asunder the oppressive fetters of the old literature. He argued that "a woman who had loosened her feet will not be willing to have her feet bound again. A man whose long hair was cut off will no longer want to wear the queue. People who have enjoyed the bliss of freedom will not want to return to bondage under the rule of a despotic emperor. The writer who is accustomed to the living literature will not be willing to compose lifeless pieces."[62]

As the Chinese audiences were hungry for a new culture, Li Dazhao became a vanguard introducing ideological and cultural ingredients from the outside world. The ideas he introduced mainly came from the West, including political theories, philosophical notions, and scholarly concepts. He did not limit himself to one country; rather, he exposed himself to all, verifying that the era was an open time for the Chinese to absorb new things. In general, Li drew ideological nutrients from the West, even if through the Japanese contour. In the process, however, he borrowed Japanese cultural elements, in particular from the Japanese language. A recent study shows that Li borrowed hundreds of Japanese phrases, among which many were freshly new to the Chinese. At the same time, Li himself created new vocabularies by following the Japanese pattern in order to introduce Western civilization.[63] Li's loan forms and alterations laid bare his pursuit of cultural renaissance through active learning, dynamic borrowing, and vigorous adaptation.

One theme of the New Culture Movement was women's liberation, in which Li Dazhao championed gender equality and women's rights. As Vera Schwarcz points out, Li "had emphasized the ideological connection between women's liberation and democracy."[64] Li declared that "only after women are liberated can true democracy be realized. . . . It is not the democratic spirit to confine and exclude women, who constitute half of the population."[65] He argued that "a fair and pleasant gender relationship solely relies on the interdependence, equality, and mutual aid between man and woman, rather than on woman's subordination and man's superiority." He praised Western women's pioneering championship of feminism and lamented Chinese women's low status. He spelled out the objectives of women's liberation, in particular equal opportunities in education, in employment, before the law, and in social life.[66] He abhorred the so-called oldest profession for its vicious effects. He pro-

Figure 5.2. Li Dazhao was employed at Beijing University beginning in early 1918. At that time, he was known in the entire country as a vanguard of the ongoing New Culture Movement, during which Chinese intellectuals criticized the Confucian tradition, championed liberalism, and pursued a new culture. (Public domain)

posed outlawing prostitution, which he argued disrespected humanism, smudged the sacred love between a man and a woman, spread venereal diseases, incited human trafficking, and deprived women of their dignity.[67] As Harriet Evans argues, indeed, Li Dazhao was "unequivocal" in his "commitment to women's equal rights with man."[68]

There has long existed an incorrect notion that the New Culture Movement was an attempt to totally negate the traditional culture. Truly, a group of Chinese scholars did intend to separate the present from the Chinese past in order to embrace Westernization in totality. But Li Dazhao was not one of them. While he warned the Chinese of the danger of clinging to the past, he adopted a rational approach in his treatment of traditional culture.[69] He pinpointed its conservative, oppressive, and stagnant features but highlighted its positive cultural nutrients, patriotic bent, sympathetic attitude, and dialectic views.[70] Other traditional values, such as morality, virtue, and the notion of Great Harmony, permeated Li's mentality.[71] He insisted on relinquishing its dross but assimilating its quintessence.[72] If an element in traditional culture contained value, it should be upgraded to fit the needs of the modern age. To Li, traditional culture functioned as a two-edged sword, because it possessed assets and because it had its own Achilles' heel. Li felt that traditional culture should be revigorated in order to retain its vitality. Take Confucianism as an example. On one hand, Li viewed it as a barrier to individual freedom, hence he rejected making it a part of China's national constitution.[73] On the other hand, however, he recognized its value and promoted turning the old Confucius into a new Confucius. Through a meaningful dialogue, negotiation, and renovation, Chinese civilization should be blended with Western civilization for the initiation of a new way of life.[74]

A neglected aspect in the study of the New Culture Movement is the close interpersonal relationship among its prominent activists. The abundant new sources now allow us to know what has passed largely unclearly and under the radar for so long. Although those activists encouraged the Chinese people to turn against the old tradition, advocated for a new culture, and pushed for national revival, they themselves often held diverse and even conflicting views. In a sense, they were ideological rivals, even though they shared a common cause and common enemies. Interestingly, though, their private relationships tended to be cordial. Li Dazhao praised Lu Xun as "a major fighting general" (*zhanjiang*) and "a great banner" (*daqi*).[75] Lu Xun's image of Li was positive, and he commented that "Li left me a good impression: he was honest and humble. He did not speak much. It is hard to portray his image, as it sometimes tended to be gentle, sometime simplistic, and sometime very ordinary. Hence, he looked like a scholar, also like an official, and sometimes like a merchant." Lu Xun respected Li as "a worthy and hard-to-gain comrade" and "a companion on the same front."[76] Li Dazhao and Hu Shi forged a special relationship, even if they were opponents on the ideological front. They worked together for *New Youth*, participated in the same activities, and pushed for common social reforms.[77] They often talked over the phone until midnight and were "a pair of extraordinary friends."[78] Hu Shi was saddened at Li's tragic death in 1927 when he heard about Li's execution while Hu was visiting Japan. Three years later, Hu remembered Li as one of his four recently lost friends.[79]

The above analysis of the New Culture Movement and Li Dazhao's role in it demonstrates the status of this movement as China's enlightenment. For many, it was China's renaissance, during which progressive intellectuals strove to construct a new civilization and for which a generation of youth was nurtured to become activists. Indeed, it is unimaginable for the May Fourth Movement in mid-1919 to have taken place without the awakening influence of the New Culture Movement. The two were connected but different, as the latter occurred during May and June 1919 as a direct response to the Paris Peace Conference. The May Fourth Movement was a success because it forced the Chinese government to refuse to sign the Treaty of Versailles. Yet it was a letdown because the protestors suffered mass arrests, imprisonment, and difficulties while the movement was being suppressed. Although it is not unreasonable to portray the New Culture Movement as the May Fourth Movement given that the two overlapped and were closely knit and interconnected, it is more helpful to consider what happened in May and June 1919 as the May Fourth Movement for the convenience of our analysis here.

One of the serious issues concerning the May Fourth Movement is whether there were any leaders of it. Some argue "the movement was launched by students spontaneously";[80] others maintain that prominent intellectuals at Beijing University, such as Chen Duxiu and Li Dazhao, were its leaders behind the scenes. Mao Zedong claimed that Chen was the commander in chief while Li played a big role in the movement.[81] In other words, the May Fourth Movement was directed, coached, and guided by those prominent intellectuals. The Chinese universities, in particular Beijing University, became "nodal points" in the converging public discussions, as Pamela Kyle Crossley contends, yet those intellectuals' role in motivating their students to action should not be ignored.[82] Chinese scholars investigating Li Dazhao have highlighted the important role he played: he exercised his influence in directing, agitating, and motivating the students. Deng Tuo, in his discourse over the leadership issue of the May Fourth Movement, argues that Li "exerted a great influence."[83] Jia Zhi claims that Li "played an extraordinary role and made an immortal contribution to the May Fourth Movement."[84] Peng Ming portrays Li as a "major general" (*zhujiang*).[85] Li Lina argues that "Li Dazhao always stood on the front line of the movement."[86] Wu Changgeng bluntly asserts that Li "directly organized and led this movement."[87] Facing so many diverse opinions, it is necessary for us to clarify Li's ties with the May Fourth Movement.

One of the reasons Li Dazhao could mobilize students was his close relationship with them. According to Xu Deheng's memory, Li was sympathetic to students of poor family backgrounds and "often dedicated a portion of his monthly salary to help them out. Once, Liu Renjing was unable to pay tuition due to a financial difficulty; Li Dazhao offered an affidavit and persuaded the administrators to allow him a late payment."[88] One time, Li's wife had just finished sewing a cotton coat for their son, but Li instantly gave it to a visiting student who suffered from the cold weather. It is said that Li often donated to poor students anonymously.[89] Thus, Li enjoyed a reputation among students, who ranked Li as one of the popular professors. Sun Fuyuan remarked, "Li Dazhao was the chief librarian. He was extremely honest. We, as students, saw him neither as a professor nor as a classmate, because we did not need to be afraid of him and because we could not be carelessly casual with him at the same time. We could always sense his cordial attitude and respected him as an elder brother."[90] Zhang Tingqian, whose penname was Chuan Dao, vividly illustrated Li's relationship with his students as "an old hen" (*laomuji*) surrounded by little chicks whom he cared for, protected, tutored, and directed.[91] This close interpersonal tie brought forth a psychological connection between Li and his students. Evan N. Dawley comments that "teacher-student relations played an especially important role in both shaping the multifarious debates and in promoting the solidarity of students within the movement" as the May Fourth Movement unfolded.[92] Vera Schwarcz remarks that "the students were able to conceive and carry out their own distinctive mission" thanks to the aid of their mentors such as Li Dazhao.[93]

Ideological guidance is another way in which Li Dazhao impacted his students and their activities. For students, the university presented them a time of change, adjustment, and transition. On one hand, they needed to acquire knowledge and sharpen their academic skills; on the other hand, their minds tended to be an empty space often predominated by the common concerns of the day. Li tried to fill the void as a guide, directing them in exploring new ideas. He delivered speeches to students at rallies or conversed with them in his office or other places. Very often, students flocked to his side to listen to his liberal ideas. According to Zhang Shenfu, his colleague at the university, Li's office in the Red Mansion "became the center or the headquarters of new thoughts."[94] For that reason, Zhang opined that "the Red Mansion at Beijing University was the origin of the May Fourth Movement."[95] More importantly, as Xu Deheng reminisced, Li urged students to take "direct action" (*zhijiexingdong*), which ideologically weaponized his students.[96] On May 1, 1919, Li published an article in which he called for "direct action" and claimed that it should be the only option for the Chinese people.[97] Indeed, this unambiguous call inspired students, stimulated their patriotic impulses, and motivated them to join the upcoming demonstrations.

Li Dazhao's leadership role in the May Fourth Movement also lies in his contributions in establishing a number of organizations that operated as an intricate web among students, faculty members, and other activists. Beijing University was an elite institution, but its students led a liberal life. Fabio Lanza creatively argues that students were "selectively disorganized." While they continued to enjoy liberty, they established diverse societies among themselves.[98] Li himself helped build organizations, promoted their missions, and offered his assistance. In late 1918, Li helped establish the Citizen Society (Guominshe) intending to refine citizens' integral character, educate them with new knowledge, and urge them to accept new ideas. In the meantime, Li assisted in organizing the New Tide Society (Xinchaoshe) for the purpose of introducing ideas from Western civilization, exposing China's problems, and seeking feasible solutions. Li contributed his articles to the movement's journal, the *New Tide*; aided its circulation; and allocated a room in his library as its editorial office.[99] In March 1919, Li assisted Deng Zhongxia in building the Citizen Education Speech Corp, a radical group, to which Li offered his support.[100]

Li Dazhao was a cofounder of the Young China Society (Shaonianzhongguoxuehui), which aimed to champion the unity of young people, help them embrace a new life, labor for national rejuvenation, and initiate a new epoch. In June 1918, Li helped push the decision to establish this organization, arranged its preparatory work, and served as an editorial director for its journal, *Young China*. Although the Young China Society was formally established on July 1, 1919, Li had contributed significantly to its one-year preparation. A diverse membership was recruited while its branches were established throughout the country and beyond. Consequently, many of its members would participate in the upcoming nationwide May Fourth Movement. According to Zhou Taixuan, Li was instrumental in initiating the Young China Society. "He was honest and amicable, and we all respected him. We consulted him on whatever we decided to do. We viewed him as an elder brother and regarded him as a moral paragon."[101]

Li Dazhao's changing attitude toward the leaders of the major powers, noticeably President Woodrow Wilson of the United States, swayed the young students.[102] At first, Li put his profound trust in Wilson and respected him as a peacemaker because Wilson had publicized his personal sympathy for weak nations.[103] In this way, Li was caught up in "the Wilsonian Moment," as Erez Manela terms it,[104] from which the whole world expected the American president to assist the reconstruction of a new and peaceful world.[105] Unfortunately, "Versailles provided a test which Wilsonian liberalism flunked," as Peter Zarrow comments.[106] When a barrage of disheartening news from the Paris Peace Conference arrived in China, Li immediately became critical of Wilson. Like other intellectuals, Li felt that his country had been betrayed, simply because China should have been respected and treated as a victorious nation. Some scholars still view it as a "diplomatic betrayal," as David Scott states.[107] According to the Treaty of Versailles, China's national interests in the former German colony in Shandong Province would be transferred to the Japanese Empire. Li angrily condemned the US president: "Wilson! Did you oppose secret diplomacy! Now where are your [fourteen] points? All have gone with the wind. I really feel sorry and ashamed of you!"[108] Li warned the Chinese not to daydream of relying on the stronger powers and accepting the Treaty of Versailles, because "today's world is a world of bandits." Li called for rejecting such a world, refusing to accept secret diplomacy, and instead pursuing national self-determination.[109] Sharply differing from his previous attitude, Li denounced Wilson as an agent of pseudo-peace.[110] Li's indignation toward the major powers, his fury at soft-talking Chinese officials, and his call to impose increasing pressure on the Beijing government prompted his students to participate in the May Fourth Movement.

It is worth noting that Li Dazhao attempted to win international support for the May Fourth Movement, in particular from Japanese intellectuals. In so doing, he struck a balance between his stance against Japanese imperialism and his move to win over Japan's progressive intellectuals. For example, Li kept friendly ties with his former professor Yoshino Sakuzo. Nearly half a year before the May Fourth Movement, Li openly supported Japan's democracy movement upon Yoshino's request. When the student demonstrations were in progress in China, Yoshino came out in defense of the Chinese students. He wrote a letter to Li Dazhao to voice his support, which Li published in Beijing to boost the students' morale.[111] Yoshino Sakuzo said in the letter that Chinese students were opposing the aggressive Japan but not the peaceful Japan and he expected the demonstration to be a success. In another letter published in Shanghai in July 1919, Yoshino Sakuzo said that he had informed a gentleman in Beijing, who was identified as Li Dazhao, that "the aggressive Japan will collapse and the peaceful Japan will establish a relationship with the Chinese youth, based on mutual aid."[112]

Whether Li Dazhao personally participated in the demonstration on May 4, 1919, remains a scholarly issue on which Chinese scholars are at odds with one another. Zhu Zhimin claims that Li's involvement on that day was limited.[113] Others concur with this view, as Guo Dehong and Zhang Minglin mention Li's support of the student demonstrators without a single word about Li's personal involvement.[114] But other scholars argue that Li joined the demonstration. Gao Yihan, Li's colleague at the university, recalled:

> Li Dazhao went along with students on the demonstration of May 4, 1919. The demonstrators marched toward the governmental building to lodge a protest demanding the release of those students who had been arrested. When they arrived at the gate of the State Council, they found that the iron gate was closed and machine guns had been set up and were aiming at them. Li was so furious that he pushed himself forward to charge against the State Council. Yet he was dragged back by other demonstrators for the reason of his personal safety. Without a doubt, Li was brave in risking his own well-being for the students.[115]

Others concur; Zhu Wentong states that Li went along with the students on May 4, 1919, and that the demonstration unfolded in an orderly progression thanks to Li's involvement. Thus, scholars in this group have touched upon three important points: Li participated, Li led, and Li acted valiantly.[116]

A Social Activist

During his Beijing University years, Li Dazhao was a prolific author of his own scholarly projects, a prominent activist for a new culture, and a tutoring coach for student demonstrators. In the meantime, he was passionate about community services and intended to put his ideas into practice in order to bring about social changes. Of course, it is impossible to enumerate all of his activities, as he kept a busy schedule of such events. However, some of the more important ones should be highlighted according to their thematic arrangement. As available sources verify, Li was energetic, enthusiastic, and vehement about devoting himself to a number of causes he believed worth pursuing. Some of them were university based, others related to the city of Beijing, and the rest were grounded in nationwide concerns. Through his activities, he enjoyed a high reputation at Beijing University, in the national capital, and throughout the whole country.

Soon after his arrival at the university, Li Dazhao joined the Virtue Promotion Society (Jindehui) established by Cai Yuanpei, who intended to nurture members of the faculty and staff in the qualities of excellence, not only as integral educators but also as moral individuals. In fact, Li could be regarded as a cofounder of this society, which he desired to turn into a fixture of the university's ethical front and to transform into a promoter of the collective good. The society demanded that members not visit prostitutes, not marry a concubine, and not become a gambler, along with other proscriptions that were added later. [117] Li became the editor of the society's journal and one of its council members. The society rallied hundreds who pledged to live up to its goals. Yet many employees refused to join in, including Hu Shi and Chen Duxiu. It is hard to assess its social impact, but its members were acclaimed as moral individuals. In particular, Li was respected as a model, and his students witnessed his loyalty to his wife. Liu Jingjun remembered, "I saw him helping his wife handle her clothes, making them neat and tidy . . . he was loyal to her and never cold-shouldered her simply because she was not very pretty and was much older."[118]

Li Dazhao's leadership role in the Salary Reclamation Movement in 1921 turned him into a celebrity among the intellectuals in Beijing. The movement was caused by the delay of salary payment to members of the faculty and staff, who had not received a single penny for three months prior to March 1921. The reasons for the delay were multiple. As the warlord regime invested 42 percent of national revenue into military expenditures, the share for education was reduced to less than 1 percent. While revenue collection became insecure, the warlord regime postponed salary payments, which did harm to vulnerable intellectuals. The faculty and staff at Beijing University organized a council, of which Li was elected a member. The council decided to stage a strike starting on March 14, 1921. Within a couple of days, eight universities and colleges established an alliance of faculty and staff to petition the government for the delayed salary. In the next month, Li Dazhao became its acting president. His reports show his staunch stance, as he accused the government of breaking its promises and condemned its officials for their deceptive behaviors. He remarked that "our strike was purely caused by the dishonest government. It is not our desire to suspend teaching. In the whole world, there is not a second country that delays educational payment and that allows educators to plunge into such a deplorable situation."[119] It is estimated that Li attended more than half of one hundred meetings and sustained a serious wound at the hands of a government guard during a protest. Through persistent struggle, the movement succeeded on July 28, at which time the alliance led by Li decided to end the strike and resume teaching on September 1, 1921.[120]

Li Dazhao participated in philanthropic campaigns also, such as disaster relief efforts, both domestically and internationally. His role in supporting Russian famine relief offers an example. In 1921, he assisted in establishing the Russian Famine Relief Society, and he served as the director of its secretariat. He wrote a notice to introduce the horrible situation in which forty million people in the Volga valley suffered from a famine caused by a drought. Because of the shortage of food, children ate grass and tree bark. Li praised the Chinese for their warmhearted character and pleaded with them to extend a hand to the suffering Russian people.[121] His portrayal of the famine in all its horrendous magnitude shocked his countrymen, and his appeal to solicit aid attracted many donors. Consequently, relief supplies were channeled to Russia. Li and his coworkers in this effort shared a common concern for humanity even though China was not a nation of plenty at that time. As an organizer, Li had to work in the relief office for two afternoons every week out of his busy schedule of teaching and library duties.[122] Li's responsibilities included drafting telegraphs, writing notices, answering letters, and authoring documents.[123] Under the society's persuasion, the Chinese government allocated twenty thousand yuan to Russia's famine victims.[124] Li's coworkers in this society came from diverse backgrounds, including Christian leaders such as Pastor Liu Tingfang, who earned his doctorate from Columbia University.[125] Working together, they put their political, social, religious, and other differences aside in a coordinated endeavor for this committed international relief campaign.

Li Dazhao's commitment to democracy prompted him to get involved in China's civil rights movement. For a while, he was a champion of the representative system. As a faculty member at Beijing University, he pushed for the injection of democratic ideals into Chinese minds and mobilized the Chinese people to fight for their own democratic rights. On August 24, 1922, Li helped establish the Great Civil Rights Movement Alliance (Minquanyundong datongmeng) in Beijing and was elected as one of the fifteen executive members. A couple months later, he coauthored its proclamation, which sought to unmask the truth that the majority of Chinese suffered from constitutional deprivation and to affirm the goals of the alliance's fight for basic civil rights: the rights of popular assembly, political elections, and labor protection. Under his influence, the alliance proposed a labor-protective law and demanded that the government ensure laborers' rights. Soon, the alliance had established branches in Nanjing (Nanking), Taiyuan, Nanchang, Chengdu, Shanghai, Guangzhou (Canton), and other places.[126]

Li Dazhao also shined a spotlight on the battle for women's rights by advocating for female liberation. In 1919, a young girl named Li Chao, a student at Beijing Female Higher Normal College, suffered from anxiety, poverty, and pressure from her family. Li Chao, a native of Guangxi Province, was determined to pursue academic excellence but was discouraged by her brother. However, she ventured a journey to Beijing, passed the examination, and enrolled at the female college. Unfortunately, she contracted a lung disease and died in the national capital. Both faculty members and students expressed sympathy for this unfortunate young woman. Li Dazhao spoke at her funeral and praised her independent spirit. To encourage young people to pursue true love, Li directed a play at the college with his own students as performers. The play was adapted from the ancient poem titled *Peacock Flying Southeast*, which extols true love free of parental control. The play inspired the youth to be modern lovers and to resist arranged marriages.[127] With Li's support, students at the college established the League for Women's Rights in 1922. Unfortunately, this league was immediately banned by the government. Students, however, successfully held a tea party at which Li spoke for women's rights, demanded suffrage for women, and appealed to the government to pass a law protecting female laborers.[128]

One student suicide case at Beijing University in 1919 saddened Li Dazhao so much that he authored a few articles to alert his fellow citizens about the suicide issue, in particular pertaining to the youth. Realizing that suicide was triggered by diverse factors, he ultimately blamed a flawed society as the major cause.[129] He exposed the truth behind a whirlwind of such cases. He portrayed modern times as a suicidal age because the cases had increased proportionately along with the progress of modern civilization. China was not exempt from it. Li pointed out that 126 persons had died of suicide in the city of Beijing alone in 1917, besides the fact that many others who had attempted suicide were rescued. Thus, Li proclaimed that "the present Chinese society has reached its apex of darkness."[130] He studied the problem and related it to seasonal change, marital status, ethnic traits, and more. He cast his argument emphatically upon the evils of the society. He tried to launch a campaign to prevent suicide, which led to "social misfortune" and "economic loss" and called on the Chinese to work to "reform this flawed society."[131] Given his grave concern over this issue, Li doubtlessly would have taken more actions on it, had he not died so young.

Li Dazhao was a prominent figure in the Anti-Christian Movement (Feijidujiaoyundong), which lasted from 1922 to 1927. It might be improper to assume that this movement shared a logical continuity with China's anti-Christian tradition such as the Boxer Rebellion which victimized Christian converts and foreign missionaries two decades before. After the Boxer Rebellion, in fact, the numbers of Chinese Christian converts had multiplied.[132] For further propagation, the World Student Christian Federation decided to convene its eleventh conference in Beijing on April 4 to 9, 1922.[133] To counterbalance this move, Chinese students and intellectuals established anti-Christian organizations and held anti-Christian rallies.[134] The Grand Anti-Religious Alliance (Feizongjiaodatongmeng) was established on March 11, 1922, in Beijing for the purpose of blockading the conference and resisting all religions, in particular Christianity, as it deemed Christianity unscientific and superstitious. Li was elected one of the directors of this alliance. The radical intellectuals, including Li, declared that religion and humankind could not coexist, and they swore to expunge the religious poison from society.[135] On the day when the Christian conference was held in Beijing, Li published an article reiterating that religion was an anti-scientific fallacy and reaffirming nonbelievers' right to be free from it.[136] On April 9, 1922, Li delivered a speech at a rally accusing religion of hampering human progress, fostering unrealistic illusions, and blocking its converts from seeking truth. This speech was published in a Japanese journal and was discovered only recently. Indeed, the rediscovery of this piece allows us to know more about Li's stance.[137] In June 1922, Li published another article in which he exposed the negative impact of religion and criticized the claim that religion could help believers achieve freedom, equality, and fraternity.[138]

Li Dazhao's social agendas included his concern for rural education, which lagged far behind the urban areas during the early republican years. He argued that the key for improving rural life and elevating the peasants from poverty was to enhance their access to education. Unfortunately, few modern schools were established in the rural areas, where the overwhelming majority of Chinese people lived. In the winter of 1919, Li started an experiment in his hometown of Daheituo Village, where not a single modern school had been built by then. He conversed with the villagers and informed them of his plan for turning the nearby Huayan Temple into a modern school, which was rejected at first by its monks. Through his persuasion, the monks eventually agreed. Li recommended a female teacher to teach girls and a male instructor to tutor boys.[139] In 1920, Li helped the school hire a female teacher, donated twenty yuan from his own pocket for her travel expenses, and assisted her and her husband in settling down.[140] This was one of Li's moves to convert religious facilities into classrooms for rural education. As Vincent Goossaert and David A. Palmer have demonstrated, the conversion of religious temples into modern schools was a trend in the early twentieth century; Li's mindset of improving rural education prompted him to act on it.[141] Needless to say, his move elicited the gratitude of the local populace.

Conclusion

No sooner had Li Dazhao landed a job at Beijing University than he found himself caught up in an avalanche of domestic and international crises that brought him into a whirlpool of political and social movements, in which he acted as a prominent figure. Indeed, "the New Culture Movement occupies an iconic place" in Chinese history,[142] while Li's eminence in this movement turned him into a rising star in the nation, in which his status was multiple: a librarian, a professor, a thinker, a teacher, an activist, and a leader. In a sense, he assisted in converting the youth into a fighting force, as Sofia Graziani argues, to prepare them for combat on the stage of the May Fourth Movement.[143] As a national campaign striving for modernity, national independence, and a new model of nation building, the New Culture Movement created a stage for Li to become a coach and guide to young, energetic, patriotic students striving for their collective goals of protecting, transforming, and renovating their country and their culture. It was during this process that Li gained a salient fame, while his path to this high reputation came at different levels: the university, the capital, and the nation. His repute stood firm, and his morale did not slide. Even if the whole nation encountered an exacerbated situation, he continued to influence a generation of youth for a persistent pursuit of their common nationalistic goals.

Li Dazhao was influential in the cultural realm during his first years at Beijing University, as his actions across a wide scope show. Yet his confidence in laboring for the public good and his efforts for a just cause attracted clamorous critics, who nitpicked him and his followers. This was a natural phenomenon, as the New Culture Movement and the May Fourth Movement witnessed the emergence of diverse groups of individuals who diverged onto different paths. Likewise, Li Dazhao could not enjoy universal endorsement for what he had done. On the contrary, he had begotten his own adversaries. For example, Li Huang, a cofounder of the Young China Society and a future anti-communist, described Li Dazhao as "a type of bureaucrat" who "ruined the Young China Society."[144] Li Dazhao and his followers resisted the Christian conference in Beijing in 1922 but could not sweep it aside, and it was held on time. Furthermore, his anti-Christian campaign was opposed by some of his colleagues, such as Zhou Zuoren, who felt that the movement itself "imposed oppression and terror," for which anti-Christians themselves should reflect on their erroneous moves and correct their misbehaviors. Qian Xuantong, another of Li's colleagues, was terrified, as he viewed the ongoing Anti-Christian Movement as an heir to the xenophobic Boxer Rebellion.[145]

Obviously, Li Dazhao's vision for China was wide ranging, and he participated in a number of popular movements. Consequently, his multiple actions overlapped with one another, causing Li to resort to manifold ways of reaching those diverse objectives. His employment at Beijing University symbolized a promising career, yet in spite of his sterling position he did not confine himself within a purely academic realm. On the contrary, his agenda for national salvation prompted him to be an energetic activist. Indeed, it was during his Beijing University years that he began his swift march toward communism. Certainly, one of the most telling aspects of his life was his status as China's first communist, which truly took shape when he worked at the university. By 1924, however, he was mired in a personal dilemma to redefine his life—whether to become an academic or a professional revolutionary—and, between the two, he chose the latter. He could have become a more prolific author, a man of ideas, and a social critic to capture a gold medal in China's academic circles, but his activism steered him toward the path of communism, which he followed in his new status as a professional revolutionary during his last years.

Chapter 6

Embracing Communism

Introduction

Li Dazhao has been acclaimed as China's first communist with a host of radiant titles, such as the glorious nomenclature of "the father of Chinese Marxism and the germinator of the Chinese Communist Party."[1] The designation "the first" is sure to recognize his eminence, but it can be troublesome when we try to verify the exact date of his self-conversion to this foreign ideology. Furthermore, the concept of "the first" engenders more questions as to why and how he embraced communism. In any case, his vital role in the establishment of the Chinese Communist Party (CCP) and the early communist movement is an undeniable, ironclad fact. Being the first communist of what was then the most populous country in the world, he is a perfect example to allow us to plumb the depths of the approach to the Chinese people's acceptance of communism and efforts to integrate this imported ideology into their own cultural setting.

Strangely enough, the precise date of Li Dazhao's self-conversion to communism remains debatable, although the majority of scholars today agree that it was sometime in 1919. Nor has the exact day of the founding of the CCP been ascertained. Although the establishment of the CCP is viewed as a milestone in modern China, the officially designated date for it, July 1, 1921, is ironically inaccurate. Nevertheless, for convenience, the Chinese government favors this date, deems it as a landmark of Chinese history, and celebrates it as an annual festival. However, the situation for the early communist activists in 1921 was deplorable at first staggering sight, because the Chinese government at that time saw communists as dangerous individuals; consequently, the party was established in secrecy to avoid political persecution. In the meantime, the Beijing government continued to oppose Soviet Russia and regarded the communist ideology as a lethal creed. Under such a circumstance, it was not at all strange for the early communist activists to hold their founding conference clandestinely. This secret meeting was remembered in multiple memoirs as taking place on a number of conflicting dates. More intriguingly, Li himself did not attend this meeting but is still respected as a cofounder and hailed as an indispensable leader of the early communist movement.

In a sense, the Chinese acceptance of communism, with Li Dazhao as the first convert, was a unique aspect of the New Culture Movement during which Chinese intellectuals enthusiastically absorbed imported ideas. Indeed, no other illuminating ideological laboratory can be compared with this movement in terms of introducing and accepting foreign ideas, which turned China's cultural landscape into a colorful kaleidoscope. Yet the Chinese encounter with national humiliation during the New Culture Movement, in particular the diplomatic debacle at the Paris Peace Conference, prompted the radical intellectuals to seek a sweeping new way toward national salvation. As Chinese American scholar Tien-wei Wu once argued, "the Chinese communist movement stemmed from nationalism"; the embracing of communism, first by Li, truly reflected his intention of saving his country and mirrored his plan for reconstructing his nation.[2] Li's self-conversion was a process of rational intake, after which he went to great lengths to validate communism as a fundamental solution to China's problems, a panacea to cure China's ills, and a feasible means of transforming China into a modern state.

Embracing Communism

Li Dazhao's path to communism was a long and tortuous trajectory, sliding from one stage to another but gradually turning onto the communist road. As for the date of his self-conversion, Gao Yihan affirms that Li accepted communism while he was in Japan, which is supported by some Japanese scholars.[3] Some Chinese scholars argue that Li demonstrated his inclination toward communism in late 1918 because he had shown his appreciation of the communist ideal by then.[4] Although Chinese scholars so far are contentious on the date of Li's self-conversion to communism, more and more today view Li's publication of "My Marxist View" in

1919 as a milestone of his faith in it.[5] It is apparent that Li's pursuit of national salvation led him to "actively" rather than "passively" embrace communism.[6] Li marched toward communism with his endeavors, from his original contact with the socialist ideology during his college years, to his membership in the Chinese Socialist Party, to his careful study of socialism, and finally to his embrace of communism.[7] His membership in the Chinese Socialist Party proves his early interest in socialist ideology, his acquaintance with Japanese socialists enabled him to understand more about it, and the Russian Revolution inspired him to seriously look into communism, all leading up to Li becoming China's first self-converted communist in 1919.

In identifying the factors in Li Dazhao's acceptance of communism, Chinese scholars emphasize the growth of China's working class as indispensable historical background. Of course, it is somewhat logical to link communism to Chinese industrial workers, whose population was two million in modern factories by the end of World War I.[8] Yet the first group of communists, including Li, were mostly intellectuals rather than industrial workers. Those intellectuals pursued the communist ideology as a means of national salvation. They were educated in Western learning and got involved in the New Culture Movement. It was the sense of nationalist duty that motivated them to explore and accept the imported ideology. Taking Li as an example, his initial plan was to democratize China by emulating the West. Then, he became disillusioned by the Great War, which created a bleeding battleground for Western countries. As the war wrecked his dream, he started to distrust the West. Furthermore, in his eyes, the imperialist powers had humiliated his country in Paris.[9] Thus, during the whirlpool of national crises in 1919, Li's ideological world coalesced into a commitment to communism.

In recent years, a number of scholars have paid attention to the connection between communism and China's traditional culture, arguing that their similarities were conducive to Li's embrace of communism. This seems ironic because the New Culture Movement called for rejecting the old tradition. However, China's cultural elements indeed served as a locus for Li to accept this foreign ideology. Specifically, the Confucian notion of the Great Harmony, as Xiufen Lu argues, was appealing to Li, as it is comparable to the communist notion of the classless society in the future. The Daoist dialectic philosophy made it easier for Li to accept the communist dialectic philosophy.[10] The Chinese were receptive to importing, absorbing, and indigenizing foreign culture; in fact, they had received Buddhism and other foreign religions throughout history. Although some Chinese citizens resisted foreign culture, a great many were interested in the imported ideologies and gradually adapted them to China's cultural setting. In a similar vein, Li embraced the communist ideology with the Chinese cultural backdrop as a milieu in which he modified what he borrowed to fit China's needs and injected traditional elements into the newly adopted ideology.

Much has been written on the impact of the communist revolution in Russia upon Li Dazhao's self-conversion to communism. Without a doubt, he was interested in what happened in Russia. Soon after the February Revolution that overthrew the czarist government, Li became one of the Chinese intellectuals who viewed it "as a foreign revolutionary model of interest to China," as Lee Feigon points out.[11] After the October Revolution, Li was the first to praise it, as Gao Yihan observes.[12] Within a few years, Li Dazhao published over thirty articles on the Russian Revolution acclaiming it.[13] He glorified the October Revolution "as a twinkling little star in the deep dark night shedding light on the road to a new life."[14] Thus, some scholars argue that the October Revolution enabled Li to acquire a "vague" (*menglong*) communist consciousness.[15] In Li's eyes, Soviet Russia represented the third civilization he himself had envisioned,[16] while he regarded the October Revolution as a bridge leading to this idealistic third civilization.[17] With his lucid, sharply drawn, and persuasive analysis, Li told the Chinese that Soviet Russia embodied genuine democracy and affectionate humanism.[18] Clearly, his infatuation with the Russian model was a major shift in his ideological transformation while he was wrestling with China's national fate. The most exciting news was the Soviet proclamation of relinquishing the privileges czarist Russia seized from China, which rekindled the hope of the Chinese intellectuals, including Li Dazhao, who viewed communism as a "gospel" and a "savior" for the Chinese national resurgence.[19]

The Japanese factor has often been neglected, underestimated, and misunderstood; however, it was as crucial as the other factors. Even before his study abroad in Japan, Li Dazhao admired Japanese socialists and held dear their socialist thoughts. During his Japan years, he got a chance to read socialism-related works and to familiarize himself with Japanese socialists. After his return to China, Li continued to retrieve related information from Japanese publications, which gradually guided him onto the path to communism.[20] It should be noted that other Chinese intellectuals also disseminated communist literature through translating

Japanese sources. For example, Li's friend Chen Puxian translated and published Marxist materials even earlier.[21] For that reason, Japanese scholars claim that "Li Dazhao's Marxism was based on Chen Puxian's translation."[22] Chinese scholars refuse to accept this argument and assert that Chen's translation was influenced by Li's guidance.[23] It should also be noted that Chen Puxian himself was not a communist, as he later went to Taiwan, where he lived until his death. In contrast, Li continued to strengthen his faith in communism, retained his ties with Japanese socialists, and joined the Japanese Socialist League in 1920, according to a source.[24]

Mao Zedong's famous statement that the salvoes of the October Revolution brought communism into China might be an exaggeration, because the Chinese, such as Li Dazhao, absorbed the communist doctrine mainly from the Japanese sources.[25] Of course, it is also incorrect to downplay the impact of the Russian Revolution. In a particular sense, Li's support of the Russian Revolution meant his initial acceptance of the communist regime. Soon after the October Revolution, the Chinese government severed its diplomatic ties with Russia and withdrew Chinese diplomats in February 1918. In this way, the Chinese government deemed communism a deadly toxin. Even in such a hostile milieu, Li enthusiastically hailed the Russian Revolution and encouraged his countrymen to endorse the Soviet regime. According to Lin Boqu's reminiscence, he received letters in March and April 1918 from Li Dazhao, who introduced communism to him by mailing pamphlets and documents about the Russian Revolution.[26]

Li Dazhao spoke, wrote, and published to defend the Russian Revolution. Just like the French Revolution that impacted the eighteenth- and nineteenth-century world, he argued, the Russian Revolution would shine upon the twentieth-century global community. He identified it as a socialist revolution that represented the spirit of humanism. He equated Soviet Russia with a model of the third civilization. He pleaded with the Chinese to welcome the arrival of the dawn of a great epoch as a result. In the last weeks of 1918, Li wrote two articles to hail Soviet Russia. In "The Common People's Victory," he celebrated the victory of the Great War in a rather different manner. To Li, two consequences of the war became obviously evident: aggressive empires collapsed and courageous laborers triumphed. From then on, Li declared that all people of the world would become a proletariat who would unfold the curtain of a new epoch, of which the Russian Revolution was just a precursor.[27]

Scholars have claimed that Li Dazhao wrote "The Victory of Bolshevism," published in late 1918, to condemn Duan Qirui, the de facto ruler of the Beijing government. However, a close examination of this article shows Li's communist message.[28] It is true that Li mocked Duan for flaunting his victory in the Great War although Duan did not dispatch a single soldier to any battlefields. But Li devoted most of this article to celebrating the Russian Revolution and saluting the communist ideal. For Li, the victory of the war was the triumph of socialism, Bolshevism, and the global proletariat. He hailed the Bolsheviks for upholding the Marxist doctrine. He claimed that the war was a clash between two classes: the world proletariat and the global bourgeoisie. Li quoted *The Manifesto of the Communist Party* to emphasize that the proletariat had nothing to lose but their own chains. He stated that the Russian Revolution was just one of many ongoing revolutions challenging the capitalist system. He extolled Bolshevism as the new spirit of the twentieth century, because of which he was confident that a new world would arrive soon.[29] He continued: "When confronted by this irresistible tide, these remnants of the past are like withered leaves facing the bitter autumn wind; one by one they will drop to the ground. On all sides one sees the victorious banner of Bolshevism, and everywhere one hears the victorious songs of Bolshevism. Everyone says that the bells are ringing! The dawn of freedom is breaking! Just take a look at the world of the future; it is sure to be a world of red flags."[30]

Evidence from Li Dazhao's writings demonstrates his familiarity with communist ideas prior to 1919. It is true that some Chinese scholars such as Liang Qichao and Zhu Zhixin, even before Li, introduced Karl Marx and communism, yet none of them had such faith in the communist ideology. Li was different, as he not only introduced communism but also believed in it. In "The New Epoch," published to celebrate New Year's Day of 1919, Li stated that the bourgeoisie, the ruling class, had created an oppressed class. By using the Marxist notion of surplus value, he exposed the way in which the capitalist class exploited the working class. He opined that "the working class should seize the weapon to defend their own rights and attack their common enemy." Li was optimistic about the future of the proletariat, and he stated that "from now on, the working class will unite with their counterparts throughout the whole world to forge a levelheaded union of laborers, smash the natural boundaries, and overthrow the global capitalist class." He endorsed violent revolutions, in particular the one in Russia, "as the great deluge—the largest flood since Noah, which will wash the world into a new epoch." Li was confident that this new epoch would bring "a new life, a new civilization, and a new world."[31]

No other works authored by Li Dazhao could match the magnitude of his "My Marxist View" in terms of his systematic introduction of communism as a foreign ideology. Although this article was published in September and November 1919 in two pieces with a total count of thirty thousand Chinese characters, it was composed a few months before. In it, Li summarized Marxism in three categories: historical materialism concerning the past, economics and class struggle concerning the present, and socialist movement and socialist reconstruction in the future. He highlighted the economic base and its impact upon the superstructure, two important notions of Marxism. While stressing the class issue, Li underscored the exploitation by the capitalist class of the working class. Li emphasized that the development of the productive forces was inevitably followed by a change in social relations. He exposed the secret of capitalism by introducing the Marxist notion of surplus value, defined as what capitalists stole from the workers, who only shared a tiny portion of what they had labored for. He posited this injustice in the entire establishment and argued that "those who exploit the workers are not capitalists but the capitalist system."[32] He contended that capitalism had created its own enemy, which was the proletarian class, whose poverty led to their intensive struggle against the capitalist class. He was confident that the downfall of capitalism was inevitable, after which public ownership of the means of production would elevate the working class to a higher status.[33]

The first impression the article gives, as Peter Zarrow points out, is that Li Dazhao was more "a commentator than a believer."[34] However, like other radical intellectuals of the day, Li rationally elaborated what he accepted without showing any sign of a quasi-religious fanaticism. This does not mean that he was not a follower; rather, he embraced what he had chosen through a rational approach. Even after his embrace of this foreign ideology, he pinpointed flaws in Marxism in spite of the fact that he affirmed its greater attributes.[35] As Zhang Rulun argues, Li accepted historical materialism but remained reserved concerning economic determinism.[36] In any case, we can see a huge milestone in this article if we superimpose it over the history of Li's gradual march towards communism. Before this article, he had already started to absorb communist ideas; after it, he vehemently defended communism, and more importantly he applied it in his analysis of China's problems. He argued that the Chinese people as a nation suffered from an agony which was similar to that of the working class throughout the entire world, although capitalism in China was not fully developed. China's anguish was caused by the indirect oppression of the capitalist class through imperialist invasions. Unless China accepted socialism, Li posited, the Chinese situation would not be changed.[37] To refute the view that socialism stifled individual freedom, he argued that "true and rational socialism will not disrespect individual freedom. Individuals versus society, and freedom versus order, are not separated under the socialist system."[38]

From that time on, Li Dazhao tried to apply communist doctrine in his scholarly explorations. Far from sophistication but on a par with communist values, he offered his analysis on a variety of topics. In an article published on December 1, 1919, Li argued that morality was not supernatural as it was based on "material" (*wuzhi*) factors: "The demands of the material base of society led to the request for an immaterial morality."[39] The transformation of Chinese ideology was a result of changes in the material base of society. The millennium-long Confucian values had reflected China's rural economic life patterns. However, the invasion of the imperialist powers and the inroads made by foreign economic forces impacted China so much that the Chinese people started to abandon Confucianism, to pursue democracy, and to fight for national liberation.[40] In analyzing ancient history, Li traced the changing gender relationship between men and women. He emphasized the role of economic changes as a leading factor in the shaping of patriarchy at the dawn of civilization. To be specific, the arrival of the agricultural revolution started to confine women at home, while men became dominant patriarchs.[41] But his overemphasis on material factors could lead him to draw an incorrect conclusion. For instance, he claimed that the Shang dynasty lingered in the Stone Age, although he acknowledged the invention of early written language on the oracle bones.[42] However, bronze utensils were soon discovered in Anyang, which proved that the Shang dynasty blossomed during China's Bronze Age.

The fierce debate between Li Dazhao and Hu Shi in 1919 on the ideology-versus-individual-issues topic, or the problem and ism topic, verified Li's stance in defending his communist faith; Jerome B. Grieder has termed it "the most celebrated exchange in an ongoing debate."[43] For Hu, what China needed was to solve problems one by one, without caring about so-called ideologies or isms. Evidently, Hu followed his teacher John Dewey's pragmatism to focus on detailed issues and to find practical solutions. Unbowed by Hu's pragmatism, Li argued that issues and isms should not be separated, that China needed a fundamental solution, and that an ideal ideology would help solve all issues.[44] This trading of barbs was not an internecine slaughter, and Li and Hu continued to be friends. Although the debate did not last long, it affirmed Li's belief in communism.[45] Yet this debate has garnered great scholarly attention. For Chinese scholars, this debate was significant because it marked a new starting point for Li and all future communists by adopting communism as a fundamental solution to China's issues and because it signaled Li's coming of age as a communist by publicizing his belief in the communist mission.[46] Scholars in Taiwan view this debate differently but highlight its significance; as Wang Yuanyi argues, this debate was the origin of the future upsurge of the Chinese revolution, even if Li and Hu did not realize the grave consequence of their debate. Wang adds that "the result would be the shaping of a left-wing totalitarian regime, if Li Dazhao's ideas were to be realized."[47]

By 1919, Li Dazhao grasped the gist of the central principles and basic tenets of the communist ideology. Yet his comprehension remained rudimentary, as he had not read a large number of the original communist classics. Nevertheless, an exaggerated overstatement concerning Li's profound comprehension is offered by some Chinese scholars who claim that "Chinese Marxist philosophy from the very beginning displayed its sophistication in the works of Li Dazhao."[48] This argument is ill founded, as Li himself acknowledged the difficulty in grasping Marxism. He cited a German statement to verify what he meant: anyone below fifty years old claiming to understand Marxism should be regarded as a swindler.[49] Other scholars argue that "non-Marxist elements in Li Dazhao's works vanished after 1924."[50] While this statement helps us understand Li's maturity as a communist by then, it is troublesome, because Li after 1924 became a professional revolutionary, authoring fewer serious scholarly works and writing mostly on revolutionary strategies and tactics.

Western scholars have studied the ways Li Dazhao carried his pre-Marxist thoughts into his newly adopted ideology. Maurice Meisner, in his 1967 monograph, probes Li's populism, nationalism, and other former thought, which penetrated into his communist mindset.[51] Arif Dirlik narrows it down to anarchism, in particular the concept of mutual aid, in Li's new world of thought.[52] Edward X. Gu shows Li's role "in the renewed popularity of Russian populism" that persisted as an idea and became intertwined with his newly embraced ideology.[53] Adrian Chan offers his criticism of Li's ignorance as he claims, "Li Dazhao was found guilty for failing to distinguish in 1918 between Marxism and Social Democracy" and for accepting other confusing notions.[54] Chinese scholars acknowledge the influence of Li's pre-Marxist thoughts. Tong Shijun claims that Li's conversion to communism did not mean that he gave up his faith in democracy.[55] Nor did Li relinquish his populism, which served as a utopian ideal and an ideological resource.[56] Zhang Jingru enumerates different aspects of Li's utopianism, such as his aversion toward urban life, his passion for the countryside, and his enthusiasm for mutual aid.[57] Indeed, after his self-conversion to communism, Li's articles retained the leftovers of his previous ideas, including liberty, equality, universal love, mutual aid, and so forth.[58] The residues of his former thoughts lingered in his works. As China's first communist, Li was not bound up by an orthodoxy, and his version of communism remained in a state of fluidity because he derived so many diverse ideas from so many different sources.

Establishing the Chinese Communist Party

For three years before the establishment of the Chinese Communist Party in 1921, Li Dazhao dedicated himself to its preparation, operations, and recruitment. His enthusiasm in disseminating communism attracted young minds to flock to this path, because they shared a common goal of national resurgence. In the China of that time, there was no way for Li and his followers to be voters; neither could they rely on any constituencies to make political and social changes. Seeing that most of the political parties became self-centered organizations, Li sensed the imperative of establishing a new political party to spread communist ideals; for this reason, he studied communism with the purpose of building a new society through implementing communist policies. In many ways, Li prepared for the birth of the CCP by organizing communist cells, establishing affiliated groups, and disseminating communist ideas. It was in this context of preparation that he assumed a historical significance as a cofounder of the CCP and was acclaimed as "a soul figure" (*linghunrenwu*)[59] and "a spiritual leader" (*jingshenlingxiu*).[60]

Li Dazhao's use of the Beijing University library as a center for nurturing young students with the communist doctrine has long attracted scholarly attention. American scholars Diane M. Nelson and Robert B. Nelson have examined "the role of the library in the promulgation of Marxism in modern China." Not only did Li purchase the communism-related books from foreign vendors for his library, but he also encouraged young students to study, discuss, and disseminate communism. "The distribution of literature and the teaching of Marxist texts" turned Li into "the individual most responsible for the radical formation of modern Chinese librarianship."[61] This argument is validated by testimonies of those who knew him. Zhang Guotao, an early communist and a prominent communist leader in the 1930s, spoke highly of Li as a guide for young students. He remarked in his memoir, "Mr. Li Dazhao was a central figure of the Marxist faith in Beijing. His library became an origin place for leftist thought." Zhang affirmed that "the priority concern of our discussions was the way of national salvation" and Li's persuasive advice enabled his followers to regard communism as a tool for their nationalistic goal.[62]

With eager learners around him, Li Dazhao started to organize young students and intellectuals into a study group called the Marxist Study Society in 1918, according to Gao Yihan, Zhu Wushan, Cheng Shewo, and others. Japanese scholars have long confirmed the founding of this group in 1918 and valued it as "the precursor of the communist group" and "the motherly body [*muti*] of the Chinese Communist Party."[63] In the 1990s, however, scholars became skeptical of its existence in the year 1918.[64] Through careful studies, more scholars now have ascertained that Li indeed helped organize a group in the winter of 1918 with the special title of the Maergesi Doctrine Study Society (*Maergesi xueshuo yanjiuhui*), intentionally using *Maergesi* to sound like *Malthus* in order to avoid censorship troubles. In March 1920, Li secretly organized the Marxist Doctrine Study Society (*Makesi xueshuo yanjiuhui*), with which he attracted over a hundred people to study communism. It remained functioning in secrecy until its public announcement in November 1921. Under Li's guidance, its members collected communism-related books in Chinese, German, English, French, Japanese, Russian, and other languages, translated them into Chinese, organized group discussions, and sponsored seminars, at which Li was a frequent speaker. It is said that Mao Zedong was strongly impacted by this society for his conversion to communism, as he told American journalist Edgar Snow that "under Li Ta-chao [Dazhao], as assistant librarian at Peking National University, I had rapidly developed towards Marxism."[65] Mao added, "By the summer of 1920 I had become, in theory and to some extent in action, a Marxist, and from this time on I considered myself a Marxist."[66]

Soon after the establishment of the Marxist Doctrine Study Society, Li Dazhao helped assemble a specialized library called the Communist Cubicle (Kangmuyizhai) in West Hall on what was then the Beijing University campus. It was a small library that also served as an office and a meeting place. According to Luo Zhanglong, Karl Marx's portrait was hung on the central wall with revolutionary slogans, poems, and axioms on other walls. The participants studied communism and celebrated communist festivals. Besides translating foreign language books, they shared their own writings among themselves. They encouraged each other to be valiant and not to be afraid of going to jail once they began engaging in revolutionary activities. To translate more foreign works, they recruited students who majored in foreign languages, including English, German, French, Japanese, Russian, Spanish, Latin, and Sanskrit.[67] It is said that a hundred young people participated in its activities, among whom many later joined the CCP.[68]

It is pertinent to mention that Li Dazhao and Zhang Ximan cofounded the Socialist Study Society (Shehuizhuyiyanjiuhui) on December 4, 1920, the establishment of which they had been preparing for during the previous year. Their objective was to gather people to study socialism, to translate foreign works, and to disseminate socialist ideas. Zhang Ximan, a Hunanese, was a professor of Russian and had translated literature concerning the October Revolution. By using this group as a public forum, Li Dazhao launched a debate against Zhang Dongsun, who publicly declared that China did not need socialism and must acquire wealth through industrialization. Li argued that China's industry could not be developed without socialism and that industrial growth under the existing system would only lead to undesirable consequences. Li advised the people to read the publications of the Socialist Study Society, in particular *The Manifesto of the Communist Party*, *Das Kapital*, and others translated works.[69] By keeping such an organization at arm's length, Li utilized it to propagate his newly acquired faith. Under his influence, a lot of members of this society later became communists.

Li Dazhao was eager to connect himself with youth groups to direct them to step onto the path of communism. During the New Culture Movement, youth groups mushroomed throughout the country. Li saw their prized potential and valuable dimension, and he extended his assistance to them whenever he was invited, even if beyond the city of Beijing. For example, Zhou Enlai, after studying for six years in Japan, returned to Tianjin, where he organized the Awakening Society

(Juewushe) among young students in September 1919. Zhou invited Li to speak to this group in Tianjin. In his speech, Li promoted national resurgence and urged its members to follow the Russian way. Upon Zhou Enlai's request, a special meeting was held at Taoranting Park in Beijing on August 16, 1920. Zhou's group traveled to Beijing to join other Beijing youth groups for this special meeting, at which Li advised them to study communism.[70] It might be an exaggeration to claim that those contacts led Zhou Enlai, the future premier of Maoist China, to become a communist, but Li's guidance was at least a factor in it. Indeed, many members of the Awakening Society later became communists, including Zhou Enlai and his future wife, Deng Yingchao. Li also supported other youth groups, and he assisted Yu Fangzhou and Han Linfu in organizing the Socialist Youth League in Beijing in January 1921 to disseminate communist doctrine.[71]

Li Dazhao's understanding of the communist concept of mobilizing the working class prompted him to interact with industrial workers. He knew that China remained an agrarian society in which the industrial working class was mainly limited to the railway enterprises and mining. He sent young students to raise those workers' class consciousness as a part of his plan for mass mobilization. At first, those workers who participated in Li's programs were merely driven by their own immediate interests rather than the communist ideal. Nevertheless, Li throbbed with energy to engage with them. To celebrate May Day in 1920, Li declared that it should be a date of awakening for China's working class.[72] On New Year's Day in 1921, Li went to Changxindian, near Beijing, to offer lectures to the newly established Laborers' Continuing School. On May Day in 1921, under Li's guidance, railway workers at Changxindian organized a trade union, which was followed by a parade in which one thousand workers took part, among whom many later joined the CCP.[73]

A widely circulated story narrates Li Dazhao and Chen Duxiu's cooperation in cofounding the CCP. It was told initially by Gao Yihan, who was Li's long-term friend. According to recent scholarly studies, this story took place in early 1920, although some suspect its truthfulness. Chen was the most wanted man in Beijing, and he planned to escape the capital city. Li thus escorted Chen from Beijing to Tianjin, from which Chen would travel to Shanghai. This famous legendary tale was first published in 1927 by Gao: "Li Dazhao shaved his mustache, wore a skullcap, held a long-stemmed tobacco pipe, and twisted his legs while sitting in a horse-driven cart. Chen Duxiu wore a kitchen worker's vest and sat inside. The two looked exactly like a cohort of merchants. Nobody doubted their identities on the way, while Li's northern accent helped."[74] In his memoir published in 1957, Gao affirmed the same story with additional information: "They dressed like merchants, carried a pile of account books, and rented a horse-driven cart. Li Dazhao sat outside, while Chen Duxiu sat inside. In this way, Li accompanied Chen to Tianjin, from which Chen took the sea route to Shanghai."[75] More importantly, Li and Chen held private discussions on the establishment of a new political party on the way, for which the well-known historical term "South Chen and North Li" (*nanchenbeili*) was later coined to emphasize the two men's significant role in the founding of the CCP.

By early 1921, Li Dazhao recognized the urgent need for building a nationwide communist party. In March 1921, he published an article titled "The Corporative Training and the Renovated Enterprise" in which he voiced his admiration of the Russian Communist Party, which had turned Russia into "a red country" (*chiseguojia*) with its 600,000 members. In contrast, he claimed, the Chinese lacked the organizational ability due to the long dynastic rule, while the existing political parties all became egoistic organizations and did not "work for the people's benefits." Although small political parties were built, they could not do anything except publicize their programs, which Li mocked as "the program movement (*zhangchengyundong*)." He argued that "we urgently need to organize a new party. It should not belong to politicians, nor should it be a traditional democratic party for the bourgeoisie. It should be a political party for the common people, the laborers. It should be a socialist party." He expected this party to forge an alliance with the communist parties of other countries and regarded the Communist International (Comintern) as the nucleus (*zhongshu*). He assured his readers that "the complete renovation of China will depend on this political party."[76]

The preliminary step for establishing such a communist party was to organize local cells in major cities, which are known in historical annals as the small communist groups (*gongchanzhuyixiaozu*). Chen Duxiu took the initiative in organizing the first such cell in Shanghai in the summer of 1920, which was followed by Li Dazhao's cell assembled at his library in September (or October) 1920 in Beijing. The original three members of Li's cell were Li Dazhao, Zhang Shenfu, and Zhang Guotao. Then, this cell started to expand after anarchists joined it. The anarchists, headed by Huang Lingshuang and Chen Derong, strongly opposed electing a leader of the cell and did not endorse keeping any meeting minutes. Later, they openly opposed Marxism, which led to an internal clash. Fortunately, according to Zhang Guotao, the anarchists peacefully withdrew.[77] Li helped this cell publish *Laodongyin* (The voice of the laborers) and *Gongrenzhoukan* (Workers' weekly) to spread communism. In the initial stage, the group encountered extreme financial difficulty, for which Li generously donated two-thirds of the income he earned as the chief librarian.[78] With just a dozen members in his cell, Li was confident that "we are just a few revolutionary seeds. We need to till the land well, plant the seeds carefully, and we will reap the harvest in the future," as he explained to Luo Zhanglong.[79] In early 1921, Li started to send his fellow communists out to build affiliated organs, such as trade unions, workers' clubs, youth leagues, and more importantly the Shandong Communist Cell in Jinan.[80]

It is reasonable to argue that the Chinese communist movement was the corollary of those early activists' determined pursuit of a transformed China, for which Li Dazhao acted as a leading figure. However, the Russian factor should not be downplayed. The Soviet regime after the October Revolution exerted a strong impact upon the building of the CCP, for which Li served as a bridge. Whether Li met a Soviet agent in the fall of 1918, as some scholars claim, is open to further study.[81] Li's meetings with N. G. Bultman in 1919 are well known, though. In 1920, Li met a number of Russian agents: S. A. Polovory, Alex Ivono, Hohonovry (a pseudonym), and Grigori Voitinsky; the last two represented the Comintern.[82] During their meetings, the Soviet agents expressed their gratefulness to Li for his support of the Russian Revolution and persuaded Li to build a nationwide communist party. Luo Zhanglong's testimony allows us to understand the initial Sino-Soviet communist interactions as he remembered them: "Voitinsky worked diligently. He held seminars to introduce Soviet Russia. He was about forty years old and was a learned man with rich experience. He always offered satisfactory answers to our questions. His English was excellent and he was well versed in German. He thus communicated with us in those two languages."[83] After their meeting, Li wrote a letter to Chen Duxiu introducing Voitinsky and arranging for him to visit Chen in Shanghai. In 1921, the Comintern agent Hendricus Sneevliet, alias G. Maring, who is known as Ma Lin in China, visited Li Dazhao. Li supported the plan of establishing a national communist party and dispatched the members of his cell to Shanghai to attend the first national congress to proclaim its founding.[84]

Without a doubt, Soviet Russia and the Comintern played a role in the establishment of the CCP, for which Li served as a middleman.

It was a pity that Li Dazhao himself did not attend the first national congress of the CCP for which he labored so much and prepared for so long. Far different from the romantic tales that glorify the conference, the first national congress was held secretly in the French Concession of Shanghai with only thirteen Chinese men in attendance, representing fifty-three communists from seven communist cells.[85] Two Comintern agents, including Maring, also attended. Although July 1 is now celebrated as the founding date of the CCP, it was not the precise day because the week-long congress started on July 23, 1921, according to recent studies. On the last day, the meeting was relocated to a boat on a lake in Jiaxing County, Zhejiang Province, to avoid police harassment in the city. Scholars have offered interpretations of the reasons why Li Dazhao did not attend. His time-consuming work at the library prevented him from making the long southbound journey. At the same time, he was the leader of the Salary Reclamation Movement, for which he had to stay in Beijing to lead the campaign against the warlord government.[86] Because of his personal reputation, his departure from Beijing would have caused troubles, as the Beijing government was monitoring his moves. In recent years, scholars have studied Li's habit of avoiding the meetings of the Beijing communist cell, for which he simply sent Bao Huisheng to attend in his name.[87] Other scholars claim that Li did not value the first national congress and did not realize its magnitude, which explains why he was not elected to the party's executive organ, the central bureau (*zhongyangju*). Li mainly invested his time and energy in his study of communism, and he tried to sidestep trivial routines.[88] Yet Li's indispensable role in the founding of the CCP is always acknowledged. More importantly, the Chinese title of the Communist Party (Gongchandang) was selected beforehand by Li Dazhao, according to a recent study.[89]

The facts that Li Dazhao did not attend the first national congress of the CCP and that he was not elected to its central bureau did not demote his prominent status as a leader in the eyes of his fellow communists. His followers respected him as the first communist, in contrast to the fact that Chen Duxiu remained skeptical of the Russian Revolution at the time of Li's self-conversion.[90] Reflecting on the glorious title of "Chen in the South and Li in the North" concerning the founding of the party, Chen Duxiu in his later years humbly commented that "South Chen enjoys an undeserved reputation, while North Li is truly the Big

Dipper."[91] One scholar commented that Li Dazhao is a rare case among the early communists because he was an extraordinary combination of "a thinker, a theorist, a revolutionary, and a famed scholar."[92] As one of the cofounders, his significance can be found in the following facts: six of the thirteen representatives who attended the first CCP national congress had ties with Beijing University, and twenty-one among the fifty-three communist members in 1921 were once either faculty members, staff members, or students at Beijing University.[93]

Li Dazhao and the Early Communist Movement

No sooner had the CCP been established than its members started to strive for the party's mission. Although Li Dazhao did not attend the first national congress, he still served as its leader, particularly in North China. Although the party was a secret political organization and its original documents were mostly lost, the remaining ones, along with members' memoirs, reveal Li's prominent role, showing that he shouldered a far greater degree of responsibility for the party. Sources prove Li's diligence in recruiting new members, disseminating the communist doctrine, leading the labor movement, coordinating with the Soviet Union, and working with the Comintern. In the first couple of years after the founding of the CCP, Li's activities covered diverse fields, in almost all of which he acted as an indispensable leader.

Although Li Dazhao was not elected to the central bureau, he remained a central figure in the party. In accordance with the central bureau's order that a district executive committee should be formed so long as twenty party members were tallied in that district, Li established the Beijing District Executive Committee to guide the communist movement not only in Beijing but also in the northern provinces. By late 1921, he established the Beijing regional committee with himself as the leader, while he assigned Luo Zhanglong to manage its organization, Gao Junyu to manage its propaganda, and Li Meigeng to arrange its finance.[94] Below the regional committee, two branches in Beijing were soon built. In November 1921, Li helped reestablish the Socialist Youth League in Beijing, through which young students were recruited as communists.[95]

Sources clearly show that Li Dazhao was a respected man among the early communists and that he often served as a mediator. Because the early communists came from different family backgrounds and various regional cultures, they carried within themselves diverse opinions and clashed inevitably over multiple issues. Hot-tempered and aggressive party members occasionally bullied mild-mannered and submissive ones. Whenever such a case occurred, Li tried to settle the dispute and bring peace through reconciliation. As Zhu Wushan recollected, Li Dazhao healed a breach between Deng Zhongxia and others during a personal conflict.[96] According to Luo Zhanglong, Li implemented his democratic policy to manage intraparty affairs and his collective leadership style won popular support, by which he endorsed thorough discussions, respected majority decisions, and opposed sectarian activities.[97]

An urgent task in addition to the overall mission for the communist ideal was to recruit new members in order to strengthen the party. The enlistment was done through personal contacts, group meetings, ideological indoctrination, and raising class consciousness. Li Dazhao emphasized high-quality recruits who had to be dedicated to the communist cause without caring much about personal gains and losses. With his efforts, more than one thousand communists were enlisted in the capital city in a few years, while many others joined the party later on. Hou Wailu was a student in Beijing from 1923 to 1926, during which he was coached in communism by Li. Although he went to France and became a communist there, he remarked that "I totally relied on Comrade Li Dazhao's guidance and followed his teaching, through which I acquired the Marxist view."[98] Li targeted the youth, guided them, and transformed their nationalistic zeal into a fervor for communism. He refused to recruit those whose thinking collided with the communist ideology. For instance, Liang Shuming kept a cordial relationship with Li and often conversed with Li at the library. Liang said that Li never tried to recruit him into the CCP. The reason, as Liang claimed in his memoir, was that "my personal qualification obviously did not meet his party's requirements."[99]

Li Dazhao's stance endorsing Soviet Russia posed a sharp contrast to the Beijing government's refusal to open diplomatic ties with it. On public occasions, Li pressed the Beijing government to extend recognition. To celebrate the fifth anniversary of the October Revolution, Li published an article pleading with the Chinese people to accept Soviet Russia unconditionally and not to follow the capitalist world in opposing it. The thrust of his argument was that Soviet Russia was "the motherland, the pioneer, and the supreme headquarters of the global working masses." While China was under "the dual oppression" of capitalism and imperialism, the Chinese people should establish a united front with the working class all over the world to support Soviet Russia and to resist global capitalism.[100] On November 7, 1922, a rally of three thousand persons at Beijing University elected Li as its chairman and invited him to deliver the first speech, in which Li hailed Soviet Russia and expected it to exert an influence upon the global community.[101] It is clear that Li's grasp of the Russian Revolution differed sharply from that of the Beijing government, because he considered Soviet Russia as a true democracy in which "officials and citizens are all managers of state affairs, while everyone is a ruler and nobody is subject to others."[102]

In contrast with his pro-Soviet stance, Li Dazhao vehemently denounced the imperialist powers and labeled them "the hated enemy" (*choudi*) of China. According to Li, the Chinese people lived in a special situation in which foreign oppressors made them suffer miserably under imperialism and capitalism.[103] Not only did the imperialist powers partition China into many spheres of influence, but they also controlled China's tariff, managed China's railways, and made decisions for China without first consulting the Chinese.[104] It was this special arrangement that turned the Chinese people into "a proletarian nation" groaning under imperialist dominance, oppression, and exploitation. Li spoke highly of Soviet Russia and regarded it "as an anti-imperialist supreme headquarters and as a good friend of the oppressed nations." He praised the Soviet gesture of relinquishing the Russian privileges seized from China by the czarist regime as a sign of "pure friendship."[105]

Another enemy of the Chinese people was the warlord regime. In 1922, Li Dazhao portrayed Chinese warlords collectively as a group of "special merchants," and he explained that ordinary merchants can only reap profits from the transaction of commodities. Yet "the special merchants, the military commanders, reap profits by gaining and strengthening personal power and by imposing all kinds of levies and taxes upon the people within their own domains."[106] Li also criticized Chinese congressmen for deceiving the nation by engaging in tricks. He put it bluntly that "the Chinese people will not recognize them as their representatives, while their congressional decisions are simply null and void."[107] According to Li, what China needed was a "fundamental reconstruction" (*genbenxingdegaizao*).[108] In particular, Li called on the Chinese youth to participate in China's political movement, as he addressed at a rally in Shanghai on September 2, 1922: "We cannot put politics aside and let the bad guys freely play with it. We must arise and seize politics in our own hands. . . . We need a political movement in which we should unite ourselves as if in an army" in order to overthrow the rule of vicious warlords, to eradicate the manipulation of brainless politicians, and to rebuild a new China.[109]

In retrospect, it is clear that the CCP in its initial stage was but an organization of intellectuals, among whom Li Dazhao established communist cells and cofounded the party. Even after its establishment, Li continued to pay attention to Chinese intellectuals who excelled in cultural circles—in particular, universities, schools, and the media. Indeed, those intellectuals shaped a special sector in Chinese society, as Eddy U elaborates. Li hoped that the intellectual class would become "champions of a mass movement working loyally for the people."[110] While intellectuals were sensitive to national humiliation, any news about the exasperating national crisis could turn them into activists, and some did become communists. According to a recent study, fifty-two out of the total of fifty-three communists at the time of the first national congress in July 1921 were intellectuals; the one exception was a man who was a skilled worker at a college in Wuhan.[111] Li did not want to lose a chance to implant the communist ideal into the minds of young intellectuals, which explains why he was enthusiastic in helping to influence Shanghai University, established in 1922, when it needed new faculty and staff members. Seizing this opportunity, Li in 1923 dispatched his student Deng Zhongxia to be its provost and other graduates from Beijing University as its faculty and staff. With a large number of communists on the campus, "Shanghai University becomes a school mainly run by the Chinese Communist Party."[112]

Li Dazhao realized the importance of ethnic issues because, although Han Chinese were the dominant group, China was in fact a multiethnic country; hence, he intended to recruit activists of other ethnicities into his party. One endeavor was his work at the Mongol-Tibetan School (Mengzangxuexiao) in Beijing, which was established by the government for the purpose of training students of these ethnicities. In 1923, Li Dazhao started to get involved in this school. He often went there to present lectures on national problems, discuss ethnic issues, deliberate on international affairs, disseminate communist ideas, and elucidate revolutionary objectives. According to a Mongol student, Jiyatai, who came from Inner Mongolia, Li often attended their meetings and advised them to study revolutionary theories, to participate in political struggle, and to forsake degenerative behaviors. Under Li's guidance, a number of students from these ethnic backgrounds became communists or joined the Socialist Youth League. In the one-year period from 1923 to 1924, according to Jiyatai, the first group of Mongol students, including Ulanhu (Wulanfu), Kuibi, Jiyatai, and others, became communists. Ulanhu later served as the vice president of the People's Republic of China, while Jiyatai became the Chinese ambassador to Mongolia. Jiyatai praised Li Dazhao for training the ethnic Mongols, introducing them to communism and hence planting the seeds for the upcoming communist movement in Inner Mongolia.[113]

Given the fact that the majority of the Chinese population at that time lived in rural areas, the peasant question was inevitably one of the most salient issues that Li Dazhao could not avoid. In fact, his populist views lingered; he remained fond of rural life and had endeavored to reform the countryside. Given this propensity, the peasant issue was bound to emerge as a major element in his communist worldview. After the founding of the CCP, the transformation of the peasantry was on his agenda.[114] In fact, Li was the first Chinese communist to seriously think over this issue, as it was not a dominant theme in the orthodox communist ideology. Li's emphasis on the peasant issue propelled him to establish communist organizations in the countryside. Gong Zhongtao was an example of this. Gong, a native of Anping County in Zhili (Hebei) Province, enrolled as a student at Beijing University of Law and Politics. He often visited Li and was inspired by Li's communist ideas. In April 1923, Li personally admitted Gong into the CCP. Four months later, Gong was dispatched by Li to return to Anping to build a night school, which was followed by the establishment of a local peasant association. Gong frequently contacted Li for advice. In the winter of 1923, upon Li's approval, Gong established a special communist branch in the village of Taicheng. According to a recent study, the Taicheng branch was the first rural communist organization in the entire history of the CCP. Gong continued to work in the same area and established the first county-level communist committee in Zhili Province the next year.[115]

Even as the CCP was established, it remained an underground organization that operated through its members' open identities, such as Li Dazhao as a professor of Beijing University. Making full use of his distinguished status, Li offered courses and lectures on the socialist ideology, published on the socialist movement, and defended the communist ideal. Nevertheless, he reaffirmed his conviction in the importance of democracy, as he elaborated in his speech at China University in

December 1921. He argued that the current phase of "democracy" should be rendered as "the doctrine of the common people" (*pingminzhuyi*).[116] While democracy meant "people's rule," socialism guaranteed the rule of the working people who made up the overwhelming majority of the society. Li claimed that democracy should be seen as "ergatocracy," which allowed the working class to hold power, guaranteed everyone a job, and ensured everybody would share whatever was needed. In this way, the class distinctions would gradually disappear.[117] He declared that "ergatocracy is the administration of the workers, for the workers, and by the workers. . . . Only ergatocracy can be called pure democracy, true democracy, and authentic democracy."[118]

Li Dazhao vehemently defended socialism whenever it was criticized. When socialism was accused of leading to poverty, Li argued that socialism would guarantee everyone the ability to lead a happy life both materially and culturally, which he declared in his speech at Shanghai University on November 7, 1923. Li insisted that "socialism will acquire wealth and will not cause poverty. Socialism is to promote production rather than destroying it." Some scorned socialism for depriving people of freedom, but Li proclaimed that nobody could live in true freedom under the capitalist system, while socialism would grant heartfelt freedom. Facing the criticism that socialism could result in personal laziness, Li asserted that socialism would liberate people from all pains and would allow everyone blissful happiness after diligent work.[119]

In the recent decades, Chinese scholars have underscored Li Dazhao's role in the Sinicization (*Zhongguohua*) of Marxism: applying the communist doctrine to meet China's needs, interpreting Marxism through Chinese vocabularies, and adapting communism to China's special national circumstances. Of course, this point could only be advanced after the end of the Cultural Revolution, before which Mao Zedong was regarded as the first man to sinicize Marxism. After Mao's death, Chinese scholars have argued that "Li Dazhao was the first Chinese to initiate the Sinicization of Marxism."[120] Others maintain that Li developed Marxism by emphasizing people's initiative, supplementing Marxism with the notion of mutual aid, declaring the inevitability of socialism, and defining China as a proletarian nation.[121] To deepen the Chinese understanding of communism, Li published articles introducing utopian socialism and emphasizing the importance of communism as the quintessential corollary of socialism.[122] He studied the Paris Commune to underscore the Russian Revolution as its successor in seizing power from the capitalist class.[123] To clarify the Chinese confusion between socialism and communism, Li used the two akin colors for elucidation, and he vividly illustrated socialism as "light red" (*qianhongse*) and communism as "pure red" (*chunchise*). According to Li, the two differed only in range but shared the same substance.[124] Yet he did not make it clear that socialism should be the initial stage leading later to communism, as today's communist doctrine circumscribes.

Li Dazhao's application of the Marxist concept of historical materialism into his scholarly research was one of his ways of propagating communism, because the acceptance of this notion could mean partial acceptance of communism. After his embrace of the Marxist concept of historical materialism, Li dropped his previous evolutionary outlook.[125] He emphasized the economic factor as the main cause of all changes, including moral change, political transformation, and social advancement. He underscored the vital role of the masses in the development of human history. Although some of his previous ideas lingered, the common thread of his historiography was historical materialism, for which he was viewed as "China's first Marxist historian."[126] Because his publications impacted his readers, his persuasive discourse led many to adopt the Marxist view. Guo Zhanbo remarked in his 1936 survey of China's ideological history, "Mr. Li Dazhao was the most accomplished historian. He also was the first and firmest promoter of historical materialism. He initiated the introduction of this new notion and should be respected as a prophet in this regard."[127]

One of Li Dazhao's contributions to the early communist movement was his initial adherence to the orthodox Marxist model in his launching of labor movements. On one hand, it demonstrates that the early activists were determined to follow the communist way, and on the other hand, it proves that the early communists were directed by the Comintern and Soviet Russia to mobilize China's industrial workers for action. Under Li Dazhao's leadership, the communists established the northern branch of the Chinese Labor Organization Secretariat (Zhongguolaodongzuheshujibu) with Li's student Luo Zhanglong as the director leading the labor movement in North China. They established trade unions, built night schools, recruited new CCP members, and staged workers' strikes along the railway line and in the mining area. After the CCP became a branch of the Comintern in 1922, Li followed its directive to contact the warlord Wu Peifu, trying to win his support. Li personally visited Wu Peifu three times in Luoyang, Henan Province, in 1922, during which Wu promised to protect workers. With Li's efforts, the CCP was able to dispatch five supervisors to the five northern railway lines, which was followed by the founding of a dozen workers' clubs and trade unions.[128] Li also supported workers in other regions. When the leaders of the labor movement in Hunan were killed in 1922, Li praised them as "the pioneers of the working class" and called on the workers to continue fighting for their unfinished cause.[129] Li devoted himself to the upsurge of the workers' movements between January 1922 and February 1923, during which the February Seventh Strike (Erqidabagong) of 1923 occurred.[130] Under Li's guidance, railway workers along the Beijing-Hankou Line organized the General Trade Union on February 1, 1923, and staged a strike three days later. As a result, the railway line was paralyzed, which posed a heavy challenge to the foreign powers who controlled railway management. Unfortunately, Wu Peifu, who had sworn to protect the workers, sent troops to suppress the strike, killing fifty-two, wounding three hundred, arresting forty, and laying off over one thousand workers.[131] The bloody crackdown taught Li a serious lesson and compelled him to seek a new way and to find a potential ally to continue the communist revolution.

Conclusion

The acceptance of communism was one of the most important historical milestones of modern China, for which Li Dazhao led the way in studying Marxism, became China's first communist, and introduced the foreign ideology to his fellow citizens. His acceptance of the ideology was the result of his long-term pursuit of China's path to national regeneration, during which he explored the works of Western civilization and deliberately exposed himself to communist literature. Hence, Mao Zedong's statement that the October Revolution instantly delivered communism to the Chinese people is only partially true, because Li had long been interested in the ideology. Moreover, the Japanese factor was equally important, as Li mainly read about Marxism from Japanese sources.[132] Facing the deluge of imported ideas, which were all regarded as "new" during the years of the early republic, Li chose Marxism at China's ideological crossroads.[133] His conscious, active, and rational acceptance was accompanied by his country's existential crisis, which heightened his sense of duty for his nation's sake and prompted him to embrace this foreign ideology. His pioneering acceptance impacted his country through his long-term influence upon his followers, including Mao Zedong, who remarked in March 1949, prior to his establishment of the People's Republic, that "it was in Beijing that I met a great man whose name was Comrade Li Dazhao. Only with his help did I become a communist. He is truly my teacher."[134]

Taiwanese scholars have lamented the decline of liberal culture due to the Chinese acceptance of communism, which they contend was "a great loss to the development of liberalism in China."[135] For those scholars, the embrace of communism changed the liberal course of the New Culture Movement, directed China onto the path of radicalism, and pushed the country closer to violent revolution. For them, the embrace of communism made those radicals stand on the cliff-like promontory of a mountain from which they poured down a reddish dye to tinge the country red. Without a doubt, Li Dazhao's conversion was the very beginning of the process that ultimately painted China with that red color. Yet Li's experience shows that his thirst for national salvation compelled him toward the communist ideology. After his self-conversion, his country experienced a new trend: national salvation superseded enlightenment, revolutionary enthusiasm outperformed reasoning, and communism dwarfed liberalism. Nevertheless, Li was not a wily thug on the peak of that mountain; rather, he was a conscientious intellectual who was never obsessed with a faulty, unsteady view but was interested in the serious business of national salvation. As a matter of fact, his self-conversion obliged him to pursue a new kind of enlightenment, a new type of rationalism, and a new model of thinking, which was truly a loss to liberalism. It would, however, be the new direction for his country to follow.

From Li Dazhao's crucial role in the establishment of the CCP and his deep involvement in the early communist movement, we can see that he served as a medium between China's radical intellectuals and Soviet Russia. As an external factor, Soviet Russia was a potent force in the early communist movement in China. With Russian support, the CCP came into being. Without it, the CCP might have been established much later. After the founding of the CCP, the early communists continued to collaborate with Soviet Russia. Therefore, the initial stage of Chinese communist history was to follow the Russian model, for which Li labored tirelessly. Li accepted an ideological alliance with Soviet Russia, not out of any geopolitical consideration but from the perspective of national salvation. In his eyes, China was not intimidated by Soviet

Russia, which had extended an olive branch; in contrast, the imperialist powers had intensified their aggression, oppression, and exploitation of his country. Grappling with the issue of national salvation while dimly aware of the totalitarian nature of the Soviet regime, Li regarded Soviet Russia as the anti-imperialist stronghold. Following the Soviet model, he first vehemently engaged himself in labor movements, but the failure of the labor movement in 1923 taught him a serious lesson.[136] After the tragedy of the February Seventh Strike and once again under Russian guidance, he moved on to forge a united front with the Nationalist Party led by Sun Yat-sen, intending to fight against their common enemies: the imperialist powers and Chinese warlords.

Chapter 7

The United Front

Introduction

Scholars have long regarded the formation of the United Front between the Nationalist Party (Kuomintang, or KMT) and the Chinese Communist Party (CCP) in early 1924 as a milestone in modern Chinese history. In particular, the convention of the First National Congress of the KMT in Guangzhou in January 1924 was viewed as "the beginning of China's new political situation," as the historian Li Jiannong remarked in the 1930s.[1] This congress not only accomplished the goal of reorganizing the KMT, but it also marked the beginning of an important alliance between the two political parties to fight against their common enemies: the imperialist powers and Chinese warlords. It was this United Front that inaugurated the National Revolution (*Guomingeming*), or the Great Revolution (*Dageming*), which lasted for a few years until the Nationalist Party eventually overthrew the Beijing regime and started to govern China. However, the United Front was not a union of love; rather, it was a political coalition allowing the two parties to count on Soviet Russia's support for their revolutionary maneuvers. At this crucial moment, Li Dazhao was a principal figure pulling the strings behind the scenes. Yet his catalyst role in shaping the United Front is not given sufficient attention because scholars habitually focus on the tie between Sun Yat-sen and the USSR, or on the relationship between the two political parties, without acknowledging individual communists, such as Li, for their substantial contributions.

In fact, Li Dazhao labored diligently on numerous occasions for the formation of the United Front. First, he coordinated with the Comintern, with which the CCP was affiliated, to conceive the birth of this coalition. Second, he established a close personal relationship with the Nationalist leader, Sun Yat-sen, to reach a mutually endorsed agenda. In fact, Sun accorded Li a high level of intimacy as part of a small coterie, among whom Li was the one to materialize the plan for the United Front. Sun trusted Li so much that he personally admitted Li into the KMT, empowered Li to be a KMT leader in North China, and appointed Li to a number of leading positions within the KMT. Li did not fail Sun's expectations; he worked diligently to reach the projected goals. Third, Li endeavored to win support from the Chinese Communists, among whom many at first strongly rejected such a political alliance, which they saw as absurd because the two political parties did not share the same ultimate destination. Facing this internal resistance, Li tried his best to convince his fellow communists to accept the United Front. Indeed, he coordinated a wide variety of efforts and swayed them to adopt a realistic approach for their party, to accept the United Front, and to push for communist growth under the Nationalist umbrella.

The partnership between the two political parties supported by Soviet Russia proved pivotal, as the United Front ultimately assisted the KMT in overthrowing the warlord regime in Beijing, unifying China, and building a new central government. It was during those years that the United Front in effect transformed Li Dazhao into a professional revolutionary who toiled for national revolution industriously and persistently. At first, his hectic schedules working for the formation of this coalition consumed much of his time and energy: he traversed southward across the Yangtze River five times, frequented Shanghai in four trips, and visited Guangzhou twice between August 1922 and February 1924.[2] After the formation of the United Front, Li handled its routine operations and served as a bridge between the United Front and Soviet Russia and between the KMT and the CCP. Li's devotion to the United Front compelled him to depart from his academic life as he dedicated himself to the revolutionary cause. He was not a commander in chief, but he managed its overall military operations. He was not a common soldier, but he fought fiercely in numerous battles until he sacrificed his own life during the anti-warlord Northern Expedition launched by the United Front between 1926 and 1928.

An Alliance with Sun Yat-sen

Although Chinese scholars argue that Li Dazhao had previously developed his ideas on the issue of potential allies for the CCP, he was not the first to propose forging the United Front with the KMT. In fact, it was Soviet Russia that initiated this policy, which predated even the founding of the CCP. In 1920, Vladimir Lenin advocated a strategy at the Comintern conference for the young communist parties to ally with the nationalist organizations in their own countries.[3] As soon as the CCP was established, the Comintern expected it to establish such an alliance with the KMT. Bruce A. Elleman comments that the "Soviet motive . . . was to direct Chinese public opinion against Beijing," to support "Soviet diplomacy" and the fight against the Western powers; this move has been regarded as "red imperialism."[4] As a branch of the Comintern, the CCP had to follow the Comintern's directive in order to secure its support. Li Dazhao carried out this order faithfully and further persuaded the Chinese Communists to obey this directive.

The domestic situation equally compelled the early communists to seek an alliance in which a potential partner would be the KMT. To be perfectly honest, the CCP's initial policy of mobilizing the Chinese workers was a failure. Immediately after the disaster of the February Seventh Strike in 1923, Li Dazhao was furious at the massacre, over which he ended his long-standing friendship with Bai Jianwu, who then served as an advisor to Wu Peifu. The unsuccessful maneuver of the labor movement saddened the communists. Deng Zhongxia admitted that "all the workers' organizations collapsed, except for just a few in Guangzhou and Hunan."[5] The cruel reality that the enemy was too strong and that the CCP was too weak prompted the communists to reflect over their revolutionary strategies. Moreover, the CCP remained a secret group that was denigrated as a dangerous party. If it were allied with Sun Yat-sen, the CCP could utilize the KMT's open status for its wider operations.[6] The CCP's financial reliance on the Comintern meant that it had to follow its order. For example, 94 percent of the CCP revenue came from the Comintern, and the total income from its own membership fees and miscellaneous earnings accounted for only a small fraction between October 1921 and June 1922, a situation that would remain roughly unchanged until 1927.[7] Therefore, the communists had no choice but to obey the Comintern directive in forging an alliance with Sun Yat-sen.

Habitually, scholars have highlighted the role of Maring (Ma Lin) as a matchmaker for the United Front, but they have neglected the fact that Li Dazhao served as a medium between Maring and Sun Yat-sen. Maring was the nickname of a Dutch communist, Hendricus Sneevliet. He lived in Dutch Indonesia for five years, during which he established a radical group and forged an alliance with other local organizations. For doing so, he was expelled from Indonesia by the Dutch authorities in 1918. Two years later, he went to Soviet Russia and became a Comintern agent. Maring was dispatched to China in 1921 to help the Chinese communists build the CCP, after which he urged the CCP to establish an alliance with the KMT. At this critical moment, it was Li Dazhao who arranged the meetings between Maring and Sun Yat-sen in late 1921. Maring proceeded to Guilin for his meetings with Sun three times, during which he persuaded Sun to accept the idea of the united front.[8] In the next couple of years, Maring lived in China and helped implement the Comintern policy of the CCP-KMT alliance. Facing the resistance of Chinese Communists, Maring carried out this policy so resolutely that he even refused to answer questions from the Chinese Communists. Testimonies are filled with anecdotes about Maring's arrogance; for instance, Zhang Guotao accused him of acting as a white supremacist.[9] Nevertheless, Maring believed that the United Front would assist the CCP to reach its potential, for the sake of which he would enforce the Comintern directive. The formation of such a united front might have been out of the question without Maring's forceful implementation and without Li Dazhao's support and arrangement.[10]

The proposal for a united front occurred during Sun Yat-sen's worst moment, and he saw this coalition, together with Soviet aid, as a source of hope for restructuring and reviving the Nationalist Party and realizing the dream of unifying China. Sun was respected as the vanguard, the leader at the forefront of the Chinese revolution who had contributed to the collapse of the Qing dynasty. Soon after the 1911 Revolution, however, he was "seen more as a liability than an asset" for his nation, according to American missionaries in China at that time, because he launched his revolution from abroad and supposedly lacked basic knowledge of his own country. Being viewed "in a negative light as an obstacle to the peaceful reunification of China," Sun was abandoned by the Western powers, which recognized the Beijing warlord regime as the legitimate Chinese government.[11] Although Sun established his own government in Guangzhou later, his regime was not recognized by any Western powers. Furthermore, Sun's ties with warlords tarnished his own reputation.[12] In Guangzhou in June 1922, Chen Jiongming mutinied, bombed Sun's presidential office, and besieged Sun in a battleship on a lake for about a month. Although Sun later escaped safely to Shanghai, he was perplexed and depressed. Unravelling the puzzle of his political future, Sun felt that he needed reliable allies domestically as well as internationally.

It is not hard to imagine Sun Yat-sen's excitement when he met Li Dazhao in Shanghai in August 1922 to discuss the issue of an alliance. Needless to say, Sun was elated that Soviet Russia had handed him an olive branch. His growing optimism in the USSR was stirred by the rapid success of the Russian regime and its quick move of power consolidation. He viewed Soviet Russia positively and saw it as a potential ally. Consequently, Sun's vision between his Three People's Principles and the communist ideology, according to some scholars, became blurred; in particular, he regarded his own principle of people's livelihood as almost equivalent to the communist objective.[13] As Alexander V. Pantsov interprets, "Sun called his program socialist and sometimes even communist."[14] Sun carefully calculated the possible benefit of an alliance with the CCP, which was a tiny organization that could be easily absorbed into the KMT. Hence, in his view, the acceptance of the communists into his party would be more a benefit than a harm.[15] According to Li Yunhan, a Taiwanese scholar, Sun intended to assimilate the Chinese Communists, put them under his control, and prevent them from instigating conspiracies in a long-term stratagem.[16] In other words, Sun's view of the prospective advantages compelled him to accept the United Front in order to maximize the gains for his party.

It is wrong to assume that all of the early communists were intrigued by the policy of a united front. In fact, the acceptance of this policy was neither easy nor undisputed. The primary sources demonstrate that there was no overt willingness to accept it from the very beginning. During the two-year intraparty debate over it, Li Dazhao was a key figure in persuading his fellow communists to accept the United Front. The issue at the heart was the early communists' aspiration to strive for communism and to labor for the proletarian revolution as an unadulterated goal. Indeed, a policy was even adopted to avoid a partnership with any other political parties at the first CCP national congress in July 1921. Yet the Comintern mandate required them to forge a united front with the KMT, which naturally confused the Chinese Communists. Li was the first one to accept it, and he pressed for its implementation. Thanks to his efforts, a new policy was adopted at the second CCP National Congress, held in Shanghai in July 1922, under which the Communists could cooperate with other political parties in order to fight for a true, democratic, and independent country. Although Li did not attend the conference, he vehemently pushed for his party to accept this policy.[17]

The policy of building a united front with the KMT continued to cause intrapartisan disputes among the Chinese Communists. The issue at stake was whether the CCP should join the KMT as a party or the communists themselves should join it as individual KMT members. To solve the problem, the Communists held the Xihu Meeting (Xihuhuiyi) in Hangzhou on August 29–30, 1922. Because Sun Yat-sen only allowed the communists to join the KMT as individual members, Maring supported this approach at the Xihu Meeting. However, it met resistance from Chen Duxiu and Zhang Guotao, who promoted bipartisan partnership or intrapartisan cooperation because they viewed the KMT as a bourgeois political organization and the CCP a proletarian party.[18] Maring acted resolutely to carry out the Comintern mandate at this meeting. Just at this critical moment, Li Dazhao gave his full support to Maring. Li argued that the KMT was a loose organization within which even anarchists had become members, and, moreover, communist participation could help the KMT make a huge change. Li told his fellow communists that Sun Yat-sen had rejected the idea of partisan partnership, so the only way to form the United Front would be for the communists to join the KMT as individual members. However, Li advised his fellow communists to retain their own identity, maintain their independence, and continue their work organizing trade unions. In other words, the CCP would continue to exist as an independent political organization. Under Li's persuasion during the two-day debate, the Xihu Meeting passed a resolution deciding that the communists would join the KMT as individual Nationalist members, but they would continue to be independent, autonomous, and disciplined communists.[19]

It must be noted that Li Dazhao and Sun Yat-sen's personal relationship played a role in the final formation of the United Front. Immediately after the Xihu Meeting, Li traveled to Shanghai to meet with the Nationalist leader in late August 1922. According to Li's own testimony, he "went to Shanghai to converse personally with Sun Yat-sen, discuss the approach to reviving the Nationalist Party, and elaborate the way of national resurgence."[20] Li stayed in Shanghai for weeks carrying out his private discussions with Sun. Li remembered that each conversation lasted for hours and that they even forgot their scheduled meals. Moreover, although the CCP was tiny, it was capable of serving as a medium between the KMT and Soviet Russia, which was a life-changing gift to the otherwise helpless Sun Yat-sen. In Shanghai, Sun presided over a special ceremony in which Li took an oath joining the KMT. A few months later, Li introduced Adolph Abramovich Joffe, a Russian diplomat, to Sun. In January 1923, Sun and Joffe issued a joint proclamation for bilateral ties between the KMT and Soviet Russia. In October 1923, Sun requested that Li secretly visit him in Shanghai to review the detailed arrangements for the United Front. The mutually cordial relationship was described by Sun's wife Song Qingling: "Sun Yat-sen especially admired and respected Li Dazhao. We always welcomed him to our home. After meeting those [communist] guests, Sun often remarked that those men were his true revolutionary comrades. He knew that he could rely on their unequivocal thoughts and their daring courage for his own upcoming revolution."[21]

The abovementioned efforts of Li Dazhao underscore his upper-level interaction with Chinese Communist leaders as well as his personal communications with the Nationalist leader. But the United Front was not a one-time, petty matter, because it required all of the Communists to endorse it. This proved to be a challenge, as many of them were unenthusiastic, nonchalant, and resistant. Thus, Li ramped up his efforts to persuade them to understand its importance. According to Bao Huisheng's memoir, Li gathered together the local communist leaders in Beijing to discuss this issue at a meeting in early 1923. The Comintern agents who attended this meeting demanded unconditional support, but most of the local leaders viewed the United Front as potentially harmful to communist unity, camaraderie, and purity. It was at this crucial point that Li strongly endorsed the United Front agreement and stressed the importance for retaining communist autonomy and independence once the United Front was forged. He reasoned that the anti-imperialist and anti-feudal revolution necessitated this alliance, because "it was too premature for the Communist Party to assume the sole leadership role for the United Front." He told the communists that the KMT would be an ally after its upcoming reorganization, although it was not a cohesive organization and it lacked strict discipline. With the Communists joining, bringing in "new blood," the United Front of the two parties would yield a positive outcome.[22] Li's impact upon his fellow Communists on this matter should not be minimized, because his fervor for the United Front did not waver and because he continued to win over his fellow Communists to its acceptance.

To mobilize Communist support for the United Front, Li Dazhao published "The Countrywide Nationalist Party" on April 18, 1923, in which he underscored the necessity of a nationwide Nationalist Party for a new national revolution. He traced the KMT's history from the overseas Chinese diaspora to Guangdong Province. Although it became a national organization after the 1911 Revolution, it was "a flower without a root" (*wugendehua*). After the Second Revolution, the party devoted too much attention to military resistance to the Beijing government without first mobilizing the masses, without an effective organization, and without an efficient propaganda machine. Li lamented that the KMT did not establish any grassroots organizations in the larger swath of Central China and North China. However, the party had a glorious history because of its role in establishing the republic. Now it was time for the Chinese people to gather together under its banner to form a united front to fight against warlords and the imperialist powers. With the people's participation, Li expected that the KMT would no longer be an organization in Guangdong or in the overseas diaspora but would become "a successful countrywide Nationalist Party."[23]

The barrier to the United Front was not totally cleared, although many Communists endorsed and accepted it after considering Li Dazhao's persuasion. Thus, the agenda of the third CCP National Congress was to make a formal decision on this issue. The congress was held in Guangzhou on June 12–20, 1923, during which the Communists continued to debate but still could not reach a unanimous consensus. Zhang Guotao and Cai Hesen opposed the idea of allowing all Communists to join the KMT, but Li Dazhao and Chen Duxiu supported it. To solve the problem, a vote was conducted through secret ballots. Among the forty who participated, twenty-one voted *yea*, sixteen voted *nay*, and three abstained.[24] With a marginal majority, the CCP passed the resolution to endorse the United Front by allowing all Communists to join the KMT as individual members. Li Dazhao's speech at the congress had been long lost in China; however, an account of it has been found in a recently discovered notebook of Maring. Li proclaimed an optimistic hope for the United Front and encouraged the Communists to stand at the forefront as the vanguard of the upcoming national revolution.[25] It was at this meeting that Li was elected a member of the CCP central committee. Five days later, Li Dazhao, Chen Duxiu, Cai Hesen, Tan Pingshan, and Mao Zedong wrote a letter to Sun Yat-sen advising the Nationalist leader to take new measures, adopt new guidelines, gather new forces, and build a new country. They suggested that Sun should build a new army in order to strengthen the KMT. They also advised Sun to move to Shanghai to convene the National Assembly. This letter was found only recently in the Maring archives in Holland, and it reveals those Communists' fervor for the national revolution under Sun Yat-sen's leadership immediately after they had decided to join the KMT.[26]

For the rest of 1923, Li Dazhao was empowered by Sun Yat-sen to establish local Nationalist units and to recruit new members. Working in the political center of the warlord regime in Beijing, Li felt the difficulty of his new role. He wrote in December 1923 that "the path of history is not always flat and smooth, as it sometimes could be full of dangers and perils." Nonetheless, he was confident of the future and encouraged his countrymen "to assume high spirits, sing the marching song, and brave the journey through a dangerous road with a solemn and stirring tune."[27] In particular, he called on the youth to "transform the country and revitalize the nation."[28] Under the leadership of Li Dazhao, many youth joined the KMT, and its membership reached three thousand in Beijing in November 1923, among whom one third were communists or members of other communism-affiliated organizations such as the Socialist Youth League.[29] By late 1923 and early 1924, Li's job was to commission a list of six representatives to attend the upcoming first KMT National Congress, to be held in Guangzhou. According to Sun Yat-sen's arrangement, Li Dazhao, Tan Xihong, and Shi Ying, who were the local Nationalist leaders in Beijing, would be the specially selected representatives. The other three would be elected by the local Nationalist members. Li Dazhao presided over the KMT membership meeting in Beijing on January 4, 1923, which was attended by a big crowd who voted to select Xu Baoju, Zhang Guotao, and Tan Kemin as the additional three representatives. Within a week, this group of six, led by Li, arrived in Guangzhou.[30]

Laboring for the United Front

As the reader will recall, the formal formation of the United Front took place at the first KMT National Congress on January 20–30, 1924. After a few days' travel from Beijing to Shanghai via the railway, Li Dazhao's entourage then took a steamship and arrived in Guangzhou on January 11. Because Li stayed at Sun Yat-sen's official residence, he was able to frequently discuss with Sun on various important issues before, during, and after the conference. Among the 196 representatives at the congress, twenty-three were communists, or more than 10 percent of the total. More importantly, communists such as Li played an important role in the reorganized Nationalist Party. For this congress, Li was one of the five members of the presidium and served as the conference chair on January 28. Also, he was a member of the supervision committee, a member of the party program committee, and a member of the propaganda committee. Indeed, he assumed the most important positions and bore the heaviest duty at this congress.[31] Because the proclamation was drafted by Michael Borodin, the Soviet agent, it reflected the Russian expectations for the Nationalist Party's anti-imperialist and anti-feudalist objectives. At this conference, Sun Yat-sen's alliance with Soviet Russia and the Communist bond with the Comintern were two parallel international ties. Inside this intricate web of relationships, the CCP played a special role in a coordinated maneuver by the three partners. It was during this conference that the news of Lenin's death arrived. Li spoke at the memorial service, hailed Lenin as a liberator of the oppressed peoples, lamented his death as a huge loss to the Chinese people, and called for his compatriots to carry on Lenin's spirit in the fight against imperialism and feudalism.[32]

Although Li Dazhao enjoyed Sun Yat-sen's trust, he encountered recalcitrant resistance from a number of KMT members at the conference. On January 28, 1924, when the party program was deliberated, Fang Ruilin, who was the Nationalist representative from Guangzhou, challenged the idea of allowing the Communists to join the KMT. Fang cited the Nationalist tradition of prohibiting transpartisan membership. Facing this defiance, Li circulated his "My Opinion" ("Yijianshu") among all representatives, in which he argued that the arduous tasks of the anti-imperialist and anti-feudalist enterprise necessitated such a united front. He declared that the Communists had a noble spirit of fighting against the common enemies without any intention of taking advantage of this coalition. He stated that the CCP aimed at serving as a bridge between the KMT and Soviet Russia, as it was a branch of the Comintern. He criticized the rumor concerning a possible Communist scheme of turning the Nationalist Party into the Communist Party. He declared that Chinese Communists joined the KMT as individual members rather than as a political organization. He swore that the Communists would abide by the KMT program and would accept punishment in case of any violations. Furthermore, he utilized Sun Yat-sen's fame to defend the United Front, which had long been endorsed by the Nationalist leader.[33] With Li's persuasion, the program was passed successfully, yet it left behind a lingering rage in the minds of the right-wing Nationalists, who sowed the seeds of the upcoming schism three years later.

The first National Congress of the KMT exerted a wide-ranging impact upon modern China, as many scholars agree. Sun Yat-sen was confident that he could obtain Russian support and that he could "absorb" the Chinese Communists into his party (*ronggong*). In any case, the first KMT congress initiated the National Revolution, which ultimately enabled the KMT to seize national power four years later. The Communists, though small in number, posited themselves as a de facto block and situated themselves within the special alliance. This extraordinary arrangement allowed the Communists to penetrate the Nationalist leadership sector, as ten among forty-one newly elected full and alternative members of the party's executive committee were Communists. Of course, Li Dazhao was a full member. Chinese historians hail this congress for anchoring the three new policies of partnering with Russia, allying with the Communists, and giving support to peasants and workers for the Nationalist program.[34] Needless to repeat, Li was a paramount communist figure whose performance was exceptional, as in the memory of He Xiangning:

> For the reorganization of the Nationalist Party, the first National Congress was held in Guangzhou in January 1924. Mr. Li Dazhao and I were representatives. His cordial attitude and honest integrity were impressive. His thorough and insightful talks were persuasive. His outstanding theory played an extremely important role in Sun Yat-sen's reorganization of the party and Sun's adoption of the three policies of partnering with Soviet Russia, allying with the communists, and giving support to peasants and workers. All his words were correct as we look back at the page of history. After the conference, Li departed from Guangzhou. Nevertheless, he always stays in our memory.[35]

To facilitate the Nationalist Party's operations and expansion, the KMT decided to establish its local executive departments (*zhixingbu*) in Beijing, Shanghai, Hankou, Harbin, and Sichuan. In reality, only three such departments were built, in Beijing, Shanghai, and Harbin, after the one in Hankou was soon disbanded.[36] The Executive Department of Beijing was founded on April 30, 1924, with Li Dazhao as a major leader. The department bore a resemblance to the central committee by establishing seven divisions, in charge of organization, propaganda, youth, workers, peasants, investigation, and women. In a way, the Executive Department of Beijing was a perfect example of the United Front between the two political parties, while Li's leadership role ensured communication, reciprocity, and collaboration.[37] The department rented a compound in Beijing to handle daily routines, established provincial branches in North China, recruited new members, and sponsored local units in more than ten northern provinces. Chinese scholars argue that Li's leadership created a new situation, as it ended the previously deplorable situation in which the Nationalist Party was only activated in South China.[38] As a result, the Nationalist membership had expanded to fourteen thousand in the northern provinces by October 1925.[39]

Following the new anti-imperialist and anti-feudal policy of the United Front, Li Dazhao vented his anger at the imperialist powers, pushed for anti-imperialist propaganda, and disseminated pro-Russian messages. In just a couple of months after the KMT congress, Li wrote to praise Lenin's spirit in liberating the oppressed nations and to grieve over his death.[40] He advised the Chinese to remember the painful history (*tongshi*) of imperialist invasions and encouraged them to restore national sovereignty, eliminate national shame, and free China from imperialist aggression. He branded "international imperialism as the only vicious enemy of our nation."[41] In early June 1924, Li published an article condemning the media of the West for spreading the rumor of Sun Yat-sen's death, which caused a panic in Guangzhou. Calling it a cultural invasion, Li proposed expelling the creators of the rumor and limiting Western reporters' activities inside China.[42] On January 17, 1925, Li delivered a speech at Beijing Normal University praising Sun Yat-sen for hoisting the banner of national liberation, exposing the evildoings of the imperialist powers, and demanding the abolition of the unequal treaties. Li criticized the wrong perception that the current anti-imperialist movement was nothing more than a revived Boxer Rebellion and argued that the ongoing revolution intended to target imperialist invaders but not to harm foreign nationals who legally resided in China.[43]

In contrast to his anti-imperialist stance, Li Dazhao supported the Soviet Union, endorsed diplomatic ties with the USSR, and pressed the Beijing government to recognize Soviet Russia. In February and March 1924, Li Dazhao along with other intellectuals in Beijing wrote two letters to Wellington Koo (Gu Weijun), the foreign minister of the Beijing government, to press him for Soviet diplomatic recognition.[44] When the ongoing negotiation with Russia was halted, Li and other intellectuals published an article to emphasize the Soviet declaration of relinquishing Russian privileges in China and calling for diplomatic ties with Soviet Russia.[45] In March 1924, Li and other Beijing University professors organized a delegation, with Li as the leader, to visit the foreign ministry. Koo met the delegation and recorded what happened in his memoir. Koo stressed the importance of the Outer Mongolia issue, because the USSR had requested that it be excluded in the bilateral negotiation. Koo wrote:

> If those treaties concerning Outer Mongolia were excluded from the unequal treaties, we may acquiesce in a situation where it is no longer the territory of China. Professor Li Dazhao's reply extremely shocked me. He said that the people there might live a better life even if Outer Mongolia were dominated and ruled by Soviet Russia. He talked in such an excited mood that I felt that he had lost his mind in terms of distinguishing right from wrong. I told him that he might express his own view or stick to his own stance, but as the foreign minister I had the duty to preserve China's territorial sovereignty and totality and to avoid the infringement of foreign forces. Seeing that Professor Li Dazhao's opinion differed completely from mine, I told him that I did not need to discuss this issue with him due to conflicting views. Therefore, I voiced my pardon and bid goodbye to the delegation.[46]

The publication of Wellington Koo's memoir in China in 2013 came as a thunderbolt to the mainland Chinese who have regarded Li Dazhao as a patriot. Thus, Koo's memoir led to diverse interpretations. Chinese scholars defended Li's Marxist view of internationalism, which they say led to Koo's "misunderstanding." They regard Koo as a narrow-minded bureaucrat, charge Koo with being an inaccurate writer, and see him as a prejudiced individual. In their eyes, Koo's memoir was unilateral tittle-tattle.[47] In any case, Li's tenacious efforts to recognize the USSR ultimately panned out well, as the Beijing government and the Soviet Union established diplomatic ties on May 31, 1924.[48]

Li Dazhao continued to offer his analysis of the national situation, elaborated on important domestic issues, and supported the National Revolution. Much that transpired in 1924 gave witness to the country being in a chaotic condition, as warlords continued to wage civil wars, in particular the Second Zhili-Fengtian War between Wu Peifu and Zhang Zuolin. Being confident of his victory after winning the First Zhili-Fengtian War against Zhang, Wu himself commanded his troops on the front line. Unexpectedly, Wu's subordinate Feng Yuxiang defected, marched back to Beijing, and overthrew the government under Wu's control, which is known as the Beijing Coup (Beijingzhengbian). Feng then reorganized his troops into the National Army (Guominjun) with three armies controlling a number of regions of North China. Feng also drove the last, briefly restored Qing emperor, Puyi, out of the Forbidden City. Feng's actions led to the military failure of Wu Peifu, who fled to Hubei Province to consolidate his power there. Facing the new situation, Li Dazhao became a lobbyist trying to lure Feng's National Army over to the Nationalist side. One move Li took was to visit Hu Jingyi, who was the commander of Feng's Second Army stationed in Kaifeng, the capital of Henan Province, in late 1924. Hu had met Sun Yat-sen in Japan and had joined the Revolutionary Alliance. Later, Hu was enlisted in Feng Yuxiang's army and soon became a military commander. During the meeting with Hu, Li Dazhao helped Hu design a plan for local affairs, promised to request Soviet advisers to train Hu's army, and promised Hu Russian munitions. Li dispatched his men to work within Hu's army with the intention of turning Hu's army into a reliable force for the National Revolution. Soon after Li's departure from Kaifeng around New Year's Day, Soviet advisers arrived in Kaifeng, and Russian-made weapons were also delivered there. Unfortunately, the unexpected death of Hu soon dashed Li's original plan.[49]

After Feng Yuxiang's "Beijing Coup," the situation in the whole country abruptly changed. To prevent either Zhang Zuolin or Duan Qirui from monopolizing power, Feng invited Sun Yat-sen to come to Beijing to deal with national affairs. Viewing it as a chance for China's unification, Sun Yat-sen departed from Guangzhou on November 13, 1924. He stopped over in Hong Kong, Shanghai, Nagasaki, and arrived in Tianjin on December 4. On the way, Sun Yat-sen delivered speeches to emphasize his struggle for national unification. Li Dazhao dispatched Zhao Shiyan to greet Sun in Tianjin. Finally, Sun arrived in Beijing on December 31. Li Dazhao participated in a huge rally at the railway station to welcome Sun and escorted him to a hotel. Following Sun's order, Li did not circulate printed leaflets that contained anti-warlord messages but withheld them in order to create a more conducive milieu for Sun's dialogue with the Beijing government, and to avoid increasing tension and ruining the opportunity.[50]

To coordinate with Sun Yat-sen, Li Dazhao led the Nationalists and Communists in Beijing to launch the National Assembly Movement to defy the ruling warlords. To an extent, it was to challenge Duan Qirui's maneuvers to convene the Reconstruction Conference (shanhouhuiyi) for a settlement after the Second Zhili-Fengtian War. Duan Qirui's refusal to make a change to the unequal treaties and Zhang Zuolin's demand that Sun Yat-sen break with Soviet Russia enraged the Nationalist leader. Subsequently, Sun Yat-sen's followers launched the National Assembly Movement. Soon after the convention of the Reconstruction Conference on February 1, 1925, which was attended by the representatives of the warlords and politicians, Li Dazhao convened the Congress of the National Assembly Promotion Association at Beijing University on March 1. More than two hundred representatives from more than twenty provinces gathered together to work on its anti-imperialist and anti-warlord agenda. Li was elected one of the five members of the presidium.[51] Li spoke at the association's meetings and served as the chair of one of the four committees. At its closing ceremony on April 16, Li was elected one of the seven members of the standing committee. The coexistence of two conferences in Beijing, one by Duan Qirui and another by Li Dazhao, demonstrates the conflicting interests of two political camps. In this way, with his persistent efforts, Li inspired the Chinese to participate in the National Revolution.

Besides the campaign against Chinese warlords and the imperialist powers, Li Dazhao had to deal with internal rivalry within the United Front, which turned out to be his other battlefield. It was not an inner partisan dispute but a partywide crisis. Because Sun Yat-sen had become sick after his arrival, the right-wing Nationalists took the opportunity to call for the decoupling of the KMT and the CCP. At first, the move for separation was led by the veteran Nationalist Feng Ziyou, who was born in Japan but became a follower of Sun Yat-sen. In January 1925, Feng Ziyou organized the League to Defend the Party (Weidangtongmeng) in Beijing to oppose Li Dazhao's leadership role. Soon, Feng expanded the league to become a larger organization called the Club of Nationalist Comrades (Tongzhijulebu). More shockingly, more than two thousand attended the founding ceremony of this club; in reaction to this threat, Li requested that the KMT central executive committee punish Feng's separatism.[52] Not very long afterward, Feng's plot to seize power encountered strong resistance from the left-wing Nationalists, which resulted in Feng's expulsion from the KMT.[53]

Li Dazhao's role in the United Front around the time of Sun Yat-sen's death deserves our attention. Needless to say, Sun's death was a huge loss to the KMT and served as a milestone in the history of the United Front. After his arrival in Tianjin, Sun's health started to deteriorate. He was diagnosed with a liver problem in Beijing in early January, which was confirmed as liver cancer after surgery on January 26, 1925. Under a weakened condition, Sun appointed nine prominent Nationalists as political commissioners (Zhengzhiweiyuan) who were obligated to carry out Sun's former duties, among whom was Li Dazhao. By early March, Sun was in a coma, and he passed away on March 12, 1925. Li served as a member of the funeral committee with the particular responsibility of drafting documents. Having been a prominent figure, Sun attracted many mourners. Consequently, the funeral committee received seven thousand wreaths, five hundred elegiac couplets, and 750,000 mourning signatures, while more than two million people paid their last respects to Sun. On March 26, Li was one of the coffin bearers who delivered Sun's coffin from the hospital to Zhongyang Park (today's Zhongshan Park). On April 2, Li participated in transporting Sun's remains to Biyun Temple at West Hill in Beijing's western suburb.[54] Li Dazhao authored a memorial elegy praising Sun as a great revolutionary who hoisted the banner of national independence, fought for forty years to free the Chinese people from imperialist dominance, assisted workers and peasants, and strove to establish a truly democratic republic.[55]

Li Dazhao's dedication to the United Front verifies the communist contribution to the ongoing National Revolution, yet this does not mean that Li did not care for the communist cause. In fact, the membership of the CCP grew at an unprecedented rate, as it expanded rapidly from early 1924 to early 1927 and in numerical data from four hundred to

57,000 persons nationwide.[56] Utilizing the opportunity of the Beijing Coup, Li Dazhao lobbied the National Army led by Feng Yuxiang to release the workers arrested previously by Wu Peifu. Under Li's leadership, trade unions were reactivated. On February 7, 1925, the rally of the General Railway Workers Union was convened in Zhengzhou, for which Li published his article entreating the workers to continue their battles against the imperialist powers and Chinese warlords.[57] However, any exaggeration in regard to the Communist growth should be forestalled, because its membership tally remained small throughout the country. The dual identity as simultaneously both Nationalists and Communists confused some, who later indeed chose to be Nationalists only and quit their Communist membership.[58] Li often complained to the Comintern in his reports that it was not easy to mobilize workers and peasants.[59] He requested that the Comintern dispatch talented Chinese students from Moscow back to China to handle local routines.[60] He asked the Comintern to mail him more communism-related publications, particularly those in English, for the purpose of propaganda.[61]

A Visit to the Soviet Union

Li Dazhao's five-month visit to the USSR from June to December 1924 should be viewed as an important episode in his life. This visit has not been neglected, but it has not attracted sufficient attention. Consequently, many of his activities there have been left out in Li Dazhao studies.[62] Of course, the lack of primary sources was the major reason. Li's visit was a secret inside China, and his assumption of a pseudonym (Qin Hua) in Soviet Russia did not help with keeping track of all his activities. The rift between the USSR and China from the early 1960s to the late 1980s was also a barrier for Chinese scholars wishing to retrieve the related primary sources from Russia. During the ten-year Cultural Revolution, nobody would dare to study Li since Mao loomed large and other early communists were overlooked. Therefore, Li's visit to Soviet Russia remained an obscure journey for a long time. The situation gradually changed after Mao's death. Not only did memoirs narrate Li's visit, but Russian sources became available after the 1980s. For example, Li Dazhao's articles published in Russian were released in 1985 and were immediately translated into Chinese.[63] Li's letters to the Comintern and Russian officials were also discovered. With these materials, Li's visit is no longer a perpetuated myth; on the contrary, a relatively clear picture has steadily appeared.

The assumption that Li Dazhao's visit to the USSR was to learn more about communism and strengthen his communist belief is logical, as he portrayed Soviet Russia as the socialist motherland and the headquarters of the global communist movements.[64] The aim of his visit, however, was to attend the fifth Comintern Conference, a special gathering of fifty communist parties from around the entire world. Nevertheless, a careful study of the primary sources shows that Li mainly worked for the anti-imperialist and anti-warlord objectives of the United Front. In his interactions with Soviet Russians and the communists from other countries, Li tried to secure their support for China's ongoing National Revolution, since some communist parties might still have regarded China as a revolutionary backwater. Of course, this is not to downgrade his visit's role in advancing his communist beliefs, since his communist faith was indeed reinforced. Nevertheless, his efforts for winning over international support were the diplomacy of sympathy for Sun Yat-sen's revolutionary cause. In Russia, Li always praised Sun for his distinguished status as "the old ancestor of revolution" (*geminglaozu*) and emphasized Sun's importance in China. To his amazement, he found that Sun Yat-sen already enjoyed a reputation in the USSR, and the Russian author of the Sun Yat-sen biography even gave a copy of it to Li.[65]

The availability of new sources now enables us to trace Li Dazhao's journey, even though not all his activities are crystal clear. For example, the dates of his departure for Russia remain a topic of debate. By scrutinizing a variety of materials, scholars claim that Li left Beijing around June 12, 1924;[66] this differs from Li's daughter's memoir, which asserts that Li arrived in Moscow a couple of weeks earlier, prior to the start of the Comintern conference.[67] If Li traveled to Moscow through Manchuria and Siberia in two weeks, he should have arrived in late June, which means that he missed the first few days of the conference that started on June 17.[68] In any case, Li attended the conference, at which he submitted his reports. After the conference, he continued to stay in Russia as the CCP representative to the Comintern. He left Moscow on December 3, according to a bulletin published by Chinese students, and was back in Beijing around mid-December after a return journey taking a couple of weeks.[69]

The next issue concerns the identities of those individuals who accompanied Li Dazhao on the journey. Li's daughter Li Xinghua's memoir states that five people went along with him to Moscow: Wang Hebo, Yao Zuomin, Liu Qingyang, Peng Zexiang, and Bu Shiqi.[70] Yet some argue that only four communists went along: Li Dazhao, Wang Hebo, Liu Qingyang, and Peng Shuzhi.[71] Luo Zhanglong claimed that he went along and witnessed Li's diligent work for the delegation.[72] Li's daughter stated that Luo did not accompany Li but arrived in Moscow a little later.[73] Some scholars contend that Luo Zhanglong's memory might be inaccurate, as no evidence so far verifies his presence.[74] According to some sources, Zhao Shiyan, who was already in Moscow, joined the delegation.[75] Diverse memoirs cannot help reach an accurate list of attendees, and this topic may continue to be of interest to scholars. But it is an ironclad fact that Li Dazhao's leadership status in the CCP enabled him to be the head of this delegation.

Despite conflicting memories and diverse documents, we at least can obtain a clear picture of the route Li took to Moscow. When he received the notice from the Comintern for the conference, Li was hiding in Wufeng Mountain to avoid arrest by the Beijing government. Then, he secretly returned to Beijing to meet other delegates. Around June 12, 1924, the delegation departed from Beijing through the railways to Harbin, where they handled paperwork with the Russian consulate. It is said that Li received financial support of five hundred yuan from his friend Yang Fuqing for this trip. After his arrival in Harbin, he stayed at Wang Fangtian's home for three days before proceeding to Manzhouli through the Chinese Eastern Railway.[76] Li and his entourage spent one night at a Russian hotel, secured horse-driven carts, hired reliable drivers, and crossed the border the next morning through a secret road to the Russian side. Without any passports, they only carried Russian consular documents to verify their identities. To the Chinese government, it was an illegal crossing. But Li's delegation steeled their nerves and arrived in the Russian territory safely.[77]

To Li Dazhao's elation, his group arrived in Moscow in late June after seven days of travel on the Trans-Siberia Railway. Although Li missed the first days of the Comintern conference, he caught the remaining program before it adjourned on July 8, 1924. According to his own writing, he witnessed the vigor of the international communist movement as the representatives from fifty countries gathered together. He himself did not draw public attention, because China was not the main topic on the Comintern agenda. The original plan allowed him to deliver an oral report on China, yet an unforeseen rearrangement by the conference chair deprived Li of this opportunity. Rather, his report was submitted to the Comintern to be included in the conference proceedings. Later, his report was summarized and published in *Pravda* and was not translated into Chinese until 1985.[78] In it, Li lamented the Chinese people's suffering under the imperialist powers and Chinese warlords, the latter being "the running dogs" of the former.[79] Li exposed the recent aggressive incidents of imperialist powers to which the Chinese government had capitulated. Li introduced the United Front, in which the KMT and the CCP fought together against their common enemies. He praised Sun Yat-sen's reorganization of his party for the purpose of mobilizing the Chinese people for the National Revolution. He praised the Chinese Communists as the vanguard but acknowledged their juvenile status. Nevertheless, he underscored the Communists' activities in the labor movement. Overall, Li focused more on the United Front, for which he called for more international support. Rather than going along with the conference's theme of Bolshevizing the communist parties participating in the Comintern, Li elaborated more on China's United Front and highlighted its importance as a new phase of the Chinese revolution.[80]

Li Dazhao's call for help during his visit to the USSR had impacted the upcoming Do Not Interfere in China Movement. After the conference ended, Li prolonged his stay as the CCP representative to the Comintern. He moved from the Lux Hotel to the dormitory of the Communist University of the Toilers of the East, known as KUTV, where a lot of Chinese nationals had registered as students.[81] What happened in China a few weeks later shocked the world. The Canton Merchants' Corps smuggled weapons from Hong Kong into Guangzhou (Canton), intending to overthrow Sun Yat-sen's revolutionary government. But the ship *Harvard* carrying those weapons was detained by Sun's troops, which caused an international sensation, as the British government dispatched nine warships to Guangzhou intending to force Sun to deliver those weapons to the corps. Li's call for supporting Sun Yat-sen received an enthusiastic response, and the Comintern launched a global movement to denounce the British interference in China's internal affairs. Li himself attended rallies and joined demonstrations, at which he was deeply moved by the Russian support.

As soon as he moved to KUTV, Li Dazhao found that the university had lapsed into its summer recess. Taking advantage of this opportunity, he visited Moscow and Leningrad (St. Petersburg). He was particularly excited to travel to Leningrad, where the October Revolution started. Li toured the city along with an interpreter and a sailor. What especially moved him was that the local council, the Soviet, in the name of the 400,000 workers of Leningrad, dispatched a telegraph to the British workers calling on them to resist Ramsay MacDonald's interventionist policy. When Li visited a local rubber factory, a large manufacturing plant of eight thousand workers, he was invited to attend a rally at which the workers denounced Britain's interventionist intentions and passed a resolution condemning any such a potential move.[82] One day, a hundred thousand workers and young children staged a huge demonstration at the Winter Palace. Li was escorted up the speaker's platform while the crowd shouted, "Long live the Chinese revolution!" During that evening, a big rally was held in the nearby park. While celebrating a children's festival, children from Russia and Germany spoke to protest the imperialist embroilment in China. During those days, according to Li, many such demonstrations were organized in Russian cities.[83] Consequently, according to Li's understanding, so much paramount pressure was placed upon the British government that it did not directly intervene in the upcoming suppression of the Canton Merchants' Corps by Sun Yat-sen.

The most memorable experience in the USSR for Li Dazhao was his interaction with the Soviet children, although he was impressed by factories, hospitals, libraries, historical relics, and other things. His visit to an orphanage in Moscow left him with an enduring memory. The children's parents had died in the Great War, the Bolshevik Revolution, and the ensuing civil war. They had led a hard life as orphans but now were taken care of. According to Li's observations, the children were well organized, acted politely, adopted a high-spirited attitude, cherished communist ideals, became aware of global affairs, and were ready to be activists. Li commented, "Those children are the fresh red flowers grown from the revolutionary storms, and their noble spirit significantly differentiates them from those who grew up in the old society." Even the children from the capitalist families joined in, as Li saw: "those small hands could not only smash their old families but also could throw away all the chains enslaving the people of the world."[84] He felt he was honored when the children put a red scarf around his neck, gave him a bundle of fresh flowers, and invited him to be an honorary captain.[85] According to his daughter, Li Dazhao treasured a photo of himself with the Soviet children, showed it to his family quite often, and disclosed his tender emotion whenever he took a look at it.[86]

One of the climactic moments of Li Dazhao's visit to the USSR was his speech at a rally held by the Do Not Interfere in China Association at the Bolshoi Theatre in Moscow on September 22, 1924, which thousands attended. The communist leaders from the United States, Britain, France, Japan, and other countries delivered speeches. Because Li was the CCP representative, he had attracted attention this time. His speech was only discovered in 1985 in an old Russian archive. Stressing the grave situation in Guangzhou where the powers' intervention had become imminent, Li proclaimed that "China has already become a huge stage for the global imperialist powers to perform." While the imperialist exploitation was appalling, China had become a lumpenproletarian nation in a dire condition. The warlords' civil wars, in Li's eyes, were a result of the conflicts of the imperialist powers. In other words, what happened in China was not only a national issue but also an international problem. Although the Chinese would cope with their own national destiny, they needed international support. Li underscored Sun Yat-sen's leadership in the Chinese revolution, and at the same time he mentioned the communist role in it. He was grateful to the global community for its condemnation of the imperialist powers and for its moral support of the Chinese struggle for freedom and independence.[87] Russian documentary producers taped his speech for just one minute, which is the only taped documentary footage of Li in his entire life and which was only discovered in a Russian archive recently.[88]

Li Dazhao did research on a variety of topics during his visit to the USSR and published a number of articles in Russian as well as in Chinese. Of course, his articles in Russian were translations made by Chinese students at KUTV, while his articles in Chinese appeared in either Nationalist or Communist publications in China. For the Russian readers, Li depicted China's trauma as being sustained under the exploitational system created by the imperialist powers and Chinese warlords. For the Chinese readers, Li intended to attest to the Russian support for their country. Those articles were not seminal scholarly inquiries but rather were intended to assist Sun Yat-sen's National Revolution by heralding a new great age ahead. He swore his loathing toward imperialism, interpreted his observation of China's misery, and pleaded with the Chinese people to participate in the ongoing anti-imperialist and anti-warlord revolution. In his article in Russian on the Chinese peasants and workers, Li offered a thundering description of China's sorrow under imperialist dominance and China's suffering in bloody civil wars that resulted from foreign aggression.[89] For the Chinese readers, he narrated his personal experiences in the USSR to highlight Russia's sympathy toward China. He respected Sun Yat-sen as a great revolutionary and called on the Chinese people to rally under Sun's banner. In his article on child labor in Shanghai, Li utilized English and Japanese sources to entreat his compatriots to pay attention to the abuse of 170,000 child laborers in the largest city of China.

Besides his interaction with Russians during his stay in Moscow, Li Dazhao retained a strong tie with the Chinese students at KUTV. Seeing that several hundred Chinese students studied at the university, the CCP established the Moscow Branch (Lumozhibu) to coordinate student activities. Because Li was the CCP representative to the Comintern, he was accepted as a leader working for this group. According to Nie Rongzhen, the Chinese students admired Li and respected him as "an internationally famed communist fighter."[90] Li attended students' meetings, delivered speeches, and offered briefings concerning the national situation.[91] He highlighted the KMT's mission and encouraged the young CCP members to support the United Front. He told them that "we came here to learn more about how to make revolution rather than to earn an overseas experience or to obtain a doctorate degree."[92] It is said that Li himself offered courses at KUTV, for which he requested his family to mail him books.[93] He helped the CCP Moscow Branch organize an editorial committee and a supervisory committee to encourage students to write about the Chinese revolution and to acquire more information about Soviet Russia. Li Dazhao was held in high regard, such that Wu Chao, a student of arts, painted a portrait of him and hung it on the wall near a public poster.[94]

Why, then, did Li Dazhao suddenly depart from Moscow on December 3, 1924, for China? Naturally, it was not a Russian decision; rather, it was the call of the CCP for him to return to handle a new situation in China, because Feng Yuxiang's coup had suddenly changed China's political landscape. Li viewed his travel back as "a return to the battlefield," as he told the Chinese students.[95] The route he took was the same as the original one, and once again he stayed at Wang Fangtian's home for three days before he left Harbin for Beijing via the railways. Wang recorded his impression of Li: "He is a man of middle-sized stature and has a round face with a pale and pink complexion. His big, blinking eyes accompany his thick eyebrows and a pair of frameless glasses. With a worker's octagonal cap on his head, he wears an old, dark suit, along with a pair of half-worn leather shoes. In his hand is a canvas bag inside which there is a white cloth quilt." To Wang's amazement, Li Dazhao "does not smoke. Neither does he drink alcohol. He does not put on the slightest of air as a professor."[96]

Li Dazhao continued to retain his positive impression of the USSR long after his return to China. Witnessing the Russian support for China and experiencing the Soviet protest against the potential imperialist intervention, Li was grateful to the country he had just visited. Perhaps it was this gratitude that prevented him from assessing the Soviet Union critically, objectively, and fairly. The narrow range of his tours impeded his interaction with the Russian citizens, while the language barrier, in spite of the limited conversational Russian vocabulary he picked up, did not allow him effective communication with the native speakers. Therefore, his image of Russia was affirmative, from the landscape to the people, and from social condition to political life. All in all, he did not notice the grim image of those meagerly clad Russians who lived in dire poverty, and he did not have any contact with those who suffered from political persecution and governmental suppression. No doubt, the tours deliberately arranged by the Russian authorities did not allow him a chance. Conceivably, his commitment to communism obscured from him an impartial assessment. As a result, his visit differed enormously from those of Chiang Kai-shek and Xu Zhimo. After a three-month visit in 1923, Chiang Kai-shek, the future Nationalist leader, lost his confidence in the Soviet model and turned himself into an anti-communist.[97] Chinese poet Xu Zhimo's visit to Soviet Russia in 1925 exposed him to a scene of stark poverty under an oppressive system so that he decried Moscow as "a manufacturing factory of nightmares" and he felt that Soviet Russia seemed to be "an echo of politics of the medieval age."[98] In contrast, Li Dazhao's revolutionary spirit was uplifted after his visit, with which he endeavored to deepen his Russian ties. Gazing back at his five-month visit, he proclaimed that his rewarding journey "had broadened my mind and steeled myself, enhancing my ability for revolutionary struggle."[99]

Conclusion

The establishment of the United Front between the KMT and the CCP was an important page of modern Chinese history. Sun Yat-sen's policy of allying with Russia and accepting the Chinese Communists into his party led to the ultimate triumph of the National Revolution in overthrowing the warlord regime, and Li Dazhao was an important contributor to this process. By grafting the young CCP onto the Nationalist apparatus, the Communists enjoyed a protective umbrella. Because Li occupied a leading position in the KMT, he assisted the Nationalists in changing their previous situation of mainly operating in South China; he helped build KMT branches and recruited new members in North China. Yet Taiwanese scholars view it differently, as one condemns Li for his "domineering behavior" (*lishizhuanshan*) in expanding the Communist forces by taking advantage of the KMT.[100] Others accuse the Communists of brewing conspiracies, adopting unscrupulous means, reaping undeserved benefits, and harming Sun Yat-sen's cause.[101] Of course, these charges derive form political convictions. The fact was that the Nationalist membership expanded more quickly than the Communist membership and that Li had labored for their mutually shared objectives. He worked out plans for the Nationalist operations and at the same time assisted the Communist growth, but he was more dedicated to the United Front and contributed significantly to the final victory of the Nationalist unification of China, for which he sacrificed his life.

Li Dazhao was deeply entangled in the network of partnerships among the KMT, the CCP, the Comintern, and the USSR. On one hand, he had to be submissive to the Comintern directives; on the other hand, he had to follow the KMT orders. This special arrangement put him in an intricate and sometimes uncomfortable situation. The primary sources demonstrate that Li elevated Sun Yat-sen to the highest status as the leader of the Chinese revolution and that Li endeavored to tighten that screw to secure Russia's support for Sun Yat-sen's revolutionary cause. Taiwanese scholars' accusation that the Communists shielded themselves under the aegis of the USSR to work on the Russian behalf is not accurate even if it seems to be logical.[102] As the above evidence shows, Li demonstrated himself to be a fighter for the United Front during his visit to Russia, as he endeavored to secure international support for China's National Revolution. He had a passion for Soviet Russia, but he did not labor for Soviet Russia. Rather, he worked for the United Front, to which he offered whatever he had, including his own life.

The national situation in postimperial China was complex, but the major political trend after 1916 was the rule of warlords. Thus, the imperialist powers and Chinese warlords became the dual enemies of the United Front, within which the KMT and the CCP became the twin sisters of the Chinese revolution. Interestingly, both parties were patronized by Soviet Russia with military, political, and financial aid, for which Li Dazhao at the onset was an intermediary. In a particular sense, the United Front was established through Li's maneuvers, support, and coordination. Li had labored on multiple fronts for this alliance. From the time when Li met Sun Yat-sen in 1922 to the day Sun died in 1925, both parties enjoyed a honeymoon period thanks to Li's continual efforts. This does not mean that problems had not existed. As a matter of fact, tough issues persisted throughout the entire process. Li's reports tell us that he could not get along with the right-wing Nationalists, whom he viewed as similar to the warlords, the equals of shameless politicians, and degenerate dropouts from the revolution (*luowuzhe*).[103] When Sun Yat-sen was still alive, the right-wing Nationalists swallowed the bitter pill, but Sun's death in March 1925 marked an end of the first phase of the United Front, after which the right-wing Nationalists started to adopt a sharp tone for decoupling. From then on, bifurcation gradually emerged. Although the United Front staggered on until 1927, it started to change, even if many, including Li, continued to labor for it.

Chapter 8

The Last Years

Introduction

Li Dazhao's last years, from 1925 to 1927, constituted an important episode of his life. He went all out to participate in the United Front, and he also contributed significantly to the ongoing National Revolution to overthrow the warlord regime and fight against the imperialist powers. In order to do so, he detached himself from his former academic life and stayed away from his teaching duties; instead, he openly, semi-openly, or secretly took part in diverse activities as a professional revolutionary on the national stage, even though he mainly operated in North China. He assumed a prominent role as a Nationalist leader inside the United Front, acted as a Communist leader within the CCP, and served as a bridge between the United Front and Soviet Russia. Without a doubt, each of his activities during this period deserves separate coverage. Although continuing to lead the revolution in the heartland of the warlord regime, Li personally faced a more dangerous situation in Beijing. As the National Revolution deepened, the conditions there became worse, which explains why a lot of his colleagues, both Nationalists and Communists, departed for South China to work for the revolutionary regime. Li did not leave. Rather, he continued to maneuver in North China, where he adopted a number of strategies for the ongoing revolution. Unfortunately for him, those years virtually paved a pathway to his tragic death in 1927.

It is erroneous to claim that Li Dazhao turned into a sophisticated theorist during his last years, but it is equally incorrect to downplay his proposition of creative ideas. Although he was more an activist than a theorist, he did offer his insightful ideas on a number of issues. He explored China's problems, examined China's national circumstance, and analyzed the nature, aims, and reliable forces of the Chinese revolution. He continued to view the revolution in his country as a cause of national liberation for which imperialism was the principal enemy. Consequently, the Chinese revolution was an inseparable component of the global revolution. Under the dominance of the imperialist powers, Chinese warlords became pawns and thus the other wicked enemy of the National Revolution. Li carefully studied the peasant issue and envisioned a new type of revolution relying on the rural folks, in whom he saw a powerful force. Pamela Kyle Crossley's statement that "Mao developed a theory he had picked up from Li Dazhao regarding the role of the farmers in the revolution" rightly ascertains Li's impact upon the upcoming communist revolution.[1]

Li Dazhao's last years shaped a vital period in his life; however, many who have written on Li have simplified those years, and, even worse, some of them offered distorted narratives out of political motives. Only in the recent decades have we witnessed progress in effecting an objective assessment. Li's writings under diverse pen names have been identified, and related primary sources and scholarly publications have become available for a deeper understanding of Li's significant contributions to the National Revolution. Li's dedication proves that the revolution in North China was as important as that in South China. It is hard to imagine the ultimate success of the Northern Expedition, which was the last stage of the National Revolution, without Li's support in the northern provinces. A careful examination brings to light three distinctive stages of his last years. The first stage, from Sun Yat-sen's death to the March 18 Massacre, witnessed Li's prominent role in the United Front; the next stage, from the March 18 Massacre to Li's arrest—a little over a year—reveals Li's underground work as he hid himself inside the Russian Embassy; and the last stage features Li's arrest and death during his final twenty-two days, about which a number of distorted stories must be straightened up.

A Professional Revolutionary in North China

Sun Yat-sen's death in March 1925 was a huge loss to the National Revolution, but his passing did not mean that the revolution he had launched was thwarted. Rather, it was carried on by his followers, including Li Dazhao. Li lamented Sun's decease as an irreplaceable loss but vowed to inherit his legacy and to realize his revolutionary goals. Li equated Sun's ideas to Lenin's theory, simply because Sun labored for China's national liberation from the imperialist powers while Lenin condemned the evilness of imperialism. Although the two men's ideas were ill suited to account for one paradigm, Li viewed them as the two sides of the same coin and argued that "Lenin's spirit is Sun Yat-sen's spirit."[2] After Sun's death, Li appeared as a successor, assuming multiple identities as a Nationalist leader publicly and as a Communist leader secretly. On the national stage, Li was as a prominent Nationalist in North China who led mass movements. Although he vanished from the public eye after March 18, 1926, he continued to guide the United Front from hiding. During his last years, his influence upon the Chinese people, his impact on the United Front, and his leadership role in bipartisan affairs left an indelible mark upon modern China.

Li Dazhao defined the Chinese revolution as an anti-imperialist cause and a national liberation enterprise. In particular, he identified Britain as the primary imperialist country that had inflicted trauma upon the Chinese people, in conjunction with several other powers. Imperialist invasions triggered China's social problems, caused high unemployment, forced the signing of the unequal treaties, seized China's national interests, assisted reactionary forces, and suppressed revolutionary movements. Through rapacious invasions, the imperialist powers agonized the Chinese people. Henceforth, the goal of the Chinese revolution was to cast away the imperialist yoke, overthrow the rule of their proxies, nullify the unequal treaties, eliminate extraterritorial privileges, and retrieve the concession areas.[3] Because the imperialist powers had built a world system, the Chinese revolution inevitably became inseparable from the global revolution,[4] and Li claimed that "the day on which the Chinese revolution succeeds will be the [first] day of the successful global revolution."[5] The imperialist powers were not monolithic, though, because they fought among themselves; thus, Li cautioned that a new imperialist war might arrive soon, and China and the Pacific Ocean would be a new battlefield. The Chinese people, according to Li, should unite with the peoples of all countries to resist the potential imperialist war.[6]

Li Dazhao's anti-imperialist rhetoric does not mean that he had become a xenophobe. On the contrary, he sought support from foreign countries; in particular, he viewed the USSR as an anti-imperialist stronghold. The primary documents found in recent years prove his deep ties with Soviet Russia, from which he constantly received financial aid. Evidence can be found in three letters donated recently to a Chinese archive by Alexander V. Pantsov from his grandfather's private collection. The letters were written in English by Li Dazhao in early 1926; in them, Li asked the Russians to remit money as compensation and for budget plans, daily disbursement, and miscellaneous expenses. For the Tianjin operation alone, according to Li's request, the budget provided from Soviet Russia was set at over one thousand US dollars per month, which verifies the substantial Russian assistance to the early communist movement in China.[7] To Western scholars, this is confirmation of "red imperialism" from Soviet Russia, which utilized lures to redirect the path of the Chinese revolution.[8] However, Li's other international ties are often ignored. For instance, he hired Rayna and William Prohmes, an American couple, in late 1925 as editors of his English-language publications in Beijing. William fell ill, so most of the assignments were done by his wife, who has recently been confirmed as being not a communist but a radical American intellectual.[9] Li was grateful to Rayna for her dedication, and he praised her: "she worked for us here for a considerable time, but never once did she express one word of complaint, even under all sorts of difficulties."[10]

The anti-imperialist mood reached a new height during the May Thirtieth Movement (Wusayundong) in 1925, in which Li Dazhao led the people in North China in staging protests, issuing proclamations, and holding rallies. This movement first started in Shanghai after Japanese factory owners killed and wounded some Chinese workers, which caused a nationwide anti-imperialist movement. During the following months and even the next year, the British forces killed over a dozen and wounded even more Chinese citizens in a number of clashes, which added fuel to the fire. Under Li's leadership, rallies were held in Beijing; the protest on June 25, 1925, was the largest rally, in which more than 300,000 participated.[11] A leaflet endorsed by Li contained anti-imperialist messages and proclaimed that "this action is a revolution to champion nationalism and fight against imperialism." In this leaflet, the Chinese demands were enumerated, including "the abolition of unequal treaties, retrieval of concession areas, and nullification of consular jurisdiction."[12] Li dispatched activists to other cities and mining areas to support the local anti-imperialist struggles. For instance, a trade union of more than two thousand workers in the Tangshan mining area was organized on

August 15, 1925, to demand that the British owners offer more benefits to Chinese workers. Then, a general strike was staged for days purporting to awaken local workers for further actions.[13]

Besides the imperialist powers, according to Li Dazhao, Chinese warlords must be considered collectively as another nefarious enemy of the ongoing National Revolution.[14] In his eyes, the warlords constituted a reactionary force because of their antagonism to revolution, their greed for more territories, and their collaboration with the imperialist powers. By the mid-1920s, a number of warlords dominated the Chinese land: Zhang Zuolin in Northeast China (Manchuria), Wu Peifu in Hunan and Hubei, Zhang Zongchang in Shandong, Yan Xishan in Shanxi, and Feng Yuxiang in the northwest. Duan Qirui, who was defeated militarily a few years earlier, remained an influential political figure of the Beijing government. In addition, a large number of local strongmen controlled small patches in discordant subnational territories. For Li, the warlords were warmongers, initiating conflicts, ravaging multiple regions, and victimizing local residents. Facing such a reality, he adopted a variety of strategies in response. First, he regarded Zhang Zuolin and Wu Peifu as the principal reactionaries due to Zhang's anti-Soviet stance and Wu's suppression of the railway workers. Second, Li refrained from condemning some warlords, hoping to split warlords up and diminish their power. Third, Li tried his best to win over some warlords into joining the United Front, for which he instigated General Guo Songling to rebel against Zhang Zuolin, which did occur but ultimately failed.[15] When Guo was killed in late 1925, Li held a memorial service in Beijing at which he spoke highly of the fallen general.[16]

Li Dazhao's winning over of the Christian warlord Feng Yuxiang consumed much of his time and energy in 1925, during which he visited Feng's headquarters in Zhangjiakou six times to discuss issues with Feng and assisted Feng's policymaking. Although some of his colleagues regarded Feng as an unreliable chameleon, Li saw a hopeful possibility in him because of Feng's previous ties with Sun Yat-sen's revolution, his imposition of strict discipline upon his soldiers, and his skillful commandership of his troops.[17] Li persuaded the USSR to offer military assistance to Feng Yuxiang. He helped Feng establish a military school and publish newspapers to spread revolutionary messages and sent his fellow communists to familiarize Feng's troops with the current national and international situation.[18] According to one scholarly calculation, Feng's army received 38,800 Soviet rifles, 17,000 Japanese rifles, 50 cannons, 18 mortars, 230 machine guns, millions of bullets, and other military equipment from 1925 to 1926.[19] More importantly, Li arranged Feng's visit to the USSR in early 1926. Some Chinese scholars might have exaggerated Li's efforts by claiming that "Feng Yuxiang became totally disillusioned with his Christian belief," which was replaced by Sun Yat-sen's Three People's Principles.[20] Nevertheless, it would be wrong to downplay Li's endeavors, which ultimately won Feng over into joining the upcoming Northern Expedition and which guaranteed the successful overthrowing of the Beijing regime.

Facing the grim reality of warlord rule in diverse regions, which enmeshed the nation in a tough situation, Li Dazhao assumed a realistic approach of wooing potential allies to strengthen the United Front. He waded into a complicated landscape but prized a number of strategic regions. Viewing the importance of Henan Province for its strategic location between the northern and the southern provinces, Li traveled to Kaifeng, the provincial capital, two times in 1925. Henan at that time was under the control of Hu Jingyi, a military commander. Li persuaded the USSR to provide Hu with weapons, equipment, and advisers. But Hu's sudden death on April 10, 1925, forced Henan into a delicate situation in which Hu's successor, Yue Weijun, an ambitious military man, intended to build a powerful base for himself through an expansionist strategy. Li visited Henan in April and again in the summer to converse with Yue, offer advice, and try to convince Yue to relinquish his unrealistic expansionist approach.[21] Although Yue promised Li that he would give it up, he soon resumed his actions to enlarge his domain. Disastrously, Yue lost his troops and escaped to another province in February 1926.[22] Obviously, Li's efforts did not pan out well there, but his endeavors in general resulted in spreading revolutionary messages throughout the region.

Soon after Sun Yat-sen's death, Li Dazhao was compelled to open another front fighting the internal enemy within the KMT: the right-wing Nationalists who opposed the Communists and who resented the alliance with Soviet Russia. Once Sun Yat-sen passed away, the right-wing Nationalists openly resisted the United Front, stimulated considerable attention, drew support from conservatives, convened meetings, and tried to seize the leadership positions within the KMT. Li had perceived this danger in Beijing and implored the party to hold the next national congress in Guangzhou rather than in Beijing as the right-wing Nationalists requested.[23] Communist scholars often lament the Communists' loss of the leadership role to the Nationalists in the United Front, which they see as a real cause for the failure of the early communist movement.[24] Yet this claim proves inaccurate in the case of Beijing, where Li continued to be the major leader. Taiwanese scholars' criticism of Li's domineering behavior, blaming Li for drifting away from the Nationalist agenda, from a particular angle, attests to Li's firm control of the United Front.[25] Indeed, Li's stance angered the right-wing Nationalists, who convened their own meeting in Beijing in November 1925 and then organized a faction known as the Western Hill clique (Xishanhuiyipai). They disavowed the alliance with Soviet Russia, demanded to purge the party, drew a sharp line with the Communists, and called for expelling them, including Li Dazhao. Facing such pressure, Li opened a new Nationalist headquarters in Beijing on January 1, 1926, and pledged to carry on Sun Yat-sen's revolutionary cause.[26]

Chinese scholars have regarded the quick growth of the KMT in North China as evidence proving Li Dazhao's successful leadership in the United Front. In early 1924, when the United Front was forged, there were barely a few hundred KMT members in North China. By January 1926, the number had jumped to 14,000. Although the tally remained small in comparison with the total national membership of 200,000 by then, it demonstrates Li's diligence in recruitment.[27] Under Li's guidance, Nationalist provincial committees were established in Henan, Suiyuan, Rehe, Hebei, Shandong, and Chahar, while more branches were built in other northern provinces, which changed the previous situation whereby the KMT had been a political organization mainly operating in South China.[28] Concurrently, of course, Li assisted the growth of the CCP. As the Communists operated secretly, it is hard to retrieve an accurate tally of their membership. A recent study provides a nuanced view showing how the Communists penetrated into diverse regions; over one hundred branches and special committees were established in North China with a total membership tally of over one thousand by late 1925.[29] Li personally admitted many individuals into the CCP, including Xu Quanzhong, a military commander, in 1925. Li dispatched Communists to diverse regions to build new branches. For example, he sent Ren Guozhen to Shenyang, Wu Lishi and Chu Tunan to Harbin, and others to diverse localities to expand the Communist underground network.[30] In October 1925, Li established a party school in Beijing to train Communists, at which he himself offered lectures. In a couple of years, according to one calculation, over one thousand CCP members in Beijing and more than three thousand in North China were under

Li's leadership.[31] Li also encouraged many to study communism, as his persuasion of Chen Hansheng reveals. Chen earned his degrees in the United States and Germany and returned to China to become a professor at Beijing University. Li convinced Chen to become familiar with the communist doctrine, and Chen finally joined the CCP in 1935.[32]

It should be noted that Li Dazhao was one of the earliest revolutionaries to pay special attention to the issue of land, on which he authored an article in late 1925. Li blamed the imperialist powers for China's transformation into a semi-colony in which the peasants who made up the majority of the Chinese population suffered from an excruciating trauma. The ruinous wars among Chinese warlords converted the peasants into soldiers, refugees, and bandits, while agricultural production deteriorated. Li analyzed the rural demographic makeup, which included landlords, rich peasants, middle peasants, small landholding farmers, tenants, and hired hands, among whom the small landholding farmers constituted the majority. Li did not expose the exploitative nature of the upper class as Mao Zedong would do in the near future; he mainly targeted the imperialist powers and Chinese warlords as the evildoers for inflicting pain upon the peasants. Li's solution was to give land to the tillers. More importantly, he saw the power of peasants who had organized their own self-defensive forces. He called on his fellow revolutionaries to go to the rural areas to improve the existing peasant organizations, build new ones, and steer them onto the revolutionary path.[33] He dispatched his followers to assist peasant organizations. Consequently, the peasant movement was in rapid progress in North China by late 1925 and early 1926. Taking Henan Province as an example, the total tally of those peasants who got involved in the peasant association there ranked number two in the entire nation, second only to Guangdong.[34]

One of the issues Li Dazhao had to handle in North China was the ethnic relationships, for which the Mongols were the priority concern. In fact, Li was one of the earliest communists to offer an in-depth analysis on the ethnic issue. In late March 1925, he published an article championing Mongol liberation. He argued that the Mongols suffered from four oppressions: foreign imperialism, Han chauvinism, Mongolian feudalism, and religious obscurantism. Pledging his support for ethnic autonomy, he envisioned a brotherly tie between Mongol and Han. The urgent task, according to Li, was to lead the Mongols to support the United Front, prevent ethnic dissension, and avoid being utilized by the imperialist powers and Chinese warlords.[35] In October 1925, with Li's support, the

People's Revolutionary Party of Inner Mongolia was established. In the same month, the Great League of Peasants, Workers, and Soldiers in Inner Mongolia was built in Zhangjiakou; Li delivered a speech at the founding ceremony and was elected a leader of the league.[36] He sponsored the publication of a journal promoting ethnic solidarity and regarding it as an important task of the United Front.[37] Indeed, Li had recruited the Mongols into both KMT and CCP.[38] Jiyatai, an ethnic Mongol, recalled that Li's speech at the founding ceremony of the league highlighted the importance of ethnic harmony between Mongol and Han.[39] In this way, Li intended to raise the Mongols' consciousness of imperialist oppression and warlords' exploitation and to persuade them to participate in the National Revolution.

Leafing through Li Dazhao's voluminous works, one can easily find that his writings were replete with anti-imperialist and anti-warlord rhetoric, yet seldom did he elaborate on the issue of China's maritime customs, which were still under foreign management. Suddenly, however, he launched the Customs Autonomy Movement (Guanshuizizhuyundong) in late 1925, during which he organized protests, assembled rallies, and addressed the crowds. This movement was a response to the warlord regime's move to invite twelve foreign powers to attend a special customs conference in Beijing on October 26, 1925. Taking this as an opportunity to demonstrate his anti-imperialist and anti-feudal message, Li organized demonstrations, participated in meetings, and spoke at rallies. On the day the international conference started, Li led more than two thousand protestors to lodge the Chinese people's grievance just outside it, which was followed by a demonstration of more than ten thousand participants in Tiananmen Square.[40] As this movement raged on, Li continued to carry out his obligatory duties as a leader. Through his efforts, a rally of more than twenty thousand was held on November 22, 1925, in Tiananmen Square to demand Chinese control of Chinese customs, to renounce potential decisions by Chinese warlords and the imperialist powers, and to request that the warlord regime respect the people's will.[41] Differing from many who acted out of spontaneously patriotic urges, Li Dazhao intermixed his nationalistic demands with his anti-imperialist and anti-warlord stance.[42]

The warlord government's stubborn refusal of the demands enumerated above enraged Li Dazhao, who believed that the time had come for a violent revolution to overthrow the regime. Li cautiously planned this uprising: he set up an action committee out of his followers, a security team among workers, a dare-to-die corps of students, and a self-defensive squad comprising nearby peasants. All of these were well-organized. Li even collaborated with soldiers to try to arrange potential military involvement. On November 28, 1925, the Capital Revolution (Shoudugeming) erupted, for which Li was both the leader and a participant. A huge rally was convened at the North Gate of the Forbidden City while leaflets were being circulated in the capital city. A resolution was passed at the rally to order Duan Qirui to resign and to call on the people to support the revolutionary government in Guangzhou. Li then led the protesters to march toward Duan's office and further to Duan's residence, for the purpose of capturing Duan. The demonstration continued until darkness fell. The next day, over fifty thousand attended the rally in Tiananmen Square to declare the dissolution of Duan's warlord regime. Nevertheless, the uprising failed because of Duan's suppression.[43] Angry protesters burned down some houses belonging to those who were related to the warlord regime or who were regarded as sympathizers of the government, including the editorial building of the *Morning Newspaper* (Chenbao), an act that was condemned by its editor, Xu Zhimo, a famous poet mentioned previously. Nevertheless, this event is still hailed by Chinese scholars as an action of the Capital Revolution.[44]

The last revolutionary movement led by Li Dazhao personally was the protest on March 18, 1926, directed against Chinese warlords and the imperialist powers. This protest occurred after Japan assisted Zhang Zuolin in the latter's clash with Feng Yuxiang's National Army at Fort Dagu on the coast. On March 12, Japan's warships escorted Zhang's battleships in approaching the fort, flouting the warning from the National Army, which fired warning shots without bullets. The Japanese shot back and inflicted casualties. The Chinese soldiers then retaliated and drove the Japanese away. Within days, the foreign powers accused China of violating the Boxer Protocol and delivered an ultimatum requesting the withdrawal of the National Army from Fort Dagu. Facing this urgent situation, Li immediately organized a protest in the name of defending China's national interests. On March 18, over 100,000 attended the rally at Tiananmen Square. In the afternoon, Li led protesters in marching toward the governmental building. Upon their arrival, protesters clashed with the guards, who opened fire at the mass of protesters, killing forty-seven and wounding over two hundred, which was dubbed the March 18 Massacre (Sanyibacan'an).[45] Li suffered a minor injury and fell into a nearby ditch, which probably saved his life. While losing one shoe, he continued to coordinate the protestors in carrying out a safe withdrawal. It is said that a policeman approached Li and directed him to a nearby store, where the workers offered him a pair of shoes. Then, he returned home safely. In the following days, Li arranged memorial services, assisted the wounded protestors, and tried to seek a safe shelter for himself because his name was now on the most wanted list.[46]

The Underground Struggle

Not many primary sources could be found to detail Li Dazhao's one year spent in the Russian Embassy between the March 18 Massacre in 1926 and his arrest on April 6, 1927. Even the date he secretly moved to the embassy remains indefinite, as many vaguely claim it as late March 1926. If this is true, it means that Li hid himself in an unspecified place in Beijing before he moved into the embassy. Immediately after the massacre, the government issued an order to arrest him, which compelled him to hide. Strangely enough, it had become a tradition for Chinese dissidents to seek the protection of a foreign embassy or consulate due to the diplomatic immunity they provided, and Li's case was just one of them. The scarcity of sources has made Li's one-year hideout a secretive occurrence; fortunately, the recently published memoirs by Li's children and others along with newly identified articles and reports by Li during that one-year period help us piece together his yearlong underground work.

Li Dazhao did not move into the Russian Embassy alone; he was followed by a group of Nationalists and Communists, among whom some soon departed for the south. According to Li, he was not under Russian control and never discussed anything directly with Russian diplomats. If needed, he sent his representatives to converse with them.[47] Neither did Li live among the Russians. His group resided in the Western Yard, which was an old military barracks inside which Li's family stayed in an independent house. His daughter Li Xinghua, who accompanied him, recalled that Li "stayed indoors working without leaving there for over a year." Yet he often "took a walk along the enclosing wall and sometimes slowly strolled to the flag post, climbed up the stand, and looked around."[48] During his last days there, his daughter saw him burning documents, perhaps to avoid the leakage of secrets that might have implicated and endangered other persons if these documents fell into the wrong hands. Of course, persons close to him tried to persuade Li to leave Beijing, and even his wife complained about the extremely isolated life there. His reply was resolute: "If I leave, who will do the work in Beijing?" His daughter remembered that her family "spent a very insecure life there."[49] Li Dazhao's son Li Baohua claimed that Li Dazhao "did not go outside for more than a year; instead, he worked inside from morning to evening every day without a single moment of rest."[50]

Li Dazhao's busy schedule turned the small compound into a new headquarters of the United Front, from which Li sent out directives to provincial branches for the two political parties (the KMT and the CCP). He collected information, authored reports, delivered them to the two central committees, and offered his advice for actions. He provided them valuable data about the changing situations in the northern provinces, such as the defeat of Yue Weijun by Jin Yun'e in Henan Province in early 1926. Jin, according to Li, had become a powerful warlord who now planned to organize a third force differing from the Beijing government in the north and the Nationalist government in the south.[51] In Beijing, Duan Qirui's government had collapsed due to the March 18 Massacre, after which Zhang Zuolin began to control the government. Yet the northern warlords were disunited because of their own complicated relationships and power-hungry ambitions, as Li pointed out to the two central committees. In such an environment, Li remained optimistic and expected a rosy prospect for his country. Li continued to interpret the Chinese revolution and published his articles under pseudonyms. Nevertheless, he encountered serious financial difficulty, could not pay his staff their salaries for months, and accumulated unpaid bills, although he acknowledged the receipt of five thousand yuan from the Nationalist government in the south, which temporarily solved the problem shortly before his arrest.[52]

Even though Li Dazhao lived in isolation, he kept his keen eyes on the changing national situation, interpreted what happened in North China, and offered his unique analysis. He continued to identify Zhang Zuolin as the principal enemy. After defeating Feng Yuxiang near Beijing in late 1926, Zhang tried to control more regions of North China. According to Li, the ambitious "Zhang Zuolin was obsessed with his presidential dream besides which he has no other interests."[53] As the Northern Expedition was in progress in South China, North China became Zhang Zuolin's domain in which "he intended to realize his dream of being president or even emperor."[54] To consolidate his power,

Zhang convened the Tianjin Conference in late 1926, intending to unite the remaining warlords. In Li's view, the conference was "an occasion for enjoying socializing banquets" and taking in frivolous pleasures.[55] To Li, "the northern warlords seem to be powerful superficially, yet from a quick glimpse at their internal issues, one can easily find that they are extremely disordered and weak."[56] Li concluded that "the unity of warlords can never be realized."[57] Thus, he argued, the ongoing National Revolution would succeed and the warlord regime would collapse.

To target Zhang Zuolin as the main enemy, Li Dazhao continued to carry on his realistic approach of wooing other warlords to join the United Front. In late 1926, Li tried to persuade Yan Xishan, the warlord of Shanxi Province, to support the United Front, for which he involved himself in secret talks with Yan's representatives in Beijing. One of Li's letters to Yan has survived, in which Li praised Yan's original relationship with Sun Yat-sen but underscored Yan's difficulties in coping with other warlords. Li advised Yan to relinquish his regional ambition inside a single province and to join "the greater enterprise." He hoped that Yan could command his several hundred thousand troops to assure the success of the National Revolution.[58] The purpose of this move, as Li himself elaborated, was "to establish a good relationship with Yan Xishan and prevent him from collaborating with Zhang Zuolin."[59] Ultimately, Yan declared his support to the Northern Expedition in July 1927, for which the importance of Li's contribution in winning him over should not be underestimated, even though it finally occurred months after Li's death.

The most successful effort to win over a warlord by Li Dazhao was the case of the Christian warlord Feng Yuxiang. One scholar argues that "Feng's joining in the revolutionary movement was inseparable from Li Dazhao's endeavors."[60] For years, Li kept up his friendly ties with Feng. Li dispatched his fellow Communists to Feng's army to promote the revolutionary cause and assist Feng's military reform. Feng's visit to the USSR, which was arranged by Li, changed Feng's political outlook. Finally, Feng declared that he would lead his forces to join the National Revolution on September 17, 1926, after which his army became part of the Nationalist forces. In his declaration, which was drafted by Liu Bojian (Li's follower), Feng proclaimed that he would accept Sun Yat-sen's nation-building plan, revealed his new identity as a member of the KMT, and pledged his support to the ongoing revolution to overthrow the rule of warlords and to expel the imperialist powers.[61] It should be noted that Li instructed those who worked in Feng's army to retain a friendly relationship with Feng, avoid criticizing him, and avert negative opinions against him.[62]

From the very beginning, Li Dazhao cautiously devised feasible strategies to support the Northern Expedition in reaching its goal of toppling the warlord regime.[63] To facilitate realizing this objective, Li collected information about Zhang Zuolin's military forces, drove a wedge between Zhang and other warlords, and assisted the Nationalist troops in controlling more territories. For Feng Yuxiang's army, Li worked out a military plan. According to Feng's own testimony, Li sent a secret letter advising Feng to consolidate his base in Gansu, reinforce the revolutionary force in Shaanxi, ally with Yan Xishan in Shanxi, and then march toward Henan (*gugan yuanshaan lianjin tuyu*), all of which Li summarized into an eight-character formula cherished by Feng as "a treasure."[64] This military plan significantly affected the outcome of the Northern Expedition, because Feng's troops indeed built a solid base in the northwest, defeated the warlord army in Xi'an in Shaanxi Province, averted a potential clash with Yan Xishan in Shanxi Province, and eventually marched toward Henan Province. On June 1, 1927, shortly after Li's death, Feng's army joined the Northern Expedition forces in Zhengzhou, today's capital of Henan Province. By then, the collapse of the warlord regime was only a matter of time.[65]

While hiding in the Russian Embassy, Li Dazhao was unable to fully participate in the policymaking of the central committee of the KMT, to which he nevertheless continued to deliver his reports. He was informed of what happened in Guangzhou, where the Nationalist government launched the Northern Expedition in mid-1926 and soon won battles in southern provinces. Suddenly, a debate arose among the two factions of the KMT in regard to the location of the new revolutionary capital: either Wuhan or Nanchang. The left-wing Nationalists chose Wuhan, but Chiang Kai-shek selected Nanchang (eventually Nanjing). In early January 1927, Li wrote a letter to the top Nationalist leaders in which he did not serve as an arbiter of the debate but expressed his strong support for the left-wing Nationalists. Li argued that "Guangzhou so far has been the revolutionary base, while Wuhan is the central point of the entire country. If the capital should be moved out of Guangzhou, the destination must be Wuhan. It is puzzling to understand the rationale for the idea to relocate the capital to Nanchang."[66] With these words, Li clearly voiced his disagreement with Chiang Kai-shek. At the same time, Li exposed problems in the north, where the paramount pressure from the warlord regime depressed some provincial Nationalist leaders, who started to lose their revolutionary aspiration and even developed a number of bad habits such as smoking opium and visiting prostitutes, which infuriated Li so much that he immediately took measures to remedy them.[67] The goal, of course, was to reinforce the National Revolution and to support the northbound Nationalist troops.

It is not right to assume that the CCP developed more rapidly by recruiting more members than the KMT did simply because Li Dazhao was a Communist leader. It is equally incorrect to downplay the Communist growth, as the CCP had indeed developed under Li's leadership. We must note that the Communists had to operate more clandestinely. The warlord regime created a dangerous milieu for them after the March 18 Massacre, and CCP recruitment became more difficult, although it continued. For example, in Anping County, Zhili (Hebei) Province, seven Communist branches and five Communist youth league branches were established by 1927.[68] During this period, Li emphasized the importance of enlisting the military commanders into the CCP. By mid-1926 in the army of Fang Zhenwu, who was a commander under Feng Yuxiang, two Communist branches with fifty members in total were built, according to Li's report.[69] Li's efforts in other units of Feng Yuxiang's forces also panned out well. By early 1927, a division commander, Shi Kexuan, and a regiment commander, Xu Quanzhong, became Communists. Another division commander, Zhang Zhaofeng, a Communist, was placed directly under Li's leadership.[70] Those military commanders played an important combined role in overthrowing the warlord regime but have been less studied because scholars have paid too much attention to the northbound revolutionary army. In particular, Chinese scholars have focused on Ye Ting, a regiment commander and a Communist, to emphasize the Communist contributions to the Northern Expedition in southern provinces.

It must be stressed that Li Dazhao continued to reflect over the role of peasants in the Chinese revolution while he hid in the Russian Embassy. To his delight, "Chinese peasants had awakened and realized the importance of relying on their own united forces to unshackle themselves from the chaotic political situation created by the imperialist powers and warlords." In this way, the peasants themselves became "a gigantic force" (*weidadeshili*) as they organized their military units in North China. Li studied the Red Spear Society (Hongqianghui), a peasant military force, linked its emergence to imperialist invasions, and hailed its anti-imperialist stance. However, Li exposed the peasants' weaknesses, such as narrow-mindedness, provincialism, and a tendency toward banditry. The peasants adhered to the local culture, indulged in the god-worshipping tradition, and tended to be irrational and superstitious. Li called on his fellow revolutionaries to contact those peasants, reform them, and guide them to the revolutionary path.[71] He dispatched his followers to the rural areas to help organize the peasant associations, which more and more peasants were joining. In Shaanxi Province alone, fifty-one county peasant associations, twelve county preparatory associations, and 3,814 village peasant associations had been established, with a total membership of over 300,000 by early 1927.[72]

Li Dazhao wasted no time in his observation of the recent imperialist invasions into his country, even though he lived in such isolated conditions at the Russian Embassy. He lamented China's status as a semi-colony in which the imperialist powers so easily seized China's national interests. In particular, Japan's new maneuvers in late 1926 drew his attention. According to Li, Japan had assumed a more aggressive posture, supporting Chinese warlords, sabotaging Chinese people's revolutionary movements, bullying Asian neighbors, and demonizing communists. More disastrously, Japan intended to sign a new treaty with China to consolidate its colonial gains. Under the guise of relinquishing consular jurisdiction, Japan aimed at grabbing more—in particular, the ownership of Chinese land, by way of a rather roundabout strategy: Japan sent speculators to Korea, confiscated Korean land, and then compelled the Koreans to immigrate to Manchuria (Northeast China), which Li termed "the ingenious ruse" of Japanese imperialism. As Li saw it, Japanese immigrants had already settled down in Manchuria, established Japanese communities, and possessed land there. He alerted the Chinese to be vigilant to Japan's three-pronged strategy: encouraging Japanese emigration, seizing the ownership of Chinese land, and then occupying Manchuria.[73] Li's prediction proved to be farsighted, as Japan indeed occupied Manchuria in just a few years.

As China suffered from the rule of warlords, the country became a fragmented political entity; consequently, national diplomacy tended to be decentralized and localized. Provincial strongmen conducted their own diplomatic negotiations, despite the fact that the Beijing government was still recognized as the central government. In such a situation, Li Dazhao actively got involved in diplomacy. Not only did he establish a working relationship with the USSR, but he also engaged in conversations with foreign nationals to familiarize them with the Chinese Nationalist stance on various issues. For relations with the United States and Britain, as his reports confirm, he worked with Tang Yueliang, who was the foreign relations officer of Feng Yuxiang's forces. Tang often visited Li and consulted Li concerning Western countries. As for Japan, Li directly held dialogues with the Japanese. In early 1927, Li met Ouchi Chozo, a Diet member, to probe the Japanese intent in China. During their meeting, Li made it clear that China's ongoing revolution was nationalistic but not egoistic and that China would not harm any other nations. In a report he authored on January 25, 1927, Li indicated that he planned to meet with a Japanese government representative, Rihachiro Bansai, to discuss a way of handling concession areas in Shanghai once the Northern Expedition forces occupied the city.[74] However, it is unclear whether the meeting ever took place because no documents have been found so far for its verification.

Arrest and Execution

The time between April 6, 1927, when Li Dazhao was arrested, and April 28, when he was executed, is a heated topic among scholars. In fact, those twenty-two days have become the most diversely recorded, the most conflictingly narrated, and the most controversially debated. The reasons are multiple. First of all, Li was not put on public trial after his arrest; rather, he was judged by a specially organized court without reporters, audience, or judicial procedures. Although major newspapers covered Li extensively, their correspondents obtained information indirectly. During those twenty-two days, Li did not have a chance to meet any visitors except for the prison guards, and thus few testimonies were left. Li himself did not write much during his incarceration besides the long statement he authored in the prison. Others' memoirs about his last days were published much later and inevitably contained inaccurate information. More deplorably, political rhetoric played a role, as Zhang Zuolin's regime demonized him and the Communist literature glorified him. In the recent decades, however, scholars have carefully examined those twenty-two days, trying to uncover the truth. Yet a number of contentious issues may still spark new debates at any time.

Chinese scholars have offered their interpretation of the reasons why Zhang Zuolin arrested Li Dazhao, such as Zhang's long-standing conflicts with the USSR, Li's support for Feng Yuxiang in opposing Zhang, Li's role in instigating Guo Songling to stage a rebellion against Zhang, the imperialists' collaboration with Zhang, and so forth.[75] A fringe theory was offered a few years ago in China that criticized Li's hiding in the Russian Embassy as "an irrational action against the then international law." Indeed, in Zhang's eyes, Li was a Russian agent who collected military information, machinated with the USSR, abetted Feng Yuxiang in fighting civil wars, and plotted to overthrow the legitimate Beijing government.[76] Zhang arrested Li in the name of fighting communism, punishing him for his collaboration with Soviet Russia, and penalizing him for disturbing the social order. Yet the arrest of Li inside the Russian Embassy was not an easy task because of the embassy's diplomatic immunity; Zhang needed special permission from the diplomatic legation to send even a single police officer into the embassy area. Furthermore, April 6, 1927, was not a random date for Zhang's action; rather, it was deliberately determined after Zhang had made sure that Li lived inside the embassy. Recent publications show that Li Dazhao's student Li Bohai's betrayal enabled the warlord to ascertain his whereabouts inside the embassy.[77] Having determined these factors, Zhang Zuolin took action on that fateful day.

Surprisingly, Li Dazhao was adamant about staying in Beijing even though he received a tip concerning Zhang Zuolin's plan to arrest him. He knew that his deeds drew the ire of Zhang, who saw him as a thorn in his flesh. Why didn't Li simply escape from Beijing and depart for South China, as many others did? A source claims that Yang Du, a well-known political gymnast who had once supported Yuan Shikai's imperial endeavors but had become a Communist collaborator and had finally joined the CCP secretly, informed Li of Zhang's plan on April 4, two days in advance.[78] According to Li's daughter's memory, "many of my father's friends came to visit him during those days and tried to persuade him to leave Beijing."[79] Li decided to stay, as his daughter recalled, in order to carry out his obligations as the leader of the United Front. Such a point has been echoed loudly in Chinese publications to lionize Li's lofty revolutionary spirit. Taiwanese scholars hold a similar view but from a different angle, as one argues that "Li refused resolutely to depart, which reveals his firm belief in the communist heresy, but, at the same time, it means that he had already prepared to sacrifice his life for his chosen cause."[80] A recent scholarly argument in China deserves mentioning: one scholar suggests that Li was overconfident of his safety in the Russian Embassy because he assumed that Zhang Zuolin dared not to dispatch his forces into the foreign embassy.[81] In other words, Li's overconfidence was a factor in his own arrest. Perhaps it was already too late for Li to escape from Beijing, over which Zhang Zuolin had cast a tight net.

Numerous news reports in China and foreign countries covered Li Dazhao's arrest, which concurred in common facts but differed in detailed narratives. Here is a brief description of the commonly accepted facts: Around 10:30 a.m. on April 6, 1927, Zhang Zuolin dispatched more than three hundred police officers, gendarmes, and plainclothes detectives to the foreign legation. After obtaining special permission from the Dutch ambassador William J. Oudendyk, the dean of the diplomatic body, they searched the Russian Embassy. Hence, Oudendyk's permission is regarded in Chinese historiography as evidence of an imperialist accomplice in Li's arrest. Boldly enough, Zhang Zuolin acted without informing the foreign ministry of his own Beijing government, while his order was carried out by his own military forces. In any case, Li Dazhao's daughter Li Xinghua kept in her memory the moment of her father's arrest. According to her, Li was busy with his work on that day. Suddenly, a gunshot was heard nearby. Li stayed calm but held a pistol in his hand. Then, "a throng of gendarmes in grey suits and long leathered boots, detectives in plainclothes, and policemen in black suits arrived in no time. They immediately flocked into the small room until it became jam-packed. Like a group of devils, they surrounded us and pointed guns at my father and me. One bad guy pushed himself forward and then seized my father's pistol."[82] Then, Li Dazhao along with his family, his colleagues, his followers, and even nearby Soviet staff members were arrested and brought to jail. Some of them were released very soon, including Li's family members. As for the number of original arrestees, different sources offer diverse data, ranging from dozens to sixty or even eighty people. The searching continued until late afternoon, during which Zhang's forces confiscated documents and other materials, loaded them into automobiles, and delivered them to the police department.[83]

Only three primary documents besides memoirs concerning Li Dazhao's time in prison have survived, which allow us to take a glance at his life during those twenty-two days. Among the three, one was his own personal statement, and the other two were testimonies written by the police. In his long statement, Li traced his childhood, education, career, and recent activities. He explained the reasons why he became a revolutionary, for which he condemned the imperialist powers that had brought forth China's misfortunes. He claimed that he joined the KMT with only one purpose, which was to achieve national liberation. He pleaded with the authorities not to punish his colleagues and followers, as he alone would bear all responsibilities.[84] The fact that he only revealed his Nationalist identity without divulging his Communist status was intended to protect his fellow Communists. The two other surviving testimonies, one short and the other long, were his replies to the questions raised by the police. He offered his answers about the KMT and its operations. Since the KMT activities were open public knowledge, Li actually relayed only information already long known to the authorities. Nonetheless, he emphasized his status as a Nationalist leader and avoided talking about the CCP.[85]

Whether Li Dazhao was tortured inside prison is a debatable topic. Some scholars have blamed a 1979 biography for initiating the rumor of torture. Indeed, that book states that "the enemy employed different kinds of penalties to brutally torture him, used bamboo needles to penetrate beneath his nails, and finally forcibly removed all his nails from his hands."[86] To highlight her father's noble spirit, Li Xinghua echoed the same story in her memoir: "The enemy used the cruelest torture and even inserted bamboo needles into his ten nails."[87] More successive publications spread the claim of torture until this very day. Yet this allegation has been traced back to the early days. A 1951 pamphlet by Lu Jian on Li Dazhao exposed his enemy's cruelty in inserting bamboo needles into Li's nails.[88] In another short book on the major Communist martyrs published in 1949, Li Ming wrote that "the enemy used bamboo needles to penetrate Comrade Li Dazhao's nails and also employed other brutal penalties."[89] All these demonstrate that the Chinese literature has persistently disseminated the torture theory; nevertheless, the origin of this claim was the widespread public chitchat in Beijing immediately after Li's arrest. To refute it as a rumor, the police department published a statement on April 20, 1927, to inform the public that torture was not applied to Li.[90] Therefore, the recent publications in China offer a revisionist statement that no evidence has been found to verify Li's torture.[91] If Li had been tortured with such a penalty, he would not have been able to author his long statement and revise it several times in such a short time span.

Immediately after Li Dazhao's arrest, a number of social groups and individual citizens launched a campaign for his release. Presidents from nine public universities held a special meeting in Beijing on April 9,

1927, to demand that the government be humane to him and to entreat a fair verdict for him at a civilian court.[92] Presidents from twenty-five public and private universities held another meeting in Beijing on April 12, hoping to rescue Li and his imprisoned followers. They emphasized Li's status as an academic and requested that he be adjudged in a regular court.[93] Civilian petitions flooded the offices of the warlord regime. It is said that Zhang Xueliang, who was known as the Young Marshal and who was the eldest son of Zhang Zuolin, received hundreds of such petitions in just a few days.[94] For example, Li Shuxia's letter to Zhang Xueliang, which was dated April 12, enumerated ten reasons to pardon Li Dazhao, who was after all an ideological violator rather than a wicked criminal. Li Dazhao's philanthropic behaviors in contributing part of his income to assist poor students were highlighted to portray him as a social exemplar. Any extreme penalties, as Li Shuxia warned, could cause strong social repercussions.[95] Yin Yanwu, a citizen from Jiangsu Province, beseeched a reasonable trial and cited the fair verdicts on communist cases in Germany and Japan as precedents.[96] Li Dazhao's friends, including Zhang Shizhao, Bai Meichu, Yang Du, and others, tried their best to rescue Li. It is said that Yang Du sold his house for four thousand yuan for the purpose of effecting Li's release.[97] The Communists in Beijing worked out a plan to attack the prison in order to save Li, but Li heard about it, deemed it a risky move, and halted this adventurous plan.[98]

Facing such a large number of petitions, Zhang Zuolin did not budge; instead, he ordered a group of confidants to compile a book titled *Soviet Plot in China*, in which he claimed that his regime had garnered sufficient evidence to validate Li Dazhao as a Russian agent.[99] Although some documents in it were later exposed as forgeries, Zhang's regime publicized it in multiple languages and soon decided to sentence Li with capital punishment.[100] Why did Zhang make the decision to kill Li so soon? Perhaps the advancing Northern Expedition forces made Zhang frantic. Li's long anti-Zhang stance infuriated the warlord. Zhang's endeavors to beef up security in Beijing necessitated a quick elimination of any potential internal threats. Zhang's consultation with other warlords, who for the most part supported executing Li, prompted Zhang to make the final decision.[101] For a long time in China, Chiang Kai-shek was accused of dispatching a telegram to Zhang Zuolin to press for Li's execution. Li's daughter put it bluntly: "Those who killed my father were not limited to Zhang Zuolin as they included the people's public enemy Chiang Kai-shek and the imperialist invaders."[102] Truly, it is reasonable to advance such a claim of Chiang Kai-shek's complicity in Li's death, as Chiang himself started to kill Communists on April 12, 1927, in Shanghai, while Li's execution occurred little more than two weeks later. Yet it is actually illogical to even think about Chiang's accountability for Li's death, because Chiang himself was fighting a war against Zhang Zuolin at the time. Furthermore, Chiang dispatched a telegraph to the foreign legation to condemn Zhang's action in Li's arrest just a few days after his apprehension.[103] An examination of the origin of this claim shows that on May 12, 1927, a newspaper in Wuhan first accused Chiang of dispatching a telegraph to Zhang urging him to kill Li.[104] This occurred during the rift between Wang Jingwei's Nationalist regime in Wuhan and Chiang Kai-shek's Nationalist regime in Nanjing. This case demonstrates the long-term influence of political rhetoric upon historical assessment. Countering this, Chinese scholars have recently advised the public not to exaggerate Chiang Kai-shek's culpability in Li's death.[105]

The diverse narratives about Li Dazhao's behavior just before his execution have attracted substantial attention but have also led to a great deal of confusion. Although all agree that Li was calm and fearless, quite a few storytellers have illustrated the moment just before his death differently. For a long time, Li's heroic image had been lofty; the biography of 1979 claimed that Li delivered his last speech and then shouted the slogan "Long live the Chinese Communist Party!"[106] But in recent decades some scholars have doubted the speech and the shouting. With no audience in front of him, Li had no chance to deliver a speech other than to his captors. He deliberately concealed his Communist identity during his imprisonment, which probably means that he would not have shouted any such slogan in his last minutes. One witness, He Jun, wrote in 1949 that Li shouted, but He Jun's memory might have been blurred, as more than twenty years had passed.[107] In any case, this claim influenced historical writings.[108] After meticulous studies, a lot of scholars today have come to an understanding that Li Dazhao did not deliver a speech and did not shout a slogan.[109] No sooner was Li brought to the execution ground than he suddenly realized his imminent death. He asked for paper, ink, and pen to author his last will, which was abruptly denied. According to one source, he uttered, "Heaven!" Zhu Chengjia, who has studied Li Dazhao throughout his scholarly career, states that the last words Li Dazhao uttered were "Alas, Father! I am delivering my soul to your hands!"[110] If this is true, these words display the strong impact of Christianity upon China's first communist.

Some scholars contend that Li Dazhao chose hanging rather than gunshot for his execution because he wanted to keep his body intact. If this is true, it reflects Li's commitment to traditional culture, which cherishes the integral entity of the human corpus. Some claim that Zhang Zuolin had particularly and intentionally imported the scaffold from the West for Li's execution, but the short time span of twenty-two days would not have allowed its transportation from a Western country to China. Perhaps Zhang used the gallows that was purchased from Britain some years before.[111] For decades, the claim that Li was hanged three times dominated the literature, as Zhang Cixi wrote: "Mr. Li climbed the scaffold and followed the executioner's order to extend his head forward a little bit. The executioner did not want Li to die immediately. Li was hanged two times through a calculated torture but was reawakened with cold water each time. Then, he was forced to walk around the scaffolds. The third hanging took another twenty minutes until he breathed his last."[112] In order to portray it as an excruciating process, Li Xinghua wrote that "the executioner intended to enlengthen his suffering and purposefully hanged him for forty minutes."[113] After careful studies, scholars today do not accept the claim of three hangings, which is regarded as an imprecise assumption.[114] It should be noted that nineteen others were also executed by hanging along with Li Dazhao, including Communists as well as Nationalists, among whom one was a woman. They were all followers of Li Dazhao in the United Front and now are respected as martyrs of the Chinese revolution by the Chinese government.

While Zhang Zuolin's regime incriminated Li Dazhao as a felon, charged him with treason, and executed him hastily, Li's death indeed caused strong repercussions throughout the country. Of course, the right-wing Nationalists had no pity for him because they hated him as a destroyer of the KMT, charged him with being a Russian lackey, and accused him of being a superstitious person for his belief in communism.[115] However, the popular sympathy for Li was pervasive. In particular, newspapers covered the miserable situation of the family he left behind, because "he left no savings, while his residence was empty without much furniture. Only some junky house fittings could be seen inside. The interior looks deplorable, while the dust overflows everywhere."[116] Li's friends and colleagues started to donate to Li's wife as an aid to her impoverished family.[117] Communists and the left-wing Nationalists grieved over Li's death. For the Communists, Li's death was equivalent to the collapse of the Great Wall, as Luo Zhanglong lamented.[118] Left-wing Nationalists like He Xiangning, the widow of Liao Zhongkai, shed tears at the sad news of Li's death.[119] A memorial service was held on May 22, 1927, in Wuhan to commemorate Li as a hero. Feng Yuxiang's army received the miserable news while marching eastward toward Henan. Feng ordered his troops to hold a traditional Chinese funeral, acclaiming Li as "a great revolutionary teacher" and bemoaning his death as "a huge loss."[120]

Li Dazhao's sudden arrest and speedy execution shocked the global community. Major Western newspapers covered the news about him from imprisonment to death. The second day after his death, the *New York Times* reported "the execution by strangling of a score of Chinese . . . Li Ta-chao [Dazhao], a widely known communist, was one of those exe-

Figure 8.1. Li Dazhao was arrested by the warlord Zhang Zuolin in Beijing on April 6, 1927. This photo was taken by the police during his imprisonment. Scholars have identified it as Li's last photo. He was promptly executed on April 28, 1927. (Public domain)

cuted."[121] The leftist writers in the West condemned the warlord regime. George Young, a British writer, denounced Zhang Zuolin as the chief of "the brutal Manchurian ex-brigands," defended the Russian protection of Li at the embassy, and praised Li as "a much-loved and valued leader.... He himself had chosen the post of danger where nothing stood between him and a painful and prolonged death."[122] Japanese communist leader Katayama Sen regarded Li's death as not only a colossal loss to China but also a big loss to the international revolutionary movement. *Pravda* of the USSR hailed Li as a hero and respected him as "a friend, a comrade, a scholar, a fighter, and a communist."[123] Vera V. Vishnyakova-Akimova, who served as an interpreter in Beijing and who knew Li personally, remarked that "the May Day celebration becomes colorless, because of the painful loss of those heroes who sacrificed their lives in Beijing." She extolled Li for "his exceptional ability and shiny personality. He was a brilliant party organizer and political activist."[124] Grigori Voitinsky, who assisted the establishment of the CCP, upon hearing the heartrending news, wrote an article to honor Li as "one of the founders of the Chinese Communist Party.... He was the bravest fighter in his struggle to overthrow the reactionary forces."[125]

It is even sadder to know that Li Dazhao's body was not given a proper burial after his execution. Immediately after his death, the warlord regime placed his corpse into a simple coffin. Thanks to his friends' donations, a new cypress coffin was purchased. According to a news report in Beijing, "the boss of the coffin shop did not know Li Dazhao and was not fond of communism. Yet after reading newspapers for days, he appreciated Li's moral deeds and treasured Li's ethical conduct. He only charged 140 yuan out of its original price of 250 yuan for the new coffin."[126] After Li's death, his wife suddenly fell ill out of sorrow. Li's uncle (his mother's brother), Mr. Zhou, who was over sixty years old, assisted Li's young children. After his execution, Li's body was delivered to Changchun Temple for a temporary stay. Then, with the new coffin, his body was transported to Zhe Temple.[127] At first, the monks there did not want to rent out a space for it, but they agreed to do so with a charge of four yuan per month.[128] One may ask, Why didn't his family transport his body to his village for a decent burial? According to a correspondent, Li's clan, out of fear of political persecution, rejected the idea of burying Li Dazhao in the clan's cemetery.[129] Perhaps local superstition was also a factor. Because Li was killed by strangulation, a burial in the cemetery would bring bad fortune to the entire extended family.[130] Thus, Li's burial was delayed, and his remains stayed in the Buddhist sanctuary for six years.

Conclusion

Revolutionaries have generally been categorized into two groups: theorists and activists. Li Dazhao acted as both at different times. He studied diverse theories, embraced communism, allied with Sun Yat-sen, published extensively, and deliberated on diverse topics. Nevertheless, he became more an activist than a theorist in his last years. He was more a doer than a thinker, although he continued to write on the Chinese revolution and offer his creative ideas. The growing literature about his last years demonstrates his revolutionary activities, detailed arrangements, and direct involvements. In many ways, Li put theory into practice. To target the imperialist powers and Chinese warlords, Li plunged into the national whirlpools, tried to bring changes, and endeavored to reach the objectives of the United Front. He did not drift away from what he set out to do; on the contrary, he placed himself in the toughest and the most dangerous spots to rally support from unfaltering followers and potential allies. Even if he elaborated theories, as he did on the role of the Chinese peasants in the revolution, he did it out of his realistic approach concerning the ongoing revolution. He was a scholar in the past but became a professional revolutionary in his last years.

Chinese scholars often assert that the failure of the CCP in the United Front was caused by the Communist leaders, who surrendered power to the Nationalists.[131] This claim might be true of Chen Duxiu, who was blamed for the Communist debacle in 1927, during which Communists were slaughtered and suppressed by Chiang Kai-shek and others. In contrast, from the very beginning in North China, Li Dazhao held the leadership role of the United Front, within which he later drew a clear line against the right-wing Nationalists. He was not an adventurer, and his steadfast leadership enabled him to become a chief manager of the two political parties. Even after he hid himself in the Russian Embassy following the March 18 Massacre, he continued to wield his power in leading the United Front. His refusal to leave Beijing meant that he was determined to continue his work for it. It was his leadership role that prompted Zhang Zuolin to arrest and execute him. Therefore, the debacle of the Communist cause in North China was not spawned by the Communists' surrender of power to the Nationalists; rather, it was caused by the stronger power of the warlord regime in the north.

One of the major issues in the study of the Northern Expedition, the last episode of the National Revolution, is the traditional overemphasis on the role of the Nationalist Revolutionary Army from Guangdong in overthrowing the warlord regime. Consequently, the endeavors of northern revolutionaries, including Li Dazhao, have been unreasonably ignored, negligently downplayed, and blithely discarded. It is true that the Nationalist Revolutionary Army under the command of Chiang Kai-shek and others was a crucial factor in the military victory. Yet Li also played a significant role in the Northern Expedition. He won over Feng Yuxiang, whose army ultimately joined the northbound Nationalist forces in Henan, exactly as Li expected. Li persuaded powerful strongmen, such as Yan Xishan, to lean toward the National Revolution, which panned out well. Li wrestled with tough issues and grappled with the complicated situation, while throughout it all he was determined to accomplish the goal of defeating the warlord regime. Although he did not have a chance to see the final victory of the Northern Expedition, his dedication and contributions to its triumph were indispensable. For these deeds, he became a vicious enemy of Zhang Zuolin, who suddenly arrested him and abruptly executed him. One could say that Li sacrificed his own life to the Northern Expedition in particular and to the National Revolution in general.

Epilogue

An abundance of scholarship on prominent figures attests to the truth that each historical era accrues an amazing inventory of influential individuals who played indispensable roles in propelling its history forward. In a sense, the macrohistory of an era can be viewed as the interplay of the deeds of those persons who are often singled out as a cluster of sequential symbols. The passage of time does not diminish them; on the contrary, their statuses remain prominently salient after years, decades, centuries, or even millennia have passed. Li Dazhao is such a man who lived during his country's transition from empire to republic and from tradition to modernity. He straddled the complex yet defining historical moment, on which he has left an indelible mark. Unlike many others, he was not a high-ranking official, not a military commander, and not a wealthy entrepreneur; instead, he was none other than an intellectual who used his pen to dispatch persuasive messages, to challenge old values, to pursue new ideas, and to defy powerful rulers. For all these reasons, he is regarded foremost as a man whose experience not only mirrored but also propelled his country's dramatic transformation. To realize his objective of national salvation, he exposed himself to multiple ideologies but ultimately embraced communism. Hence, he became China's first communist, cofounded the Chinese Communist Party, led the early communist movement, forged the United Front with Sun Yat-sen, and played a key role in the National Revolution.

Setting Li Dazhao in the historical context of modern China, one can easily envisage his importance in remolding his country even during such a short life, but the brevity of his life also makes it difficult to delineate a precise periodization. However, scholars need to utilize momentous events to sketch out a broadly delimited gauge denoting the start as well as the end of a distinctive period in a person's life. In Li's case, he had traversed through such clear-cut milestones since he had lived through the late Qing imperial decay, experienced the early republican turmoil, and participated in the postimperial radical movements. In other words, his early years could be periodized into a number of distinctive eras. His childhood and adolescent years prior to 1905 shaped his early life, which was characterized by his unfortunate upbringing and his pursuit of a classical education. Between 1905 and 1913, he received a modern education, which allowed him to step out of restrictive traditional barriers to greet Western civilization. From 1913 to 1916, his Japan years opened a new vista for him to continue his exploration of Western civilization through the Japanese channel and to become an activist. From 1916 to 1918, as an editor and a writer, he vehemently championed democracy, constitutional rule, individual freedom, and cultural renaissance. His pre-1918 life can in fact be periodized into those four unique eras in full harmony with what he did and achieved. However, his post-1918 experience has been interpreted in diverse ways through different approaches.[1] Here, the thematic approach, in chronological order, is adopted to trace his career at Beijing University, his embrace of communism, his alliance with Sun Yat-sen, his leadership role in the United Front, and his final days. Only in this way can Li's unique role in directing his nation into a new trajectory be accentuated.

Spurred by the call of his times, Li Dazhao enthusiastically participated in the New Culture Movement. It was during this movement that he came into the spotlight of the national arena, drawing public attention to his advocacy of a new culture for the purpose of saving his country and rejuvenating his nation. As products of a classical and modern education, his linguistic proficiency and critical thinking skills allowed him to become a broker of new knowledge, an importer of foreign ideas, and a challenger of old values. Indeed, most of the vanguard leaders of the New Culture Movement were young, energetic, and Western-oriented intellectuals, such as Li Dazhao, Hu Shi, and Chen Duxiu. Collectively, these intellectuals shared a common mission of jettisoning the tyrannical tradition, upholding the republican system, spreading the democratic ideal, and introducing new ideas. It was in this new milieu that Li staunchly safeguarded the republic and played an important role in promoting constitutional rule, for which he was acclaimed "a fighter for democracy" (*minzhudoushi*).[2] His firm stance against the old values won him fame in "ideological leadership."[3] His call to dismantle the Confucian edifice that assisted despotism did not mean that he intended to completely discard Confucianism; rather, his call to retain certain Confucian values so long as they fit the needs of modernization demonstrates his purpose of rejuvenating Chinese culture but incorporating it into a new civilization.[4]

The claim that Li Dazhao's grasp of communist theory revealed its "sophistication" (*chengshuxing*) at the very beginning of his embrace of it, as some assert, should be regarded as an exaggeration.[5] Without Li having read a large number of communist classics, his understanding of this foreign ideology could not have been so profound, although he had grasped its fundamentals. Consequently, his communist ideology was not a full-blown structure inside which diverse elements intermingled. It remained a developing thought, adaptable, adoptable, and still with the ability to change into a better entity. Maurice Meisner's and Arif Dirlik's scholarship demonstrates how Li's pre-Marxist ideas penetrated into his communist mindset. Democratic ideas, constitutionalism, anarchism, liberalism, and traditional culture all crisscrossed the boundaries within his new world of thought. Women's liberation, sympathy for the working class, individual rights, and other notions all left a mark on his newly acquired ideology. All of these serve as an impetus for interested scholars to devote further research to Li's thought. Nevertheless, Li accepted communism at the crucial moment of national crisis with the intention of utilizing it as a tool to solve China's problems. Indeed, what he did throughout his life was to hunt for a newer paradigm for national salvation. Whatever he chose, the underlying driving force was his nationalistic zeal: reviving his nation, modernizing his country, and rejuvenating his culture. To him, communism was almost a panacea, more suitable to China's circumstance and more fitting for a superlative outcome than other options. It was his nationalism along with other elements that deeply affected his concept of communism.

Li Dazhao's embrace of communism exposes the truth that the Chinese acceptance of communism was the result of a long-term ideological pursuit through manifold routes. Li's membership in the Socialist Party during 1912–13 demonstrates his initial interest in the socialist ideology. His friendship with Japanese socialists and his familiarity with their ideas directed him toward the socialist path. More importantly, he retrieved his communism-related materials through diverse channels but particularly through Japan. In this respect, Li's case contradicts the influential historiographical paradigm regarding the Chinese acceptance of communism, namely Mao Zedong's statement that "the salvoes of the October Revolution brought us Marxism-Leninism."[6] Mao's assertion overstated the Russian influence and created an impression that the Chinese accepted communism from Russia immediately after the breakout of the Bolshevik Revolution. Of course, the denial of this revolution as a factor would be ahistorical, but it is also not proper to exaggerate its influence. Li's personal experience goes beyond such a simplistic interpretation. Without a doubt, Li was inspired by the Russian Revolution and maintained useful contacts with Soviet Russia, which indeed impacted his acceptance of communism. Yet his interest in the ideology existed long before the Russian Revolution because, truly, he had traversed a long journey toward communism. His comprehension of the communist ideology via the Japanese sources means that Mao's statement was only partially true. In the end, the claim that communism was solely imported from Russia in a rapid manner is not historically accurate.

Li Dazhao continued to explore communism-related issues after he cofounded the CCP, but he became gradually more an activist than a theorist. During his last years, he drifted away from his former academic life and chose to be a professional revolutionary. Between 1924, when he forged the United Front with Sun Yat-sen, and 1927, when he was executed by Zhang Zuolin, he dedicated himself to the goals of the United Front: overthrowing the warlord regime, expelling the imperialist powers, and achieving national independence. Under his leadership, his United Front branch in Beijing turned out to be "a crucial joint" (*guanjiedian*) during the National Revolution for which he labored bravely in the heartland of the warlord regime.[7] To weaken Zhang Zuolin, Li adopted a number of strategies to woo other warlords into joining the United Front. His maneuvers with Feng Yuxiang were a great success, while similar stories abound concerning his other activities. As the Northern Expedition forces gathered momentum and occupied more regions, Li ratcheted up his pressure on Feng and others to adopt a workable strategy for the revolutionary cause. Facing his sagging power, Zhang Zuolin shifted his fury toward Li, dispatched his troops to storm the Russian Embassy, arrested Li, and executed him shortly afterward.

Li Dazhao's death was followed by a long burial delay, and his body deteriorated in a coffin at Zhe Temple in Beijing for six years, which went against the Chinese mortuary tradition requiring the corpse to be soon interred in a tomb with the proper ritual after a well-arranged memorial service. The political situation at that time did not allow for such a funeral, as Zhang Zuolin continued to control Beijing until June 1928, when he was killed by Japanese soldiers during his retreat to Manchuria. Zhang Zuolin's eldest son, Zhang Xueliang, became his successor but decided to side with the victorious Nationalist regime headed by Chiang Kai-shek, which helped the latter unify China. During those six years when Li's coffin stayed in the Buddhist temple, civil wars towered above Chinese political life, and the Communists suffered heavily from Chiang Kai-shek's merciless extermination campaigns. Nevertheless, the Chinese Communists continued to operate actively. When the warlord era was finally banished, upon the request of Li's widow, Zhao Renlan, along with support from a wide swath of society, a funeral for Li Dazhao was finally held on April 23, 1933. Nationalist leaders and social elites donated to it, including Wang Jingwei (one thousand yuan), Chen Gongbo (three hundred yuan), Dai Jitao (one hundred yuan), Lu Xun (fifty yuan), and many others.[8] Li Dazhao's former colleagues, friends, and others in Beijing attended the funeral. However, the Communists orchestrated an attempt to turn the funeral into a rally against Chiang Kai-shek. It is hard to know the number of attendees, as the estimates ranged between seven hundred and ten thousand.[9] What is certain is that it was a spectacular scene as Li's coffin was carried from the temple through the busy streets to the final destination of Wan'an Public Cemetery (Wan'angongmu) in Beijing. According to one report, dozens of protestors were arrested, while others sustained wounds during their clash with the police.[10] Finally, however, Li was buried in a sepulchre in a permanent location. Sadly enough, his postmortem history was quickly followed by the death of his spouse, Zhao Renlan, who passed away thirty-five days after his belated entombment.

Li Dazhao's dedication to the United Front overshadowed his contributions to the Communist cause. After all, he was a Communist leader. In the vast land of North China, Li recruited more members, established new branches, and supervised the Communist operations. Unfortunately for him, this was a region ruled by warlords who mostly assumed an anti-Communist stance. Under such a circumstance, it was not easy for him to expand the Communist membership. Numerically, the north indeed lagged behind the south in building up its roster. During the years from 1924 to 1927, the Communist membership increased dramatically, from 400 to 57,000,[11] among which only about 3,000 were activated in North China. It seems that in this respect, Li did not do enough. A close examination shows that the unfavorable situation was to blame. In contrast to the party's open or semi-open status in the south, its secret operation in the northern provinces made it difficult to achieve a speedy enlistment. Yet Li worked diligently to recruit new members, dispatched his followers to South China to support the revolutionary regime, and sent his adherents into the northern provinces for actions. His urgent task, however, was to coordinate with the south to win the National Revolution, in which he invested most of his time, energy, and expertise. Significantly, his continual control of the United Front in North China was impressive: among the nine executive members of the Nationalist Party branch in Beijing in early 1927, four were Communists, four were left-wing Nationalists, and only one was a right-wing Nationalist.[12]

On the national level, Li Dazhao's status as a contributor to the communist movement was equally indispensable. His theoretical elucidation of communism attracted many into accepting this foreign ideology. According to Mao Zedong's testimony, Mao swiftly embraced the ideology because of Li's guidance.[13] Li laid a solid foundation for the Communist organization, particularly in North China, as he steered early activists into adopting the communist faith, and many of them became future Communist leaders. The fact that the communist revolution was won first in North China, not South China, during the Chinese Civil War in the 1940s, could be seen in part as an attestation of Li's long-standing influence. His attempt to redefine the Chinese revolution with the realistic approach of relying on the peasants redirected his nation to a new path, which his disciple, Mao Zedong, would follow during the impending rural revolution.[14] Li's tragic death deprived him of his top leadership role in the CCP; as one academic writer assumed, "if Li Dazhao had not died . . . he would have inevitably become the next leader of the Chinese Communist Party, and then he would have been able to avoid many upcoming mistakes and failures of the party."[15] Unfortunately, Li died along with many other early communists during Chiang Kai-shek's brutal campaigns and the warlords' ruthless crackdowns. This means that the first group of Communists, who lived in the urban areas, received a modern education, possessed humanist values, assumed broad mindsets, and adapted their thinking to the recent global trends, were mostly eliminated by Chiang Kai-shek and the warlords. Amazingly, however, the next generation of communists carried on Li's workable paradigm of relying on the peasants as the main force for making a new type of revolution throughout the vast countryside.

Li Dazhao's sudden death did not eliminate him from the memory of those who had worked with him or befriended him. From the existing primary sources, we can sense their tender feelings, their authentic impressions, and their affectionate passion for him. Ding Weifen, who was a Nationalist leader and who worked with Li Dazhao in Beijing, remarked that "Mr. Li was an upright statesman. His death was a colossal loss to the revolutionary cause in the north."[16] Bao Huiseng, a cofounder of the Chinese Communist Party, praised Li as "an outstanding activist of the revolutionary movement."[17] Lu Xun, a famous writer and Li's colleague, remarked that "after I received the news of his death, his oval face, his delicate eyes and mustache, and his blue robe and black jacket often pop up in front of my eyes, along with an ominous guillotine as the backdrop."[18] Hu Shi, an ideological rival but a colleague, heard about Li's death during his visit to Japan, and he was shocked and saddened. In 1930, Hu commemorated his four lost friends, among whom was Li Dazhao.[19] Li's colleague at Beijing University Zhang Shenfu stated that "Li Dazhao should be respected as a perfect man of modern China."[20] Chen Zhongfan, another colleague, composed a poem on the tenth anniversary of Li's death to recall his friendship with Li and to express his profound respect for Li. Chen said that Li often appeared in his dreams and woke him up during the nighttime.[21] All these were personal memories, but they were spontaneous, genuine, and straightforward in delivering their affection for Li, an affection etched deeply in their minds and preserved well in their memories.

The next generation of authors who wrote about Li Dazhao endeavored to construct a new image of him. They did not have a chance to work with him and never even met him, but they had heard the stories about him. They collected information from diverse sources meant to praise Li as a hero. In this way, a collective memory gradually emerged. Their writings were intended to fit the need of the time—specifically, to enhance their own revolutionary spirit. Their efforts spanned the 1949 divide, while a number of writers continued to reconstruct Li's lofty image. Zhang Ruxin published an article in Yan'an in 1943 extolling Li Dazhao as "a great revolutionary," "a progressive fighter," and "the newest individual ever since the beginning of Chinese history." Zhang encouraged his fellow Communists to learn from Li's "proletarian purity, resoluteness, and bravery."[22] In 1947, Cai Shangsi published an article to commemorate the twentieth anniversary of Li's death, praising him for his creative thinking, his communist actions, and his fearless spirit. For Cai, Li was one of the greatest thinkers in Chinese history in terms of sacrificing a life for a faith.[23] After 1949, more similar publications came out; for instance, Zang Kejia gleaned materials, visited the places where Li had worked, and published a book-length poetic biography in 1959 acclaiming Li as a heroic martyr.[24]

Yet the Cultural Revolution between 1966 and 1976 stalled any moves to write on Li Dazhao as a cofounder of the Chinese Communist Party and cast a completely different light on him. In order to lend legitimacy to Mao Zedong's absolutism and deify his holiness, Mao cultists aimed at erasing the collective memory of Li Dazhao, who was valued as little to nothing. Even worse, an overtly anti-Li rhetoric came to the surface. It seems that Communist China had reneged on its own commitment to the ideology Li introduced, developed, and disseminated. The immediate motive and the underlying drive to foment such a mood was to exalt the Mao cult. Consequently, historical relics related to Li were removed from museums, his role in Communist history disappeared from the publications of that era, and even mentioning his name became taboo.[25] Kang Sheng, a follower of the Gang of Four, along with other radicals during the Cultural Revolution, defamed Li more blatantly, accusing Li of desecrating Mao, labeling Li as "at most a bourgeoisie democrat," and charging Li as "a traitor during his late years."[26] As more extremist actions were taken, Li's tomb stele was toppled and other related relics were damaged.[27] Susanne Weigelin-Schwiedrzik observed that "Li Dazhao's hiding in the Soviet embassy came close, in the eyes of some, to betraying his country as well as the Chinese Communist movement,"[28] because the Soviet Union was indeed seen as an enemy of Maoist China at that time.

The post-Mao political reform witnessed a rehabilitation of Li Dazhao's reputation. Although scholarly debates continued to produce diverse points of view concerning Li's life, ideas, and activities, the general mood was to raise Li's fame to a new height, which still continues to grow exponentially. In a sense, the post-Mao era transformed Li into a fated messenger who embraced communism, expanded its tenets, and spread its principles, for which he holds recognition as China's first communist. He is hailed as a great pioneer who constantly draws ideological, nationalistic, and emotional resonance. He retains a special status as a notable forerunner, a brave fighter, a moral paragon, and an immortal martyr. His tomb at Wan'an Public Cemetery was turned into a memorial mausoleum, and a new stele with a new inscription was erected. Officially, he has earned a quadruple title: "the pioneer of the Chinese communist movement, a great Marxist, an outstanding proletarian revolutionary, and one of the major founders of the Chinese Communist Party."[29] The places where he lived or worked are now tagged as heritage sites, while memorial halls and parks have been designated in his honor. Commemorative conferences are convened and related books published to glorify him as a bright beacon shedding light upon China's national path and his life as a milestone in modern Chinese history.[30]

Although Li Dazhao sacrificed his life as a leader of the United Front and openly exposed his identity as a Nationalist to the warlord regime after his arrest, he has not been well studied in Taiwan, where the Nationalist Party continued to rule until the beginning of the twenty-first century. For a long time, whenever issues related to Li Dazhao were mentioned, negative remarks often popped up. Scholars in Taiwan grieved over the May Fourth Movement intellectuals' march toward communism and regarded it as a great loss to the development of liberalism.[31] Some scholars downplayed the Communist role in the New Culture Movement and deemed it insignificant.[32] Other Taiwanese scholars accused the Communists of distorting history by claiming themselves the May Fourth Movement vanguards.[33] Some condemned the Communists for nearly ruining the great enterprise of Sun Yat-sen due to their egoism in taking advantage of the United Front.[34] Some regretted the formation of the United Front and the unexpected death of Sun Yat-sen, which gave the CCP a chance to grow.[35] Some expressed their pity for Li because, although he allegedly perceived the USSR as a new czarist empire, he could not quit his job as a Russian agent.[36] As for the United Front, some denounced Li for being a tyrant who firmly controlled the Nationalist branch in North China.[37] After the turn of the twenty-first century, however, this political rhetoric has been replaced by a more rational historical evaluation, as Fang-yen Yang's scholarly analysis of Li's search for a new civilization shows.[38]

No other loss to Li Dazhao's family was as titanic as his unexpected death. Suddenly, his execution left his widow and children helplessly stranded in Beijing. Similar to his own early years, his children immediately became quasi-orphans leading a miserable life, perhaps worse than his own childhood due to the immensity of trauma his horrific death left to them. His disheartened widow and children departed from Beijing for Daheituo Village in May 1927, leaving behind Li's body in a coffin at the Buddhist temple. Li's eldest son, Li Baohua, however, was hidden in the writer Zhou Zuoren's home for a while.[39] Soon, Li Baohua, with Li Dazhao's friends' help, was sent to Japan under the alias Yang Zhen to receive a higher education. According to one source, Li Baohua joined the Chinese Communist Party in early 1931 and returned to China that year because of Japan's occupation of Manchuria.[40] After the establishment of the People's Republic of China, Li Baohua became a top leader of Anhui Province and then a governor of the People's Bank in Beijing. Li Dazhao's young children, after the death of Zhao Renlan in 1933, became a group of orphans, but they were fortunately supported by Li's friends and other social elites. For example, Xiong Xiling, a former premier of the Republic of China, ran an orphanage in Beijing and took care of Li Dazhao's young children free of charge.[41] Later on, some of Li Dazhao's children went to Yan'an or joined the Communist forces in other locations. Li's daughter Li Xinghua, who was trained as a writer, authored a vivid memoir about her father, which was published posthumously in 1981. Unfortunately, Li's grown children were adversely impacted during the Cultural Revolution because their father was reviled. After 1976, however, Li Dazhao's descendants have enjoyed the respect of the Party. Li Dazhao's grandson Li Hongta, a retired government official, was bestowed the highest medal at the one hundredth anniversary of the founding of the Chinese Communist Party in July 2021 for carrying on the Li family's Communist tradition.[42]

Scholars have long complained about "the absence of a complete biography" of Li Dazhao in the English-speaking world.[43] The reasons for the nonexistence until now of such an important book are multiple. The lack of sufficient sources made it impossible to do so prior to 1976, after which more scholars have drifted away from the history of communism to focus on other diverse scholarly topics. However, a plethora of primary and secondary sources became available after 1976, which offered a chance for a scholar to undertake the massive task of writing such a comprehensive biography. Yet the mood in the late twentieth century was to enjoy a getaway from "an excessive focus on revolution" in order to diversify scholarly interests in social, economic, religious, frontier, and cultural issues.[44] Consequently, Li Dazhao, China's first communist, remains still far from familiar in the West, and a thorough biography of Li has remained unaccomplished. Recent events in the world, in particular the collapse of the Communist regimes in Eastern Europe and the USSR, have made many scholars and writers understandably oblivious to the importance of any communist figures, let alone Li Dazhao. Nevertheless, while Eastern Europe and Russia stepped out of communism, China continues to carry on the communist ideology first embraced by Li. It is a special form of communism that was accepted by Li, interpreted by Li, disseminated by Li, and recast by Li. His passion for national salvation permeated into this imported ideology, which was further developed into a sinicized version of communism. As Joseph W. Esherick argues, the Chinese revolution is "an evolving historical process," which inevitably involves a number of stages.[45] A careful analysis shows that Li was the first to inaugurate the entire process, helping to initiate its first stage and playing a principal role in the early communist movement. Given his importance, this monograph is intended to examine the life of Li Dazhao, analyze his ideas, highlight his roles, and unfold a neglected page regarding the genesis of the communist movement and the development of the first United Front in one of the most populous countries in the world.

Abbreviations

CCP	The Chinese Communist Party
Comintern	The Communist International
KMT	The Nationalist Party (Kuomintang)
KUTV	The Communist University of the Toilers of the East
LDZBXAZ	*Li Dazhao beibu xisheng anzang ziliaoxuanbian* (Selected materials concerning Li Dazhao's arrest, death, and burial), edited by Li Jihua, Chang Jinjun, and Li Quanxing (2011)
LDZQJ	*Li Dazhao quanji* (The complete works of Li Dazhao; 2013)
LDZYTJ	*Li Dazhao yu Tianjin* (Li Dazhao in Tianjin), edited by Liu Minshan (1989)
USSR	The Union of Soviet Socialist Republics
YMCA	The Young Men's Christian Association

Glossary

Beifanggonghehui 北方共和会
Beijingzhengbian 北京政变
Beixinshuju 北新书局
Beiyangfazhengxuehui 北洋法政学会
Beiyangfazhengzhuanmenxuexiao 北洋法政专门学校
Beiyangsanjie 北洋三杰
bozhongzhe 播种者
bupingdengtiaoyue 不平等条约
buren 不仁
buxin 不信
buyi 不义
buyong 不勇
buzhi 不智
Cai Yuanpei 蔡元培
Chen Duxiu 陈独秀
Chen Yilong 陈翼龙
Chenbao 晨报
chengshuxing 成熟性
Chenzhong 晨钟
Chiang Kai-shek (Jiang Jieshi) 蒋介石
chiseguojia 赤色国家
chongchu beiyang de fanli 冲出北洋的樊篱
choudi 仇敌
chunchise 纯赤色
Dageming 大革命
Dagongbao 大公报
Daheituo 大黑坨

dangsi 党私
daqi 大旗
Deng Yingchao 邓颖超
di'ertianxing 第二天性
Duan Qirui 段祺瑞
dudu 都督
Erqidabagong 二七大罢工
Feijidujiaoyundong 非基督教运动
Feizongjiaodatongmeng 非宗教大同盟
Feng Yuxiang 冯玉祥
Feng Ziyou 冯自由
Gao Yihan 高一涵
geminglaozu 革命老祖
genbenxingdegaizao 根本性的改造
Gongchandang 共产党
gongchanzhuyixiaozu 共产主义小组
gongdi 公敌
Gongrenzhoukan 工人周刊
guanggaodewenxue 广告的文学
Guangzhou (Canton) 广州
guanjiedian 关节点
Guanshuizizhuyundong 关税自主运动
gugan yuanshaan lianjin tuyu 固甘援陕联晋图豫
guihundeminguo 鬼混的民国
guihundeshenghuo 鬼混的生活
Guomingeming 国民革命
Guominjun 国民军
Guominshe 国民社
Guozijian 国子监
hanjiaqi 汉家旗
Hantou 憨头
heimu 黑幕
Honglou 红楼
Hongqianghui 红枪会
Hu Jingyi 胡景翼
Hu Shi 胡适
huahui 花会
Huaidetang 怀德堂
huangjinzhihongshui 黄金之洪水

Hufayundong 护法运动
Huguozhanzheng 护国战争
Jiang Weiping 蒋卫平
Jiayin 甲寅
Jiayinrikan 甲寅日刊
Jieshi 碣石
Jindehui 进德会
Jing Ke 荆轲
jingshenlingxiu 精神领袖
jingtu 净土
jiushichou 九世仇
Jiyatai 吉雅泰
Juewushe 觉悟社
junhuo 君祸
juren 巨人
juren (degree) 举人
Kaifeng 开封
Kang Sheng 康生
Kang Youwei 康有为
Kangmuyizhai 亢慕义斋
Kejuzhidu 科举制度
Kuomintang 国民党
Laodongyin 劳动音
laomuji 老母鸡
Laoting 乐亭
Li Dazhao 李大钊
Li Dazhao quanji 李大钊全集
Li Dazhao xuanji 李大钊选集
Li Guoqiu 李国秋
Li Renrong 李任荣
Li Rubi 李如璧
Li Ruzhen 李如珍
Li Ruzhu 李如珠
Li Weimo 李为模
Li Yuanhong 黎元洪
Liang Qichao 梁启超
linghunrenwu 灵魂人物
lishizhuanshan 李氏专擅
Litiezui 李铁嘴

Liurixueshengzonghui 留日学生总会
Lu Xun 鲁迅
Lumozhibu 旅莫支部
luowuzhe 落伍者
Ma Lin (G. Maring; Hendricus Sneevliet) 马林
Maergesi xueshuo' yanjiuhui 马尔格士学说研究会
Makesi xueshuo yanjiuhui 马克思学说研究会
Mao Zedong 毛泽东
menglong 朦胧
Mengzangxuexiao 蒙藏学校
minchang 民常
Minquanyundongdatongmeng 民权运动大同盟
minxian 民宪
minyi 民彝
minzhudoushi 民主斗士
muti 母体
nanchenbeili 南陈北李
pingminzhuyi 平民主义
pinjiexuecui 品洁学粹
pinyin 拼音
piyingxi 皮影戏
Puyi 溥仪
qianhongse 浅红色
Qianziwen 千字文
qieguo 窃国
Qin Shihuang 秦始皇
qingchun 青春
qiren 旗人
quandi 圈地
ronggong 容共
Sangu 三姑
Sanyibacan'an 三一八惨案
Sanzijing 三字经
shanhouhuiyi 善后会议
Shaonianzhongguoxuehui 少年中国学会
Shehuizhuyiyanjiuhui 社会主义研究会
shengsi 省私
Shenzhouxuehui 神州学会
Shenzhouxuekan 神州学刊

Shoudugeming 首都革命
shoushuderen 守书的人
shuyuan 书院
Sun Hongyi 孙洪伊
Sun Yat-sen (Sun Zhongshan) 孙中山
Tang Hualong 汤化龙
tongshi 痛史
Tongzhijulebu 同志俱乐部
Tushuguanzhuren 图书馆主任
tuyu 土语
Ulanhu (Wulanfu) 乌兰夫
Wan'angongmu 万安公墓
weidadeshili 伟大的势力
Weidangtongmeng 卫党同盟
weitiaohe 伪调和
wenmingzhibing 文明之病
Wu Peifu 吴佩孚
Wufengshan 五峰山
wugendehua 无根的花
Wusayundong 五卅运动
Wusiyundong 五四运动
wuzhi 物质
Xianfagongyan 宪法公言
xianghuodi 香火地
Xihuhuiyi 西湖会议
Xinchaoshe 新潮社
Xinqingnian 新青年
Xinwenhuayundong 新文化运动
Xinzheng 新政
Xinzhonghuaminzu 新中华民族
Xishanhuiyipai 西山会议派
xiucai 秀才
Xu Zhimo 徐志摩
Yan Xishan 阎锡山
Yang Du 杨度
Yan-Zhao wenhua 燕赵文化
Yanzhi 言治
Yijianshu 意见书
Yimaoxuehui 乙卯学会

yonggandeqiangshou 勇敢的枪手
Yongpingfuzhongxuetang 永平府中学堂
Yu Shude 于树德
yuan'e 元恶
Yuan Shikai 袁世凯
Yunnanxuanyan 云南宣言
zaishuren 栽树人
zaizaozhongguo 再造中国
Zhang Cixi 张次溪
Zhang Guotao 张国涛
Zhang Shizhao 章士钊
Zhang Xueliang 张学良
Zhang Xun 张勋
Zhang Zuolin 张作霖
Zhangchengyundong 章程运动
Zhangjiakou 张家口
zhanjiang 战将
Zhao Renlan 赵纫兰
zhengzhiweiyuan 政治委员
zhijiexingdong 直接行动
Zhili 直隶
zhixingbu 执行部
Zhongguohua 中国化
Zhongguojingjicaizhengxuehui 中国经济财政学会
Zhongguolaodongzuheshujibu 中国劳动组合书记部
Zhongguoshehuidang 中国社会党
Zhonghuaxuehui 中华学会
zhongshu 中枢
zhongxinshili 中心势力
zhongyangju 中央局
Zhongyangribao 中央日报
Zhou Enlai 周恩来
Zhou Zuoren 周作人
Zhu Shunshui 朱舜水
zhuangzhongren 撞钟人
zhujiang 主将
zichanmu 子产母
zizhong 自重
zuji 祖籍

Notes

Introduction

1. Sun Yat-sen, "*Jianshe* fakanci" [Introduction of the inaugural issue of *Jianshe*], *Jianshe* [Reconstruction] 1, no. 1 (1919): 1.

2. Ishikawa Yoshihiro, *The Formation of the Chinese Communist Party*, trans. Joshua A. Fogel (New York: Columbia University Press, 2013), 8.

3. Zhen Jiang, "Li Dazhao: Zhongguo de 'Puluomixiusi'" [Li Dazhao: China's Prometheus], *Guojiarenwenlishi* [National humanity history], December 2017, 17.

4. Zhu Zhimin, *Li Dazhao zhuan* [Biography of Li Dazhao] (Beijing: Hongqichubanshe, 2009), 2.

5. Li Ming, *Zhonggong liulieshi xiaozhuan* [Short biographies of the six communist martyrs] (Hong Kong: Xinzhongguoshuju, 1949), 4.

6. Zhang Jianguo, *Weidade bozhongzhe* [The great seed-sower] (Wuhan: Hubeirenminchubanshe, 1980), 1.

7. Zhonggongzhongyangdangshiyanjiushi, *Li Dazhao yanjiu wenji* [A collection of research articles on Li Dazhao] (Beijing: CCP History Press, 1991), 3.

8. Zhonggongzhongyangdangshiyanjiushi, *Li Dazhao yanjiu wenji*, 7.

9. Zhonggongzhongyangdangshiyanjiushi, 18.

10. Tai Wan-chin, "Chen Duxiu's Conversion from a Liberal Democrat to a Marxist-Leninist: Motivation and Impact," *Tamkang Journal of International Affairs* 11, no. 1 (2007): 115.

11. Jonathan D. Spence, *The Search for Modern China*, 3rd ed. (New York: W. W. Norton, 2013), 222.

12. Dahua Zhang, "On Modern Chinese Nationalism and Its Conceptualization," *Journal of Modern Chinese History* 6, no. 2 (December 2012): 217.

13. Dong Baorui, "Li Dazhao de wentanhaoyou Gao Yihan" [Gao Yihan: Li Dazhao's good friend in the literary circle], *Dangshizongheng*, no. 4 (2003): 17.

14. Zhang Jingru and Wu Hanquan, "Zhongguo jiang 'dierci dagongxianyu shijiezhijinbu': Li Dazhao yu Zhongguomeng" [China will make "another contribution to the world's progress": Li Dazhao and the Chinese Dream], *Tangshanxueyuanxuebao* [Journal of Tangshan University] 29, no. 4 (July 2016): 9.

15. Han Yide and Wang Shudi, *Li Dazhao yanjiu lunwenji* [Collection of publications on the study of Li Dazhao] (Shijiazhuang: Hebeirenminchubanshe, 1984), 1:44.

16. Shao Guoying, "Li Dazhao wenzhang 'shenhoushi'" [The follow-up stories concerning Li Dazhao's writings], *Huaihuaxueyuanxuebao* [Journal of Huaihua University] 33, no. 12 (December 2014): 58.

17. Zhang Cixi, *Li Dazhao xiansheng zhuan* [Biography of Mr. Li Dazhao] (Beijing: Xuanwenshudian, 1951), 2.

18. Zang Kejia, *Li Dazhao* (Beijing: Zuojiachubanshe, 1959), 149.

19. Wang Chaomei, ed., *Li Dazhao yanjiu lunwenji* [A collection of articles on the study of Li Dazhao] (Beijing: Zhonggongdangshichubanshe, 1991), 26.

20. Lidazhaozhuanbianxiezu, *Li Dazhao zhuan* [Biography of Li Dazhao] (Beijing: Renminchubanshe, 1979), 265.

21. Chang-tai Hung, "The Cult of the Red Martyr: Politics of Commemoration in China," *Journal of Contemporary History* 43, no. 2 (April 2008): 287.

22. Wu Hanquan, "Jinshinian Li Dazhao yanjiu de jinzhan ji xiangguan wenti de taolun" [The discourse over the new research on Li Dazhao and other related issues in the past ten years], *Jindaishiyanjiu* [Modern history studies], no. 4 (2006): 146.

23. Peng Hongwei and Li Yuzhen, "Guanyu Li Dazhao zai sulian jianghua he wenzhang de shuoming" [A note on the speeches and articles by Li Dazhao while he was in the Soviet Union], *Jindaishiyanjiu* [Modern history studies] 30, no. 6 (1985): 5–10.

24. Han Chunyun, "Li Dazhao xiegei Sun Zhongshan de xindeng zai helan guojiadang'anguan faxian" [The findings of the letter by Li Dazhao to Sun Yat-sen and other items in the Dutch National Archives], *Lantaishijie* [The Lantai world], no. 1 (May 2011): 48.

25. Han Yide and Yao Weidou, "Jinnian faxian de Li Dazhao yiwen jiqi jiazhi" [The value of Li Dazhao's recently discovered writings], in Wang Chaomei, *Li Dazhao yanjiu lunwenji*, 356.

26. "Publisher's notes," in Li Dazhao, *Li Dazhao quanji* [The complete works of Li Dazhao] (Beijing: Renminchubanshe, 2013), 1:4 (hereafter cited as *LDZQJ*).

27. Zhu Chengjia, "*Li Dazhao wenji* zhong jipianwenzhang de biankao" [The examination of a few articles in *The Selected Works of Li Dazhao*], *Jindaishi yanjiu* [Modern history studies], no. 1 (1998): 267–77.

28. Li Jihua, "Yetan dui Li Dazhao jipianwenzhang de biankao—jiujiaoyu Zhu Chengjia xiansheng" [My remarks on the examination of a few articles of Li Dazhao—a scholarly dialogue with Mr. Zhu Chengjia], *Dangshibolan* [Party history expo], no. 7 (2006): 48–59.

29. Yang Hu and Wang Xianming, "Xueshu zhushi qiangushi, xunguizunxianshiyoucheng—dui Li Dazhao lunzhu zhong sige waiguo renming zhushi ji xiangguanwenti de zai tantao" [Reexamination of the annotations to four foreign names in Li Dazhao's works and some questions related to the annotations], *Qinghuadaxuexuebao* 25, no. 3 (2010): 51–63.

30. Li Jihua, "Dui xinban *Li Dazhao quanji* bufenzhushi de shangque" [A suggestion to some notes in *The Complete Works of Li Dazhao*], *Hebeixuekan* [Hebei academic journal] 27, no. 2 (March 2007): 115–18.

31. Maurice Meisner, *Li Ta-chao and the Origins of Chinese Marxism* (Cambridge, MA: Harvard University Press, 1967), xii.

Chapter 1

1. Charles Carlton, *Royal Childhoods* (London: Routledge / K. Paul, 1986), 1.

2. Qin Aimin and Guo Zhenxiang, "Li Dazhao yu zhongguo nongmin wenti" [Li Dazhao and China's peasant problems], *Wenshijinghua* [Essence of literature and history], no. 2 (1999): 26–28.

3. Li Dazhao, "You Jieshi shan zaji" [Miscellany concerning my travel to Mount Jieshi], November 1, 1913, *LDZQJ*, 1:144.

4. Li Dazhao, "Wufengshan ji" [My travel to Wufengshan], August 31 and September 7, 1919, *LDZQJ*, 3:62.

5. Zhou Jingbao, "Li Dazhao zuji tanxi" [An analysis of the ancestral locale of Li Dazhao], *Tangshanxueyuanxuebao* 30, no. 1 (January 2017): 18–21.

6. Wang Yanping, *Li Dazhao zuji chutan* [Survey of Li Dazhao's ancestral locale], *Dang'antiandi* [Archives world], no. 11 (2012): 30–33.

7. Du Quanzhong, *Li Dazhao yandu* [A study of Li Dazhao] (Beijing: Zhongyangbianyichubanshe, 2006), 85.

8. Zhu Zhimin, *Li Dazhao zhuan* [Biography of Li Dazhao], 7.

9. Li Dazhao, "Wanshui jiyou" [To a friend during the year's end], winter 1909, *LDZQJ*, 5:309.

10. Zhang Tongle, "Shilun Li Dazhao aiguozhuyisixiang de Yan-Zhaowenhua yuanyuan" [Li Dazhao's patriotic thought and its origin in the Yan-Zhao culture], *Hebeiguangbodianshidaxuexuebao* [Journal of Hebei Radio and Television University] 16, no. 1 (February 25, 2011): 7–11.

11. Zhang Jianguo, *Weidade bozhongzhe* [The great seed-sower], 85.

12. Zhu Wentong, "Li Dazhao yu jidujiaowenhua" [Li Dazhao and Christian culture], *Hebeishifandaxuexuebao* [Journal of Hebei Normal University] 37, no. 1 (January 2014): 28–29.

13. Zhu Wentong, "Li Dazhao yu jidujiaowenhua," 33.

14. Zhonggongtangshanshiweidangshiyanjiushi, *Li Dazhao yu guxiang* [Li Dazhao and his hometown] (Beijing: Zhongyangwenxianchubanshe, 1994), 10–14.

15. Li Xinghua, *Huiyi wodefuqin Li Dazhao* [My memory of my father Li Dazhao] (Shanghai: Shanghaiwenyichubanshi, 1981), 16.

16. Zhu Zhimin, *Li Dazhao zhuan* [Biography of Li Dazhao], 10.

17. Du Quanzhong, *Li Dazhao yandu* [A study of Li Dazhao], 60.

18. Li Yibin, "Guanyu Li Dazhao tongzhi de shengnianyueri wenti" [The issue concerning the time of Comrade Li Dazhao's birth], *Lishiyanjiu* [Historical research], no. 9 (1978): 93.

19. Meisner, *Li Ta-chao and the origins of Chinese Marxism*, 1.

20. Charles A. Desnoyers, *Patterns of East Asian History* (New York: Oxford University Press, 2018), 278.

21. Zhu Chengjia, *Li Dazhao zhuan* [Biography of Li Dazhao] (Beijing: Zhongguoshehuikexuechubanshe, 2009), 10.

22. Li Dazhao, "Yuzhongzishu" [Personal statement in the jail], *LDZQJ*, 5:297.

23. Some scholars argue that Li Dazhao's father died in April 1889. Du Quanzhong, *Li Dazhao yandu*, 12.

24. Zhu Chengjia, *Li Dazhao zhuan*, 10.

25. Huang Zhen and Yao Weidou, *Li Dazhao de gushi* [The story of Li Dazhao] (Shijiazhuang: Hebeirenminchubanshe, 1980), 3.

26. Li Xinghua, *Huiyi wodefuqin Li Dazhao*, 23.

27. Li Xinghua, 19.

28. Li Xinghua, 19.

29. Li Dazhao, "Yuzhongzishu," *LDZQJ*, 5:297.

30. Fang Siji, "Shaonian Li Dazhao de zhuangzhihaoqing" [The motivated aspiration of young Li Dazhao], *Xiaoxueshengshidai* [Schoolkid times], no. 2 (2011): 5.

31. Zhu Zhimin, *Li Dazhao zhuan*, 11.

32. Li Xinghua, *Huiyi wodefuqin Li Dazhao*, 28.

33. Zhu Zhimin, *Li Dazhao zhuan*, 14.

34. Du Quanzhong, *Li Dazhao yandu*, 93.

35. Li Dazhao, "Yuzhongzishu," *LDZQJ*, 5:297.

36. Ichisada Miyazaki, *China's Examination Hell: The Civil Service Examinations of Imperial China* (New York: Weatherhill, 1976), 1.

37. Benjamin A. Elman, *Civil Examinations and Meritocracy in Late Imperial China* (Cambridge, MA: Harvard University Press, 2013), 319.

38. Benjamin A. Elman, "Political, Social, and Cultural Reproduction via Civil Service Examinations in Late Imperial China," *Journal of Asian Studies* 50, no. 1 (February 1991): 8.

39. Du Quanzhong, *Li Dazhao yandu*, 103, 105, 222.

40. Zhonggongtangshanshiweidangshiyanjiushi, *Li Dazhao yu guxiang*, 44–45.

41. Li Xinghua, *Huiyi wodefuqin Li Dazhao*, 24.

42. Du Quanzhong, *Li Dazhao yandu*, 110.

43. Fu Shaochang, "Li Dazhao zaoqi aiguosixiang jiqi tedian" [The characteristics of Li Dazhao's early patriotic thoughts], *Hongsewenhuaxuekan* [Journal of Red Culture], no. 2 (September 2017): 69.

44. Du Quanzhong, *Li Dazhao yandu*, 111.

45. He Zongyu, "Woyeyaodang Hong Xiuquan" [I also want to be Hong Xiuquan], in *Li Dazhao rengefengfan* [The noble character of Li Dazhao], ed. Zhonggonghebeishengweidangshiyanjiushi and Tangshanshi Li Dazhao yanjiuhui (Beijing: Hongqichubanshe, 1999), 76.

46. Fu Shaochang, "Li Dazhao zaoqi aiguosixiang jiqi tedian," 69.

47. Du Quanzhong, *Li Dazhao yandu*, 104.

Chapter 2

1. Zhang Jingru et al., *Li Dazhao shengping shiliao biannian* [Chronicle of historical materials concerning Li Dazhao's life] (Shanghai: Shanghairenminchubanshe, 1984), 2.

2. Zhu Wentong, *Li Dazhao zhuan* [Biography of Li Dazhao] (Tianjin: Tianjin Gujichubanshe, 2005), 24.

3. Zhu Wentong, *Li Dazhao zhuan*, 34–35.

4. Zhu Wentong, *Li Dazhao zhuan*, 27, 29.

5. Zhonggongtangshanshiweidangshiyanjiushi, *Li Dazhao yu guxiang* [Li Dazhao and his hometown], 282.

6. Fu Shaochang, "Li Dazhao zaoqi aiguosixiang jiqi tedian" [The characteristics of Li Dazhao's early patriotic thoughts], 70.

7. Wang Jing, "Minguo dilixueren Bai Meichu dui nanhaijiangyu de lunshu" [Bai Meichu, a geographer in the Republic of China, discussed the territory of the South China Sea], *Nanhaixuekan* [Journal of South China Sea studies] 9, no. 2 (2023): 59.

8. Zhonggongtangshanshiweidangshiyanjiushi, *Li Dazhao yu guxiang*, 60.

9. Ma Mao, "Liu He jiazuwangshi" [The old stories of Liu He's extended family], Universities Service Centre for China Studies Collection (website), accessed August 5, 2021, http://mjlsh.usc.cuhk.edu.hk/Book.aspx?cid=4&tid=5059; Taihangyingxiong, "Liu He de fuqin Liu Zhiyan" [Liu He's father Liu Zhiyan], January 19, 2020, https://web.archive.org/web/20200212224456/http://taihang-summit.com/28dc001ec0/.

10. Feng Ziyou, "Guanwai daxia Jiang Datong" [A brave warrior in Northeast China], in *Li Dazhao yu Tianjin*, ed. Liu Minshan (Tianjin: Tianjinshehuikexueyuanchubanshe, 1989), 287 (hereafter *LDZYTJ*).

11. Li Dazhao, "Ti Jiang Weiping yixiang" [Inscription to the portrait of late Jiang Weiping], winter 1910, *LDZQJ*, 5:311; Li Dazhao, "Ku Jiang Weiping" [Weeping over Jiang Weiping], 1911, *LDZQJ*, 5:312.

12. Li Xinghua, *Huiyi wodefuqin Li Dazhao* [My memory of my father Li Dazhao], 25–26.

13. Li Dazhao, "Yuzhongzishu" [Personal statement in jail], April 1927, *LDZQJ*, 5:297.

14. Li Dazhao, "Yuzhongzishu," 5:302.

15. Li Dazhao, "Wufeng youji" [A travel to Wufeng], August 31 and September 7, 1919, *LDZQJ*, 3:61.

16. Li Dazhao, "You Jieshi shan zaji" [Miscellany concerning my travel to Mount Jieshi], November 1, 1913, *LDZQJ*, 1:144.

17. *Beiyangfazhengxuetang zhangcheng* [The program of North China College of Laws and Politics], 1907, in Liu Minshan, *LDZYTJ*, 224–28.

18. Li Xinghua, *Huiyi wode fuqin Li Dazhao*, 26.

19. Yu Shude, "Wo suozhidaode Li Dazhao tongzhi" [Comrade Li Dazhao as I know him], in *Huiyi Li Dazhao* [In memory of Li Dazhao], by Xu Deheng et al. (Beijing: Renminchubanshe, 1980), 23.

20. Zhu Wentong, *Li Dazhao zhuan*, 45.

21. Yu Yi, "Song Li Guinian youxue riben xu" [A note on sending Li Guinian to study in Japan], 1913, in Liu Minshan, *LDZYTJ*, 263.

22. Zhou Hongxing and Li Ruluan, *Li Dazhao shi qianshi* [A concise interpretation of Li Dazhao's poems] (Chengdu: Sichuanrenminchubanshe, 1979), 1–2.

23. Marjorie Dryburgh, "Rewriting Collaboration: China, Japan, and the Self in the Diaries of Bai Jianwu," *Journal of Asian Studies* 68, no. 3 (August 2009): 689–714.

24. Li Dazhao, "Zeng Youfang, Shoushan" [To Youfang (Ni Dingyun) and Shoushan (Liu Xiling)], Fall 1913, *LDZQJ*, 5:316.

25. Li Dazhao, "Shibanianlaizhihuigu" [Retrospection over the past eighteen years], December 23, 1923, *LDZQJ*, 4:495.

26. Liu Minshan, *LDZYTJ*, 10.

27. Liu Minshan, 13–14.

28. Zhou Xinjuan and Qin Ling, "Li Dazhao yu xinhaigeming" [Li Dazhao and the 1911 Revolution], *Chizhoushizhuanxuebao* [Journal of Chizhou Teachers' College] 21, no. 4 (August 2007): 61–63.

29. Li Dazhao, "Luxing riji" [A traveling diary], May 9–11, 1917, *LDZQJ*, 2:206.

30. Liu Minshan, *LDZYTJ*, 20.

31. Zhu Chengjia, *Li Dazhao zhuan*, 119.

32. Liu Minshan, *LDZYTJ*, 33, 237.

33. Liu Minshan, 252.

34. John King Fairbank, Edwin O. Reischauer, and Albert M. Craig, *East Asia: Tradition and Transformation* (Houghton Mifflin, 1989), 435, 558.

35. Li Dazhao, "Denglouzagan" [Assorted feelings on the tower], 1908, *LDZQJ*, 5:307.

36. Li Dazhao, "Zhu Shunshui zhihaitianhongzhua" [The life in exile of Zhu Shunshui], April 1, 1913, *LDZQJ*, 1:23.

37. Li Dazhao, "Suiwanjiyou," *LDZQJ*, 5:309.

38. Zhang Cixi, *Li Dazhao xianshengzhuan*, 3.

39. Li Dazhao, "Yinyoupian" [Hidden worries], June 1912, *LDZQJ*, 1:1.

40. Li Dazhao, "Da'aipian" [The great lamentation], April 1, 1913, *LDZQJ*, 1:9.

41. Li Dazhao, "Da'aipian," 7.

42. Zhu Chengjia, "Li Dazhao dui Yuan Shikai de renshi guocheng" [A history of Li Dazhao's changing attitudes toward Yuan Shikai], *Lishiyanjiu* [Historical research], no. 6 (1983): 12–21.

43. Li Dazhao, "Nantian dongluan, shijiangquguo, yi Tianwen junzhong" [My friend Tianwen went to join the army in the turbulent South], August 1913, *LDZQJ*, 5:314–15.

44. Li Dazhao, "Shifeipian" [Correct and wrong], September 1, 1913, *LDZQJ*, 1:102.

45. Li Dazhao, "Yinyoupian," 1:1–2.

46. Li Dazhao, "Da'aipian," 1:8.

47. Li Dazhao, "Lunminquan zhipangluo" [On the loss of the people's rights], June 1, 1913, *LDZQJ*, 1:73.

48. Li Dazhao, "Cai dudu hengyi" [My remarks on the removal of military governors], June 1, 1913, 1:61–64.

49. Li Dazhao, "Ansha yu qunde" [Assassination and mass morality], May 1, 1913, *LDZQJ*, 1:43–44.

50. Li Dazhao, "Yuansha" [The cause of killing], September 1, 1913, *LDZQJ*, 1:79.

51. Li Dazhao, "Ouzhou geguo xuanjuzhi kao" [An exploration into the election system in European states], November 1, 1913, *LDZQJ*, 1:132–36.

52. Li Dazhao, "Geguo yiyuan fenggei kao" [The salaries of congressmen in diverse countries], November 1, 1913, *LDZQJ*, 1:139–42.

53. Li Dazhao, "Lun guanliaozhuyi" [On the civil service system], September 1, 1913, *LDZQJ*, 1:86–88.

54. Li Dazhao, "Tanhe yongyu zhi jiefen" [An explanation of the notion of impeachment], early March 1913, *LDZQJ*, 1:12–15.

55. Li Dazhao, "Yiyuanzhi yu eryuanzhi" [The unicameral legislature and the bicameral legislature], September 1, 1913, *LDZQJ*, 1:95.

56. Li Dazhao, "Lun xianfa gongbuquan dangshu xianfahuiyi" [The power to proclaim the constitution should be in the hands of the constitution-making body], October 1, 1913, *LDZQJ*, 1:107.

57. Wu Hanquan, "Tuo'ersitai dui Li Dazhao zaoqisixiang de yingxiang" [Leo Tolstoy's impact on Li Dazhao's early thoughts], *Xueshujiaoliu* [Academic exchanges], no. 6 (1993): 125–30.

58. Li Dazhao, trans., "Tuo'ersitai zhuyi zhi gangling" [The program of Leo Tolstoy], April 1, 1913, *LDZQJ*, 5:543–45.

59. Li Dazhao, "Yuansha," 1:81; Li Dazhao, "Wenhao" [The eminent writers], November 1, 1913, *LDZQJ*, 1:121.

60. Li Dazhao, "Zhengke zhi quwei" [The interests of the politicians], September 1, 1913, *LDZQJ*, 1:98.

61. Li Dazhao, "You Jieshishan zaji," 1:149.

Chapter 3

1. Zhu Chengjia, *Li Dazhao zhuan* [Biography of Li Dazhao], 219.

2. Spence, *Search for Modern China*, 269–73.

3. Han Yide, "Li Dazhao liuxueshiqi de shishikaocha" [A survey of historical facts concerning Li Dazhao's study abroad in Japan], *Jindaishiyanjiu* [Modern Chinese history studies] 1989, no. 1 (1989): 303.

4. Li Dazhao, "You Jieshishan zaji," *LDZQJ*, 1:149.

5. Li Dazhao, "Jinggao quanguo fulao shu" [Proclamation to alert all our compatriots], early February 2016, *LDZQJ*, 1:218.

6. Gao Zhonghua, "Li Dazhao de jiawuguan" [Li Dazhao's perspective on the First Sino-Japanese War], *Tangshanxueyuanxuebao* [Journal of Tangshan University] 30, no. 2 (March 2017): 31.

7. Li Fengbin and Wang Wei, "Qingmo zhongguo xuesheng liuri yuanyinchutan" [A preliminary study of the reasons why the Chinese students went to Japan during the late Qing period], *Yinshanxuekan* [Yinshan academic journal], no. 2 (1996): 77.

8. Zhu Chengjia, *Li Dazhao zhuan*, 222–24.

9. Yu Yi, "Song Li Guinian youxue riben xu," in Liu Minshan, *LDZYTJ*, 263.

10. Dong Baorui, "Liuxueriben zai Li Dazhao yishengzhong suoqidezuoyong" [The impact of Li Dazhao's study in Japan upon his whole life], *Hebeixuekan* [Journal of Hebei], no. 1 (1990): 44.

11. Zhu Wentong, *Li Dazhao zhuan*, 71.

12. Zhang Weimin, "Qingmo zhongguo xuesheng de liurilangchao" [The wave of Chinese students in Japan during the late Qing period], *Zhongguoqingnianyanjiu* [China youth study], no. 1 (1998): 47.

13. Zhu Zhimin, *Li Dazhao zhuan*, 58–60.

14. Li Dazhao, "Ziranlu yu hengpinglu shi" [Natural laws and balance laws], November 1, 1913, *LDZQJ*, 1:154.

15. Jia Tianyun and Liu Aiying, "Li Dazhao fu ribenliuxue shijiankao" [An examination of the time when Li Dazhao arrived in Japan for his study abroad], *Jindaishiyanjiu*, no. 2 (1995): 281.

16. Zhu Wentong, "Li Dazhao fu ribenliuxue shijian bianxi" [An analysis of the timing of Li Dazhao's arrival in Japan for his study abroad], *Jindaishiyanjiu*, no. 2 (1996): 279.

17. Han Yide, "Li Dazhao liuxueshiqi de shishikaocha," 303.

18. Meisner, *Li Ta-chao and the Origins of Chinese Marxism*, 2.

19. Zhu Chengjia, *Li Dazhao zhuan*, 230.

20. Mori Masao, "Li Dazhao zai zaodaotian daxue" [Li Dazhao studied at Waseda University], *Qiluxuekan* [Qilu journal], no. 1 (1987): 74–75.

21. Zhu Chengjia, *Li Dazhao zhuan*, 232.

22. Li Dazhao, "Shibanianlaizhihuigu" [Retrospection over the past eighteen years], *LDZQJ*, 4:497.

23. Zhu Wentong, *Li Dazhao zhuan*, 73.

24. Yang Shusheng, "Liuxueriben dui Li Dazhao de yingxiang" [The impact of study abroad in Japan upon Li Dazhao], in Zhonggongzhongyangdangshiyanjiushi, *Li Dazhao yanjiu wenji*, 125.

25. Li Dazhao, "Zhi Jiyezuozao" [To Yoshino Sakuzo], June 15, 1919, *LDZQJ*, 5:385.

26. Li Dazhao, "Zhongguo guoji falun yixu" [Preface to the Chinese version of *China's International Laws*], April 1915, *LDZQJ*, 1:229–30.

27. Li Dazhao, "Buziyou zhi beiju" [The tragedy of not being free], April 19, 1917, *LDZQJ*, 2:157.

28. Zhu Zhimin, *Li Dazhao zhuan*, 104.

29. Li Dazhao, "Xinshu guanggao sanze" [Three advertisements concerning new books], April 1915, *LDZQJ*, 1:233.

30. Li Xinghua, *Huiyi wodefuqin Li Dazhao*, 141.

31. Li Xinghua, 145.

32. Zhu Wentong, "Li Dazhao yu jidujiaowenhua" [Li Dazhao and Christian culture], 32.

33. Zhu Wentong, 33.

34. Mori Masao, "Li Dazhao zai zaodaotian daxue," 75.

35. Liu Yuwei, "Liuxueribenshidai de Li Dazhao" [Li Dazhao as a foreign student in Japan], *Zhongguominhangxueyuanxuebao* [Journal of the Civil Aviation Institute of China] 11, no. 1 (March 1993): 64.

36. Han Yide, "Li Dazhao liuxueshiqi shishihesixiang guijidekaocha," 52.

37. The Japanese government offered to impose stricter control over anti-Yuan Chinese revolutionaries in Japan once Yuan Shikai accepted the Japanese demands, which was termed a "sweetener" by scholars. See W. G. Beasley, *Japanese Imperialism 1894–1945* (New York: Oxford University Press, 1987), 112.

38. Li Dazhao, "Ziranlu yu hengpinglu shi," *LDZQJ*, 1:154.

39. Li Dazhao, "Jinggao quanguo fulao shu," 1:218.

40. Li Dazhao, "Guoqing" [The national condition], November 10, 1914, *LDZQJ*, 1:204.

41. Zhang Cixi, *Li Dazhao xiansheng zhuan*, 1.
42. Li Dazhao, *Song Youheng* [Farewell to Youheng], spring 1916, *LDZQJ*, 5:327.
43. Li Dazhao, *Song Xiangwu* [Farewell to Xiangwu], spring 1916, *LDZQJ*, 5:329.
44. Li Dazhao, *Ji Huo Lubai* [A note to Huo Lubai], May 1916, *LDZQJ*, 5:330. In his later writings, Li Dazhao also rendered Huo Lubai's name as Huo Libai, which was another name of Huo.
45. Patrick Fuliang Shan, *Yuan Shikai: A Reappraisal* (Vancouver, BC: University of British Columbia Press), 198.
46. Zhu Chengjia, *Li Dazhao zhuan*, 340.
47. Li Dazhao, "Jinggao quanguofulao shu," 1:211–20.
48. Li Dazhao, "Guomin zhi xindan" [The concealed vengeance], June 1915, *LDZQJ*, 1:243.
49. Li Dazhao, "Guomin zhi xindan," 244.
50. Zhu Wentong, *Li Dazhao zhuan*, 78.
51. Li Dazhao, "Yimaocanla, youhengbindafalunfuchunshen, zaitaipingyangzhouzhongzuo" [Composed on the French ship from Yokohama, Japan, to Shanghai in the last lunar month of 1915], January 1916, *LDZQJ*, 5:323.
52. Zhang Jingru et al., *Li Dazhao shengping shiliao biannian* [Chronicle of historical materials concerning Li Dazhao's life], 15.
53. Dong Baorui, "'Gaozhu shenzhou fengyulou': Li Dazhao yu shenzhouxuehui huiyou Yi Xiang" [Working for China: Li Dazhao and Yi Xiang, who was a member of the China Society], *Dangshizongheng* [On the party history] 181, no. 3 (2001): 4–7.
54. Han Yide and Yao Weidou, *Li Dazhao shengping jinian* [A chronicle of Li Dazhao's life] (Harbin: Heilongjiangrenminchubanshe, 1987), 29.
55. Zhu Chengjia, *Li Dazhao zhuan*, 361.
56. Song Fangchun and Li Quanxing, *Li Dazhao yanjiu cidian* [The dictionary of Li Dazhao studies] (Beijing: Hongqichubanshe, 1994), 190.
57. Zhu Chengjia, *Li Dazhao zhuan*, 360.
58. Song Fangchun and Li Quanxing, *Li Dazhao yanjiu cidian*, 932.
59. Zhu Wentong, *Li Dazhao nianpuchangbian* [The extended chronicle of Li Dazhao's life] (Beijing: Zhongguoshehuikexuechubanshe, 2009), 174.
60. Song Fangchun and Li Quanxing, *Li Dazhao yanjiu cidian*, 705.
61. Zhu Chengjia, *Li Dazhao zhuan*, 368.
62. Zhang Jingru et al., *Li Dazhao shengping shiliao biannian*, 16.
63. Zhu Chengjia, *Li Dazhao zhuan*, 443.
64. Zhu Wentong, *Li Dazhao zhuan*, 87.
65. Zhu Wentong, *Li Dazhao nianpuchangbian*, 179.
66. Li Dazhao, "Fengsu" [The custom], August 10, 1914, *LDZQJ*, 1:159.
67. Li Dazhao, "Zhengzhiduikangli zhi yangcheng" [The formation of opposing political forces], November 1, 1914, *LDZQJ*, 1:178–90.

68. Li Dazhao, "Fengsu," 1:160.
69. Li Dazhao, "Yanshixin yu zijuexin" [The sick of life and self-consciousness], August 10, 1915, LDZQJ, 1:252–53.
70. Li Dazhao, "Minyi yu zhengzhi" [People's sovereignty and politics], May 15, 1916, LDZQJ, 1:287.
71. Li Dazhao, "Minyi yu zhengzhi," 1:268–71.
72. Li Dazhao, 1:274.
73. Li Dazhao, 1:273.
74. Li Dazhao, 1:275.
75. Li Dazhao, 1:277.
76. Li Dazhao, 1:279.
77. Li Dazhao, 1:280.
78. Li Dazhao, 1:271.
79. Li Dazhao, 1:284.
80. Li Dazhao, 1:286.
81. Claudia Pozzana, "Spring, Temporality, and History in Li Dazhao," *Position* 3, no. 2 (Fall 1995): 287.
82. Ishikawa Yoshihiro, "Li Dazhao zaoqisixiangzhong de ribenyinsu—yi Maoyuanhuashan weili" [The Japanese elements in Li Dazhao's early thoughts—examples from the writings of Kayahara Kazan], *Shehuikexueyanjiu* [Social science studies], no. 3 (2007): 141–42.
83. Han Yide and Yao Weidou, *Li Dazhao shengping jinian*, 35.
84. Li Dazhao, "Qingchun" [The youth], LDZQJ, 1:313.
85. Li Dazhao, "Qingchun," 1:314.
86. Li Dazhao, 1:317.
87. Li Dazhao, 1:318.
88. Li Dazhao, "Wujia yu huobigoumaili" [Price and the purchasing power of the currency], August 10, 1914, LDZQJ, 1:174.
89. Song Fangchun and Li Quanxing, *Li Dazhao yanjiu cidian*, 9.
90. Gao Yihan, "Huiyi wusishiqi de Li Dazhao tongzhi" [My memory of Comrade Li Dazhao during the May Fourth era], in Xu Deheng et al., *Huiyi Li Dazhao* [In memory of Li Dazhao], 165.
91. Yang Shusheng, "Liuxueriben dui Li Dazhao de yingxiang" [The impact of study abroad in Japan upon Li Dazhao], in Zhonggongzhongyangdangshiyanjiushi, *Li Dazhao yanjiu wenji* [A collection of research articles on Li Dazhao], 121.
92. Liu Minshan, "Li Dazhao yu Xingdeqiushui" [Li Dazhao and Kotoku Shusui], *Jindaishiyanjiu* 1995, no. 4 (1995): 253.

Chapter 4

1. Li Dazhao, "Zhi Huo Libai" [To Huo Libai], May 1916, LDZQJ, 5:351.

2. Li Dazhao, "Zhi Huo Libai" [To Huo Libai], May 21, 1916, *LDZQJ*, 5:352. These are two different letters.

3. Zhang Jingru et al., *Li Dazhao shengping shiliao biannian* [Chronicle of historical materials concerning Li Dazhao's life], 17.

4. Zhang Cixi, *Li Dazhao xiansheng zhuan*, 5.

5. Zhang Jianguo, *Weidade bozhongzhe: Li Dazhao de gushi* [The great seed-sower: The story of Li Dazhao], 64.

6. Zhang Jingru et al., *Li Dazhao shengping shiliao biannian*, 19.

7. Li Dazhao, "Chenzhong zhi shiming—qingchunzhonghua zhi chuangzao" [The mission of the *Morning Bell*—The creation of young China], August 15, 1916, *LDZQJ*, 1:329–30.

8. Li Dazhao, "Disan" [The third], *LDZQJ*, 1:340.

9. Li Dazhao, "Chenzhong zhi shiming," 1:333.

10. Zhu Chengjia, *Li Dazhao zhuan* [Biography of Li Dazhao], 464.

11. Li Dazhao, "Fendou zhi qingnian" [The high-spirited youth], September 3, 1916, *LDZQJ*, 1:351.

12. Li Dazhao, "Jieshao zheren Tuoersitai" [Introducing Philosopher Leo Tolstoy], August 20, 1916, *LDZQJ*, 1:342.

13. Li Dazhao, "Dake'er zhi 'ai' guan" [The view of love by Tagore], August 23, 1916, *LDZQJ*, 1:348.

14. Li Dazhao, "Beigen zhi ouxiang shuo" [The theory on idols by Francis Bacon], August 31, 1916, *LDZQJ*, 1:350.

15. Li Dazhao, "Jieshao zheren Nicai" [Introducing Philosopher Friedrich Nietzsche], August 22, 1916, *LDZQJ*, 1:344.

16. Li Dazhao, "Zhu jiuyuewuri" [Celebrating September 5], September 5, 1916, *LDZQJ*, 1:360.

17. Li Dazhao, "Zhengtanyanshuohui zhi biyao" [The necessity of orations on the political arena], August 30, 1916, *LDZQJ*, 1:347.

18. Li Dazhao, "Quan" [Power], August 29, 1916, *LDZQJ*, 1:346.

19. Li Dazhao, "Xinxianxiang" [A new phenomenon], September 4, 1916, *LDZQJ*, 1:356.

20. Li Dazhao, "Bielei" [Bye-bye with tears], September 4, 1916, *LDZQJ*, 1:358–59.

21. Zhu Chengjia, *Li Dazhao zhuan*, 477.

22. Gao Yihan, "He Li Dazhao tongzhi xiangchu de shihou" [My time with Comrade Li Dazhao], *Gongrenribao* [Workers' daily], April 27, 1957.

23. Han Yide and Yao Weidou, *Li Dazhao shengping jinian* [A chronicle of Li Dazhao's life], 32.

24. Li Dazhao, "Shengzhi yu xianfa" [The provincial system and the constitution], November 9, 1916, *LDZQJ*, 1:388.

25. Li Dazhao, "Xianfa yu sixiangziyou" [The constitution and free ideas], December 10, 1916, *LDZQJ*, 1:403–4.

26. Wu Hanquan, "Shilun zaoqi Li Dazhao dui chuantongwenhua de shenshi" [Li Dazhao's analysis of the traditional culture in his early thought], *Xuzhoushifandaxuexuebao* [Journal of Xuzhou Normal University] 24, no. 4 (December 1998): 91.

27. Li Dazhao, "Guoqing jinian" [The celebration of the National Day], October 10, 1916, *LDZQJ*, 1:363–64.

28. Li Dazhao, "Xianfa yu sixiangziyou," 1:401.

29. Li Dazhao, "Zhidingxianfa zhi zhuyi" [Attention to the making of the constitution], October 20, 1916, *LDZQJ*, 1:367.

30. Li Dazhao, "Zhidingxianfa zhi zhuyi," 1:369.

31. Gao Yihan, "Huiyi 'wusi' shiqi de Li Dazhao tongzhi" [My memory of Comrade Li Dazhao during the May Fourth era], in *Wusiyundong huiyilu* [Memoirs concerning the May Fourth Movement], by Zhongguoshehuikexueyuan Jindaishiyanjiusuo (Beijing: Zhishichanquanchubanshe, 2013), 154.

32. Li Dazhao, "Xinzhonghuaminzuzhuyi" [The New Chinese Nation], February 19, 1917, *LDZQJ*, 1:479.

33. Li Dazhao, "Meiyugao" [Excellence and strength], April 1, 1917, *LDZQJ*, 2:99.

34. Li Dazhao, "Lixianguomin zhi xiuyang" [Nurturing the citizens under the constitution], March 11, 1917, *LDZQJ*, 1:519.

35. Li Dazhao, "Luxingriji" [A diary of my travel], May 9–11, 1917, *LDZQJ*, 2:205.

36. Li Dazhao, "Zui'e yu chanhui" [Evil and repent], April 21, 1917, *LDZQJ*, 2:169.

37. Li Dazhao, "Jianyishenghuo zhi biyao" [The necessity of a simple life], April 22, 1917, *LDZQJ*, 2:171–72.

38. Ping Zhu, "Becoming Laborers: The Identification with Labor during the Chinese New Culture Movement," *Journal of Asian Studies* 82, no. 1 (2023): 33.

39. Li Dazhao, "Kelian zhi renlichefu" [The pitiful rickshaw drivers], February 10, 1917, *LDZQJ*, 1:454–55.

40. Li Dazhao, "Luxingriji," 2:207.

41. Li Dazhao, "Laoting tongxin" [A letter from Laoting], May 23, 1917, *LDZQJ*, 2:217.

42. Li Dazhao, "Qingnian yu laoren" [The youth and the old men], April 1, 1917, *LDZQJ*, 2:46.

43. Li Dazhao, "Xuesheng wenti" [The problem of students], pt. 1, April 3, 1917, *LDZQJ*, 2:121.

44. Li Dazhao, "Xuesheng wenti" [The problem of students], pt. 2, April 5, 1917, *LDZQJ*, 2:126–29.

45. Li Dazhao, "Buziyou zhi beiju" [The tragedy of not being free], April 19, 1917, *LDZQJ*, 2:161.

46. Li Dazhao, "Zhongxinshili chuangzaolun" [The creation of the central political force], April 23, 1917, *LDZQJ*, 2:175–76.

47. Li Dazhao, "Aiguo zhi fanduidang" [The patriotic oppositional party], March 7, 1917, *LDZQJ*, 1:517.

48. Li Dazhao, "Kongzi yu xianfa" [Confucius and the constitution], January 30, 1917, *LDZQJ*, 1:423.

49. Li Dazhao, "Jiangyanhui zhi biyao" [The need for oratory meetings], April 8, 1917, *LDZQJ*, 2:135.

50. Li Dazhao, "Shouhui'an yu lixianzhengzhi" [The bribery case and constitutional politics], April 20, 1917, *LDZQJ*, 2:165–66.

51. Li Dazhao, "Tiaohe zhi faze" [The rule of compromise], spring 1917, *LDZQJ*, 2:36.

52. Li Dazhao, "Tiaohe zhi faze," 2:36.

53. Li Dazhao, "Tiaohe zhi faze," 2:37–40.

54. Li Dazhao, "Zhengzhi zhi lixinli yu xiangxinli" [The centrifugal force and the centripetal force in politics], April 29, 1917, *LDZQJ*, 2:204.

55. Li Dazhao, "Meidebangjiaojijue woguobukebuyousuobiaoshi" [Now the United States and Germany severed their diplomacy and our country should act too], February 9, 1917, *LDZQJ*, 1:447.

56. Li Dazhao, "Jinhouguomin zhi zeren" [The responsibility of our citizens from now on], February 11, 1917, *LDZQJ*, 1:457.

57. Li Dazhao, "Woguowaijiao zhi shuguang" [The dawn of our nation's diplomacy], February 9, 1917, *LDZQJ*, 1:450.

58. Li Dazhao, "Lunguorenbukeyiwaijiaowenti weirangquan zhi wuqi" [Our nationals should not use diplomacy as a weapon against one another], February 17, 1917, *LDZQJ*, 1:473.

59. Li Dazhao, "Zhongdebangjiao juelichou zhi zhongzhongwenti" [The multiple problems after the Sino-German diplomatic breakup], March 5, 1917, *LDZQJ*, 1:511–12.

60. Li Dazhao, "Dazhanzhong ouzhougeguo zhi zhengbian" [The political changes of European countries during the Great War], April 1, 1917, *LDZQJ*, 2:102–20.

61. Li Dazhao, "Ouzhougeguo shehuidang zhi pingheyundong" [The peace movement launched by the socialist parties in European countries], April 24, 1917, *LDZQJ*, 2:178.

62. Li Dazhao, "Dazhanzhongzhi minzhuzhuyi" [Democracy during the Great War], April 16, 1917, *LDZQJ*, 2:143.

63. Li Dazhao, "Mianbao yu hepingyundong" [Bread and the peace movement], March 25, 1917, *LDZQJ*, 2:24.

64. Li Dazhao, "Beimei zhi fengyun'er—Luosifu qingyuanchuzheng" [The brave man of North America—Roosevelt requested to be a soldier], February 18, 1917, *LDZQJ*, 1:475.

65. Li Dazhao, "Dazhanzhongzhi minzhuzhuyi," *LDZQJ*, 2:142.

66. Li Dazhao, "Eguogonghezhengfu zhi chenglijiqizhenggang" [The establishment of the Russian republican government and its program], March 27, 1917, *LDZQJ*, 2:25.

67. Li Dazhao, "Eguo geming zhi yuanyinjinyin" [The diverse factors leading to the Russian Revolution], March 19–21, 1917, *LDZQJ*, 2:1–11.

68. Li Dazhao, "Eguodageming zhi yingxiang" [The influence of the Great Russian Revolution], March 29, 1917, *LDZQJ*, 2:30.

69. Li Dazhao, "Huangjinleilei zhi riben" [The wealthy Japan], February 10, 1917, *LDZQJ*, 1:453.

70. Li Dazhao, "Jidongmenluozhuyi" [The Far Eastern Monroe Doctrine], February 21, 1917, *LDZQJ*, 1:483.

71. Li Dazhao, "Dayaxiyazhuyi" [Pan-Asianism], April 18, 1917, *LDZQJ*, 2:155.

72. Li Dazhao, "Dongdeshenghuo yu jingdeshenghuo" [Moving life and quiet life], April 12, 1917, *LDZQJ*, 2:138.

· 73. Li Dazhao, "Dongdeshenghuo yu jingdeshenghuo," *LDZQJ*, 2:138.

74. Li Dazhao, "Zhanzheng yu renkou wenti" [War and the population issue], March 30, 1917, *LDZQJ*, 2:34.

75. Li Dazhao, "Zhanzheng yu renkou" [War and population], April 1, 1917, *LDZQJ*, 2:68.

76. Li Dazhao, "Zhanzheng yu renkou," 78.

77. Li Dazhao, "Lunshouhuizhiqianyiyouzhunbei" [It is proper to be prepared in collecting and halting the circulation of copper coins], February 6, 1917, *LDZQJ*, 1:433–35.

78. Li Dazhao, "Zhanzheng yu tong" [War and copper], February 14, 1917, *LDZQJ*, 1:463.

79. Li Dazhao, "Zhi Li Taifen" [To Li Taifen], mid-August 1917, *LDZQJ*, 5:356.

80. Li Dazhao, "Piweitiaohe" [Exposing the pseudo compromise], August 15, 1917, *LDZQJ*, 2:221–33.

81. Li Dazhao, "Baoli yu zhengzhi" [Violence and politics], October 15, 1917, *LDZQJ*, 2:239.

82. Li Dazhao, "Baoli yu zhengzhi," *LDZQJ*, 2:249.

83. Li Dazhao, "Ciri" [The Day], October 10, 1917, *LDZQJ*, 2:254–56.

84. Zhu Wentong, *Li Dazhao nianpuchangbian* [The extended chronicle of Li Dazhao's life], 239.

85. Zhu Wentong, 235.

Chapter 5

1. Jin Yufu, "Li Dazhao yu wusiyundong" [Li Dazhao and the May Fourth Movement], in Han Yide and Wang Shudi, *Li Dazhao yanjiu lunwenji*, 1:75.

2. Li Dazhao, "Benxiaochengli diershiwunian jinian ganyan" [Remarks on the 25th anniversary of the founding of Beijing University], December 17, 1922, *LDZQJ*, 4:134.

3. Li Baohua, "Huiyi fuqin Li Dazhao de yixie geminghuodong" [In memory of my father Li Dazhao's revolutionary activities], in Xu Deheng et al., *Huiyi Li Dazhao* [In memory of Li Dazhao], 11–12.

4. Wang Shiru, "Li Dazhao tongzhi zai Beijingdaxue de renzhishijian kaobian" [An examination of the date of Comrade Li Dazhao's appointment at Beijing University], *Beijingdaxuexuebao* [Journal of Beijing University], no. 5 (1980): 82.

5. Li Dazhao, "Li Shouchang qishi" [Notice from Li Dazhao], December 2, 1922, *LDZQJ*, 4:133.

6. Jin Yufu, "Li Dazhao yu wusiyundong," 1:76.

7. Wang Yanping and Li Quanxing, *Li Dazhao shishitanwei* [An exploration of historical facts concerning Li Dazhao] (Shijiazhuang: Hebeirenminchubanshe, 2016), 100.

8. Li Dazhao, "Xiuzheng tushuguan jieshuguize" [The revised library loan rules], April 11, 1918, *LDZQJ*, 2:281–82.

9. Li Dazhao, "Xiuzheng tushuguan jieshuguize" [The revised library loan rules], December 23, 1920, *LDZQJ*, 3:284–85.

10. Jing Liao, "The New Culture Movement and the Breakthrough in Chinese Academic Library Reform," *Library History* 24, no. 1 (March 2008): 44.

11. Li Dazhao, "Tushuguan zhuren bugao" [Notice from the chief librarian], December 12, 1919, *LDZQJ*, 3:171.

12. Li Dazhao, "Tushuguan zhuren bugao" [Notice from the chief librarian], November 15, 1919, *LDZQJ*, 3:114.

13. Li Dazhao, "Canguan Qinghuaxuexiao zaji" [Miscellanies concerning the visit to Qinghua School], March 19–20, 1918, *LDZQJ*, 2:276.

14. Li Dazhao, "Guanyu tushuguan de yanjiu" [A study of the library enterprise], October 24, 1921, *LDZQJ*, 3:437.

15. Li Dazhao, "Guanyu tushuguan de yanjiu," 3:439; Li Dazhao, "Meiguo tushuguanyuan zhi xunlian" [The training of American librarians], December 1, 1921, *LDZQJ*, 3:449.

16. Zhu Wentong, *Li Dazhao nianpuchangbian* [The extended chronicle of Li Dazhao's life], 350.

17. Jing Liao, "The New Culture Movement," 45.

18. Zhu Wentong, *Li Dazhao nianpuchangbian*, 255.

19. Chen Weiping, "Youguan Li Dazhao tongzhi de yizexinshiliao" [A new historical document concerning Comrade Li Dazhao], *Lilunxuekan* [Theory journal], no. 2 (1992): 86.

20. Li Dazhao, "Zai Beijinggaodengshifanxuexiao tushuguan erzhounian jinianhui shang de yanjiang" [Speech at the second anniversary of the estab-

lishment of the library of Beijing Higher Normal School], December 13, 1919, *LDZQJ*, 3:172–74.

21. Jing Liao, "New Culture Movement," 46.

22. Diane M. Nelson and Robert B. Nelson, "Li Ta-chao," in *World Encyclopedia of Library and Information Services*, ed. Robert Wedgeworth, 3rd ed. (Chicago: American Library Association, 1993), 521. Also see Wang Shiru, "Li Dazhao dui Zhongguo tushuguanshiye de gongxian" [Li Dazhao's contributions to China's library enterprise], in Han Yide and Wang Shudi, 2:602.

23. Yao Zhang, "The Development of Library and Information Science in China (1840–2009)," *IFLA Journal* 40, no. 4 (2014): 299.

24. Wang Shiru, "Li Dazhao tongzhi shoupinjiaoshou jisuokaikecheng kaoshi" [An examination of Comrade Li Dazhao's appointment as a professor and the courses he taught], *Journal of Beijing University* 18, no. 4 (1981): 93.

25. Zhang Cixi, *Li Dazhao xiansheng zhuan* [Biography of Mr. Li Dazhao], 3.

26. Li Yanbo, *Li Dazhao Beijing shinian: Jiaoxuepian* [Li Dazhao's ten years in Beijing: Teaching] (Beijing: Central Compilation and Translation Press, 2016), 305–12.

27. Jiang Lijing, "Teachers Are Key Factors of Universities: Peking Female Higher Normal College 1917–1922," *History Research* 7, no. 2 (March/April 2017): 87.

28. Li Xinghua, *Huiyi wode fuqin Li Dazhao* [My memory of my father Li Dazhao], 70.

29. Zhang Wensheng, "Li Dazhao shixuesixiangxingcheng de zhiyetiaojian" [Analysis of the occupational background and the formation of Li Dazhao's thoughts on history], *Nankaixuebao* [Journal of Nankai University], no. 2 (2015): 127.

30. Zhang Wensheng, *Li Dazhao shixuesixiang yanjiu* [A study of Li Dazhao's thoughts on history] (Beijing: Zhongguoshehuikexuechubanshe, 2006), 10.

31. Li Dazhao, *Shixueyaolun* [The essentials of history], May 1924, *LDZQJ*, 4:531, 4:559–62.

32. Li Dazhao, "Jin yu gu" [The present and the ancient], February 1923, *LDZQJ*, 4:326–27.

33. Li Dazhao, "Jin yu gu: Zai Beijing kongdexuexiao de yanjiang" [The present and the ancient: Speech at Beijing Kongde School], January 8, 1922, *LDZQJ*, 4:16.

34. Li Dazhao, "Shixue yu zhexue: Zai fudandaxue de yanjiang" [History and philosophy: Speech at Fudan University], April 17–19, 1923, *LDZQJ*, 4:205.

35. Li Dazhao, "Jin yu gu," 4:326.

36. Li Dazhao, "Jin yu gu: Zai Beijing kongdexuexiao de yanjiang," 4:16.

37. Li Dazhao, "Shixue yu zhexue: Zai fudandaxue de yanjiang," 4:205.

38. Li Dazhao, 4:194.

39. Yin Xiangxia, "Li Dazhao dui zhongguo jindaishehui de yanjiu" [Li Dazhao's study of modern Chinese society], *Shixueshiyanjiu* [The study of historiography], no. 2 (1995): 17.

40. Gao Zhonghua, "Li Dazhao de jiawuguan" [Li Dazhao's perspective on the First Sino-Japanese War], 31.

41. Li Dazhao, "Jiaoji tielu lueshi" [A concise history of the railway line between Qingdao and Jinan], March 5, 1922, *LDZQJ*, 4:67.

42. Li Dazhao, "Zhongguo gudai jingjisixiang zhi tedian" [The characteristics of ancient Chinese economic thoughts], 1920, *LDZQJ*, 3:286.

43. Li Dazhao, "Chamaoyi yu mengzang zhi guanxi" [The tea trade and the Han ties with the Mongols and the Tibetans], December 7–8, 1923, *LDZQJ*, 4:478. This article was discovered by Zhang Jianjun of Inner Mongolia Normal University in 2012 and shows the depth of Li Dazhao's careful study of Chinese history.

44. Li Dazhao, "Baodan de lishisixiang" [Jean Bodin's historical thoughts], September 1923–early 1924, *LDZQJ*, 4:346–60.

45. Li Dazhao, "Mengdesijiu de lishisixiang" [Montesquieu's historical thoughts], September 1923–early 1924, *LDZQJ*, 4:365–85.

46. Li Dazhao, "Weike jiqi lishisixiang" [Vico and his historical thoughts], September 1923–early 1924, *LDZQJ*, 4:391–95.

47. Li Dazhao, "Kongdaoxi de lishiguan" [Condorcet's historical views], November 1923, *LDZQJ*, 4:398–403.

48. Ouyang Zesheng, *Wusiyundong de lishiquanshi* [Historical interpretation of the May Fourth Movement] (Beijing: Beijing University Press, 2012), 220.

49. Li Dazhao, "*Qingdai tongshi* xu" [Preface to *The History of the Qing dynasty*], December 11, 1923, *LDZQJ*, 4:486. Xiao Yishan was also known as Xiaozi Yishan.

50. Dong Yali, "Li Dazhao linsiqian zuoleshenme? Caifang Li Dazhao zhangzi Li Baohua, cizi Li Guanghua" [What did Li Dazhao do before his death? An interview with Li Dazhao's oldest son, Li Baohua, and second son, Li Guanghua], *Zhanghuixiaoshuo* [The traditional Chinese fiction], no. 3 (2010): 92.

51. Liu Yang, "Li Dazhao dejiahenjianlou, shufangbuxiao" [Li Dazhao's home is simple, but his study is not small], *Bolanqunshu* [Chinese book review monthly], no. 6 (2018): 95.

52. Bao Huiseng, "Huiyi Li Dazhao tongzhi" [My memory of Comrade Li Dazhao], in Xu Deheng et al., *Huiyi Li Dazhao*, 150.

53. Tse-tsung Chow, *The May Fourth Movement: Intellectual Revolution in Modern China* (Cambridge, MA: Harvard University Press, 1964), 1–5.

54. Zhang Qingxiang, "Li Dazhao wusishiqi xinwenhuajiangou de xiandaifang'an" [Li Dazhao's modern plan for reconstructing a new culture during the May Fourth era], *Gansushehuikexue* [Social sciences of Gansu], no. 2 (2004): 33.

55. Leigh Jenco, "Culture as History: Envisioning Change across and beyond 'Eastern' and 'Western' Civilization in the May Fourth Era," *Twentieth-Century China* 38, no. 1 (January 2013): 34.

56. Ya-pei Kuo, "The Making of the New Culture Movement: A Discursive History," *Twentieth-Century China* 42, no. 1 (January 2017): 69.

57. Li Dazhao, "Dongxiwenming genben zhi yidian" [The fundamental differences between Eastern and Western civilization], June–July 1918, *LDZQJ*, 2:311–13.

58. Jenco, "Culture as History," 35.

59. Bai Xiaotian, "Li Dazhao yu xinwenhuayundong de qianjin fangxiang" [Li Dazhao and the direction of the New Culture Movement], *Tangshanxueyuanxuebao* [Journal of Tangshan University] 30, no. 2 (March 2017): 63–65.

60. Li Dazhao, "Jinzhishuohua" [Prohibiting to speak], December 14, 1919, *LDZQJ*, 3:177.

61. Li Dazhao, "Shenme shi xinwenxue?" [What is the new literature?], December 8, 1919, *LDZQJ*, 3:169.

62. Li Dazhao, "Jiefanghouderenren" [The people after their liberation], April 13, 1919, *LDZQJ*, 2:449.

63. Zhang Li, "*Xinqingnian* zuozhequn yu zhongri jindai cihuijiaoliu: Yi Li Dazhao weili" [The authors of *New Youth* and the modern linguistic exchanges between Chinese and Japanese: The case of Li Dazhao], *Sanxiadaxuexuebao* [Journal of China Three Gorges University] 41, no. 5 (September 2019): 113–16.

64. Vera Schwarcz, *The Chinese Enlightenment: Intellectuals and the Legacy of the May Fourth Movement of 1919* (Berkeley: University of California Press, 1986), 116.

65. Li Dazhao, "Funujiefang yu minzhu" [Women's liberation and democracy], October 15, 1919, *LDZQJ*, 3:90.

66. Li Dazhao, "Xiandai de nuquan yundong" [The modern feminist movement], January 18, 1922, *LDZQJ*, 4:21.

67. Li Dazhao, "Feichangwenti" [The issue of prohibiting prostitution], April 27, 1919, *LDZQJ*, 2:454.

68. Harriet Evans, "The Language of Liberation: Gender and *Jiefang* in Early Chinese Communist Party Discourse," in *Twentieth-Century China: New Approaches*, ed. Jeffrey N. Wasserstrom (London: Routledge, 2003), 198.

69. Li Dazhao, "Zuiweixian de dongxi" [The most dangerous thing], July 6, 1919, *LDZQJ*, 2:486.

70. Zhao Guofeng, "Lun Li Dazhao dui chuantongsixiangwenhua de taidu" [Li Dazhao's attitude toward traditional ideology and culture], *Jiangxishehuikexue* [Jiangxi social sciences], no. 7 (2005): 117–20.

71. Wang Jin, "Li Dazhao sixiangzhong de chuantongyinsu jiqi dangdaiyiyi" [On the traditional elements in Li Dazhao's thought and their contemporary implications], *Tangshanxueyuanxuebao* 30, no. 5 (September 2017): 41.

72. Zhang Tongle, "Lun Li Dazhao dui zhongguochuantongwenhua de pipan yu jicheng" [Li Dazhao's criticism and inheritance of Chinese traditional culture], *Hebeishidaxuebao* [Journal of Hebei Normal University] 23, no. 4 (October 2000): 102–6.

73. Li Dazhao, "Xinde! Jiude!" [New! Old!], May 15, 1918, *LDZQJ*, 2:290.

74. Song Zhijian, "Li Dazhao de fankongshijiao" [Li Dazhao's anti-Confucian perspectives], *Yanhuangzongheng* [History of China], no. 10 (2016): 40–43.

75. Huang Zhen and Yao Weidou, *Li Dazhao de gushi* [The story of Li Dazhao], 49–50.

76. Xu Yufeng, "Li Dazhao yu Lu Xun" [Li Dazhao and Lu Xun], *Zhumadianshizhuanxuebao* [Journal of Zhumadian Normal College], no. 2 (1988): 1.

77. Zhu Zhimin, "Li Dazhao yu Hu Shi" [Li Dazhao and Hu Shi], *Jindaishiyanjiu* [Modern history studies], no. 2 (1997): 278.

78. Gong Shuduo and Huang Xingtao, "Hu Shi yu Li Dazhao guanxilun" [An analysis of the relationship between Hu Shi and Li Dazhao], *Shixueyuekan* [History monthly], no. 1 (1996): 62.

79. Wang Shiru, "Hu Shi shi Li Dazhao de haopengyou" [Hu Shi was Li Dazhao's good friend], *Wenshijinghua* [Essence of literature and history] 270, no. 11 (2012): 38.

80. Liang Shiqiu, "Wokan wusiyundong" [The May Fourth Movement in my eyes], in *Wocanjialiao wusiyundong* [I participated in the May Fourth Movement], by Lianhebao (Taipei: Lianhebaoshe, 1980), 48.

81. Mao Zedong, "Speech on the Guidelines for the Seventh National Congress of the Chinese Communist Party," April 21, 1945, accessed October 5, 2018, http://cpc.people.com.cn/GB/64184/64186/66647/4491001.html.

82. Pamela Kyle Crossley, *The Wobbling Pivot: China since 1800* (West Sussex, UK: Wiley-Blackwell, 2010), 166.

83. Deng Tuo, "Shui lingdaoliao wusiyundong?" [Who led the May Fourth Movement?], in Han Yide and Wang Shudi, 1:68.

84. Jia Zhi, "Jinian wusiyundong, xiang Li Dazhao xuexi" [Remembering the May Fourth Movement and learning from Li Dazhao], in *Li Dazhao zai wusishiqi de sixianghuodong* [Li Dazhao's thoughts and activities during the May Fourth era], ed. Xin Ding (Hong Kong: Longtengchubanshe, 1979), 9.

85. Peng Ming, "Li Dazhao yanjiuzhong de jigewenti" [Some issues on Li Dazhao studies], in Zhonggongzhongyangdangshiyanjiushi, *Li Dazhao yanjiu wenji* [A collection of articles on the study of Li Dazhao], 111.

86. Li Lina, "Li Dazhao yu wusiyundong" [Li Dazhao and the May Fourth Movement], *Zhongguodang'an* [Chinese archives], no. 5 (2009): 78.

87. Wu Changgeng, "Guanghuiyeji, zhandouyisheng: Jinian Li Dazhao tongzhi danchen jiushizhounian" [A glorious achievement and a fighting life: The celebration of the ninetieth anniversary of Li Dazhao's birthday], in Xin Ding, 3.

88. Xu Deheng, "Jinian weidade gemingxianqu Li Dazhao tongzhi" [Commemorating the great revolutionary pioneer Comrade Li Dazhao], in Xu Deheng et al., *Huiyi Li Dazhao* [In memory of Li Dazhao], 9.

89. Fan Shulin, "Li Dazhao zizhu beida pinkunsheng" [Li Dazhao helped the poor student at Beijing University], *Wenshibolan* [Literature and history expo], no. 1 (2017): 20.

90. Sun Fuyuan, "Huiyi wusi qingnian" [Remembering the youth of the May Fourth era], in Zhongguoshehuikexueyuan Jindaishiyanjiusuo, *Wusiyundong huiyilu* [Memoirs concerning the May Fourth Movement], 35.

91. Zhang Tingqian, "Guanyu Li Dazhao xiansheng" [About Mr. Li Dazhao], in Xu Deheng et al., *Huiyi Li Dazhao*, 110.

92. Evan N. Dawley, "Changing Minds: American Missionaries, Chinese Intellectuals, and Cultural Internationalism, 1919–1921," *Journal of American-East Asian Relations* 12, no. 1/2 (Spring/Summer 2003): 20.

93. Vera Schwarcz, *Chinese Enlightenment*, 56.

94. Zhang Shenfu, "Yi Shouchang" [Remembering Li Dazhao], in Xu Deheng et al., *Huiyi Li Dazhao*, 63.

95. Zhang Shenfu, "Hongloushiqi de Li Dazhao" [Li Dazhao during the Red Mansion era], *Gonghuixinxi* [Information concerning the worker's union], no. 22 (2017): 27.

96. Xu Deheng, "Jinian weidade gemingxianqu Li Dazhao tongzhi," 7.

97. Li Dazhao, "Wuyijie zagan" [Random thoughts on the May Day], May 1, 1919, LDZQJ, 2:455.

98. Fabio Lanza, "The Beijing University Students in the May Fourth Era: A Collective Biography," in *The Human Tradition in Modern China*, ed. Kenneth J. Hammond and Kristin Stapleton, 117–34 (New York: Rowman & Littlefield, 2008).

99. Zhu Zhimin, *Li Dazhao zhuan* [Biography of Li Dazhao], 241.

100. Xu Deheng, "Zatan wusi" [Random talks on the May Fourth Movement], in Zhongguoshehuikexueyuan Jindaishiyanjiusuo, *Wusiyundong huiyilu*, 187.

101. Zhou Taixuan, "Tan shaonianzhongguoxuehui" [Remarks on the Young China Society], in Zhongguoshehuikexueyuan Jindaishiyanjiusuo, 189.

102. Patrick Fuliang Shan, "From Admirer to Critic: Li Dazhao's Changing Attitudes toward the United States," in *Sino-American Relations: A New Cold War*, ed. Xiaobing Li and Qiang Fang, 31–54 (Amsterdam: University of Amsterdam Press, 2022).

103. Jiang Hongyan and Hu Minghui, "Gemingxianqu Li Dazhao yanzhongde diyicishijiedazhan" [World War I in the eyes of Li Dazhao the revolutionary pioneer], *Qiqiharshifangaodengzhuankexuexiaoxuebao* [Journal of Qiqihar Junior Teachers College] 95, no. 1 (2007): 5.

104. Erez Manela, "Asia in the Global 1919: Reimagining Territory, Identity, and Solidarity," *Journal of Asian Studies* 78, no. 2 (May 2019): 409.

105. H. W. Brands, *Woodrow Wilson* (New York: Times Books, 2003),104.
106. Peter Zarrow, *China in War and Revolution, 1895–1949* (London: Routledge, 2005), 155.
107. David Scott, *China and the International System, 1840–1949: Power, Presence, and Perceptions in a Century of Humiliation* (Albany: State University of New York Press, 2008), 205.
108. Yuan Ming, "Chinese Intellectuals and the United States: The Dilemma of Individualism vs. Patriotism," *Asian Survey* 29, no. 7 (July 1989): 651.
109. Li Dazhao, "Mimiwaijiao yu qiangdaoshijie" [Secret diplomacy and the bandit world], May 18, 1919, *LDZQJ*, 2:459.
110. Li Dazhao, "Wei xiansheng gankai heru?" [Mr. Wilson, how do you feel?], June 29, 1919, *LDZQJ*, 2:479.
111. Yang Shusheng, "Liuxueriben dui Li Dazhao de yingxiang" [Li Dazhao's study abroad in Japan and its impact upon him], in Zhonggongzhongyangdangshiyanjiushi, *Li Dazhao yanjiu wenji*, 125.
112. Lu Wanhe, "Li Dazhao yu Jiyezuozao" [Li Dazhao and Yoshino Sakuzo], in Han Yide and Wang Shudi, 2:289–90.
113. Zhu Zhimin, *Li Dazhao zhuan*, 253.
114. Guo Dehong and Zhang Minglin, *Li Dazhao zhuan* [Biography of Li Dazhao] (Beijing: Hongqichubanshe, 2016), 168–69.
115. Zhang Jingru et al., *Li Dazhao shengping shiliao biannian* [Chronicle of historical materials concerning Li Dazhao's life], 75.
116. Zhu Wentong, *Li Dazhao nianpuchangbian*, 274.
117. Zhu Zhimin, *Li Dazhao zhuan*, 192.
118. Liu Jingjun, "Jiyilide Li Shouchang xiansheng" [Mr. Li Dazhao in my memory], in Xu Deheng et al., *Huiyi Li Dazhao*, 178–79.
119. Li Dazhao, "Jiubeijingzhuanmenyishang xuexiaojiaozhiyuan zongbakewenti fabiao de tanhua" [Speech concerning the general strike by faculty and staff from the universities and colleges in Beijing], May 22, 1921, *LDZQJ*, 3:394.
120. Zhu Zhimin, *Li Dazhao zhuan*, 199.
121. Li Dazhao, "Eguo zaihuangzhenjihui qishi" [Notice of the Russian Famine Relief Society], February 27, 1922, *LDZQJ*, 5:501.
122. Wang Yanping, "Li Dazhao yu eguozaihuangzhenjihui" [Li Dazhao and the Russian Famine Relief Society], *Dang'antiandi* [Archives world], no. 4 (2017): 21.
123. Li Shuxin, "Xinfaxiande Li Dazhao zhenji ezai huodong shiliao" [Newly discovered historical documents concerning Li Dazhao's activities for the Russian famine relief], *Dangshiyanjiuyujiaoxue* [Party history research and teaching] 237, no. 1 (2014): 108.
124. Wang Yanping, "Li Dazhao yu eguozaihuangzhenjihui," 21.
125. Zhu Wentong, "Li Dazhao yu jidujiaowenhua" [Li Dazhao and Christian culture], 34.

126. Wang Jie, *Li Dazhao Beijing shinian: Shijianpian* [Li Dazhao's ten years in Beijing: Events] (Beijing: Central Compilation and Translation Press, 2012), 191–95.

127. Wang Yanping and Li Quanxing, *Li Dazhao shishitanwei*, 111–12.

128. Li Dazhao, "Zainuquanyundongtongmenghui zhaodaibaojie chahuahui shangde jianghua" [Speech at the tea party for the media sponsored by the League for Women's Rights], August 13, 1922, *LDZQJ*, 4:109.

129. Li Dazhao, "Yige zisha de qingnian" [A youth who committed suicide], November 23, 1919, *LDZQJ*, 3:120.

130. Li Dazhao, "Qingnianyanshizishawenti" [The pessimism and suicidal issues among the youth], December 1, 1919, *LDZQJ*, 3:155–59.

131. Li Dazhao, "Lunzisha" [On suicide], January 30, 1922, *LDZQJ*, 4:41–42.

132. Patrick Fuliang Shan, "Triumph after Catastrophe: Church, State and Society in Post-Boxer China, 1900–1937," *Peace and Conflict Studies* 16, no. 2 (Fall 2009): 33–50.

133. Tang Xiaofeng and Wang Shuai, eds., *Minguoshiqi feijidujiaoyundong zhongyaowenxian huibian* [A collection of important documents on the Anti-Christian Movement during the republican era] (Beijing: Shehuikexuechubanshe, 2015), 183.

134. Patrick Fuliang Shan, "The Anti-Christian Movement Revisited: A Centennial Reflection," *American Review of China Studies* 23, no. 2 (Fall 2022): 25–51.

135. Tatsuro Yamamoto and Sumiko Yamamoto, "The Anti-Christian Movement in China, 1922–1927," *Far Eastern Quarterly* 12, no. 2 (February 1953): 133–47.

136. Li Dazhao, "Feizongjiaozhe xuanyan" [The anti-religious proclamation], April 4, 1922, *LDZQJ*, 4:79.

137. Li Dazhao, "Zongjiao fang'ai jinbu" [Religion hampers progress], April 9, 1922, *LDZQJ*, 4:81–83.

138. Li Dazhao, "Zongjiao yu ziyoupingdengbo'ai" [Religion and freedom, equality, and fraternity], June 1922, *LDZQJ*, 4:98.

139. Xu Jinpu, Li Jinzhi, Li Yuzhi, and Zhao Suzhen, "Li Dazhao tongzhi chuangban xinxuetang" [Comrade Li Dazhao built a modern school], in Xu Deheng et al., *Huiyi Li Dazhao*, 183.

140. Li Dazhao, "Wei pin nujiaoxishi jiaxin" [Family letter concerning the female teacher], May 5, 1920, *LDZQJ*, 5:400.

141. Vincent Goossaert and David A. Palmer, *The Religious Question in Modern China* (Chicago: University of Chicago Press, 2012), 49.

142. Ya-pei Kuo, "New Culture Movement," 52.

143. Sofia Graziani, "Youth and the Making of Modern China: A Study of the Communist Youth League's Organisation and Strategies in Times of Revolution (1920–1937)," *European Journal of East Asian Studies* 13, no. 1 (2014): 117.

144. Wang Jie, *Li Dazhao Beijing shinian: Jiaowangpian* [Li Dazhao's ten years in Beijing: Social connections] (Beijing: Central Compilation and Translation Press, 2010), 115.

145. Wang Jie, *Li Dazhao Beijing shinian: Shijianpian*, 200–201.

Chapter 6

1. Wong Young-tsu (Wang Rongzu), "Congwenhua yu zhengzhi jiaodujiedu wusiqianhou de Li Dazhao" [An interpretation of Li Dazhao before and after the May Fourth Movement: The cultural and political perspective], *Wenshizhe* [Literature, history, and philosophy] 372, no. 3 (2019): 14.

2. Tien-wei Wu, "A Review of the Wuhan Debacle: The Kuomintang-Communist Split of 1927," *Journal of Asian Studies* 29, no. 1 (November 1969): 125.

3. Li Haichun, "Lun Li Dazhao jieshou makesizhuyi de guocheng" [The progression of Li Dazhao's acceptance of Marxism], *Henanshifandaxuexuebao* [Journal of Henan Normal University], no. 1 (2004): 117.

4. Zhang Qingxiang, "Li Dazhao 'wusi'shiqi xinwenhuajiangou de xiandaifang'an" [Li Dazhao's modern plan for reconstructing a new culture during the May Fourth era], 33.

5. Zuo Ying and Song Yuzhong, "Cong Li Dazhao makesizhuyiguan qianxi 'wentiyuzhuyi' lunzheng" [An analysis of the debate over issues and isms from Li Dazhao's Marxist perspective], *Xuelilun* [Theory research], no. 4 (2018): 42.

6. Li Yanlin, "Li Dazhao 'genbenjiejue' de sixiang yu makesizhuyi zhongguohua de lishiqidian" [Li Dazhao's thought on a "fundamental solution" and the historical starting point of the sinicization of Marxism], *Jilinshengshehuizhuyixueyuanxuebao* [Journal of Jilin Provincial College of Socialism], no. 2 (2009): 32–36.

7. Li Haichun, "Lun Li Dazhao jieshou makesizhuyi de guocheng," 117–19.

8. Li Xiaosan, *Xinminzhuzhuyigeming jianshi* [A concise history of China's new democratic revolution] (Beijing: Zhonggongdangshichubanshe, 2010), 63.

9. Shen Yaqiong, "Shilun wusishiqi zhongguoxianjinrenshi jieshou makesizhuyi de lishi chengyin" [The historical factors leading China's progressive intellectuals to accept Marxism during the May Fourth era], *Huaihaiwenhui* [Huaihai review], no. 6 (2010): 33.

10. Xiufen Lu, "The Confucian Ideal of Great Harmony (*Datong*), the Daoist Account of Change, and the Theory of Socialism in the Work of Li Dazhao," *Asian Philosophy* 21, no. 2 (May 2011): 171–92.

11. Lee Feigon, *Chen Duxiu, Founder of the Chinese Communist Party* (Princeton, NJ: Princeton University Press, 2014), 138.

12. Gao Yihan, "Huiyi wusishiqi de Li Dazhao tongzhi" [Remembering Comrade Li Dazhao during the May Fourth era], in Xu Deheng et al., *Huiyi Li Dazhao* [In memory of Li Dazhao], 165.

13. Zhang Yanguo, "Li Dazhao, Qu Qiubai dui eguodaolu de renzhi" [Li Dazhao and Qu Qiubai's analysis of the Russian way], *Zhongguoshehuikexue* [Social sciences of China], no. 10 (2016): 175.

14. Liang Zhu, "Makesizhuyi chuanbozhongde tansuo yu sikao—yi Li Dazhao de shehuizhuyiguan weijidian" [Dissemination of Marxism: Li Dazhao's view of socialism], *Tangshanxueyuanxuebao* [Journal of Tangshan University] 30, no. 2 (March 2017): 3.

15. Peng Ming, "Li Dazhao yanjiuzhong de jigewenti" [Some issues in Li Dazhao studies], in Zhonggongzhongyangdangshiyanjiushi, *Li Dazhao yanjiu wenji* [A collection of research articles on Li Dazhao], 103.

16. Mu Yunjun, "Cong Li Dazhao 'disanwenming'shuo kan makesizhuyi yu ruxue guanxi de chongzhuan" [Li Dazhao's third civilization and the relationship between Marxism and Confucianism], *Shandongshehuikexue* [Shandong social sciences] 243, no. 11 (2015): 22.

17. Liu Yougu, "Lun Li Dazhao 'disan' wenming zhishuo" [Li Dazhao's theory of the third civilization], *Zhongzhouxuekan* [Academic journal of Zhongzhou] 123, no. 3 (May 2001): 144.

18. Wong Young-tsu (Wang Rongzu), "Congwenhua yu zhengzhi jiaodujiedu wusiqianhou de Li Dazhao," 18.

19. Lin Xianzhi, "Wusishiqi Mao Zedong zoushang makesizhuyizhilu de tanyuan" [An exploration into Mao Zedong's march toward the Marxist road during the May Fourth era], *Fengjiarenwenshehuixuebao* [Feng Chia journal of humanities and social science], no. 3 (November 2001): 159.

20. Ishikawa Yoshihiro, "Wusishiqi Li Dazhao de sixiang yu Maoyuanhuashan, Chen Puxian" [Li Dazhao's thoughts during the May Fourth era and Kayahara Kazan and Chen Puxian], trans. Wang Jie and Tian Ziyu, *Wenshizhe*, no. 5 (1993): 15.

21. Ishikawa Yoshihiro, *Formation of the Chinese Communist Party*, 10.

22. Hideaki Kikuchi, *Modaiwangchao yu jindai zhongguo* [The last dynasty and modern China], trans. Ma Xiaojuan (Guilin: Guangxishifandaxuechubanshe, 2018), 208.

23. Wang Xianming and Yang Hu, "Wusishiqi Li Dazhao chuanbo makesizhuyi de dier zhendi—'*Chenbaofukan*' chuanbo makesizhuyi de gongxian yu yiyi" [The second front for Li Dazhao to disseminate Marxism during the May Fourth era—the contribution and significance of *Chenbao Supplement* in disseminating Marxism], in *Zhongguogongchandang chuangjianshiyanjiuwenji, 2002–2012* [A collection of articles on the history of the establishment of the Chinese Communist Party, 2002–12], ed. Zhonggongyidahuizhijinianguan (Shanghai: Shanghairenminchubanshe, 2013), 284.

24. Ishikawa, *The Formation of the Chinese Communist Party*, 20.

25. Patrick Fuliang Shan, "Li Dazhao and the Chinese Embracement of Communism," in *Chinese Ideology*, ed. Shiping Hua (London: Routledge, 2022), 94.

26. Xie Fulin, "Shixi Li Dazhao shumindeshengli he Bolshevism de shengli de sixiangzhuzhi" [An analysis of the main theme of Li Dazhao's "Victory of the Common People" and "Victory of Bolshevism"], *Qinghuadaxuexuebao* [Journal of Qinghua University] 14, no. 3 (1999): 117.

27. Li Dazhao, "Shumin de shengli" [Victory of the common people], November 1918, *LDZQJ*, 2:359.

28. Xie Fulin, "Shixi Li Dazhao shumindeshengli he Bolshevism de shengli de sixiangzhuzhi," 118.

29. Li Dazhao, "Bolshevism de shengli" [Victory of Bolshevism], *LDZQJ*, 2:362–68.

30. Pei-kai Cheng and Michael Lestz, *The Search for Modern China: A Documentary Collection*, with Jonathan D. Spence (New York: W. W. Norton, 1999), 241.

31. Li Dazhao, "Xinjiyuan" [The new epoch], New Year's Day, 1919, *LDZQJ*, 2:375–77.

32. Li Dazhao, "Wode makesizhuyiguan" [My Marxist view], September and November 1919, *LDZQJ*, 3:28.

33. Li Dazhao, "Wode makesizhuyiguan," 3:40.

34. Peter Zarrow, *China in War and Revolution, 1895–1949*, 176.

35. Li Dazhao, "Wode makesizhuyiguan," 3:19.

36. Zhang Rulun, "Historiography and Chinese Modernity—A Study of the Historiographical Ideas of Li Dazhao," *Chinese Studies in History* 49, no. 2 (2016): 84.

37. Li Dazhao, "Zhongguode shehuizhuyi yu shijiede zibenzhuyi" [China's socialism and the world's capitalism], March 20, 1921, *LDZQJ*, 3:359–60.

38. Li Dazhao, "Ziyou yu zhixu" [Freedom and order], January 15, 1921, *LDZQJ*, 3:327.

39. Li Dazhao, "Wuzhibiandong yu daodebiandong" [The material change and the change in moral values], December 1, 1919, *LDZQJ*, 3:145.

40. Li Dazhao, "You jingjishang jieshi zhongguojindai sixiangbiandong de yuanyin" [Interpreting the factors of modern China's ideological changes from the economic perspective], January 1, 1920, *LDZQJ*, 3:189, 3:191.

41. Li Dazhao, "Yuanrenshehui yu wenzishuqishang zhi weiwudefanying" [The materialistic evidence in written documents and contacts of the ancient men], 1920, *LDZQJ*, 3:307.

42. Li Dazhao, "Yuanrenshehui yu wenzishuqishang zhi weiwudefanying," 3:300–301.

43. Jerome B. Grieder, "The Question of 'Politics' in the May Fourth Era," in *Reflections on the May Fourth Movement: A Symposium*, ed. Benjamin I. Schwartz (Cambridge, MA: East Asian Research Center, Harvard University, 1973), 95.

44. Li Dazhao, "Zailun wenti yu zhuyi" [The second debate over issues and ism], August 17, 1919, *LDZQJ*, 3:49, 3:53.

45. Zhang Cui, "Wenti yu zhuyi zhizheng yu makesizhuyi zhongguohua" [The issue-versus-ism debate and the sinicization of Marxism], *Hunanminzuzhiyexueyuanxuebao* [Journal of Hunan Vocational College for Nationalities] 5, no. 3 (2009): 26.

46. Zuo Ying and Song Yuzhong, "Cong Li Dazhao makesizhuyiguan qianxi 'wentiyuzhuyi' lunzheng," 42.

47. Wang Yuanyi, "Huozainali—xinjie Hu Shi yu Li Dazhao 'wentiyuzhuyi' de lunbian jiqi lishiyiyi" [Where are the doubts? A new interpretation of the significance of the issue-versus-ism debate between Hu Shi and Li Dazhao], *Taidalishixuebao* [Historical inquiry], no. 50 (December 2012): 155, 240.

48. Jin Rongdong, *Li Dazhao zhexue yanjiu* [A study of Li Dazhao's philosophy] (Shanghai: Huadongshidachubanshe, 2000), 11.

49. Li Dazhao, "Wode makesizhuyiguan," 3:1.

50. Lu Mingzhuo, "Li Dazhao dui 'haozhengfuzhuyi' de renshi" [Li Dazhao's analysis of the idea to build a good government], in *Li Dazhao yanjiu lunwenji* [Collection of publications on the study of Li Dazhao], ed. Han Yide and Wang Shudi (Shijiazhuang: Hebeirenminchubanshe), 2:458.

51. Meisner, *Li Ta-chao and the Origins of Chinese Marxism*, 197.

52. Arif Dirlik, *The Origins of Chinese Communism* (Oxford: Oxford University Press, 1989), 51.

53. Edward X. Gu, "Populistic Themes in May Fourth Radical Thinking: A Reappraisal of the Intellectual Origins of Chinese Marxism (1917–1922)," *East Asian History*, no. 10 (December 1995): 116.

54. Adrian Chan, "The Liberation of Marx in China," *Journal of Contemporary Asia* 25, no. 1 (January 1995): 95.

55. Tong Shijun, "Li Dazhao yu Mule" [Li Dazhao and John S. Miller], *Ershiyishiji* [Twenty-first century] 69, no. 2 (2002): 41–45.

56. Gao Like, "Li Dazhao yu mincuiminzhuzhuyi" [Li Dazhao and populist democracy], *Ershiyishiji* 70, no. 4 (2002): 55.

57. Zhang Jingru, "Li Dazhao xiandaihuayishi" [Li Dazhao's ideas on modernity], in Zhonggongzhongyangdangshiyanjiushi, *Li Dazhao yanjiu wenji*, 79.

58. Li Dazhao, "Yao ziyoujihede guomindahui" [Demanding for the National Assembly through free arrangements], August 17, 1920, *LDZQJ*, 3:263.

59. Wang Jie, *Li Dazhao Beijing shinian: Shijianpian* [Li Dazhao's ten years in Beijing: Events], 125–27.

60. Cheng Jinjiao, "Chen Duxiu heyidangxuan 'yida' zhongyangzongshuji—jianlun Li Dazhao weineng jinru 'yida' zhongyangju zhi yuanyin" [Why could Chen Duxiu be elected the general secretary of the central bureau at the first congress? An interpretation of the reasons Li Dazhao was not elected into the central bureau at this first congress], *Anqingshifanxueyuanxuebao* [Journal of Anqing Teachers College] 26, no. 1 (January 2007): 75.

61. Diane M. Nelson and Robert B. Nelson, "'The Red Chamber': Li Ta-chao and Sources of Radicalism in Modern Chinese Librarianship," *Journal of Library History* 14, no. 2 (Spring 1979): 121, 122.

62. Zhang Guotao, *Wodehuiyi* [My recollections] (Hong Kong: Mingbaoyuekan, 1971), 79, 80.

63. Wang Jie, *Li Dazhao Beijing shinian: Shijianpian*, 90.

64. Peng Ming, "Li Dazhao yanjiuzhong de jigewenti," 105, 108.

65. Edgar Snow, *Red Star over China: The Rise of the Red Army* (New York: Modern Library, 1944), 157.

66. Snow, *Red Star over China*, 155.

67. Luo Zhanglong, "Kangzhaihuiyilu—Yihe Shouchang tongzhi zaiyiqi de rizi" [Remembering Kangmuyizhai: The days with Comrade Li Dazhao], in Xu Deheng et al., *Huiyi Li Dazhao*, 45.

68. Wang Jie, *Li Dazhao Beijing shinian: Shijianpian*, 92–94.

69. Li Dazhao, "Zhongguo de shehuizhuyi jiqi shixingfangfa de kaocha" [A survey of China's socialism and its ways of implementation], January 27, 1921, *LDZQJ*, 3:329.

70. Chen Xiaocen, "Li Dazhao xiansheng yu juewushe" [Mr. Li Dazhao and the Awakening Society], in Xu Deheng et al., *Huiyi Li Dazhao*, 91, 93.

71. Wang Jie, *Li Dazhao Beijing shinian: Shijianpian*, 136.

72. Li Dazhao, "'Wuyi yundong shi" [A history of May Day and the following movements], May 1, 1920, *LDZQJ*, 3:246.

73. Han Yide and Yang Shusheng, "Lun Li Dazhao yu zhongguogongchandang de chuangli" [Li Dazhao and the establishment of the CCP], in Han Yide and Wang Shudi, 2:368–69.

74. Dong Baorui, "Li Dazhao de wentan haoyou Gao Yihan" [Gao Yihan: Li Dazhao's good friend in the literary circle], *Dangshizongheng* [On the party history], no. 4 (2003): 18.

75. Gao Yihan, "Huiyi wusishiqi de Li Dazhao tongzhi," 166.

76. Li Dazhao, "Tuantide xunlian yu gexinde shiye" [The corporative training and the renovated enterprise], March 1921, *LDZQJ*, 3:348–50.

77. Zhang Guotao, *Wodehuiyi*, 108.

78. Zhu Qiaosen, "Genggaodi juqi gongchanzhuyi he aiguozhuyi de qizhi" [Raising the banners of communism and patriotism even higher], in Zhonggongzhongyangdangshiyanjiushi, *Li Dazhao yanjiu wenji*, 32.

79. Wang Jie, *Li Dazhao Beijing shinian: Jiaowangpian* [Li Dazhao's ten years in Beijing: Social connections], 236.

80. Zhou Zixin, "Li Dazhao yu zhongguogongchandang de chuangli" [Li Dazhao and the founding of the CCP], in Han Yide and Wang Shudi, 2:346.

81. Liu Jianyi, "The Origin of the Chinese Communist Party and the Role Played by Soviet Russia and the Comintern" (PhD diss., University of York, March 2000), 11.

82. Wang Yanping and Li Quanxing, *Li Dazhao shishitanwei* [An exploration of historical facts concerning Li Dazhao], 170–99.

83. Luo Zhanglong, "Kangzhaihuiyilu—Yihe Shouchang tongzhi zaiyiqi de rizi," 37.

84. Zhou Zixin, "Li Dazhao yu zhongguogongchandang de chuangli," 346.

85. Those thirteen men represented the communist cells in Shanghai, Beijing, Changsha, Wuhan, Jinan, Guangzhou, and Tokyo. Gong Shuduo, *Zhongguojindaishi* [Modern history of China, 1919–49] (Beijing: Zhonghuashuju, 2010), 29.

86. Wang Shun, "Li Dazhao weihe wei canjia dangde yida?" [Why did Li Dazhao not attend the first congress of the CCP?], *Lishijiaoxue* [History teaching], no. 12 (1989): 26.

87. Lu Haijiang and Lin Xiumin, "Li Dazhao weihe weichuxi zhonggong yida?" [Why didn't Li attend the first CCP national congress?], *Dangshizongheng*, no. 1 (1991): 43.

88. Cheng Jinjiao, "Chen Duxiu heyidangxuan 'yida' zhongyangzongshuji," 75.

89. Zhou Zixin, "Li Dazhao yu zhongguogongchandang de chuangli," 345.

90. Zhu Chengjia, "Denggaoyihuqunshanying—Zhonggongchuangliguocheng de tedian yu Li Dazhao de lishizuoyong" [The call received response—The characteristics of the establishment of the CCP and the historical role of Li Dazhao], in Zhonggongyidahuizhijinianguan, *Zhongguogongchandang chuangjianshiyanjiuwenji, 2002–2012*, 420–21.

91. Wang Chaozhu, *Li Dazhao* (Beijing: Zhongguoqingnianchubanshe, 1989), 848.

92. Zhu Chengjia, "Denggaoyihuqunshanying," 417.

93. Xiao Chaoran, "Zhongguogongchandang de chuangli yu beijingdaxue" [The founding of the CCP and Beijing University], *People's Daily*, accessed June 14, 2020, http://cpc.people.com.cn/BIG5/218984/218997/219021/14817918.html.

94. Song Fangchun and Li Quanxing, *Li Dazhao yanjiu cidian* [The dictionary of Li Dazhao studies], 172.

95. Zhu Zhimin, *Li Dazhao zhuan* [Biography of Li Dazhao], 296.

96. Zhu Wushan, "Huiyi Shouchang tongzhi," in Xu Deheng et al., *Huiyi Li Dazhao*, 160.

97. Luo Zhanglong, "Kangzhaihuiyilu—Yihe Shouchang tongzhi zaiyiqi de rizi," 46–47.

98. Zhang Wensheng, "Li Dazhao shixuesixiangxingcheng de zhiyetiaojian" [Analysis of the occupational background and the formation of Li Dazhao's thoughts on history], 132.

99. Liang Shuming, "Huiyi Li Dazhao xiansheng" [In memory of Mr. Li Dazhao], in Xu Deheng et al., *Huiyi Li Dazhao*, 89.

100. Li Dazhao, "Shiyuegeming yu zhongguorenmin" [The October Revolution and the Chinese people], November 7, 1922, *LDZQJ*, 4:124.

101. Li Dazhao, "Zai beijinggetuanti faqide su'e shiyuegeming jinianhui shangde yanjiang" [The speech at the rally organized by various organizations in Beijing to celebrate the anniversary of the October Revolution], November 7, 1922, *LDZQJ*, 4:126.

102. Li Dazhao, "Pingminzhuyi" [Democracy], January 1923, *LDZQJ*, 4:143.

103. Li Dazhao, "Zai shanghai shehuizhuyiqingniantuan 'guojishaonianri jinianhui' shangde yanjiang" [Speech at the rally to celebrate 'the international youth day' organized by the Shanghai Socialist Youth League], September 3, 1922, *LDZQJ*, 4:113.

104. Li Dazhao, "Guojide zibenzhuyixiade zhongguo (jiuguojigongguan yu xinguojigongguan)" [China under the international capitalist system (the old internationally shared control and the new internationally shared control)], December 1, 1922, *LDZQJ*, 4:131.

105. Li Dazhao, "'Daguomin' de waijiao" [The diplomacy of "the great nation"], September 16, 1923, *LDZQJ*, 4:443.

106. Li Dazhao, "Jiu sun wu liangshi tongyi zhongguo de fangce yu *Beijingzhoubao* jizhe de tanhua" [Conversation with reporters of *Beijing Weekly* concerning Sun Yat-sen and Wu Peifu's strategies to unify China], September 17, 1922, *LDZQJ*, 4:116.

107. Li Dazhao, "Zhongguo jinhoude zhengzhiyundong" [The future political movements in China], July 22, 1923, *LDZQJ*, 4:230–31.

108. Li Dazhao, "Jiu zhongguo shijigaizaode zhongxinshiliwenti yu *Beijingzhoubao* jizhe de tanhua" [Conversation with reporters of *Beijing Weekly* concerning the central force issue to reconstruct China], May 17, 1923, *LDZQJ*, 4:222.

109. Li Dazhao, "Zai shanghai shehuizhuyiqingniantuan 'guojishaonianri jinianhui' shangde yanjiang," 4:112–13.

110. Eddy U, "Reification of the Chinese Intellectuals: On the Origins of the CCP Concept of *Zhishifenzi*," *Modern China* 35, no. 6 (November 2009): 614.

111. Zhou Liangshu, "1921 nian–1923 nian zhonggong zai gaoxiaozhong dangdejianshe" [CCP development at Chinese universities between 1921 and 1923], *Beijingdangshi* [Party history of Beijing], no. 1 (2006): 20.

112. Wang Jie, *Li Dazhao Beijing shinian: Shijianpian*, 183.

113. Jiyatai, "Li Dazhao tongzhi he neimenggu chuqi de geminghuodong" [Comrade Li Dazhao and the early revolutionary activities in Inner Mongolia], in Xu Deheng et al., *Huiyi Li Dazhao*, 170.

114. Zhao Zhenzhen, "Lun Li Dazhao de nongmin guominxing gaizaosixiang" [Li Dazhao's thoughts on the transformation of peasants' national character], *Chongqingyoudiandaxuexuebao* [Journal of Chongqing University of Posts and Communications] 25, no. 3 (May 2013): 48.

115. Wang Jie, *Li Dazhao Beijing shinian: Jiaowangpian*, 65.

116. Li Dazhao, "You pingminzhengzhi dao gongrenzhengzhi—Zai beijingzhongguodaxue de yanjiang" [From democracy to workers' politics—A speech at China University], December 15–17, 1921, *LDZQJ*, 4:1.

117. Li Dazhao, "You pingminzhengzhi dao gongrenzhengzhi," 4–5.

118. Li Dazhao, "Pingminzhengzhi yu gongrenzhengzhi" [Democracy and ergatocracy], July 1, 1922, *LDZQJ*, 4:104–5.

119. Li Dazhao, "Shehuizhuyi shiyi—Zai shanghaidaxue de yanjiang" [Interpreting socialism: A speech at Shanghai University], November 7, 1923, *LDZQJ*, 4:457–59.

120. Cheng Mingxin and Yuan Cun, "Li Dazhao yu makesizhuyi zhongguohua de kaiduan" [Li Dazhao and the beginning of the Sinicization of Marxism], *Hebeixuekan* [Hebei academic journal], no. 2 (1996): 111.

121. Zuo Yuhe and Wang Ruifang, "Li Dazhao yu makesizhuyi zhongguohua" [Li Dazhao and the Sinicization of Marxism], *Shixueyuekan* [History monthly], no. 1 (1993): 68–70.

122. Li Dazhao, "Shehuizhuyi yu shehuiyundong" [Socialism and social movements], September 1923–April 1924, *LDZQJ*, 4:243.

123. Li Dazhao, "Yibaqiyi nian de bali 'kangmiao'en: Wushinian de huigu, shehuigeming de xiansheng'" [The Paris Commune of 1871: A remembrance at its fiftieth anniversary to emphasize it as the pioneer of the social revolution], *LDZQJ*, 4:170.

124. Li Dazhao, "Pingminzhengzhi yu gongrenzhengzhi," 4:106.

125. Cao Muqing, "Lun wusishiqi Li Dazhao de lishiguan" [Li Dazhao's historical perspectives during the May Fourth era], in Han Yide and Wang Shudi, 2:579.

126. Yang Peng, "Analysis of Japanese Influence on the Three Major Historiographical Trends in Early Modern China," *Chinese Studies in History* 49, no. 1 (2016): 34.

127. Chen Wenxu, "Minzhugemingshiqide Li Dazhao yu makesizhuyi zhongguohua: Congwusishiqi Li Dazhao sixiangfazhan guijideshijiao lai kaocha". [Li Dazhao and the Sinicization of Marxism in the period of the democratic revolution: An analysis from the perspective of Li Dazhao's ideological growth during the May Fourth era], *Lilunxuekan* [Theory journal] 187, no. 9 (September 2009): 38.

128. Bao Huisheng, "Huiyi Li Dazhao tongzhi" [Remembering Comrade Li Dazhao], in Xu Deheng et al., *Huiyi Li Dazhao*, 152.

129. Li Dazhao, "'Huang Pang liuxueji' xu" [Preface to "The event of Huang Ai and Pang Renquan's sacrifice"], March 23, 1922, *LDZQJ*, 4:73.

130. Xiong Huaiji, "Li Dazhao—Zhongguo gongrenyundong de weidaxianqu" [Li Dazhao: The great pioneer of China's workers' movement], in Han Yide and Wang Shudi, 2:26.

131. Gong Shuduo, *Zhongguojindaishi*, 54.

132. Ishikawa Yoshihiro, "Wusishiqi Li Dazhao de sixiang yu Maoyuanhuashan, Chen Puxian," 17.

133. Chen Wangdao, "Huiyi dangchenglishiqi de yixie qingkuang" [My recollection of some information around the time when the party was established], in *Yidaqianhou* [Before and after the first national congress], ed. Zhongguoshehuikexueyuanxiandaishiyanjiushi (Beijing: Renminchubanshe, 1980), 2:19–20.

134. Wang Jie, *Li Dazhao Beijing shinian: Jiaowangpian*, 163.

135. Tai Wan-chin, "Chen Duxiu's Conversion," 115.

136. Luo Zhanglong, *Chunyuanzaiji* [The remarks from the Toona Garden] (Beijing: Sanlianchubanshe, 1984), 240–67.

Chapter 7

1. Li Jiannong, *Zhongguo jinbainian zhengzhi shi* [The history of Chinese politics in the past hundred years] (Taipei: Taiwanshangwushuguan, 1975), 602.

2. Zhonggongbeijingshiweidangshiyanjiushi, *Li Dazhao yu diyici guogonghezuo* [Li Dazhao and the first united front between the Nationalist Party and the Communist Party] (Beijing: Beijingchubanshe, 1989), 31.

3. Zhu Wentong, *Li Dazhao zhuan* [Biography of Li Dazhao], 171.

4. Bruce A. Elleman, "Soviet Diplomacy and the First United Front in China," *Modern China* 21, no. 4 (October 1995): 451, 473.

5. Li Chao, "Sun Zhongshan yu zhonggong sanda" [Sun Yat-sen and the Third CCP National Congress], *Guangzhoushehuizhuyixueyuan* [Journal of Guangzhou Institute of Socialism] 55, no. 4 (2016): 50.

6. Han Jun and Cao Junxue, "Guogong diyicihezuode yuanyin tanxi" [An analysis of the reasons of the first united front between the Nationalist Party and the Communist Party], *Chifengxueyuanxuebao* [Journal of Chifeng University] 32, no. 11 (November 2011): 23.

7. Yang Tianhong, "Jiaru guomindang zhihou gongchandangren de shenfen rentong wenti" [The identity of communists after joining the Nationalist Party], *Jindaishiyanjiu* [Modern Chinese history studies], no. 6 (2010): 19.

8. Lidazhaozhuanbianxiezu, *Li Dazhao zhuan* [Biography of Li Dazhao], 151.

9. Zhang Guotao, *Wodehuiyi* [My recollections], 136.

10. Cai Lesu, "Yetan Malin zaidiyici guogonghezuo xingchengzhongde zuoyong" [An analysis of G. Maring's role in the shaping of the first united front between the Nationalist Party and the Communist Party], *Qinghuadaxuexuebao* [Journal of Tsinghua University] 1, no. 2 (1988): 74.

11. Michael V. Metallo, "American Missionaries, Sun Yat-sen, and the Chinese Revolution," *Pacific Historical Review* 47, no. 2 (May 1978): 281–82.

12. Li Dazhao, "Jiuzhongguoxianzhuang dajizhewen" [Replying to a correspondent's questions concerning China's national situation], October 20, 1923, *LDZQJ*, 4:448.

13. Jiang Junwei, "Sun Zhongshan he Li Dazhao guogonghezuo sixiangyitong bijiao" [Comparison of similarities and differences between Sun Yat-sen's ideas and Li Dazhao's thoughts on the united front between the Nationalist Party and the Communist Party], *Zhonggongfujianshengweidangxiaoxuebao* [Journal of Fujian CCP provincial party school], no. 12 (2001): 53–56. Some Chinese American scholars argue differently, however: Immanuel C. Y. Hsü argues that Sun "refused to substitute Communism for his Three People's Principle" although he accepted the Russian aid. See Hsü, *The Rise of Modern China* (New York: Oxford University Press, 2000), 521.

14. Alexander V. Pantsov, *Victorious in Defeat: The Life and Times of Chiang Kai-shek, China, 1887–1975* (New Haven, CT: Yale University Press, 2023), 32–33.

15. Lei Xiaocen, *Sanshinian dongluan zhongguo* [China in the turbulent thirty years] (Hong Kong: Yazhouchubanshe, 1955), 23.

16. Li Yunhan, *Congronggongdaoqingdang* [From the acceptance of the communists to the party purge] (Taipei: Taiwanshangwuyinshuguan, 1973), 1–2.

17. Lidazhaozhuanbianxiezu, *Li Dazhao zhuan*, 150.

18. Xiao Shen, "Zhonggongdangnei duiyu shouci guogonghezuode zhenglunjiqijieju" [The debate and outcome within the Communist Party over the united front between the Nationalist Party and the Communist Party], *Dangshiyanjiuyujiaoxue* [Communist Party of China history research and teaching] 195, no. 2 (2007): 56.

19. Wu Jialin, "Li Dazhao yu diyici guogonghezuode jianli" [Li Dazhao and the establishment of the first united front between the Nationalist Party and the Communist Party], *Dangxiaojiaoxue* [Teaching at the party schools], no. 5 (1988): 34.

20. Li Dazhao, "Yuzhongzishu" [Personal statement in the jail], April 1927, *LDZQJ*, 5:298.

21. Song Qingling, "Sun Zhongshan he tatonggongchandang de hezuo" [Sun Yat-sen and his cooperation with the Chinese Communist Party], *Renminribao* [People's daily], November 12, 1962; Liu Changhui, "Diyici guogonghezuoshiqide Li Dazhao" [Li Dazhao during the first united front between the Nationalist Party and the Chinese Communist Party], *Xuzhoushifanxueyuanxuebao* [Journal of Xuzhou Normal University], no. 4 (1985): 29.

22. Bao Huisheng, "Huiyi Li Dazhao tongzhi" [Remembering Comrade Li Dazhao], in Xu Deheng et al., *Huiyi Li Dazhao* [In memory of Li Dazhao], 155.

23. Li Dazhao, "Pubianquanguode guomindang" [The countrywide Nationalist Party], April 18, 1923, *LDZQJ*, 4:208–10.

24. Li Chao, "Sun Zhongshan yu zhonggong sanda," 51.

25. Li Dazhao, "Zaizhonggong disancidaibiaodahuishang guanyu guogonghezuowenti de yijian" [My opinion on the issue of the cooperation between the Nationalist Party and the Communist Party at the third CCP national congress], June 1923, *LDZQJ*, 4:226.

26. Li Dazhao et al., "Zhi Sun Zhongshan de xin" [A letter to Sun Yat-sen], June 25, 1923, *LDZQJ*, 5:523.

27. Li Dazhao, "Jiannande guoyun yu xiongjiande guomin" [The unfortunate national situation and the exuberant citizens], December 20, 1923, *LDZQJ*, 4:488.

28. Li Dazhao, "Shibanianlaizhihuigu" [Retrospection over the past eighteen years], December 30, 1923, *LDZQJ*, 4:498.

29. Wang Jie, *Li Dazhao Beijing shinian: Shijianpian* [Li Dazhao's ten years in Beijing: Events], 226.

30. Zhu Wentong, *Li Dazhao zhuan*, 176.

31. Zhu Wentong, 177.

32. Li Dazhao, "Zai guangzhou zhuidao lienin bing jinian 'erqi' dahui shang de yanjiang" [Speech at the rally to mourn Lenin's passing and to commemorate the February Seventh Strike], February 7, 1924, *LDZQJ*, 4:511.

33. Li Dazhao, "Zai zhongguoguomindang diyicidaibiaodahui shangde fayan" [Speech at the first national congress of the Nationalist Party], January 28, 1924, *LDZQJ*, 4:505, 4:508.

34. Li Yunhan, *Congronggongdaoqingdang*, 2.

35. He Xiangning, "Zhongzhichengcheng bukecui" [The united people could not be defeated], in Xu Deheng et al., *Huiyi Li Dazhao*, 140.

36. Liu Jianqing, Wang Jiadian, and Xu Liangbo, *Zhongguo guomindang shi* [History of the Nationalist Party] (Nanjing: Jiangsugujichubanshe, 1992), 201.

37. Wang Jie, *Li Dazhao Beijing shinian: Shijianpian*, 243.

38. Zhou Jin, "Li Dazhao yu diyiciguogonghezuo" [Li Dazhao and the first united front between the Nationalist Party and the Communist Party], *Beijingdang'an* [Beijing archives], no. 8 (2011): 10.

39. Zhu Wentong, *Li Dazhao zhuan*, 183.

40. Li Dazhao, "Lienin busi" [Lenin never dies], March 30, 1924, *LDZQJ*, 4:514.

41. Li Dazhao, "Zheyizhou" [This week], May 1, 1924, *LDZQJ*, 4:517.

42. Li Dazhao, "Xinwen de qinlue" [The invasion of the media], June 11, 1924, *LDZQJ*, 4:581.

43. Li Dazhao, "Diguozhuyiqinluezhongguo houzhi guominyundong" [The national movement as a consequence of the imperialist invasion], January 17, 1925, *LDZQJ*, 5:48–49.

44. Li Dazhao et al., "Zhi Gu Shaochuan, Wang Rutang yanyiji xuanbu huifu zhong'e jiaoshu" [A letter to Wellington Koo and Wang Rutang for restoring the diplomatic relationship between China and Russia], February 15, 1924, *LDZQJ*, 5:525; Li Dazhao et al., "Zhi guwaizhang han" [A letter to Foreign Minister Gu], March 13, 1924, *LDZQJ*, 5:527.

45. Li Dazhao et al., "Zhong'e jiaoshe poliehou getuanti taidu" [The attitudes from diverse organizations after the breakup of the diplomatic negotiation between China and Russia], March 22, 1924, *LDZQJ*, 5:531.

46. Gu Weijun (Wellington Koo), *Gu Weijun huiyilu* [The memoir of Wellington Koo] (Beijing: Zhonghuashuju, 2013), 1:324.

47. Wang Jie, *Li Dazhao Beijing shinian: Jiaowangpian* [Li Dazhao's ten years in Beijing: Social connections], 69.

48. Zhu Wentong, *Li Dazhao zhuan*, 185.

49. Zhang Jiang, "Li Dazhao zai Kaifeng" [Li Dazhao in Kaifeng], *Shixueyuekan* [History monthly], no. 5 (1982): 58.

50. Wang Jie, *Li Dazhao Beijing shinian: Shijianpian*, 262–64.

51. Li Dazhao, "Zai guominhuiyichuchenghui quanguodaibiaodahui kaimushishangde yanjiang" [Speech at the opening ceremony of the National Congress of the National Assembly Promotion Association], March 1, 1925, *LDZQJ*, 5:54.

52. Li Dazhao, "Zhuzhangdizhi guomindangtongzhijulebu de chengli" [Advocating to resist the founding of the Nationalist Party Comrade Club], March 10, 1925, *LDZQJ*, 5:539.

53. Zhou Jin, "Li Dazhao yu diyiciguogonghezuo," 10.

54. Wang Jie, *Li Dazhao Beijing shinian: Shijianpian*, 266–68.

55. Li Dazhao, "Wan Sun Zhongshan lian" [Memorial elegy for Sun Yat-sen], March 1925, *LDZQJ*, 5:55.

56. Xiao Shen, "Zhonggongdangnei duiyu shouci guogonghezuode zhenglunjiqijieju," 60.

57. Li Dazhao, "Wu Peifu yapo jinghanlaogongyundong de yuanyin" [The reasons why Wu Peifu suppressed the workers' movement along the Beijing-Hankou line], February 7, 1925, *LDZQJ*, 5:52.

58. Yang Tianhong, "Jiaruguomindangzhihou gongchandangrende shenfenrentong wenti," 22.

59. Li Dazhao, "Shouchang jiaolai de baogao (zhisan)" [Li Dazhao's report (3)], July 1924, *LDZQJ*, 5:582.

60. Li Dazhao, "Zhi gongchanguoji dongfangbu de shenqingshu" [Requests to the Comintern's Oriental Department], July 17, 1924, *LDZQJ*, 5:538.

61. Li Dazhao, "Zhi gongchanguoji dongfangbu" [A letter to the Oriental Department of the Comintern], February 14, 1925, *LDZQJ*, 5:446.

62. Zhang Cixi, *Li Dazhao xiansheng zhuan* [Biography of Mr. Li Dazhao], 107.

63. Peng Hongwei and Li Yuzhen, "Guanyu Li Dazhao zai sulian jianghua he wenzhang de shuoming" [An explanation concerning Li Dazhao's speeches and articles during his visit to the USSR], *Jindaishiyanjiu*, no. 6 (1985): 5.

64. Lidazhaozhuanbianxiezu, *Li Dazhao zhuan*, 165.

65. Li Dazhao, "Su'e minzhong duiyu zhongguogemingde tongqing" [The Soviet people's sympathy with the Chinese revolution], September 24, 1924, *LDZQJ*, 5:23.

66. Wang Jie, *Li Dazhao Beijing shinian: Shijianpian*, 249.

67. Li Xinghua, *Huiyi wode fuqin Li Dazhao* [My memory of my father Li Dazhao], 105.

68. Dong Baorui, "Li Dazhao de sulianzhixing (shang)" [Li Dazhao's travel to the Soviet Union (1)], *Dangshibocai* [Extensive collection of the party history], no. 12 (2000): 18.

69. Li Min, "Kaozheng Li Dazhao 1924 nian de sulianzhixing" [An examination of Li Dazhao's visit to the Soviet Union in 1924], *Dangshibocai*, no. 7 (2011): 55.

70. Li Xinghua, *Huiyi wode fuqin Li Dazhao*, 100.

71. Dong Baorui, "Li Dazhao zai sulian liuxiade zhengui dianyingjingtou" [The precious film footage left by Li Dazhao during his trip to the Soviet Union], *Dangshizongheng* [On the party history], no. 3 (2006): 17.

72. Luo Zhanglong, "Kangzhaihuiyilu—Yihe Shouchang tongzhi zaiyiqi de rizi" [Remembering Kangmuyizhai: The days with Comrade Li Dazhao], in Xu Deheng et al., *Huiyi Li Dazhao*, 53.

73. Li Xinghua, *Huiyi wode fuqin Li Dazhao*, 100.

74. Li Min, "Kaozheng Li Dazhao 1924 nian de sulianzhixing," 55.

75. Dong Baorui, "Li Dazhao de sulianzhixing (shang)," 18.

76. Wang Fangtian, "Li Dazhao zai haerbin" [Li Dazhao in Harbin], in Xu Deheng et al., *Huiyi Li Dazhao*, 187.

77. Li Xinghua, *Huiyi wode fuqin Li Dazhao*, 103.

78. Dong Baorui, "Li Dazhao de sulianzhixing (shang)," 18–19.

79. Li Dazhao, "Zai gongchanguoji diwucidaibiaodahui diershiercihuiyi shangde baogao" [Report for the twenty-second meeting of the fifth conference of the Comintern], July 1, 1924, *LDZQJ*, 5:1.

80. Cai Siwei, "Shiping Li Dazhao tijiao gongchanguoji wuda shumianbaogao de zuoyong" [An analysis of the role of Li Dazhao's report submitted as a written missive at the fifth Comintern conference], *Yunnanjiaoyuxueyuanxuebao* [Journal of Yunnan Education College], no. 2 (1990): 45–47.

81. Dong Baorui, "Li Dazhao zai sulian liuxiade zhengui dianyingjingtou," 18.

82. Li Dazhao, "Su'e minzhong duiyu zhongguogemingde tongqing," 5:25.
83. Li Dazhao, 5:26.
84. Li Dazhao, 5:24.
85. Li Xinghua, *Huiyi wode fuqin Li Dazhao*, 113.
86. Li Xinghua, 115.
87. Li Dazhao, "Zai mosikedajuyuan 'buxuganshezhongguoxiehui' zuzhidedahuishangde yanjiang" [Speech for the rally organized by the Don't Interfere in China Association at Moscow's Bolshoi Theatre], September 22, 1924, *LDZQJ*, 5:19–21.
88. Dong Baorui, "Li Dazhao zai sulian liuxiade zhengui dianyingjingtou," 20.
89. Li Dazhao, "Zhongguo neizhan yu zhongguo nongmin" [The Chinese civil war and the Chinese peasants], September–October 1924, *LDZQJ*, 5:35, 5:40.
90. Dong Baorui, "Li Dazhao de sulianzhixing (shang)," 20.
91. Li Dazhao, "Zhongguo zuijinde zhengbian" [The recent political changes in China], September 12, 1924, *LDZQJ*, 5:8.
92. Li Dazhao, "Zhongguode shibian he bentuande xunlian" [The changes in China and our party's training], October 30, 1924, *LDZQJ*, 5:45–46.
93. Li Xinghua, *Huiyi wode fuqin Li Dazhao*, 109.
94. Dong Baorui, "Li Dazhao de sulianzhixing (shang)," 21.
95. Lidazhaozhuanbianxiezu, *Li Dazhao zhuan*, 165.
96. Wang Fangtian, "Li Dazhao zai haerbin," 185–86.
97. Li Yunhan, *Congronggongdaoqingdang*, 230.
98. Su Ming, "Zhiyi yu xiaojie: Cong 'ouyou manlu' kan Xu Zhimo su'e guan zhi zhuanbian" [Doubt and certainty: An analysis of Xu Zhimo's changing attitude toward Soviet Russia in his *Random Remarks on the Travel to Europe*], *Nanjingdaxuexuebao* [Journal of Nanjing University], no. 5 (2008): 108–9.
99. Li Xinghua, *Huiyi wode fuqin Li Dazhao*, 109.
100. Li Yunhan, *Congronggongdaoqingdang*, 255.
101. Jiang Yongjing, *Baoluoting yu wuhanzhengquan* [Borodin and the Wuhan regime] (Taipei: Zhuanjiwenxuechubanshe, 1972), 1.
102. Jiang Yongjing, *Baoluoting yu wuhanzhengquan*, 1.
103. Li Dazhao, "Shouchang jiaolai de baogao (zhier)" [Li Dazhao's report (2)] July 1924, *LDZQJ*, 5:575.

Chapter 8

1. Crossley, *Wobbling Pivot*, 173.
2. Li Dazhao, "Zai Lenin shishi erzhounianjiniandahui shangde yanjiang" [Speech at the meeting for the second anniversary of Lenin's death], January 21, 1926, *LDZQJ*, 5:122.

3. Chen Kenong, "Li Dazhao xiansheng ersan shi" [Stories about Mr. Li Dazhao], *Nanchongshiyuanxuebao* [Journal of Nanchong Teachers College], no. 2 (1979): 49.

4. Li Dazhao, "Makesi de zhongguo minzugeming guan" [Marx's view of China's national revolution], May 1926, *LDZQJ*, 5:143.

5. Li Dazhao, "Da yingdiguozhuyizhe qinluezhongguo shi" [A history of British imperialist invasions into China], August 1925, *LDZQJ*, 5:69.

6. Li Dazhao, "Xin diguozhuyi zhanzheng de yunniang" [The looming of a new imperialist war], January 6, 1926, *LDZQJ*, 5:119.

7. Li Dazhao, "Gei moutongzhi de xin" [A letter to a certain comrade], March 2, 1926, *LDZQJ*, 5:452.

8. Bruce A. Elleman, "Soviet Diplomacy," 473.

9. Nancy F. Cott, *Fighting Words: The Bold American Journalists Who Brought the World Home between the Wars* (New York: Basic Books, 2020), 362.

10. Baruch Hirson and Arthur J. Knodel, *Reporting the Chinese Revolution: The Letters of Rayna Prohme* (London: Pluton Press, 2007), 12.

11. Lidazhaozhuanbianxiezu, *Li Dazhao zhuan* [Biography of Li Dazhao], 180.

12. Shanghaishehuikexueyuan, *Wusayundongshiliao* [Historical documents concerning the May Thirtieth Movement] (Shanghai: Shanghairenminchubanshe, 1981), 1:190.

13. Xue Shixiao, "Li Dazhao yu kailuanmeikuang gongrenyundong" [Li Dazhao and the workers' movement in the Kailuan mining area], *Henanligongdaxuexuebao* [Journal of Henan Polytechnic University] 8, no. 4 (October 2007): 378.

14. Li Dazhao, "Da yingdiguozhuyizhe qinluezhongguo shi," 69.

15. Wang Jie, *Li Dazhao Beijing shinian: Shijianpian* [Li Dazhao's ten years in Beijing: Events], 275.

16. Song Fangchun and Li Quanxing, *Li Dazhao yanjiu cidian* [The dictionary of Li Dazhao studies], 564.

17. Li Shanyu and Yang Shusheng, "Li Dazhao yu guominjun" [Li Dazhao and the National Army], *Qiluxuekan*, no. 2 (1985): 72.

18. Zuo Bao, "Li Dazhao liudao zhangjiakou" [Li Dazhao's six visits to Zhangjiakou], *Dangshibocai* [Extensive collection of the party history], no. 3 (2002): 40–41.

19. Du Wenhuan, "Feng Yuxiang jiaru guogongtongyizhanxian zhi zhuli" [The helping hand for Feng Yuxiang to join the Nationalist-Communist United Front], *Dangshizongheng* [On the party history], no. 4 (1989): 33.

20. Chen Minyu and Zeng Shaoling, "Li Dazhao yu Feng Yuxiang de gemingyouyi" [The revolutionary friendship between Li Dazhao and Feng Yuxiang], *Fujiandangshiyuekan* [Fujian party history monthly], no. 9 (2003): 6.

21. Zhang Jiang, "Li Dazhao zai Kaifeng" [Li Dazhao in Kaifeng], 58.

22. Wang Yanping, "Li Dazhao sanfu Henan Kaifeng shishishuzheng" [An investigation into historical facts concerning Li Dazhao's three visits to Kaifeng, Henan Province], *Lantaishijie* [The Lantai world], July 2011, 17.

23. Li Dazhao, "Zhuzhang zai Guangzhou zhaokai guomindang dierjie daibiaodahui" [Proposal of holding the second national congress of the Nationalist Party in Guangzhou], early April 1925, *LDZQJ*, 5:61.

24. Wang Li and Ma Junnian, "Gongchanguoji yu diyici guogonghezuo de xingcheng" [The Comintern and the shaping of the first United Front between the Nationalist Party and the Communist Party], *Fujiandangshiyuekan*, no. 4 (2011): 30–32.

25. Li Yunhan, *Congronggongdaoqingdang* [From the acceptance of the communists to the party purge], 255.

26. Li Dazhao, "Qingtianbairi qizhi zhixia" [Under the blue-sky-and-white-sun flag], January 1, 1926, *LDZQJ*, 5:113.

27. Leng Yujian, "Li Dazhao yu diyici guogonghezuo" [Li Dazhao and the first United Front between the CCP and the KMT], *Zhongguotongyizhanxian* [China's United Front], no. 11 (2004): 44.

28. Zhou Jin, "Li Dazhao yu diyiciguogonghezuo" [Li Dazhao and the first United Front between the Nationalist Party and the Communist Party], 10.

29. Tian Chao and Wang Haoyao, "Li Dazhao yu zhonggongbeifang zaoqi dangzuzhi" [Li Dazhao and the early communist organizations in North China], *Tangshanxueyuanxuebao* [Journal of Tangshan University] 31, no. 4 (July 2018): 26.

30. Zhang Guang'en, "Li Dazhao tongzhi he dongbeidiqu dangde zaoqihuodong" [Comrade Li Dazhao and the early communist activities in Northeast China], *Shehuikexuejikan* [Social science journal] 68, no. 3 (1990): 109; Tang Runlin, "Li Dazhao yu dongbeidiqu dangzuzhi de chuangjian yu fazhan" [Li Dazhao and the creation and development of the party organizations in Northeast China], *Lantaishijie* [The Lantai world], no. 7 (2020): 11–12.

31. Zhao Xiude, "Li Dazhao yu zhonggong beijingdangzuzhi de chuangli he fazhan" [Li Dazhao and the establishment and development of the Communist Party organizations in Beijing], *Dangshijiaoxue* [Party history teaching], no. 5 (1989): 16–20.

32. Xiaoqing Diana Lin, *Peking University: Chinese Scholarship and Intellectuals, 1898–1937* (Albany: State University of New York Press, 2005), 175.

33. Li Dazhao, "Tudi yu nongmin" [Land and peasants], December 30, 1925–February 3, 1926, *LDZQJ*, 5:95–109.

34. Nie Yuansu and Shi Xiaosheng, "Li Dazhao yu henan gongnong gemingyundong" [Li Dazhao and the workers' and peasants' movements in Henan], *Lishijiaoxue* [History teaching], no. 7 (1984): 18.

35. Li Dazhao, "Menggu minzu de jiefangyundong" [The liberation movement of the ethnic Mongols], March 1925, *LDZQJ*, 5:57–59.

36. Xiao Chaoran, Sha Jiansun, and Liang Zhu, "Li Dazhao zai zhongguogongchanzhuyiyundong zhongde lishidiwei" [The historical position of Li Dazhao in the Chinese communist movement], *Beijingdaxuexuebao* [Journal of Beijing University], no. 6 (1979): 12.

37. Jin Ge, "Neimenggu minzujiefangyundong de xianqu Li Dazhao" [Li Dazhao: The pioneer of the national liberation movement in Inner Mongolia], *Neimengguxuanchuan* [Inner Mongolia propaganda], no. 3 (2003): 43.

38. Hao Weimin and Qiqige, "Li Dazhao yu Neimenggu geming" [Li Dazhao and the revolution in Inner Mongolia], in *Li Dazhao yanjiu lunwenji* [Collection of publications on the study of Li Dazhao], ed. Han Yide and Wang Shudi (Shijiazhuang: Hebeirenminchubanshe, 1984), 2:410.

39. Jiyatai, "Li Dazhao tongzhi he Neimenggu chuqide geming huodong" [Comrade Li Dazhao and the initial revolutionary activities in Inner Mongolia], in Xu Deheng et al., *Huiyi Li Dazhao* [In memory of Li Dazhao], 173.

40. Zhang Cixi, *Li Dazhao xiansheng zhuan* [Biography of Mr. Li Dazhao], 52.

41. Zhang Jingru and Ma Mozhen, *Li Dazhao* (Shanghai: Shanghairenminchubanshe, 1981), 128.

42. Liang Zhu, "Guanshuizizhuyundong shimo" [A history of the Customs Autonomy Movement], *Beijingdangshi* [The party history of Beijing], no. 5 (1988): 2–7.

43. Yang Hongzhang, "Li Dazhao yu Duan Qirui shinianjian de zhengzhi guanxi shulue" [An analysis of the decade-long political relationship between Li Dazhao and Duan Qirui], *Binzhoujiaoyuxueyuanxuebao* [Journal of Binzhou Education College] 7, no. 2 (June 2001): 28.

44. Zhang Jingru and Ma Mozhen, *Li Dazhao*, 131.

45. Zhang Jingru and Ma Mozhen, 142.

46. Li Xinghua, *Huiyi wode fuqin Li Dazhao* [My memory of my father Li Dazhao], 121–22.

47. Li Dazhao, "Yuzhongzishu" [My statement in prison], April 1927, *LDZQJ*, 5:299–300.

48. Li Xinghua, *Huiyi wode fuqin Li Dazhao*, 184–85.

49. Li Xinghua, 187.

50. Dong Yali, "Li Dazhao linsiqian zuoleshenme? Caifang Li Dazhao zhangzi Li Baohua, cizi Li Guanghua" [What did Li Dazhao do before his death? An interview with Li Dazhao's eldest son, Li Baohua, and second son, Li Guanghua], 95.

51. Li Dazhao, "Gei guomindang zhongyangzhengzhihuiyi de baogao (zhisan)" [The third report to the Central Political Council of the Nationalist Party], January 22, 1927, *LDZQJ*, 5:255.

52. Li Dazhao, "Yuzhongzishu," 5:301.

53. Li Dazhao, "Gei guomindang zhongyangzhengzhihuiyi de baogao (zhisi)" [The fourth report to the Central Political Council of the Nationalist Party], January 22, 1927, *LDZQJ*, 5:279.

54. Li Dazhao, "Fengxi zuijin junshijihua" [The recent military plan of the Fengtian clique], January 1927, *LDZQJ*, 5:228.

55. Li Dazhao, "Tianjin huiyi yu shiju de jianglai" [The Tianjin Conference and the future national situation], June 19, 1926, *LDZQJ*, 5:588.
56. Li Dazhao, "Gei guomindang zhongyangzhengzhihuiyi de baogao (zhisan)," 5:266.
57. Li Dazhao, "Tianjin huiyi yu shiju de jianglai," 5:590.
58. Li Dazhao, "Shoutongzhi laixin" [Comrade Li Dazhao's letter], December 5, 1926, *LDZQJ*, 5:202.
59. Li Dazhao, "Guomin erjun zhong gongzuo ying zhuyizhishi" [Attention to some important issues for those who work within the Second Army], December 5, 1926, *LDZQJ*, 5:209.
60. Yan Zhixin, *Li Dazhao he Feng Yuxiang* [Li Dazhao and Feng Yuxiang] (Beijing: Jiefangjunchubanshe, 1987), 1.
61. Yan Zhixin, *Li Dazhao he Feng Yuxiang*, 186.
62. Li Dazhao, "Guomin erjun zhong gongzuo ying zhuyizhishi," 5:209–10.
63. Li Dazhao, "Beifang junshi zhengzhi zhuangkuang" [The military and political conditions in the North], October 1, 1926, *LDZQJ*, 5:597.
64. Xiao Yusheng, *Li Dazhao de junshihuodong* [Li Dazhao's military activities] (Beijing: Junshikexuechubanshe, 1988), 112.
65. Xiao Yusheng, *Li Dazhao de junshihuodong*, 165.
66. Li Dazhao, "Zhi Bai Wenwei, Wang Faqin, Xu Qian, Gu Mengyu" [A letter to Bai Wenwei, Wang Faqin, Xu Qian, and Gu Mengyu], January 24, 1927, *LDZQJ*, 5:235.
67. Li Dazhao, "Beifangqu duiyu santebiequ ji xibeijun zhong gongzuo de yijian" [Some advice for the work in the Third Special Region and among the Northwest Army], October 18, 1926, *LDZQJ*, 5:187.
68. Niu Yanan and Li Guihua, "Zhongguo diyige nongcun dangzhibu de jianli" [The establishment of the first rural branch of the CCP], *Dang'antiandi* [Archives world], no. 5 (2020): 12.
69. Li Dazhao, "Tong gongchanguoji zhixingweiyuanhui qingbaochu gongzuorenyuan de tanhua" [Conversation with the intelligent officers of the Comintern], June 30, 1926, *LDZQJ*, 5:154.
70. Xiao Yusheng, *Li Dazhao de junshihuodong*, 134.
71. Li Dazhao, "Lu yu shaan dengsheng de hongqianghui" [The Red Spear Society in Shandong, Henan, and Shaanxi Provinces], August 8, 1926, *LDZQJ*, 5:163–69.
72. Shi Jie and Zhang Shouxian, "Li Dazhao he Shaanxi gemingyundong" [Li Dazhao and the revolutionary movement in Shaanxi Province], *Xibeidaxuexuebao* [Journal of Northwest University], no. 3 (1984): 24.
73. Li Dazhao, "Riben diguozhuyi zuijin jingong zhongguo de fangce" [The most recent strategies of Japanese imperialism to invade China], July 22, 1926, *LDZQJ*, 5:160.

74. Li Dazhao, "Gei guomindang zhongyangzhengzhihuiyi de baogao (zhiwu)" [The fifth report to the Central Political Council of the Nationalist Party], January 25, 1927, *LDZQJ*, 5:282–92.

75. Wang Hai, "Zhang Zuolin busha Li Dazhao dengren dongyin qianxi" [An analysis of the motives of Zhang Zuolin to arrest and kill Li Dazhao and others], *Zhongguojinianguanyanjiu* [Studies of China's memorial museums], no. 2 (2017): 165–71.

76. Si Gong, "Zhang Zuolin weihe shahai Li Dazhao" [Why did Zhang Zuolin kill Li Dazhao], *Quanguoxinshumu* [National new books information], no. 21 (2009): 45.

77. Li Jihua, Chang Jinjun, and Li Quanxing, eds., *Li Dazhao beibu xisheng anzang ziliaoxuanbian* [Selected materials concerning Li Dazhao's arrest, death, and burial] (Beijing: Xianzhuangshuju, 2011), 539 (hereafter cited as *LDZBXAZ*).

78. *LDZBXAZ*, 541.

79. Li Xinghua, *Huiyi wode fuqin Li Dazhao*, 187.

80. *LDZBXAZ*, 486.

81. Meng Zhaogeng, "Zhonggong zaoqi lingdaoren Li Dazhao yingyong jiuyi qianhou" [The early communist leader Li Dazhao sacrificed his life bravely], *Wenshichunqiu* [Spring and autumn of literature and history], no. 11 (2019): 18.

82. Li Xinghua, *Huiyi wode fuqin Li Dazhao*, 189.

83. *LDZBXAZ*, 45.

84. Li Dazhao, "Yuzhongzishu," 5:301.

85. *LDZBXAZ*, 397–411.

86. Lidazhaozhuanbianxiezu, *Li Dazhao zhuan*, 215.

87. Li Xinghua, *Huiyi wode fuqin Li Dazhao*, 205.

88. Lu Jian, *Li Dazhao he Qu Qiubai* [Li Dazhao and Qu Qiubai] (Beijing: Shangwuyinshuguan, 1951), 14.

89. Li Ming, *Zhonggong liulieshi xiaozhuan* [Short biographies of the six communist martyrs], 8.

90. *LDZBXAZ*, 7.

91. Zhu Zhimin, *Li Dazhao zhuan* [Biography of Li Dazhao], 353.

92. *LDZBXAZ*, 227.

93. *LDZBXAZ*, 229.

94. *LDZBXAZ*, 273.

95. *LDZBXAZ*, 158.

96. *LDZBXAZ*, 271.

97. *LDZBXAZ*, 546.

98. Zhang Jingru and Ma Mozhen, *Li Dazhao*, 163.

99. Jingshijingchating [Metropolitan Police Headquarters], *Soviet Plot in China*, English ed. (Beijing: Metropolitan Police Headquarters, 1928), 1.

100. *LDZBXAZ*, 463–67.

101. Zhu Zhimin, *Li Dazhao zhuan*, 358.

102. Li Xinghua, *Huiyi wode fuqin Li Dazhao*, 204.
103. LDZBXAZ, 225.
104. LDZBXAZ, 623.
105. LDZBXAZ, 620.
106. Lidazhaozhuanbianxiezu, *Li Dazhao zhuan*, 220.
107. He Jun, "Li Dazhao xunnan muduji" [My witness of Li Dazhao's death], *Gemingrenwu* [Revolutionary personages], no. 1 (1985): 44.
108. Wang Tongce, "Zhishifengzi de chonggaodianfan: jinian gemingxianlie Li Dazhao tongzhi xunnan ershijiu zhounian" [The lofty paragon for intellectuals: In memory of the revolutionary martyr Li Dazhao at the twenty-ninth anniversary of his death], in Han Yide and Wang Shudi, 1:113.
109. Zhang Jingru, "Li Dazhao linxingqian meiyou fabiao yanshuo" [Li Dazhao did not deliver a speech before his execution], *Dangshiyanjiuyujiaoxue* [Party history studies and teaching], no. 2 (2011): 111.
110. Gu Dapeng, "Zhu Chengjia yinshen ershinian huanyuan Li Dazhao" [Zhu Chengjia hid himself for twenty years to study in order to restore the true Li Dazhao], *Dagongbao*, July 10, 2016, A19.
111. LDZBXAZ, 532.
112. Zhang Cixi, *Li Dazhao xiansheng zhuan* [Biography of Mr. Li Dazhao], 77.
113. Li Xinghua, *Huiyi wode fuqin Li Dazhao*, 206.
114. LDZBXAZ, 13.
115. An Pingjun, "1927: Li Dazhao de lieshi zhilu" [1927: The path of Li Dazhao as a martyr], *Guojiarenwenlishi* [National humanity history], July 2017, 109.
116. LDZBXAZ, 98.
117. Liang Shuming, *Yiwang tan jiulu* [Remarks on my old memories] (Beijing: Jinchengchubanshe, 2006), 104.
118. Luo Zhanglong, "Kangzhai huiyilu: Jihe shouchang tongzhi zaiyiqi de rizi" [My memory of Kangzhai: My days with Comrade Li Dazhao], in Xu Deheng et al., *Huiyi Li Dazhao*, 57.
119. He Xiangning, "Zhongzhichengcheng bukecui" [United we stand], in Xu Deheng et al., 140.
120. Yan Zhixin, *Li Dazhao he Feng Yuxiang*, 257.
121. "Tried by a Secret Court," *New York Times*, April 29, 1927, 1.
122. George Young, "The Murders in China," *Lansbury's Labour Weekly* 3, no. 114 (May 14, 1927): 5.
123. Zhang Jian and Pei Cuimin, "Li Dazhao tongzhi yuhaihou de guojifanying" [The international response to Comrade Li Dazhao's death], *Fudanxuebao* [Journal of Fudan University], no. 6 (1979): 111.
124. Vera V. Vishnyakova-Akimova, "Zhongguogeming jianwen" [My witness of the Chinese Revolution], in LDZBXAZ, 479.
125. Wang Jie, *Li Dazhao Beijing shinian: Jiaowangpian* [Li Dazhao's ten years in Beijing: Social connections], 237.

126. *LDZBXAZ*, 235.
127. *LDZBXAZ*, 316.
128. *LDZBXAZ*, 320.
129. *LDZBXAZ*, 323.
130. *LDZBXAZ*, 260.
131. Wang Shunsheng, *Zhongguogemingshi* [History of the Chinese Revolution] (Beijing: Zhongguorenmindaxuechubanshe, 1991), 231.

Epilogue

1. Liu Shaomeng, "Lun Li Dazhao de zaoqisixiang jiqi tedian" [Li Dazhao's early thoughts and their characteristics], in *Li Dazhao yanjiu lunwenji*, ed. Han Yide and Wang Shudi (Shijiazhuang: Hebeirenminchubanshe, 1984), 1:366.
2. Wu Hanquan, "Xifangjindaiwenhua yu Li Dazhao de zaoqisixiang" [Modern Western culture and Li Dazhao's early thoughts], *Ningxiadaxuexuebao* [Journal of Ningxia University] 20, no. 2 (1998): 36.
3. Bai Xiaotian, "Li Dazhao yu xinwenhuayundong de qianjin fangxiang" [Li Dazhao and the direction of the New Culture Movement], 63.
4. Zhang Qingxiang, "Li Dazhao 'wusi' shiqi xinwenhua jiangou de xiandaifang'an" [Li Dazhao's modern plan for reconstructing a new culture during the May Fourth era], 33.
5. Jin Rongdong, *Li Dazhao zhexue yanjiu* [A study of Li Dazhao's philosophy], 11.
6. Mao Zedong, "Lun renminminzhu zhuanzheng: Jinian zhongguogongchandang ershibazhounian" [On people's democratic dictatorship: In commemoration of the twenty-eighth anniversary of the establishment of the Chinese Communist Party], June 30, 1949, in *Mao Zedong xuanji* [Collected works of Mao Zedong] (Beijing: Renminchubanshe, 1968), 1360.
7. Li Jihua, Chang Jinjun, and Li Quanxing, *LDZBXAZ*, 538.
8. Song Lin, "Li Dazhao he tade furen Zhao Renlan" [Li Dazhao and his wife Zhao Renlan], *Dangshizonglan* [Overview of party history], no. 3 (1999): 10.
9. Dong Yali, "Li Dazhao linsiqian zuoleshenme?" [What did Li Dazhao do before his death?], 96; Li Jihua, Chang Jinjun, and Li Quanxing, *LDZBXAZ*, 417.
10. *LDZBXAZ*, 420.
11. Xiao Shen, "Zhonggongdangnei duiyu shouci guogonghezuode zhenglunjiqijieju" [The debate and outcome within the CCP over the United Front between the Nationalist Party and the Communist Party], 60.
12. Liu Changhui, "Diyici guogonghezuoshiqide Li Dazhao" [Li Dazhao during the first United Front between the Nationalist Party and the CCP], 32.
13. Du Yanhua, "Li Dazhao wenhuasixiang dui Mao Zedong zaoqi wenhuaguan xingcheng he fazhan de yingxiang" [The impact of Li Dazhao's cultural

thoughts upon the shaping and development of early Mao Zedong's cultural perspective], *Zhonggongdangshiyanjiu* [Study of the history of the CCP], no. 1 (2003): 85.

14. Crossley, *Wobbling Pivot*, 173.

15. Cheng Long, "Li Dazhao he Mao Zedong" [Li Dazhao and Mao Zedong], *Dangshibocai* [Extensive collection of the party history], no. 11 (1999): 7.

16. Wang Jie, *Li Dazhao Beijing shinian: Jiaowangpian* [Li Dazhao's ten years in Beijing: Social connections], 44.

17. Bao Huiseng, "Huiyi Li Dazhao tongzhi" [My memory of Comrade Li Dazhao], in Xu Deheng et al., *Huiyi Li Dazhao* [In memory of Li Dazhao], 157.

18. Lu Xun, "Shouchang xiansheng he tade yiwen" [Li Dazhao and his surviving writings], in Xu Deheng et al., *Huiyi Li Dazhao*, 138.

19. Wang Shiru, "Hu Shi shi Li Dazhao de haopengyou" [Hu Shi was Li Dazhao's good friend], 38.

20. Zhang Shenfu, "Yi Shouchang" [My memory of Li Dazhao], in Xu Deheng et al., *Huiyi Li Dazhao*, 61.

21. Wang Jie, *Li Dazhao Beijing shinian: Jiaowangpian*, 31.

22. Zhang Ruxin, "Jinian zhonghuaminzu buxiude gemingweiren Li Dazhao tongzhi" [In memory of the eternally great revolutionary of the Chinese nation Comrade Li Dazhao], in Han Yide and Wang Shudi, 1:48.

23. Cai Shangsi, "Li Dazhao de sixiang pingjie" [Introduction and assessment of Li Dazhao's thought], in Han Yide and Wang Shudi, 1:60.

24. Zang Kejia, *Li Dazhao* (Beijing: Zuojiachubanshe, 1959), 132.

25. Liu Juanxun, *Gemingshijia Hu Hua* [The revolutionary historian Hu Hua] (Beijing: Dangdaizhongguochubanshe, 2011), 371.

26. Han Yide and Wang Shudi, "Li Dazhao yanjiu zongshu" [A comprehensive review of the Li Dazhao studies], in Han Yide and Wang Shudi, 2: 630.

27. Chen Kenong, "Li Dazhao ersan shi" [Stories about Li Dazhao], 50.

28. Susanne Weigelin-Schwiedrzik, "What Is Wrong with Li Dazhao?" in *New Perspectives on the Chinese Communist Revolution*, ed. Tony Saich and Hans van de Ven (Armonk, NY: M. E. Sharpe, 1995), 69.

29. *LDZQJ*, 1:7.

30. Guo Jicheng, *Zhongguo jindaiminzuweiji xiade xiandaixing xuanze yu jiangou: Li Dazhao sixiang xinjie* [The selection and reconstruction of modernity under the national crisis of modern China: A new interpretation of Li Dazhao's thought] (Beijing: Zhongguozhengfadaxuechubanshe, 2011), 1.

31. Tai, "Chen Duxiu's Conversion," 115; Wang Yuanyi, "Yuzhou geming lun"[An examination of the global revolution], in *Wusiyundong bashizhounian xueshuyantaohui lunwenji* [A collection of papers from the seminar to commemorate the eightieth anniversary of the May Fourth Movement], ed. Lu Fangshang and Zhang Zhelang (Taipei: Hongbaiyinshuashiye, 1999), 596.

32. Liang Shiqiu, "Wokan wusi" [The May Fourth Movement in my eyes], in Lianhebao, *Wocanjialiao wusiyundong* [I participated in the May Fourth Movement], 149.

33. Chen Lifu, "Zhonggong yu wusi chebushangguangxi" [The CCP has nothing to do with the May Fourth Movement], in Lianhebao, *Wocanjialiao wusiyundong*, 84.

34. Jiang Yongjing, *Baoluoting yu wuhanzhengquan* [Michael Borodin and the Wuhan regime], 1.

35. Lei, *Sanshinian dongluan zhongguo* [China in the turbulent thirty years], 23.

36. Shen Yunlong, "Minshiliu Beijing shoucha eshiguan zhi jingguo" [The history of searching the Soviet Russian embassy in 1927], in *LDZBXAZ*, 496.

37. Li Yunhan, *Congronggongdaoqingdang* [From the acceptance of the Communists to the party purge], 255.

38. Fang-yen Yang, "Zaizao xinwenming: Li Dazhao zaoqi sixiangzhongde pubianyuteshu" [Toward a new civilization: The universal and the particular in the early thoughts of Li Dazhao], *Zhengzhikexueluncong*, no. 63 (March 2015): 43.

39. Dong Yali, "Li Dazhao linsiqian zuoleshenme?" [What did Li Dazhao do before his death?], 95.

40. Wang Yanping, "Jidong kangzhanzhongde Li Dazhao houdai" [Li Dazhao's descendants during the anti-Japanese war in East Hebei], *Dang'antiandi* [Archives world], no. 11 (2015): 19.

41. Wang Jie, *Li Dazhao Beijing shinian: Jiaowangpian*, 251.

42. Liu Debin, "Qiyixunzhang huodezhe—Li Hongta: Gongchandangren gemingchuantong youxiujiafeng de chuanchengren" [The receiver of the July 1 Medal—Li Hongta: The inheritor of the revolutionary tradition and the excellent family style], Sina Corporation, Domestic News, June 29, 2021, https://news.sina.com.cn/c/2021-06-29/doc-ikqciyzk2479502.shtml.

43. Huang Sung-k'ang, *Li Ta-chao and the Impact of Marxism in Modern Chinese Thinking* (The Hague: Mouton, 1965), 4.

44. Joseph W. Esherick, "Ten Theses on the Chinese Revolution," *Modern China* 21, no. 1 (January 1995): 69.

45. Esherick, "Ten Theses," 64.

Bibliography

An Pingjun. "1927: Li Dazhao de lieshi zhilu" [1927: The path of Li Dazhao as a martyr]. *Guojiarenwenlishi* [National humanity history], July 2017, 104–9.
Bai Xiaotian. "Li Dazhao yu xinwenhuayundong de qianjin fangxiang" [Li Dazhao and the direction of the New Culture Movement]. *Tangshanxueyuanxuebao* [Journal of Tangshan University] 30, no. 2 (March 2017): 63–65.
Beasley, W. G. *Japanese Imperialism 1894–1945*. New York: Oxford University Press, 1987.
Brands, H. W. *Woodrow Wilson*. New York: Times Books, 2003.
Cai Lesu. "Yetan Malin zaidiyici guogonghezuo xingchengzhongde zuoyong" [An analysis of G. Maring's role in the shaping of the first united front between the Nationalist Party and the Communist Party]. *Qinghuadaxuexuebao* [Journal of Tsinghua University] 1, no. 2 (1988): 74–81.
Cai Siwei. "Shiping Li Dazhao tijiao gongchanguoji wuda shumianbaogao de zuoyong" [An analysis of the role of Li Dazhao's report submitted as a written missive at the fifth Comintern conference]. *Yunnanjiaoyuxueyuanxuebao* [Journal of Yunnan Education College], no. 2 (1990): 45–47.
Carlton, Charles. *Royal Childhoods*. London: Routledge / K. Paul, 1986.
Chan, Adrian. "The Liberation of Marx in China." *Journal of Contemporary Asia* 25, no. 1 (January 1995): 93–108.
Chen Kenong. "Li Dazhao xiansheng ersan shi" [Stories about Mr. Li Dazhao]. *Nanchongshiyuanxuebao* [Journal of Nanchong Teachers College], no. 2 (1979): 48–50.
Chen Minyu and Zeng Shaoling. "Li Dazhao yu Feng Yuxiang de gemingyouyi" [The revolutionary friendship between Li Dazhao and Feng Yuxiang]. *Fujiandangshiyuekan* [Fujian party history monthly], no. 9 (2003): 5–6.
Chen Weiping. "Youguan Li Dazhao tongzhi de yizexinshiliao" [A new historical document concerning Comrade Li Dazhao]. *Lilunxuekan* [Theory journal], no. 2 (1992): 85–87.
Chen Wenxu. "Minzhugemingshiqide Li Dazhao yu makesizhuyi zhongguohua: Congwusishiqi Li Dazhao sixiangfazhan guijideshijiao lai kaocha" [Li

Dazhao and the Sinicization of Marxism in the period of the democratic revolution: An analysis from the perspective of Li Dazhao's ideological growth during the May Fourth era]. *Lilunxuekan* [Theory journal] 187, no. 9 (September 2009): 34–38.

Cheng Jinjiao. "Chen Duxiu heyidangxuan 'yida' zhongyangzongshuji—jianlun Li Dazhao weineng jinru 'yida' zhongyangju zhi yuanyin" [Why could Chen Duxiu be elected the general secretary of the central bureau at the first congress? An interpretation of the reasons Li Dazhao was not elected into the central bureau at this first congress]. *Anqingshifanxueyuanxuebao* [Journal of Anqing Teachers College] 26, no. 1 (January 2007): 72–76.

Cheng Long. "Li Dazhao he Mao Zedong" [Li Dazhao and Mao Zedong]. *Dangshibocai* [Extensive collection of the party history], no. 11 (1999): 4–7.

Cheng Mingxin and Yuan Cun. "Li Dazhao yu makesizhuyi zhongguohua de kaiduan" [Li Dazhao and the beginning of the Sinicization of Marxism]. *Hebeixuekan* [Hebei academic journal], no. 2 (1996): 110–11.

Cheng, Pei-kai, and Michael Lestz. *The Search for Modern China: A Documentary Collection.* With Jonathan D. Spence. New York: W. W. Norton, 1999.

Chow, Tse-tsung. *The May Fourth Movement: Intellectual Revolution in Modern China.* Cambridge, MA: Harvard University Press, 1964.

Cott, Nancy F. *Fighting Words: The Bold American Journalists Who Brought the World Home between the Wars.* New York: Basic Books, 2020.

Crossley, Pamela Kyle. *The Wobbling Pivot: China since 1800.* West Sussex, UK: Wiley-Blackwell, 2010.

Dawley, Evan N. "Changing Minds: American Missionaries, Chinese Intellectuals, and Cultural Internationalism, 1919–1921." *Journal of American-East Asian Relations* 12, no. 1/2 (Spring/Summer 2003): 1–31.

Desnoyers, Charles A. *Patterns of East Asian History.* New York: Oxford University Press, 2018.

Dirlik, Arif. *The Origins of Chinese Communism.* Oxford: Oxford University Press, 1989.

Dong Baorui. "'Gaozhu shenzhou fengyulou': Li Dazhao yu shenzhouxuehui huiyou Yi Xiang" [Working for China: Li Dazhao and Yi Xiang, a member of the China Society]. *Dangshizongheng* [On the party history] 181, no. 3 (2001): 4–7.

———. "Li Dazhao de sulianzhixing (shang)" [Li Dazhao's travel to the Soviet Union (1)]. *Dangshibocai* [Extensive collection of the party history], no. 12 (2000): 17–21.

———. "Li Dazhao de wentanhaoyou Gao Yihan" [Gao Yihan: Li Dazhao's good friend in the literary circle]. *Dangshizongheng* [On the party history], no. 4 (2003): 15–18, 41.

———. "Li Dazhao zai sulian liuxiade zhengui dianyingjingtou" [The precious film footage left by Li Dazhao during his trip to the Soviet Union]. *Dangshizongheng* [On the party history], no. 3 (2006): 16–20.

———. "Liuxueriben zai Li Dazhao yishengzhong suoqidezuoyong" [The impact of Li Dazhao's study in Japan upon his whole life]. *Hebeixuekan* [Journal of Hebei], no. 1 (1990): 43–46.

Dong Yali. "Li Dazhao linsiqian zuoleshenme? Caifang Li Dazhao zhangzi Li Baohua, cizi Li Guanghua" [What did Li Dazhao do before his death? An interview with Li Dazhao's eldest son, Li Baohua, and second son, Li Guanghua]. *Zhanghuixiaoshuo* [The traditional Chinese fiction], no. 3 (2010): 92–96.

Dryburgh, Marjorie. "Rewriting Collaboration: China, Japan, and the Self in the Diaries of Bai Jianwu." *Journal of Asian Studies* 68, no. 3 (August 2009): 689–714.

Du Quanzhong. *Li Dazhao yandu* [A study of Li Dazhao]. Beijing: Zhongyangbianyichubanshe, 2006.

Du Wenhuan. "Feng Yuxiang jiaru guogongtongyizhanxian zhi zhuli" [The helping hand for Feng Yuxiang to join the Nationalist-Communist United Front]. *Dangshizongheng* [On the party history], no. 4 (1989): 32–34.

Du Yanhua. "Li Dazhao wenhuasixiang dui Mao Zedong zaoqi wenhuaguan xingcheng he fazhan de yingxiang" [The impact of Li Dazhao's cultural thoughts upon the shaping and development of early Mao Zedong's cultural perspective]. *Zhonggongdangshiyanjiu* [Study of the history of the Chinese Communist Party], no. 1 (2003): 75–79, 85.

Elleman, Bruce A. "Soviet Diplomacy and the First United Front in China." *Modern China* 21, no. 4 (October 1995): 450–80.

Elman, Benjamin A. *Civil Examinations and Meritocracy in Late Imperial China.* Cambridge, MA: Harvard University Press, 2013.

———. "Political, Social, and Cultural Reproduction via Civil Service Examinations in Late Imperial China." *Journal of Asian Studies* 50, no. 1 (February 1991): 7–28.

Esherick, Joseph W. "Ten Theses on the Chinese Revolution." *Modern China* 21, no. 1 (January 1995): 45–76.

Evans, Harriet. "The Language of Liberation: Gender and *Jiefang* in Early Chinese Communist Party Discourse." In *Twentieth-Century China: New Approaches*, edited by Jeffrey N. Wasserstrom, 193–220. London: Routledge, 2003.

Fairbank, John King, Edwin O. Reischauer, and Albert M. Craig. *East Asia: Tradition and Transformation.* Houghton Mifflin, 1989.

Fan Shulin. "Li Dazhao zizhu beida pinkunsheng" [Li Dazhao helped the poor student at Beijing University]. *Wenshibolan* [Literature and history expo], no. 1 (2017): 20.

Fang Siji. "Shaonian Li Dazhao de zhuangzhihaoqing" [The motivated aspiration of young Li Dazhao]. *Xiaoxueshengshidai* [Schoolkid times], no. 2 (2011): 4–8.

Feigon, Lee. *Chen Duxiu, Founder of the Chinese Communist Party.* Princeton, NJ: Princeton University Press, 2014.

Fu Shaochang. "Li Dazhao zaoqi aiguosixiang jiqi tedian" [The characteristics of Li Dazhao's early patriotic thoughts]. *Hongsewenhuaxuekan* [Journal of Red Culture], no. 2 (September 2017): 69–77.

Gao Like. "Li Dazhao yu mincuiminzhuzhuyi" [Li Dazhao and populist democracy]. *Ershiyishiji* [Twenty-first century] 70, no. 4 (2002): 44–55.

Gao Yihan. "He Li Dazhao tongzhi xiangchu de shihou" [My time with Comrade Li Dazhao]. *Gongrenribao* [Workers' daily], April 27, 1957.

Gao Zhonghua. "Li Dazhao de jiawuguan" [Li Dazhao's perspective on the First Sino-Japanese War]. *Tangshanxueyuanxuebao* [Journal of Tangshan University] 30, no. 2 (March 2017): 28–32.

Gong Shuduo. *Zhongguojindaishi* [Modern history of China, 1919–49]. Beijing: Zhonghuashuju, 2010.

Gong Shuduo and Huang Xingtao. "Hu Shi yu Li Dazhao guanxilun" [An analysis of the relationship between Hu Shi and Li Dazhao]. *Shixueyuekan* [History monthly], no. 1 (1996): 62–70.

Goossaert, Vincent, and David A. Palmer. *The Religious Question in Modern China*. Chicago: University of Chicago Press, 2012.

Graziani, Sofia. "Youth and the Making of Modern China: A Study of the Communist Youth League's Organisation and Strategies in Times of Revolution (1920–1937)." *European Journal of East Asian Studies* 13, no. 1 (2014): 117–49.

Grieder, Jerome B. "The Question of 'Politics' in the May Fourth Era." In *Reflections on the May Fourth Movement: A Symposium*, edited by Benjamin I. Schwartz, 95–102. Cambridge, MA: East Asian Research Center, Harvard University, 1973.

Gu Dapeng. "Zhu Chengjia yinshen ershinian huanyuan Li Dazhao" [Zhu Chengjia hid himself for twenty years to study in order to restore the true Li Dazhao]. *Dagongbao*, July 10, 2016, A19.

Gu, Edward X. "Populist Themes in May Fourth Radical Thinking: A Reappraisal of the Intellectual Origins of Chinese Marxism (1917–1922)." *East Asian History*, no. 10 (December 1995): 99–126.

Gu Weijun (Wellington Koo). *Gu Weijun huiyilu* [The memoir of Wellington Koo]. Beijing: Zhonghuashuju, 2013.

Guo Dehong and Zhang Minglin. *Li Dazhao zhuan* [Biography of Li Dazhao]. Beijing: Hongqichubanshe, 2016.

Guo Jicheng. *Zhongguo jindaiminzuweiji xiade xiandaixing xuanze yu jiangou: Li Dazhao sixiang xinjie* [The selection and reconstruction of modernity under the national crisis of modern China: A new interpretation of Li Dazhao's thought]. Beijing: Zhongguozhengfadaxuechubanshe, 2011.

Han Chunyun. "Li Dazhao xiegei Sun Zhongshan de xindeng zai helan guojiadang'anguan faxian" [The findings of the letter by Li Dazhao to Sun Yat-sen and other items in the Dutch National Archives]. *Lantaishijie* [The Lantai world], no. 9 (May 2011): 48.

Han Jun and Cao Junxue. "Guogong diyicihezuode yuanyin tanxi" [An analysis of the reasons of the first united front between the Nationalist Party and the Communist Party]. *Chifengxueyuanxuebao* [Journal of Chifeng University] 32, no. 11 (November 2011): 22–23.

Han Yide. "Li Dazhao liuxueshiqi de shishikaocha" [A survey of historical facts concerning Li Dazhao's study abroad in Japan]. *Jindaishiyanjiu* [Modern Chinese history studies], no. 1 (1989): 303–12.

Han Yide and Wang Shudi, editors. *Li Dazhao yanjiu lunwenji* [Collection of publications on the study of Li Dazhao]. Shijiazhuang: Hebeirenminchubanshe, 1984. 2 vols.

Han Yide and Yao Weidou. *Li Dazhao shengping jinian* [A chronicle of Li Dazhao's life]. Harbin: Heilongjiangrenminchubanshe, 1987.

He Jun. "Li Dazhao xunnan muduji" [My witness of Li Dazhao's death]. *Gemingrenwu* [Revolutionary personages], no. 1 (1985): 43–45.

Hideaki Kikuchi. *Modaiwangchao yu jindai zhongguo* [The last dynasty and modern China]. Translated by Ma Xiaojuan. Guilin: Guangxishifandaxuechubanshe, 2018. Originally published as *Rasuto enpera to kindai Chugoku*.

Hirson, Baruch, and Arthur J. Knodel. *Reporting the Chinese Revolution: The Letters of Rayna Prohme*. London: Pluton Press, 2007.

Hsü, Immanuel C. Y. *The Rise of Modern China*. New York: Oxford University Press, 2000.

Huang Sung-k'ang. *Li Ta-chao and the Impact of Marxism in Modern Chinese Thinking*. The Hague: Mouton, 1965.

Huang Zhen and Yao Weidou. *Li Dazhao de gushi* [The story of Li Dazhao]. Shijiazhuang: Hebeirenminchubanshe, 1980.

Hung, Chang-tai. "The Cult of the Red Martyr: Politics of Commemoration in China." *Journal of Contemporary History* 43, no. 2 (April 2008): 279–304.

Ishikawa Yoshihiro. *The Formation of the Chinese Communist Party*. Translated by Joshua A. Fogel. New York: Columbia University Press, 2013.

———. "Li Dazhao zaoqisixiangzhong de ribenyinsu—yi Maoyuanhuashan weili" [The Japanese elements in Li Dazhao's early thoughts—examples from the writings of Kayahara Kazan]. *Shehuikexueyanjiu* [Social science studies], no. 3 (2007): 141–49.

———. "Wusishiqi Li Dazhao de sixiang yu Maoyuanhuashan, Chen Puxian" [Li Dazhao's thoughts during the May Fourth era and Kayahara Kazan and Chen Puxian]. Translated by Wang Jie and Tian Ziyu. *Wenshizhe* [Literature, history, and philosophy], no. 5 (1993): 12–19.

Jenco, Leigh. "Culture as History: Envisioning Change across and beyond 'Eastern' and 'Western' Civilization in the May Fourth Era." *Twentieth-Century China* 38, no. 1 (January 2013): 34–52.

Jia Tianyun and Liu Aiying. "Li Dazhao fu ribenliuxue shijiankao" [An examination of the time when Li Dazhao arrived in Japan for his study abroad]. *Jindaishiyanjiu* [Modern Chinese history studies], no. 2 (1995): 280–82.

Jiang Hongyan and Hu Minghui. "Gemingxianqu Li Dazhao yanzhongde diyicishijiedazhan" [World War I in the eyes of Li Dazhao the revolutionary pioneer]. *Qiqiharshifangaodengzhuankexuexiaoxuebao* [Journal of Qiqihar Junior Teachers College] 95, no. 1 (2007): 5–7.

Jiang Junwei. "Sun Zhongshan he Li Dazhao guogonghezuo sixiangyitong bijiao" [Comparison of similarities and differences between Sun Yat-sen's ideas and Li Dazhao's thoughts on the united front between the Nationalist Party and the Communist Party]. *Zhonggongfujianshengweidangxiaoxuebao* [Journal of Fujian CCP Provincial Party School], no. 12 (2001): 53–56.

Jiang Lijing. "Teachers Are Key Factors of Universities: Peking Female Higher Normal College 1917–1922." *History Research* 7, no. 2 (March/April 2017): 78–89.

Jiang Yongjing. *Baoluoting yu wuhanzhengquan* [Michael Borodin and the Wuhan regime]. Taipei: Zhuanjiwenxuechubanshe, 1972.

Jin Ge. "Neimenggu minzujiefangyundong de xianqu Li Dazhao" [Li Dazhao: The pioneer of the national liberation movement in Inner Mongolia]. *Neimengguxuanchuan* [Inner Mongolia propaganda], no. 3 (2003): 42–43.

Jin Rongdong. *Li Dazhao zhexue yanjiu* [A study of Li Dazhao's philosophy]. Shanghai: Huadongshidachubanshe, 2000.

Jingshijingchating [Metropolitan Police Headquarters]. *Soviet Plot in China*. English ed. Beijing: Metropolitan Police Headquarters, 1928.

Kuo, Ya-Pei. "The Making of the New Culture Movement: A Discursive History," *Twentieth-Century China* 42, no. 1 (January 2017): 52–71.

Lanza, Fabio. "The Beijing University Students in the May Fourth Era: A Collective Biography." In *The Human Tradition in Modern China*, edited by Kenneth J. Hammond and Kristin Stapleton, 117–34. New York: Rowman & Littlefield, 2008.

Lei Xiaocen. *Sanshinian dongluan zhongguo* [China in the turbulent thirty years]. Hong Kong: Yazhouchubanshe, 1955.

Leng Yujian. "Li Dazhao yu diyici guogonghezuo" [Li Dazhao and the first United Front between the CCP and the KMT]. *Zhongguotongyizhanxian* [China's United Front], no. 11 (2004): 41–44.

Li Chao. "Sun Zhongshan yu zhonggong sanda" [Sun Yat-sen and the Third CCP National Congress]. *Guangzhoushehuizhuyixueyuan* [Journal of Guangzhou Institute of Socialism] 55, no. 4 (2016): 48–53.

Li Dazhao. *Li Dazhao quanji* [The complete works of Li Dazhao]. Beijing: Renminchubanshe, 2013. 5 vols.

Li Fengbin and Wang Wei. "Qingmo zhongguo xuesheng liuri yuanyinchutan" [A preliminary study of the reasons why the Chinese students went to Japan during the late Qing period]. *Yinshanxuekan* [Yinshan academic journal], no. 2 (1996): 73–78.

Li Haichun. "Lun Li Dazhao jieshou makesizhuyi de guocheng" [The progression of Li Dazhao's acceptance of Marxism]. *Henanshifandaxuexuebao* [Journal of Henan Normal University], 31, no. 1 (2004): 117–20.
Li Jiannong. *Zhongguo jinbainian zhengzhi shi* [The history of Chinese politics in the past hundred years]. Taipei: Taiwanshangwushuguan, 1975.
Li Jihua. "Dui xinban *Li Dazhao quanji* bufenzhushi de shangque" [A suggestion to some notes in *The Complete Works of Li Dazhao*]. *Hebeixuekan* [Hebei academic journal] 27, no. 2 (March 2007): 115–18.
———. "Yetan dui Li Dazhao jipianwenzhang de biankao—jiujiaoyu Zhu Chengjia xiansheng" [My remarks on the examination of a few articles of Li Dazhao—a scholarly dialogue with Mr. Zhu Chengjia]. *Dangshibolan* [Party history expo], no. 7 (2006): 48–59.
Li Jihua, Chang Jinjun, and Li Quanxing, editors. *Li Dazhao beibu xisheng anzang ziliaoxuanbian* [Selected materials concerning Li Dazhao's arrest, death, and burial]. Beijing: Xianzhuangshuju, 2011.
Li Lina. "Li Dazhao yu wusiyundong" [Li Dazhao and the May Fourth Movement]. *Zhongguodang'an* [Chinese archives], no. 5 (2009): 78–79.
Li Min. "Kaozheng Li Dazhao 1924 nian de sulianzhixing" [An examination of Li Dazhao's visit to the Soviet Union in 1924]. *Dangshibocai* [Extensive collection of the party history], no. 7 (2011): 54–55.
Li Ming. *Zhonggong liulieshi xiaozhuan* [Short biographies of the six communist martyrs]. Hong Kong: Xinzhongguoshuju, 1949.
Li Shanyu and Yang Shusheng. "Li Dazhao yu guominjun" [Li Dazhao and the National Army]. *Qiluxuekan*, no. 2 (1985): 72–78.
Li Shuxin. "Xinfaxiande Li Dazhao zhenji ezai huodong shiliao" [Newly discovered historical documents concerning Li Dazhao's activities for the Russian famine relief]. *Dangshiyanjiuyujiaoxue* [Party history research and teaching] 237, no. 1 (2014): 107–10.
Li Xiaosan. *Xinminzhuzhuyigeming jianshi* [A concise history of China's new democratic revolution]. Beijing: Zhonggongdangshichubanshe, 2010.
Li Xinghua. *Huiyi wode fuqin Li Dazhao* [My memory of my father Li Dazhao]. Shanghai: Shanghaiwenyichubanshe, 1981.
Li Yanbo. *Li Dazhao Beijing shinian: Jiaoxuepian* [Li Dazhao's ten years in Beijing: Teaching]. Beijing: Central Compilation and Translation Press, 2016.
Li Yanlin. "Li Dazhao 'genbenjiejue' de sixiang yu makesizhuyi zhongguohua de lishiqidian" [Li Dazhao's thought on a "fundamental solution" and the historical starting point of the sinicization of Marxism]. *Jilinshengshehuizhuyixueyuanxuebao* [Journal of Jilin Provincial College of Socialism], no. 2 (2009): 32–36.
Li Yibin. "Guanyu Li Dazhao tongzhi de shengnianyueri wenti" [The issue concerning the time of Comrade Li Dazhao's birth]. *Lishiyanjiu* [Historical research], no. 9 (1978): 93.

Li Yunhan. *Congronggongdaoqingdang* [From the acceptance of the Communists to the party purge]. Taipei: Taiwanshangwu, 1973.

Liang Shuming. *Yiwang tan jiulu* [Remarks on my old memories]. Beijing: Jinchengchubanshe, 2006.

Liang Zhu. "Guanshuizizhuyundong shimo" [A history of the Customs Autonomy Movement]. *Beijingdangshi* [The party history of Beijing], no. 5 (1988): 2–7.

———. "Makesizhuyi chuanbozhongde tansuo yu sikao—yi Li Dazhao de shehuizhuyiguan weijidian" [Dissemination of Marxism: Li Dazhao's view of socialism]. *Tangshanxueyuanxuebao* [Journal of Tangshan University] 30, no. 2 (March 2017): 1–8.

Lianhebao. *Wo canjialiao wusiyundong* [I participated in the May Fourth Movement]. Taipei: Lianhebaoshe, 1980.

Liao, Jing. "The New Culture Movement and the Breakthrough in Chinese Academic Library Reform." *Library History* 24, no. 1 (March 2008): 37–47.

Lidazhaozhuanbianxiezu. *Li Dazhao zhuan* [Biography of Li Dazhao]. Beijing: Renminchubanshe, 1979.

Lin Xianzhi. "Wusishiqi Mao Zedong zoushang makesizhuyizhilu de tanyuan" [An exploration into Mao Zedong's march toward the Marxist road during the May Fourth era]. *Fengjiarenwenshehuixuebao* [Feng Chia Journal of humanities and social science], no. 3 (November 2001): 143–60.

Lin, Xiaoqing Diana. *Peking University: Chinese Scholarship and Intellectuals, 1898–1937*. Albany: State University of New York Press, 2005.

Liu Changhui. "Diyici guogonghezuoshiqide Li Dazhao" [Li Dazhao during the first united front between the Nationalist Party and the Chinese Communist Party]. *Xuzhoushifanxueyuanxuebao* [Journal of Xuzhou Normal University], no. 4 (1985): 29–32.

Liu Debin. "Qiyixunzhang huodezhe—Li Hongta: Gongchandangren gemingchuantong youxiujiafeng de chuanchengren" [The receiver of the July 1 Medal—Li Hongta: The inheritor of the revolutionary tradition and the excellent family style]. Sina Corporation, Domestic News, June 29, 2021. https://news.sina.com.cn/c/2021-06-29/doc-ikqciyzk2479502.shtml.

Liu Jianqing, Wang Jiadian, and Xu Liangbo. *Zhongguo guomindang shi* [History of the Nationalist Party]. Nanjing: Jiangsugujichubanshe, 1992.

Liu Jianyi. "The Origin of the Chinese Communist Party and the Role Played by Soviet Russia and the Comintern." PhD diss., University of York, March 2000.

Liu Juanxun. *Gemingshijia Hu Hua* [The revolutionary historian Hu Hua]. Beijing: Dangdaizhongguochubanshe, 2011.

Liu Minshan, editor. *Li Dazhao yu Tianjin* [Li Dazhao in Tianjin]. Tianjin: Tianjinshehuikexueyuanchubanshe, 1989.

———. "Li Dazhao yu Xingdeqiushui" [Li Dazhao and Kotoku Shusui]. *Jindaishiyanjiu* [Modern Chinese history studies], no. 4 (1995): 253–61.

Liu Yang. "Li Dazhao dejiahenjianlou, shufangbuxiao" [Li Dazhao's home is simple, but his study is not small]. *Bolanqunshu* [Chinese book review monthly], no. 6 (2018): 95–98.

Liu Yougu. "Lun Li Dazhao 'disan' wenming zhishuo" [Li Dazhao's theory of the third civilization]. *Zhongzhouxuekan* [Academic journal of Zhongzhou] 123, no. 3 (May 2001): 143–45.

Liu Yuwei. "Liuxueribenshidai de Li Dazhao" [Li Dazhao as a foreign student in Japan]. *Zhongguominhangxueyuanxuebao* [Journal of the Civil Aviation Institute of China] 11, no. 1 (March 1993): 56–70.

Lu Fangshang and Zhang Zhelang, editors. *Wusiyundong bashizhounian xueshuyantaohui lunwenji* [A collection of papers from the seminar to commemorate the eightieth anniversary of the May Fourth Movement]. Taipei: Hongbaiyinshuashiye, 1999.

Lu Haijiang and Lin Xiumin. "Li Dazhao weihe weichuxi zhonggong yida?" [Why didn't Li attend the first CCP national congress?]. *Dangshizongheng* [On the party history], no. 1 (1991): 42–43.

Lu Jian. *Li Dazhao he Qu Qiubai* [Li Dazhao and Qu Qiubai]. Beijing: Shangwuyinshuguan, 1951.

Lu, Xiufen. "The Confucian Ideal of Great Harmony (*Datong*), the Daoist Account of Change, and the Theory of Socialism in the Work of Li Dazhao." *Asian Philosophy* 21, no. 2 (May 2011): 171–92.

Luo Zhanglong. *Chunyuanzaiji* [The remarks from the Toona Garden]. Beijing: Sanlianchubanshe, 1984.

Ma Mao. "Liu He jiazuwangshi" [The old stories of Liu He's extended family]. Universities Service Centre for China Studies Collection (website). Accessed August 5, 2021. http://mjlsh.usc.cuhk.edu.hk/Book.aspx?cid=4&tid=5059.

Manela, Erez. "Asia in the Global 1919: Reimagining Territory, Identity, and Solidarity." *Journal of Asian Studies* 78, no. 2 (May 2019): 409–16.

Mao Zedong. "Lun renminminzhu zhuanzheng: Jinian zhongguogongchandang ershibazhounian" [On people's democratic dictatorship: In commemoration of the twenty-eighth anniversary of the establishment of the Chinese Communist Party]. June 30, 1949. In *Mao Zedong xuanji* [Collected works of Mao Zedong], 1357–71. Beijing: Renminchubanshe, 1968.

———. "Speech on the Guidelines for the Seventh National Congress of the Chinese Communist Party." April 21, 1945. Accessed October 5, 2018. http://cpc.people.com.cn/GB/64184/64186/66647/4491001.html.

Meisner, Maurice. *Li Ta-chao and the Origins of Chinese Marxism*. Cambridge, MA: Harvard University Press, 1967.

Meng Zhaogeng. "Zhonggong zaoqi lingdaoren Li Dazhao yingyong jiuyi qianhou" [The early communist leader Li Dazhao sacrificed his life bravely]. *Wenshichunqiu* [Spring and autumn of literature and history], no. 11 (2019): 16–20.

Metallo, Michael V. "American Missionaries, Sun Yat-sen, and the Chinese Revolution." *Pacific Historical Review* 47, no. 2 (May 1978): 261–82.
Miyazaki, Ichisada. *China's Examination Hell: The Civil Service Examinations of Imperial China.* New York: Weatherhill, 1976.
Mori Masao. "Li Dazhao zai zaodaotian daxue" [Li Dazhao studied at Waseda University]. *Qiluxuekan* [Qilu journal], no. 1 (1987): 74–75.
Mu Yunjun. "Cong Li Dazhao 'disanwenming'shuo kan makesizhuyi yu ruxue guanxi de chongzhuan" [Li Dazhao's third civilization and the relationship between Marxism and Confucianism]. *Shandongshehuikexue* [Shandong social sciences] 243, no. 11 (2015): 21–25.
Nelson, Diane M., and Robert B. Nelson. "Li Ta-chao." In *World Encyclopedia of Library and Information Services*, edited by Robert Wedgeworth, 3rd ed., 521. Chicago: American Library Association, 1993.
———. "'The Red Chamber': Li Ta-chao and Sources of Radicalism in Modern Chinese Librarianship." *Journal of Library History* 14, no. 2 (Spring 1979): 121–28.
New York Times. "Tried by a Secret Court." April 29, 1927, 1.
Nie Yuansu and Shi Xiaosheng. "Li Dazhao yu henan gongnong gemingyundong" [Li Dazhao and the workers' and peasants' movements in Henan]. *Lishijiaoxue* [History teaching], no. 7 (1984): 13–18.
Niu Yanan and Li Guihua. "Zhongguo diyige nongcun dangzhibu de jianli" [The establishment of the first rural branch of the Chinese Communist Party]. *Dang'antiandi* [Archives world], no. 5 (2020): 10–12.
Ouyang Zesheng. *Wusiyundong de lishiquanshi* [Historical interpretation of the May Fourth Movement]. Beijing: Beijing University Press, 2012.
Pantsov, Alexander V. *Victorious in Defeat: The Life and Times of Chiang Kai-shek, China, 1887–1975.* New Haven, CT: Yale University Press, 2023.
Peng Hongwei and Li Yuzhen. "Guanyu Li Dazhao zai sulian jianghua he wenzhang de shuoming" [An explanation concerning Li Dazhao's speeches and articles during his visit to the USSR]. *Jindaishiyanjiu* [Modern Chinese history studies], no. 6 (1985): 1–10.
Pozzana, Claudia. "Spring, Temporality, and History in Li Dazhao." *Position* 3, no. 2 (Fall 1995): 283–305.
Qin Aimin and Guo Zhenxiang. "Li Dazhao yu zhongguo nongmin wenti" [Li Dazhao and China's peasant problems]. *Wenshijinghua* [Essence of literature and history], no. 2 (1999): 26–28.
Schwarcz, Vera. *The Chinese Enlightenment: Intellectuals and the Legacy of the May Fourth Movement of 1919.* Berkeley: University of California Press, 1986.
Scott, David. *China and the International System, 1840–1949: Power, Presence, and Perceptions in a Century of Humiliation.* Albany: State University of New York Press, 2008.
Shan, Patrick Fuliang. "The Anti-Christian Movement Revisited: A Centennial Reflection." *American Review of China Studies* 23, no. 2 (Fall 2022): 25–51.

———. "From Admirer to Critic: Li Dazhao's Changing Attitudes toward the United States." In *Sino-American Relations: A New Cold War*, edited by Xiaobing Li and Qiang Fang, 31–54. Amsterdam: University of Amsterdam Press, 2022.

———. "Li Dazhao and the Chinese Embracement of Communism." In *Chinese Ideology*, edited by Shiping Hua, 94–110. London: Routledge, 2022.

———. "Triumph after Catastrophe: Church, State and Society in Post-Boxer China, 1900–1937." *Peace and Conflict Studies* 16, no. 2 (Fall 2009): 33–50.

———. *Yuan Shikai: A Reappraisal*. Vancouver: University of British Columbia Press, 2018.

Shanghaishehuikexueyuan. *Wusayundongshiliao* [Historical documents concerning the May Thirtieth Movement]. Vol. 1. Shanghai: Shanghairenminchubanshe, 1981.

Shao Guoying. "Li Dazhao wenzhang 'shenhoushi'" [The follow-up stories concerning Li Dazhao's writings]. *Huaihuaxueyuanxuebao* [Journal of Huaihua University] 33, no. 12 (December 2014): 57–60.

Shen Yaqiong. "Shilun wusishiqi zhongguoxianjinrenshi jieshou makesizhuyi de lishi chengyin" [The historical factors leading China's progressive intellectuals to accept Marxism during the May Fourth era]. *Huaihaiwenhui* [Huaihai review], no. 6 (2010): 32–35.

Shi Jie and Zhang Shouxian. "Li Dazhao he Shaanxi gemingyundong" [Li Dazhao and the revolutionary movement in Shaanxi Province]. *Xibeidaxuexuebao* [Journal of Northwest University], no. 3 (1984): 17–25.

Si Gong. "Zhang Zuolin weihe shahai Li Dazhao" [Why did Zhang Zuolin kill Li Dazhao]. *Quanguoxinshumu* [National new books information], no. 21 (2009): 44–45.

Snow, Edgar. *Red Star over China: The Rise of the Red Army*. New York: Modern Library, 1944.

Song Fangchun and Li Quanxing. *Li Dazhao yanjiu cidian* [The dictionary of Li Dazhao studies]. Beijing: Hongqichubanshe, 1994.

Song Lin. "Li Dazhao he tade furen Zhao Renlan" [Li Dazhao and his wife Zhao Renlan]. *Dangshizonglan* [Overview of party history], no. 3 (1999): 6–10.

Song Qingling. "Sun Zhongshan he tatonggongchandang de hezuo" [Sun Yat-sen and his cooperation with the Chinese Communist Party]. *Renminribao* [People's daily], November 12, 1962.

Song Zhijian. "Li Dazhao de fankongshijiao" [Li Dazhao's anti-Confucian perspectives]. *Yanhuangzongheng* [History of China], no. 10 (2016): 40–43.

Spence, Jonathan D. *The Search for Modern China*. 3rd ed. New York: W. W. Norton, 2013.

Su Ming. "Zhiyi yu xiaojie: Cong 'ouyou manlu' kan Xu Zhimo su'e guan zhi zhuanbian" [Doubt and certainty: An analysis of Xu Zhimo's changing attitude toward Soviet Russia in his *Random Remarks on the Travel to Europe*]. *Nanjingdaxuexuebao* [Journal of Nanjing University], no. 5 (2008): 106–13.

Sun Yat-sen. "Jianshe fakanci" [Introduction to the inaugural issue of *Jianshe*]. *Jianshe* [Reconstruction] 1, no. 1 (1919): 1.
Tai Wan-chin. "Chen Duxiu's Conversion from a Liberal Democrat to a Marxist-Leninist: Motivation and Impact." *Tamkang Journal of International Affairs* 11, no. 1 (2007): 115–48.
Taihangyingxiong. "Liu He de fuqin Liu Zhiyan" [Liu He's father Liu Zhiyan]. January 19, 2020. https://web.archive.org/web/20200212224456/http://taihangsummit.com/28dc001ec0/.
Tang Runlin. "Li Dazhao yu dongbeidiqu dangzuzhi de chuangjian yu fazhan" [Li Dazhao and the creation and development of the party organizations in Northeast China]. *Lantaishijie* [The Lantai world], no. 7 (2020): 10–12.
Tang Xiaofeng and Wang Shuai, editors. *Minguoshiqi feijidujiaoyundong zhongyaowenxian huibian* [A collection of important documents on the Anti-Christian Movement during the republican era]. Beijing: Shehuikexuechubanshe, 2015.
Tian Chao and Wang Haoyao. "Li Dazhao yu zhonggongbeifang zaoqi dangzuzhi" [Li Dazhao and the early communist organizations in North China]. *Tangshanxueyuanxuebao* [Journal of Tangshan University] 31, no. 4 (July 2018): 22–27.
Tong Shijun. "Li Dazhao yu Mule" [Li Dazhao and John S. Miller]. *Ershiyishiji* [Twenty-first century] 69, no. 2 (2002): 41–45.
U, Eddy. "Reification of the Chinese Intellectuals: On the Origins of the CCP Concept of *Zhishifenzi*." *Modern China* 35, no. 6 (November 2009): 604–31.
Wang Chaomei, editor in chief. *Li Dazhao yanjiu lunwenji* [A collection of articles on the study of Li Dazhao]. Beijing: Zhonggongdangshichubanshe, 1991.
Wang Chaozhu. *Li Dazhao*. Beijing: Zhongguoqingnianchubanshe, 1989.
Wang Hai. "Zhang Zuolin busha Li Dazhao dengren dongyin qianxi" [An analysis of the motives of Zhang Zuolin to arrest and kill Li Dazhao and others]. *Zhongguojinianguanyanjiu* [Studies of China's memorial museums], no. 2 (2017): 165–71.
Wang Jie. *Li Dazhao Beijing shinian: Jiaowangpian* [Li Dazhao's ten years in Beijing: Social connections]. Beijing: Central Compilation and Translation Press, 2010.
———. *Li Dazhao Beijing shinian: Shijianpian* [Li Dazhao's ten years in Beijing: Events]. Beijing: Central Compilation and Translation Press, 2012.
Wang Jin. "Li Dazhao sixiangzhong de chuantongyinsu jiqi dangdaiyiyi" [On the traditional elements in Li Dazhao's thought and their contemporary implications]. *Tangshanxueyuanxuebao* [Journal of Tangshan University] 30, no. 5 (September 2017): 41–45.
Wang Jing. "Minguo dilixueren Bai Meichu dui nanhaijiangyu de lunshu" [Bai Meichu, a geographer in the Republic of China, discussed the territory of

the South China Sea]. *Nanhaixuekan* [Journal of South China Sea studies] 9, no. 2 (2023): 52–60.
Wang Li and Ma Junnian. "Gongchanguoji yu diyici guogonghezuo de xingcheng" [The Comintern and the shaping of the first united front between the Nationalist Party and the Communist Party]. *Fujiandangshiyuekan* [Fujian party history monthly], no. 4 (2011): 30–32.
Wang Shiru. "Hu Shi shi Li Dazhao de haopengyou" [Hu Shi was Li Dazhao's good friend]. *Wenshijinghua* [Essence of literature and history] 270, no. 11 (2012): 36–39.
———. "Li Dazhao tongzhi shoupinjiaoshou jisuokaikecheng kaoshi" [An examination of Comrade Li Dazhao's appointment as a professor and the courses he taught]. *Beijingdaxuexuebao* [Journal of Beijing University] 18, no. 4 (1981): 93–94.
———. "Li Dazhao tongzhi zai Beijingdaxue de renzhishijian kaobian" [An examination of the date of Comrade Li Dazhao's appointment at Beijing University]. *Beijingdaxuexuebao* [Journal of Beijing University], no. 5 (1980): 82–84.
Wang Shun. "Li Dazhao weihe wei canjia dangde yida?" [Why did Li Dazhao not attend the first congress of the CCP?]. *Lishijiaoxue* [History teaching], no. 12 (1989): 26.
Wang Shunsheng. *Zhongguogemingshi* [History of the Chinese Revolution]. Beijing: Zhongguorenmindaxuechubanshe, 1991.
Wang Yanping. "Jidong kangzhanzhongde Li Dazhao houdai" [Li Dazhao's descendants during the anti-Japanese war in East Hebei]. *Dang'antiandi* [Archives world], no. 11 (2015): 19–21.
———. "Li Dazhao sanfu Henan Kaifeng shishishuzheng" [An investigation into historical facts concerning Li Dazhao's three visits to Kaifeng, Henan Province]. *Lantaishijie* [The Lantai world], July 2011: 16–17.
———. "Li Dazhao yu eguozaihuangzhenjihui" [Li Dazhao and the Russian Famine Relief Society]. *Dang'antiandi* [Archives world], no. 4 (2017): 20–23.
———. *Li Dazhao zuji chutan* [Survey of Li Dazhao's ancestral locale]. *Dang'antiandi* [Archives world], no. 11 (2012): 30–33.
Wang Yanping and Li Quanxing. *Li Dazhao shishitanwei* [An exploration of historical facts concerning Li Dazhao]. Shijiazhuang: Hebeirenminchubanshe, 2016.
Wang Yuanyi. "Huozainali—xinjie Hu Shi yu Li Dazhao 'wentiyuzhuyi' de lunbian jiqi lishiyiyi" [Where are the doubts? A new interpretation of the significance of the issue-versus-ism debate between Hu Shi and Li Dazhao]. *Taidalishixuebao* [Historical inquiry], no. 50 (December 2012): 155–250.
———. "Yuzhou geming lun" [An examination of the global revolution]. In Lu Fangshang and Zhang Zhelang, 573–97.

Weigelin-Schwiedrzik, Susanne. "What Is Wrong with Li Dazhao?" In *New Perspectives on the Chinese Communist Revolution*, edited by Tony Saich and Hans van de Ven, 56–74. Armonk, NY: M. E. Sharpe, 1995.

Wong Young-tsu (Wang Rongzu). "Congwenhua yu zhengzhi jiaodujiedu wusiqianhou de Li Dazhao" [An interpretation of Li Dazhao before and after the May Fourth Movement: The cultural and political perspective]. *Wenshizhe* [Literature, history, and philosophy] 372, no. 3 (2019): 14–23.

Wu Hanquan. "Jinshinian Li Dazhao yanjiu de jinzhan ji xiangguan wenti de taolun" [The discourse over the new research on Li Dazhao and other related issues in the past ten years]. *Jindaishiyanjiu* [Modern history studies], no. 4 (2006): 146–57.

———. "Shilun zaoqi Li Dazhao dui chuantongwenhua de shenshi" [Li Dazhao's analysis of the traditional culture in his early thought]. *Xuzhoushifandaxuexuebao* [Journal of Xuzhou Normal University] 24, no. 4 (December 1998): 90–92.

———. "Tuo'ersitai dui Li Dazhao zaoqisixiang de yingxiang" [Leo Tolstoy's impact on Li Dazhao's early thought]. *Xueshujiaoliu* [Academic exchanges], no. 6 (1993): 125–30.

———. "Xifangjindaiwenhua yu Li Dazhao de zaoqisixiang" [Modern Western culture and Li Dazhao's early thought]. *Ningxiadaxuexuebao* [Journal of Ningxia University] 20, no. 2 (1998): 36–39.

Wu Jialin. "Li Dazhao yu diyici guogonghezuode jianli" [Li Dazhao and the establishment of the first united front between the Nationalist Party and the Communist Party]. *Dangxiaojiaoxue* [Teaching at the party schools], no. 5 (1988): 32–37.

Wu, Tien-wei. "A Review of the Wuhan Debacle: The Kuomintang-Communist Split of 1927." *Journal of Asian Studies* 29, no. 1 (November 1969): 125–43.

Xiao Chaoran. "Zhongguogongchandang de chuangli yu beijingdaxue" [The founding of the CCP and Beijing University]. *People's Daily*. Accessed June 14, 2020. http://cpc.people.com.cn/BIG5/218984/218997/219021/14817918.html.

Xiao Chaoran, Sha Jiansun, and Liang Zhu. "Li Dazhao zai zhongguogongchanzhuyiyundong zhongde lishidiwei" [The historical position of Li Dazhao in the Chinese communist movement]. *Beijingdaxuexuebao* [Journal of Beijing University], no. 6 (1979): 2–15.

Xiao Shen. "Zhonggongdangnei duiyu shouci guogonghezuode zhenglunjiqijieju" [The debate and outcome within the Communist Party over the united front between the Nationalist Party and the Communist Party]. *Dangshiyanjiuyujiaoxue* [Communist Party of China history research and teaching] 195, no. 2 (2007): 55–61.

Xiao Yusheng. *Li Dazhao de junshihuodong* [Li Dazhao's military activities]. Beijing: Junshikexuechubanshe, 1988.

Xie Fulin. "Shixi Li Dazhao shumindeshengli he Bolshevism de shengli de sixiangzhuzhi" [An analysis of the main theme of Li Dazhao's *Victory of the*

Common People and Victory of Bolshevism]. *Qinghuadaxuexuebao* [Journal of Qinghua University] 14, no. 3 (1999): 117–24.
Xin Ding, editor. *Li Dazhao zai wusishiqi de sixianghuodong* [Li Dazhao's thoughts and activities during the May Fourth era]. Hong Kong: Longtengchubanshe, 1979.
Xu Deheng et al. *Huiyi Li Dazhao* [In memory of Li Dazhao]. Beijing: Renminchubanshe, 1980.
Xu Yufeng. "Li Dazhao yu Lu Xun" [Li Dazhao and Lu Xun]. *Zhumadianshizhuanxuebao* [Journal of Zhumadian Normal College], no. 2 (1988): 1–4.
Xue Shixiao. "Li Dazhao yu kailuanmeikuang gongrenyundong" [Li Dazhao and the workers' movement in the Kailuan mining area]. *Henanligongdaxuexuebao* [Journal of Henan Polytechnic University] 8, no. 4 (October 2007): 374–79.
Yamamoto, Tatsuro, and Sumiko Yamamoto. "The Anti-Christian Movement in China, 1922–1927." *Far Eastern Quarterly* 12, no. 2 (February 1953): 133–47.
Yan Zhixin. *Li Dazhao he Feng Yuxiang* [Li Dazhao and Feng Yuxiang]. Beijing: Jiefangjunchubanshe, 1987.
Yang, Fang-yen. "Zaizao xinwenming: Li Dazhao zaoqi sixiangzhongde pubianyuteshu" [Toward a new civilization: The universal and the particular in the early thought of Li Dazhao]. *Zhengzhikexueluncong*, no. 63 (March 2015): 1–54.
Yang Hongzhang. "Li Dazhao yu Duan Qirui shinianjian de zhengzhi guanxi shulue" [An analysis of the decade-long political relationship between Li Dazhao and Duan Qirui]. *Binzhoujiaoyuxueyuanxuebao* [Journal of Binzhou Education College] 7, no. 2 (June 2001): 25–28.
Yang Hu and Wang Xianming. "Xueshu zhushi qiangushi, xunguizunxianshiyoucheng—dui Li Dazhao lunzhu zhong sige waiguo renming zhushi ji xiangguanwenti de zai tantao" [Reexamination of the annotations to four foreign names in Li Dazhao's works and some questions related to the annotations]. *Qinghuadaxuexuebao* [Journal of Qinghua University] 25, no. 3 (2010): 51–63.
Yang Peng. "Analysis of Japanese Influence on the Three Major Historiographical Trends in Early Modern China." *Chinese Studies in History* 49, no. 1 (2016): 28–38.
Yang Tianhong. "Jiaru guomindang zhihou gongchandangren de shenfen rentong wenti" [The identity of communists after joining the Nationalist Party]. *Jindaishiyanjiu* [Modern Chinese history studies], no. 6 (2010): 16–34.
Yin Xiangxia. "Li Dazhao dui zhongguo jindaishehui de yanjiu" [Li Dazhao's study of modern Chinese society]. *Shixueshiyanjiu* [The study of historiography], no. 2 (1995): 17–22.
Young, George. "The Murders in China." *Lansbury's Labour Weekly* 3, no. 114 (May 14, 1927): 5.
Yuan Ming. "Chinese Intellectuals and the United States: The Dilemma of Individualism vs. Patriotism." *Asian Survey* 29, no. 7 (July 1989): 645–54.
Zang Kejia. *Li Dazhao*. Beijing: Zuojiachubanshe, 1959.

Zarrow, Peter. *China in War and Revolution, 1895–1949*. London: Routledge, 2005.
Zhang Cixi. *Li Dazhao xiansheng zhuan* [Biography of Mr. Li Dazhao]. Beijing: Xuanwenshudian, 1951.
Zhang Cui. "Wenti yu zhuyi zhizheng yu makesizhuyi zhongguohua" [The issue-versus-ism debate and the sinicization of Marxism]. *Hunanminzuzhiyexueyuanxuebao* [Journal of Hunan Vocational College for Nationalities] 5, no. 3 (2009): 26–28.
Zhang, Dahua. "On Modern Chinese Nationalism and Its Conceptualization." *Journal of Modern Chinese History* 6, no. 2 (December 2012): 217–34.
Zhang Guang'en. "Li Dazhao tongzhi he dongbeidiqu dangde zaoqihuodong" [Comrade Li Dazhao and the early communist activities in Northeast China]. *Shehuikexuejikan* [Social science journal] 68, no. 3 (1990): 108–11.
Zhang Guotao. *Wodehuiyi* [My recollections]. Hong Kong: Mingbaoyuekan, 1971.
Zhang Jian and Pei Cuimin. "Li Dazhao tongzhi yuhaihou de guojifanying" [The international response to Comrade Li Dazhao's death]. *Fudanxuebao* [Journal of Fudan University], no. 6 (1979): 111.
Zhang Jiang. "Li Dazhao zai Kaifeng" [Li Dazhao in Kaifeng]. *Shixueyuekan* [History monthly], no. 5 (1982): 57–60.
Zhang Jianguo. *Weidade bozhongzhe: Li Dazhao de gushi* [The great seed-sower: The story of Li Dazhao]. Wuhan: Hubeirenminchubanshe, 1980.
Zhang Jingru. "Li Dazhao linxingqian meiyou fabiao yanshuo" [Li Dazhao did not deliver a speech before his execution]. *Dangshiyanjiuyujiaoxue* [Party history studies and teaching], no. 2 (2011): 110–11.
Zhang Jingru and Ma Mozhen. *Li Dazhao*. Shanghai: Shanghairenminchubanshe, 1981.
Zhang Jingru, Ma Mozhen, Liao Ying, and Qian Ziqiang. *Li Dazhao shengping shiliao biannian* [Chronicle of historical materials concerning Li Dazhao's life]. Shanghai: Shanghairenminchubanshe, 1984.
Zhang Jingru and Wu Hanquan. "Zhongguo jiang 'dierci dagongxianyu shijiezhijinbu': Li Dazhao yu Zhongguomeng" [China will make 'another contribution to the world's progress': Li Dazhao and the Chinese Dream]. *Tangshanxueyuanxuebao* [Journal of Tangshan University] 29, no. 4 (July 2016): 1–9.
Zhang Li. "*Xinqingnian* zuozhequn yu zhongri jindai cihuijiaoliu: Yi Li Dazhao weili" [The authors of *New Youth* and the modern linguistic exchanges between Chinese and Japanese: The case of Li Dazhao]. *Sanxiadaxuexuebao* [Journal of China Three Gorges University] 41, no. 5 (September 2019): 113–16.
Zhang Qingxiang. "Li Dazhao wusishiqi xinwenhuajiangou de xiandaifang'an" [Li Dazhao's modern plan for reconstructing a new culture during the May Fourth era]. *Gansushehuikexue* [Social science of Gansu], no. 2 (2004): 33–36.

Zhang Rulun. "Historiography and Chinese Modernity—A Study of the Historiographical Ideas of Li Dazhao." *Chinese Studies in History* 49, no. 2 (2016): 80–89.

Zhang Shenfu. "Hongloushiqi de Li Dazhao" [Li Dazhao during the Red Mansion era]. *Gonghuixinxi* [Information concerning the worker's union], no. 22 (2017): 27.

Zhang Tongle. "Lun Li Dazhao dui zhongguochuantongwenhua de pipan yu jicheng" [Li Dazhao's criticism and inheritance of Chinese traditional culture]. *Hebeishidaxuebao* [Journal of Hebei Normal University] 23, no. 4 (October 2000): 102–6.

———. "Shilun Li Dazhao aiguozhuyisixiang de Yan-Zhaowenhua yuanyuan" [Li Dazhao's patriotic thought and its origin in the Yan-Zhao culture]. *Hebeiguangbodianshidaxuexuebao* [Journal of Hebei Radio and Television University] 16, no. 1 (Febuary 25, 2011): 7–11.

Zhang Weimin. "Qingmo zhongguo xuesheng de liurilangchao" [The wave of Chinese students in Japan during the late Qing period]. *Zhongguoqingnianyanjiu* [China youth study], no. 1 (1998): 44–47.

Zhang Wensheng. "Li Dazhao shixuesixiangxingcheng de zhiyetiaojian" [Analysis of the occupational background and the formation of Li Dazhao's thought on history]. *Nankaixuebao* [Journal of Nankai University], no. 2 (2015): 126–33.

———. *Li Dazhao shixuesixiang yanjiu* [A study of Li Dazhao's thought on history]. Beijing: Zhongguoshehuikexuechubanshe, 2006.

Zhang Yanguo. "Li Dazhao, Qu Qiubai dui eguodaolu de renzhi" [Li Dazhao and Qu Qiubai's analysis of the Russian way]. *Zhongguoshehuikexue* [Social sciences of China], no. 10 (2016): 175–200, 206.

Zhang, Yao. "The Development of Library and Information Science in China (1840–2009)." *IFLA Journal* 40, no. 4 (2014): 296–306.

Zhao Guofeng. "Lun Li Dazhao dui chuantongsixiangwenhua de taidu" [Li Dazhao's attitude toward traditional ideology and culture]. *Jiangxishehuikexue* [Jiangxi social sciences], no. 7 (2005): 117–20.

Zhao Xiude. "Li Dazhao yu zhonggong beijingdangzuzhi de chuangli he fazhan" [Li Dazhao and the establishment and development of the Communist Party organizations in Beijing]. *Dangshijiaoxue* [Party history teaching], no. 5 (1989): 16–20.

Zhao Zhenzhen. "Lun Li Dazhao de nongmin guominxing gaizaosixiang" [Li Dazhao's thoughts on the transformation of peasants' national character]. *Chongqingyoudiandaxuexuebao* [Journal of Chongqing University of Posts and Communications] 25, no. 3 (May 2013): 48–51.

Zhen Jiang. "Li Dazhao: Zhongguo de 'Puluomixiusi'" [Li Dazhao: China's Prometheus]. *Guojiarenwenlishi* [National humanity history], December 2017, 16–17.

Zhonggongbeijingshiweidangshiyanjiushi. *Li Dazhao yu diyici guogonghezuo* [Li Dazhao and the first united front between the Nationalist Party and the Communist Party]. Beijing: Beijingchubanshe, 1989.

Zhonggonghebeishengweidangshiyanjiushi and Tangshanshi Li Dazhao yanjiuhui, editors. *Li Dazhao rengefengfan* [The noble character of Li Dazhao]. Beijing: Hongqichubanshe, 1999.

Zhonggongtangshanshiweidangshiyanjiushi. *Li Dazhao yu guxiang* [Li Dazhao and his hometown]. Beijing: Zhongyangwenxianchubanshe, 1994.

Zhonggongyidahuizhijinianguan. *Zhongguogongchandang chuangjianshiyanjiuwenji, 2002–2012* [A collection of articles on the history of the establishment of the Chinese Communist Party, 2002–2012]. Shanghai: Shanghairenminchubanshe, 2013.

Zhonggongzhongyangdangshiyanjiushi. *Li Dazhao yanjiu wenji* [A collection of research articles on Li Dazhao]. Beijing: CCP History Press, 1991.

Zhongguoshehuikexueyuan Jindaishiyanjiusuo. *Wusiyundong huiyilu* [Memoirs concerning the May Fourth Movement]. Beijing: Zhishichanquanchubanshe, 2013.

Zhongguoshehuikexueyuanxiandaishiyanjiushi. *Yidaqianhou* [Before and after the first national congress]. Vol. 2. Beijing: Renminchubanshe, 1980.

Zhou Hongxing and Li Ruluan. *Li Dazhao shi qianshi* [A concise interpretation of Li Dazhao's poems]. Chengdu: Sichuanrenminchubanshe, 1979.

Zhou Jin. "Li Dazhao yu diyiciguogonghezuo" [Li Dazhao and the first united front between the Nationalist Party and the Communist Party]. *Beijingdang'an* [Beijing archives], no. 8 (2011): 9–10.

Zhou Jingbao. "Li Dazhao zuji tanxi" [An analysis of the ancestral locale of Li Dazhao]. *Tangshanxueyuanxuebao* [Journal of Tangshan University] 30, no. 1 (January 2017): 18–21.

Zhou Liangshu. "1921 nian–1923 nian zhonggong zai gaoxiaozhong dangdejianshe" [CCP development at Chinese universities between 1921 and 1923]. *Beijingdangshi* [Party history of Beijing], no. 1 (2006): 19–23.

Zhou Xinjuan and Qin Ling. "Li Dazhao yu xinhaigeming" [Li Dazhao and the 1911 Revolution]. *Chizhoushizhuanxuebao* [Journal of Chizhou Teachers' College] 21, no. 4 (August 2007): 61–63.

Zhu Chengjia. "Li Dazhao dui Yuan Shikai de renshi guocheng" [A history of Li Dazhao's changing attitudes toward Yuan Shikai]. *Lishiyanjiu* [Historical research], no. 6 (1983): 12–21.

———. "*Li Dazhao wenji* zhong jipianwenzhang de biankao" [The examination of a few articles in *The Selected Works of Li Dazhao*]. *Jindaishiyanjiu* [Modern history studies], no. 1 (1998): 267–77.

———. *Li Dazhao zhuan* [Biography of Li Dazhao]. Beijing: Zhongguoshehuikexuechubanshe, 2009.

Zhu, Ping. "Becoming Laborers: The Identification with Labor during the Chinese New Culture Movement." *Journal of Asian Studies* 82, no. 1 (2023): 25–43.

Zhu Wentong. "Li Dazhao fu ribenliuxue shijian bianxi" [An analysis of the timing of Li Dazhao's arrival in Japan for his study abroad]. *Jindaishiyanjiu* [Modern Chinese history studies], no. 2 (1996): 279–84.

———. *Li Dazhao nianpuchangbian* [The extended chronicle of Li Dazhao's life]. Beijing: Zhongguoshehuikexuechubanshe, 2009.

———. "Li Dazhao yu jidujiaowenhua" [Li Dazhao and Christian culture]. *Hebeishifandaxuexuebao* [Journal of Hebei Normal University] 37, no. 1 (January 2014): 28–35.

———. *Li Dazhao zhuan* [Biography of Li Dazhao]. Tianjin: Tianjingujichubanshe, 2005.

Zhu Zhimin. "Li Dazhao yu Hu Shi" [Li Dazhao and Hu Shi]. *Jindaishiyanjiu* [Modern history studies], no. 2 (1997): 266–80.

———. *Li Dazhao zhuan* [Biography of Li Dazhao]. Beijing: Hongqichubanshe, 2009.

Zuo Bao. "Li Dazhao liudao zhangjiakou" [Li Dazhao's six visits to Zhangjiakou]. *Dangshibocai* [Extensive collection of the party history], no. 3 (2002): 40–41.

Zuo Ying and Song Yuzhong. "Cong Li Dazhao makesizhuyiguan qianxi 'wentiyuzhuyi' lunzheng" [An analysis of the debate over issues and isms from Li Dazhao's Marxist perspective]. *Xuelilun* [Theory research], no. 4 (2018): 42–44.

Zuo Yuhe and Wang Ruifang. "Li Dazhao yu makesizhuyi zhongguohua" [Li Dazhao and the Sinicization of Marxism]. *Shixueyuekan* [History monthly], no. 1 (1993): 66–73, 85.

Index

Abe Isoo, 60, 78
American Revolution, 64, 90, 101
Amur River, 33
An Jung-geun, 16
Anhui, 15, 47, 102, 222
Anping, 153, 199
Anti-Christian Movement, 129, 131
Awakening Society, 144, 145

Bacon, Francis, 86
Bai Jianwu, 38, 70, 102, 161
Bai Meichu, 33, 205
Bai Yayu, 40
Balkan Peninsula, 61
Bao Huisheng, 148, 165
Beidaihe, 14
Beijing Coup, 172, 175
Beijing Female Higher Normal College, 112, 128
Beijing Higher Normal College, 112
Beijing University
  Li's employment, 10; Zhang Shizhao's recommendation, 65; Li's relationship with Kang Shuaiqun, 77; Li's overseas experience, 79; Li's new job at Beijing University, 102; the chief librarian, 105–111; Li's appointment as a professor, 111–115; the May Fourth Movement, 115–125; Li's social activities, 125–131
Beijing University library
  Li as director of the library, 81; his job at the most prestigious university in China, 105; a photo of Li at the Beijing University Library, 108; international professional exchanges, 110–111; a center for learning communism, 142
Bodin, Jean, 114
Bohai Bay, 14
Bolshevik Revolution, 138, 179, 216
Borodin, Michael (Mikhail), 168
Boxer Rebellion, 27, 31, 55, 129, 131, 170
Britain (British), 31, 48, 75, 82, 83, 84, 96, 109, 178, 179, 180, 187, 188, 189, 201, 207, 209
Buddhism (Buddhist), 17, 51, 136, 210, 217, 222

Cai E, 67
Cai Hesen, 166, 167
Cai Shangsi, 219
Cai Yuanpei, 105, 112, 126
Capital Revolution, 194

CCP Moscow Branch, 181
Chan, Adrian, 141
Changchun Temple, 209
Changli, 31, 55
Changxindian, 145
Chaoyang University, 112
Carlyle, Thomas, 61
Chen Derong, 146
Chen Duxiu, 60, 72, 85, 121, 126, 145, 146, 147, 148, 164, 166, 167, 210, 214
Chen Gongbo, 217
Chen Hansheng, 192
Chen Jintao, 94
Chen Jiongming, 163
Chen Puxian, 137
Chen Yilong, 41, 51, 53
Chen Zhongfan, 219
Cheng Shewo, 143
Chiang Kai-shek (Jiang Jieshi), 5, 6, 182, 198, 205, 206, 210, 211, 217, 218
China Society, 68
China University, 112, 153
Chinese civilization, 36, 114, 116, 117, 120
Chinese Communist Party (CCP), 2, 7, 9, 10, 133, 142, 143, 144, 145, 146, 147, 148, 149, 150, 152, 153, 155, 156, 157, 159, 160, 161, 162, 163, 164, 165, 166, 168, 173, 174, 176, 177, 178, 180, 181, 182, 183, 185, 191, 192, 193, 196, 199, 202, 204, 206, 209, 210, 213, 216, 218, 219, 220, 221, 222
Chinese Labor Organization Secretariat, 155
Chinese Scholarly Society, 67, 68
Chinese Socialist Party, 41, 135
Chinese Society of Economy and Finance, 68

Chu Tunan, 191
Citizen Society, 123
Civil Service Examination System, 17, 21, 24, 25, 26, 30, 36, 55
Columbia University, 127
Communist Cubicle, 144
Communist International (Comintern), 146, 147, 148, 149, 155, 160, 161, 162, 164, 165, 168, 175, 176, 177, 178, 181, 183
Condorcet, Marquis de, 115
Confucianism, 17, 22, 26, 74, 82, 90, 91, 94, 120, 140, 215
Confucius, 31, 74, 90, 114, 120
Constitutional Protection Movement, 100
Crossley, Pamela Kyle, 121, 186
Cultural Revolution, 6, 7, 19, 154, 175, 220, 222
Customs Autonomy Movement, 193

Daheituo, 15, 17, 18, 69, 81, 130, 221
Dai Jitao, 217
Daoism, 135
Dawley, Evan N., 122
Deng Tuo, 121
Deng Yingchao, 145
Deng Zhongxia, 123, 150, 152, 161
Dewey, John, 140
Dicey, Albert Venn, 61
Ding Weifen, 219
Dirlik, Arif, 141, 215
Duan Qirui, 87, 89, 96, 99, 100, 102, 138, 172, 173, 189, 194, 196

Elleman, Bruce A., 161
Elman, Benjamin A., 24
Emerson, Ralph Waldo, 61
Enlightenment, 85, 120, 157
Esherick, Joseph W., 223

Evans, Harriet, 119

Fairbank, John King, 43
Fang Ruilin, 168
Fang Zhenwu, 199
February Seventh Strike, 156, 158, 161
Feigon, Lee, 136
Feng Guozhang, 99, 102
Feng Yuxiang, 39, 172, 175, 189, 190, 194, 196, 197, 198, 199, 201, 202, 208, 211, 216
Feng Ziyou, 33, 174
First Sino-Japanese War, 55, 114
Forbidden City, 109, 172, 194
Fort Dagu, 194
France (French), 8, 90, 92, 96, 97, 101, 114, 137, 143, 144, 148, 150, 180
French Revolution, 137

Gang of Four, 7, 220
Gansu, 198
Gao Yihan, 6, 69, 77, 89, 92, 125, 134, 136, 143, 145
General Association of Chinese Students in Japan, 66, 67, 69
Germany (German), 8, 65, 66, 89, 92, 95, 96, 97, 101, 114, 124, 141, 143, 144, 147, 179, 192, 205
Gong Zhongtao, 153
Goodnow, Franklin Johnson, 64
Goossaert, Vincent, 130
Grand Anti-Religious Alliance, 129
Graziani, Sofia, 130
Great Civil Rights Movement Alliance, 128
Great Harmony, 119, 135
Great War (First World War, or World War One, or World War I), 61, 65, 82, 95, 96, 97, 98, 114, 135, 137, 138, 179

Greeley, Horace, 86
Grieder, Jerome B., 140
Gu, Edward X., 141
Gu Zonghai, 24
Guangdong, 47, 166, 192, 211
Guangxi, 128
Guangzhou (Canton, Cantonese), 65, 128, 159, 160, 161, 162, 163, 166, 167, 168, 169, 170, 173, 178, 179, 180, 190, 194, 198
Guilin, 162
Guo Songling, 189, 202
Guo Zhanbo, 6, 155

Han dynasty, 91
Han Feizi, 114
Han Yide, 62
Han Xiangting, 32
Harbin, 170, 177, 181, 191
Harvard University
   Li Dazhao's autobiography, 58; Li's introduction of a French mother, 97
He Jun, 206
He Xiangning, 169, 208
Hebei, 14, 153, 191, 199
Henan, 15, 155, 172, 190, 191, 192, 196, 198, 208, 211
Holland (Dutch), 8, 162, 167, 203
Hong Xiuquan, 27
Hu Jingyi, 172, 190
Hu Qiaomu, 3
Hu Sheng, 3
Hu Shi, 117, 120, 126, 140, 214, 219
Huang Baolin, 25, 26, 27
Huang Lingshuang, 146
Huang Xing, 89
Huayan Temple, 17, 18, 130
Hunan (Hunanese), 38, 47, 64, 83, 144, 156, 161, 189
Hundred Days' Reform of 1898, 26
Huo Lubai (also Huo Libai), 65, 83

Imai Yoshiyuki, 36, 60
Indonesia, 162
Inner Mongolia, 152, 153, 193
Ishikawa Yoshihiro, 76
Ito Hirobumi, 16

Japan (Japanese), 5, 8, 10, 16, 17, 18, 36, 39, 42, 44, 49, 53–80, 81, 82, 83, 85, 93, 97, 102, 110, 116, 118, 120, 124, 125, 129, 134, 135, 136, 137, 143, 144, 156, 172, 174, 180, 181, 188, 189, 194, 200, 201, 205, 209, 214, 215, 216, 217, 219, 222
Japanese Empire, 63, 66, 79, 124
Jenco, Leigh, 116
Jia Zhi, 121
Jiang Kanghu, 41
Jiang Qing, 7
Jiang Weiping, 33
Jiang Zemin, 2
Jiangxi, 47
Jiaxing, 148
Jieshi, 14, 35, 55
Jin Yufu, 107
Jin Yun'e, 196
Jinan, 114, 147
Jing Ke, 16, 38, 44
Jiyatai, 152, 153, 193
Joffe, Adolph Abramovich, 165
Johns Hopkins University, 57
Junges Deutschland, 85

Kaifeng, 172, 190
Kang Sheng, 7, 220
Kang Shuaiqun, 77
Kang Youwei, 26, 32, 90
Katayama Sen, 209
Kawakami Hajime, 77, 78
Kayahara Kazan, 76
Kobe, 57

Koo, Wellington (Gu Weijun), 171, 172
Korea (Koreans), 14, 16, 200
Kotoku Shusui, 78
Kuibi, 153
Kuo, Ya-pei, 116
KUTV, 178, 180, 181

Lady Cui, 19, 20
Lady Zhou, 19
Lanza, Fabio, 123
Laoting (Leting in Mandarin), 14, 15, 16, 21, 25, 28, 29, 31, 88, 93, 99
Laozi, 114
Lenin, Vladimir, 161, 168, 170, 187
Leningrad, 178, 179
Li Baohua, 196, 222
Li Bohai, 202
Li Chao, 128
Li Chun, 102
Li Dazhao
  Impact upon China, 2, 213–216; nationalism, 4–5; Li Dazhao studies, 6–9; Li's family, 13–18; early years, 18–23; classical education, 23–27; modern education, 29–43; early ideas, 43–49, 70–78; study abroad in Japan, 55–63; editor and writer in Beijing, 82–98; chief librarian at Beijing University, 106–115; the May Fourth Movement, 115–125; social activities, 125–130; becoming a communist, 133–142; establishing the CCP, 142–149; leading the early Communist movement, 149–156; the United Front with Sun Yat-sen, 161–175; visiting the Soviet Union, 175–182; a professional

revolutionary, 186–195; hiding in the Russian Embassy, 195–201; Li's arrest and execution, 201–210; the funeral for Li, 216–217
Li Guoqiu, 15
Li Hongta, 222
Li Huang, 131
Li Jiannong, 100, 159
Li Leguang, 6
Li Ming, 204
Li Qingfang, 88
Li Renrong, 17, 19
Li Rubi, 17
Li Ruzhen, 17, 18, 22
Li Ruzhu, 17
Li Shuxia, 205
Li Weimo, 17
Li Xinghua, 7, 9, 20, 34, 61, 176, 195, 203, 204, 207, 222
Li Yuanhong, 95, 99
Liang Qichao, 26, 32, 72, 89, 92, 99, 100, 138
Liang Shuming, 150
Liao, Jing, 111
Liao Zhongkai, 208
Library of Congress, 109, 110
Lin Boqu, 65, 137
Liu Bojian, 197
Liu Jingjun, 126
Liu Renjing, 122
Liu Tingfang, 127
Liu Xiangwu, 65
Liu Xiling, 39
Liu Yulou, 33
Lu Jian, 204
Lu, Xiufen, 135
Lu Xun, 6, 117, 120, 217, 219
Luan River, 14, 15
Luanzhou Uprising, 40
Lulong, 29, 31

Luo Zhanglong, 144, 147, 149, 150, 155, 177, 207
Luoyang, 155
Lvov, Georgy, 97

MacDonald, Ramsay, 179
Maergesi Doctrine Study Society, 143
Malthus, Thomas, 98, 143
Manchu (Manchus, Manchurian), 15, 16, 28, 33, 39, 40, 44, 50, 90, 99, 209
Manchuria (Northeast China), 14, 17, 22, 33, 65, 93, 176, 189, 200, 217, 222
Manela, Erez, 124
Mao Zedong
    Mao's claim of being Li's student, 2; Mao's status as a demigod during the Cultural Revolution, 6; Mao as Li's assistant, 7; Mao praised Li for his role in the May Fourth Movement, 111; Li's impact upon Mao, 121; Mao's assessment of the Russian Revolution, 137; Li's influence upon Mao, 143; Sinicization of Marxism, 154; the October Revolution, 156; Li as Mao's teacher, 157; Li, Mao, and others' letter to Sun Yat-sen, 167; rural classes, 192; the Russian Revolution, 216; Li's theoretical influence upon Mao, 218; Mao's holy status, 220
March 18 Massacre, 186, 194, 195, 196, 199, 210
Maring, G. (Hendricus Sneevliet, known as Ma Lin in China), 147, 148, 162, 164, 166, 167
Marx, Karl, 138

Marxism (Marxist), 2, 77, 78, 113, 133, 134, 137, 138, 139, 141, 142, 143, 147, 150, 154, 155, 156, 171, 215, 216, 221
Marxist Doctrine Study Society, 143, 144
Mashenmiao, 109
Mathews, Shailer, 61
May Fourth Movement, 9, 106, 115, 116, 121, 122, 123, 124, 130, 131, 221
May Thirtieth Movement, 188
Meisner, Maurice, 8, 9, 18, 58, 141, 215
Mill, John Stuart, 61
Ming dynasty, 15, 44
Minobe Tatsukichi, 60
Minyi, 69, 73, 74
Mongol-Tibetan School, 152
Mongolia (Mongolian), 14, 42, 152, 153, 171, 192, 193
Montesquieu, Charles, 114
Mori Masao, 58
Morning Bell, 82, 84, 85, 86, 87, 88
Moscow, 175, 176, 177, 178, 179, 180, 181, 182
Mozi, 114

Nagao Ariga, 64
Nakajima Tan, 41–42
Nakano Kaizan, 49
Nanchang, 128, 198
Nanjing, 102, 128, 198, 206
Napoleon (Napoleon Bonaparte), 75
National Army, 172, 175, 194
National Assembly Movement, 173
National Protection Army, 67
National Protection War, 67, 90
National Revolution, 2, 10, 159, 169, 172, 173, 174, 176, 178, 180, 183, 185, 186, 189, 193, 197, 199, 211, 213, 216, 218

Nationalist Party (KMT), 2, 33, 41, 47, 72, 88, 89, 100, 158, 159, 160, 161, 162, 163, 164, 165, 166, 167, 168, 169, 170, 173, 174, 178, 181, 182, 183, 190, 191, 193, 196, 197, 198, 199, 204, 207, 218, 221
Nelson, Diane M. and Robert B. Nelson
  Li as "the father of modern Chinese librarianship," 111; the role of Li's library in spreading communism, 142
New Chinese Nation, 92
New Culture Movement, 76, 81, 85, 105, 106, 116, 117, 118, 119, 120, 121, 130, 131, 134, 135, 144, 157, 214, 221
New Policy, 25
New Tide Society, 123
New York City, 86
New York Times, 208
New Youth, 85, 116, 120
Ni Dingyun, 39
Nietzsche, Friedrich, 86
North China, 14, 15, 16, 35, 36, 41, 42, 57, 149, 155, 160, 166, 170, 172, 183, 185, 186, 187, 188, 191, 192, 196, 210, 217, 218, 221
North China College of Law and Politics, 35
North China Society of Law and Politics, 41
Northern Expedition, 160, 186, 190, 196, 197, 198, 199, 201, 205, 211, 216

October Revolution, 136, 137, 144, 147, 150, 156, 179, 216
Oudendyk, William J., 203
Outer Mongolia, 171

Pacific Ocean (journal), 100
Pacific Ocean, 187
Palmer, David A., 130
Pan-Asianism, 97
Pantsov, Alexander V., 163, 188
Paris Peace Conference, 106, 116, 121, 124, 134
Peng Jieshi, 88
Peng Ming, 121
People's Republic of China, 2, 111, 153, 222
Pozdneev, A. M., 42
Pozzana, Claudia, 76
Progressive Party, 41, 47, 56, 72, 89, 100
Public Review of the Constitution, 88, 92
Puyi, 99, 172

Qi Xieyuan, 117
Qian Xuantong, 131
Qin dynasty, 91
Qin Guangli, 88
Qin Shihuang, 16
Qing dynasty (The Qing Empire), 3, 4, 24, 28, 29, 36, 39, 40, 90, 99, 115, 162
Qingdao, 66, 114
Qinghua School (later Tsinghua University), 109

Reconstruction Conference, 173
Red Mansion, 109, 111, 122
Red Spear Society, 199
Ren Guozhen, 191
Republic of China, 2, 42, 48, 88, 94, 222
Revolutionary Alliance, 33, 88, 172
Robinson, Arthur G., 58
Roosevelt, Theodore, 97
Russia (Russian), 3, 8, 33, 42, 97, 127, 134, 135, 136, 137, 138, 139, 141, 143, 144, 145, 146, 147, 148, 150, 151, 154, 155, 157, 158, 160, 161, 162, 163, 165, 168, 169, 170, 171, 172, 173, 175, 176, 177, 178, 179, 180, 181, 182, 183, 184, 185, 186, 188, 190, 191, 195, 198, 199, 200, 202, 203, 205, 207, 209, 210, 216, 221, 223
Russian Embassy (Soviet Embassy), 186, 195, 198, 199, 200, 202, 203, 210, 216, 220
Russian Famine Relief Society, 127
Russian Revolution, 3, 135, 136, 137, 138, 147, 148, 151, 154, 216

Salary Reclamation Movement, 126, 148
Schwarcz, Vera, 118, 122
Scott, David, 124
Shaanxi, 198, 200
Shan Zi'ao, 24, 25
Shandong, 15, 25, 65, 66, 106, 124, 147, 189, 191
Shang dynasty, 31, 140
Shanghai, 6, 62, 67, 70, 83, 84, 99, 100, 102, 124, 128, 145, 146, 147, 148, 151, 152, 154, 160, 163, 164, 165, 167, 168, 170, 173, 181, 188, 201, 206
Shanxi, 5, 189, 197, 198
Shatan, 109, 111
Shi Kexuan, 199
Shi Ying, 167
Smith, Adam, 27
Snow, Edgar, 143
Socialist Study Society, 144
Socialist Youth League, 145, 149, 153, 167
Song Jiaoren, 47, 48
Song Qingling, 165
Song Zhongbin, 33

Soviet Russia, 134, 136, 137, 147, 148, 150, 151, 155, 157, 158, 159, 160, 161, 162, 163, 165, 168, 169, 171, 173, 175, 176, 181, 182, 183, 184, 185, 188, 190, 191, 202, 216
Soviet Union, 8, 149, 171, 172, 175, 182, 220
Spence, Jonathan D., 4
Sun Fuyuan, 122
Sun Guidan, 112
Sun Hongyi, 56, 83, 88, 100, 102
Sun Yat-sen (Sun Zhongshan, Sun Yixian), 2, 8, 10, 33, 48, 72, 88, 89, 100, 101, 112, 158, 159, 160, 161, 162, 163, 164, 165, 167, 168, 169, 170, 172, 173, 174, 176, 178, 179, 180, 181, 182, 183, 184, 186, 187, 189, 190, 191, 197, 210, 213, 214, 216, 221

Ta Kung Pao, 6, 45
Tagore, Rabindranath, 86
Taicheng, 153
Taiping Rebellion, 27
Taiwan (Taiwanese), 8, 137, 141, 157, 163, 183, 191, 202, 221
Tan Kemin, 167
Tan Pingshan, 167
Tan Xihong, 167.
Tang Hualong, 56, 57, 67, 70, 83, 84, 87, 88.
Tang Peisong, 57
Tang Shaoyi, 88
Tang Yueliang, 201
Tangshan, 188
Third Aunt (Sangu), 20, 34
Three People's Principles, 163, 190
Tiananmen Square, 193, 194
Tianjin, 6, 14, 29, 34, 35, 36, 38, 39, 41, 42, 45, 49, 56, 57, 60, 88, 144, 145, 146, 173, 174, 188, 197
Tianjin Conference, 197
Tiger, 64, 92
Tiger Daily, 92
Tokyo, 19, 42, 57, 62, 63, 64, 65, 66, 68, 69, 71, 72, 74, 77, 78, 82, 92
Tolstoy, Leo, 49, 51, 80, 86, 93, 101, 103
Tong Shijun, 142
Treaty of Versailles, 116, 121, 124
Turkey, 96
Twenty-One Demands, 54, 62, 65, 67, 78, 79, 97

U, Eddy, 152
Ulanhu (Wulanfu), 153
United Front, 2, 10, 151, 158, 159–184, 185, 186, 187, 189, 190, 191, 192, 193, 196, 197, 202, 207, 210, 213, 214, 216, 217, 218, 221, 223
United States (USA), 59, 71, 91, 95, 109, 110, 123, 180, 192, 201
USSR, 159, 163, 171, 172, 175, 176, 178, 179, 180, 181, 182, 183, 187, 189, 190, 197, 200, 202, 209, 221, 222

Vico, Giovanni Battista, 114
Virtue Promotion Society, 126
Vishnyakova-Akimova, Vera V., 209
Voitinsky, Grigori, 147, 209

Wan'an Public Cemetery, 217, 220
Wang Fangtian, 177, 181
Wang Jingwei, 206, 217
Wang Senran, 6
Wang Zhengting, 89
Waseda University, 54, 57, 58, 59, 60, 61, 62, 63, 69, 71, 77, 78, 79, 82, 112

Washington, George, 46, 71, 75
Wead, Katharine H., 110
Weigelin-Schwiedrzik, Susanne, 220
Wen Shilin, 39, 88, 89
Western civilization, 10, 29, 54, 82, 96, 97, 98, 103, 116, 118, 120, 123, 156, 214
Western Hill clique, 191
Wilson, Woodrow, 61, 123, 124
World Student Christian Federation, 129
Wu Changgeng, 121
Wu Lishi, 191
Wu Peifu, 155, 156, 161, 172, 175, 189
Wu, Tien-wei, 134
Wufeng (Wufengshan), 14, 35, 177
Wuhan, 6, 152, 198, 206, 208

Xiao Yishan, 115
Xihu Meeting, 164
Xinjiang, 39
Xiong Xiling, 222
Xu Deheng, 121, 122
Xu Quanzhong, 191, 199
Xu Zhimo, 182, 194

Yale University, 94
Yan Xishan, 189, 197, 198, 211
Yan'an, 219, 222
Yang Du, 202, 205
Yang Fuqing, 177
Yangtze (Yangzi) River, 15, 83, 160
Yan-Zhao culture, 16
Yasukuni, 63
Ye Ting, 199
Yin Rugeng, 110
Yin Yanwu, 205
Yongle, 15
Yongping, 30, 31, 32, 33, 34, 35, 49
Yoshino Sakuzo, 36, 60, 124
Young China, 76, 77, 80, 85, 92

Young China (journal), 123
Young China Society, 123, 131
Young, George, 209
Young Men's Christian Association (YMCA), 57, 58, 61, 69
Young Turks, 85
Yu Shude, 37, 39, 40
Yu Yi, 37, 38, 56
Yuan Shikai, 31, 36, 46, 47, 48, 53, 54, 59, 63, 64, 65, 66, 67, 68, 69, 70, 71, 73, 75, 78, 79, 83, 87, 90, 91, 102, 202
Yuan Tongli, 109
Yue Weijun, 190, 196
Yunnan Proclamation, 89
Yushukan, 63

Zang Kejia, 6, 220
Zarrow, Peter, 124, 139
Zhang Cixi, 6, 44, 83, 207
Zhang Dongsun, 144
Zhang Gongpu, 25
Zhang Guotao, 143, 146, 147, 162, 164, 166, 167
Zhang Jianguo, 84
Zhang Jingru, 142
Zhang Rulun, 139
Zhang Runzhi, 60
Zhang Ruxin, 219
Zhang Shenfu, 122, 146, 219
Zhang Shizhao, 64, 65, 92, 106, 112, 205
Zhang Tingqian (Chuan Dao), 122
Zhang Ximan, 144
Zhang Xueliang, 205, 217
Zhang Xun, 99, 100
Zhang Zhaofeng, 199
Zhang Zongchang, 189
Zhang Zuolin
    Zhang issued the order to arrest and kill Li Dazhao, 10; Zhang and civil wars, 172; Zhang

Zhang Zuolin *(continued)*
asked Sun Yat-sen to sever ties with Soviet Russia, 173; the warlord of Manchuria, 189; Zhang's ties with Japan, 194; Zhang's control of North China, 196; Li's view of Zhang as the main enemy, 197; Li's report on Zhang's military forces, 198; the reasons why Zhang arrested and executed Li, 201–202; Li's arrest, 203; Zhang's decision to execute Li, 205; Zhang during the Northern Expedition, 206; Li's death, 207; Li's last photo, 208; Western writers denounced Zhang, 209; Zhang's execution of Li, 210; Li became Zhang's vicious enemy, 211; Li's strategies against Zhang, 216; Zhang's death, 217
Zhangjiakou, 189, 193
Zhao Huidou, 25
Zhao Renlan, 23, 217, 222
Zhao Shiyan, 173, 177
Zhao Wenlong, 22
Zhe Temple, 209, 216
Zhejiang, 148
Zhili (Hebei), 14, 31, 40, 102, 153, 172, 173, 191, 199
Zhou Enlai, 144, 145
Zhou Taixuan, 123
Zhou Zuoren, 131, 222
Zhu Chengjia, 46, 53, 66, 206
Zhu, Ping, 93
Zhu Shunshui, 44, 56
Zhu Wushan, 143, 150
Zhu Zhixin, 138